FLAGLER

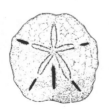

A Florida Sand Dollar Book

Henry M. Flagler, 1907

FLAGLER:
Rockefeller Partner and Florida Baron

Edward N. Akin

University Press of Florida
Gainesville Tallahassee Tampa Boca Raton
Pensacola Orlando Miami Jacksonville

Copyright 1988 by Kent State University Press
Paperback edition, 1991, University Press of Florida
00 99 98 97 96 95   6 5 4 3
Printed in the USA on acid-free paper

Library of Congress Cataloging-in-Publication Data

Akin, Edward N.
    Flagler, Rockefeller partner and Florida baron / Edward N. Akin. —
Pbk. ed.
        p.   cm. — (A Florida sand dollar book)
    Includes bibliographical references and index.
    ISBN 0-8130-1108-6 (alk. paper)
    1. Flagler, Henry Morrison, 1830–1913.   2. Businessmen—Florida—
Biography.   3. Capitalists and financiers—Florida—Biography.
4. Standard Oil Company—History.   5. Florida—History—1865–
6. Rockefeller, John D. (John Davison), 1839–1937.   I. Title.
II. Series.
HC102.5.F55A75   1991
338′.04′092—dc20
[B]   91-27086
                                                                                          CIP

This book was selected for publication by the Florida Atlantic
University editorial committee.

University Press of Florida is the scholarly publishing agency for the
State University System of Florida, comprised of Florida A&M
University (Tallahassee), Florida Atlantic University (Boca Raton),
Florida International University (Miami), Florida State University
(Tallahassee), University of Central Florida (Orlando), University of
Florida (Gainesville), University of North Florida (Jacksonville),
University of South Florida (Tampa), University of West Florida
(Pensacola).

Order books from University Press of Florida, 15 NW 15th Street,
Gainesville, FL 32611.

To
Gail and David

Contents

Illustrations

Preface

WITH THE BUSINESS TRENDS of the 1980s—mergers, leveraged buy-outs, deregulation of the trucking and airline industries, and the loosening of government restrictions on business—the general public now seems to have a renewed interest in the American economy. In fact, for the first time, business history seems to have come into its own. The change in the general attitude toward business history may be symbolized by the Pulitzer prizes for history recently awarded to business historians Alfred D. Chandler and Thomas McCraw.[1] Maybe, in a strange sort of way, people are taking the oft-quoted phrase "the business of America is business" to have new historical significance. Certainly, the number of textbooks on American business history is growing.[2]

In keeping with this renewed interest—if not trend—it is time to reevaluate the workings of late nineteenth-century American business. This book will attempt this through a biographical approach to one of John Rockefeller's business associates, Henry Flagler. In doing so, it is my goal to add to the information heretofore available on Flagler's business career, while giving new meaning to his activities at Standard Oil and on the Florida east coast.

Saint or Sinner? Robber Baron or Industrial Statesman? Philanthropist or Exploiter? These, and other questions of a similar nature, are usually asked of the biographer of a late nineteenth-century businessman. More disturbing than such questions is that most of what has been written on the career of Henry Flagler has tended to be in that "either/or" vein. Since most of the information concerning Flagler's first career is contained in accounts of John Rockefeller and the Standard Oil Company, let us begin with a review of those.

During the late nineteenth century, the meteoric rise of Standard inspired contemporary critics. I do not wish to burden the narrative with all of those; therefore, only the ones who enjoyed a wide following are discussed here. Henry Demarest Lloyd, in his 1881 article "The Story of a Great Monopoly" for the *Atlantic Monthly*, was the first journalist to launch an attack of any significance toward Standard.[3] It was primarily a polemical diatribe, based on only superficial research. It was timely, however, for the following year, Standard's leaders created the Standard Oil Trust. The specter of unbridled monopoly created a public desire to know more about the "soulless, grasping" corporation and its leaders.

Lloyd met the public appetite with the 1894 publication of *Wealth against Commonwealth*.[4] As one would guess from the title, Lloyd saw Standard ("Wealth") as serving its own selfish ends against the public good ("Commonwealth"). Once again, Lloyd was well received. A major theme of his narrative was the personification of the corporation through John Rockefeller. Therefore, at that early date, it became fashionable— although erroneous—for the public to easily interchange the names "John D. Rockefeller" and "Standard Oil." In spite of a much longer narrative contained in his book, Lloyd had done little to change the interpretative bent of his earlier writing. The book received mixed reviews when it appeared. The newly emerging muckraking journals thought it was a first-rate exposure of monopolistic practices. The more conservative press accused Lloyd of purple-prose techniques.[5]

It was Ida Minerva Tarbell, a writer for the muckraking journal *McClure's*, who did the most to establish Standard's long-lasting reputation as the epitome of a large monopoly out to destroy the nation's free enterprise system. Tarbell already had an excellent reputation as a writer as a result of her biography of Napoleon. She had a personal interest in the oil industry as an area of study, since she herself was from the Oil Regions of northwestern Pennsylvania, and her brother and father were oilmen. Therefore, when S. S. McClure asked her to research the piece on Standard, she immediately accepted. She hired an able assistant from the Cleveland area to assist her in the research. The result of the project was both commercially successful and enduring.[6]

Right on the heels of a major investigation of Standard by the United States Industrial Commission, the serialization of Tarbell's story began to appear in *McClure's* in November 1902. By the time her two-volume *His-*

tory of the Standard Oil Company appeared in 1904, Tarbell had firmly established her study as the basic interpretation of Standard and Rockefeller. During the early research phase of her project, she had received the cooperation of Standard officials, but they were much more cautious as the serialization progressed.[7]

Unlike Lloyd, Tarbell exhausted the public record on Standard Oil. She and her assistant read every available newspaper, court record, and published account of the company. She also interviewed Standard opponents and officials, including Flagler. Although one may disagree with some of her interpretations—as is sometimes the case in the following chapters—when one considers the constraints she was under, especially the lack of internal evidence from Standard, she did an admirable job.[8]

Throughout his active career with Standard, John Rockefeller had refused to answer any of the company's critics. Although Flagler was, at times, not as quiet as Rockefeller, and Standard did pursue a public relations policy after the publication of Tarbell's work (discussed in detail in chapter 5), it was not until 1917 that Rockefeller himself took an active role in such countermeasures. In that year, his son convinced him to cooperate with William O. Inglis in the preparation of an authorized biography to offset the negative public image that had continued since the days of the *McClure's* project.[9]

Inglis's biography was never completed. His research, however, did serve as the basis of the Rockefeller version of events. Off and on over a period beginning in 1917 and ending in 1922, Inglis conducted a series of interviews with John Rockefeller. When John T. Flynn wrote *God's Gold: The Story of Rockefeller and His Times* in the depths of the Great Depression (1932), he had access to the typescripts of the Inglis conversations with Rockefeller, but carefully avoided a pro-Rockefeller bias.[10]

The Rockefeller family then convinced Allan Nevins, a leading historian of the Civil War and an excellent writer, to undertake a biography of John Rockefeller. Although Nevins maintained a heavily documented approach to his task, his narrative, which appeared as the two-volume *John D. Rockefeller: The Heroic Age of American Enterprise* in 1940, was as much a brief in Rockefeller's defense as Tarbell's had been for the "prosecution." At critical points, Nevins was forced to rely on the Inglis material, which was often merely Rockefeller's off-the-cuff refutation of Lloyd and Tarbell attacks.[11]

The first major breakthrough in our understanding of the Standard story was when Nevins gained access to a large number of internal Standard materials, including minute books and letter books of correspondence.

This discovery allowed Nevins to publish another two-volume biography, *Study in Power: John D. Rockefeller, Industrialist and Philanthropist,* in 1953.[12] Although the new story was much more detailed, Nevins still pursued the role of apologist for Rockefeller. For the purposes at hand, this new work had one significant interpretative difference when compared with Nevins's earlier biography. *Study in Power,* in spite of its biographical nature, emphasized the role Flagler had played at Standard during the 1870s and early 1880s, the period of Standard's most critical—and criticized—growth. Nevins convincingly, and correctly, portrayed Flagler as the chief architect and enforcer of practices such as rebates and drawbacks. In spite of Nevins's treatment of Standard, historians have continued to portray the organization as the creation of one individual, rather than as what it really was: an enlarged partnership, at least during its creative early years.

Since the Nevins biographies of Rockefeller, there has been no large-scale study of the early years of Standard. There have appeared, however, some studies that have increased our understanding of the organization. Ralph and Muriel Hidy, in their *Pioneering in Big Business,* added to our knowledge of the Standard organization of the 1880s and 1890s, but they gave only passing attention to the company before the 1882 organization of the Standard Oil Trust. Also, the Hidys' study is primarily concerned with an internal analysis of the Standard organization, but lacks a human dimension.[13]

During the 1970s, two studies appeared that foreshadow my own. In 1974, Jerome T. Bentley wrote his dissertation at the University of Pittsburgh on the contribution of transportation to the rise of Standard in the period after 1872. Five years later, the study was published as a book in Stuart Bruchey's series, *Energy in the American Economy.*[14] The same year, 1979, another highly technical work appeared on Rockefeller and Standard, Bruce Bringhurst's *Antitrust and the Oil Monopoly: The Standard Oil Cases, 1890–1911.* This volume argued rather forcefully that the breakup of Standard showed the weakness of American antitrust policy.[15] However, because Bringhurst chose not to follow closely Standard's path from laissez-faire competition in the 1860s through the combinations of the 1870s, his work is of only limited use to the Flagler biographer.

An interpretative work added to the Standard Oil history shelf in 1980 was David Freeman Hawke's *John D.: The Founding Father of the Rockefellers*. In that one-volume treatment, Hawke presented Rockefeller's life in a tone that reflects a calm detachment and an unbiased appraisal. Although Mr. Hawke did not see the manuscript for this book at any stage, his encouragement has been constant and his insights have been duly noted—at times within the text, but especially in the endnotes.[16]

While one could argue that Flagler's Standard Oil career has been covered in detail, the same cannot be said of his Florida years. There have been two biographies of Flagler. The first to appear was Sidney Walter Martin's *Florida's Flagler* in 1949. Without access to Flagler's personal papers, Martin was forced to rely on newspaper and secondary sources. Although he did interview Flagler's only son, Harry, father and son had become estranged in the middle of the 1890s and had never reconciled. In 1986, David Leon Chandler wrote *Henry Flagler: The Astonishing Life and Times of the Visionary Robber Baron Who Founded Florida,* a biography aimed at a popular audience. Chandler, author of several previous popular historical studies, including *The Natural Superiority of Southern Politicians*, gives a spirited presentation of Flagler's life. He adds to Martin's account with well-drawn stories of Flagler's early years in Ohio. However, he does little with the all-important business aspects of Flagler's career, both at Standard Oil and on the Florida east coast.[17]

With Flagler's Standard Oil career chronicled by studies such as those of Tarbell, Nevins, and Hawke, and with basic material of Flagler's Florida years covered in the Martin and Chandler biographies, why have a new, book-length study of this Gilded Age businessman? There are several reasons for such a study: (1) By concentrating on the leaders of late nineteenth-century industry, we often forget that many of the organizations, especially Standard Oil, were cooperative efforts and not merely individual empires. A study of a secondary figure, rather than the principal person, in such a business helps us reformulate our questions. (2) Even in the heavily mined primary source material of Standard, new material often surfaces, both within materials already surveyed and in previously unknown material. In particular, chapter 1 of this book is the first, full-scale account of Rockefeller, Andrews & Flagler, since the letter books of the partnership, now housed at the Rockefeller Archives, have only been used by David Freeman Hawke, and then not extensively. (3) With the materials available from The Henry Morrison Flagler Museum archives at Palm Beach, Florida, we can now fully explore Flagler's impact on Florida during his second full career as he developed that state's east coast. Flagler's Florida career was certainly his most individual contribution to America's social and economic scene. But in order to fully understand Flagler the aging businessman, one must see him within the context of a full biographical treatment. Many of his Florida activities make no sense without an understanding of his first fifty-five years.

Prologue:
Young Entrepreneur

HENRY FLAGLER stood on the platform of his private railroad car as the crowd below gave him a tumultuous welcome. In a sense, the January 22, 1912, occasion was a belated birthday party. Three weeks earlier, on January 2, Flagler, owner of the Florida East Coast Railway, had celebrated his eighty-second birthday. His once-intense blue eyes now had a cloudy, gray cast. In spite of this evidence of age, some of the features that had made Flagler a rather handsome young man were still pronounced. His stature, although stooped, portrayed an air of command. He kept his short, white hair parted in the middle; and his mustache, below a straight, classic nose, was bushy, tending to cover his upper lip.[1]

The celebration was far more than a birthday party, for Flagler's train stood at Key West, an island city far removed from the mainland. Two dreams were fulfilled that day. The citizens of Key West, isolated for so long off the tip of Florida, now felt united with the mainstream of American commerce. The oft-maligned Henry Flagler, wealthy Standard Oil pioneer and Florida east coast developer, now felt his much-criticized business decisions vindicated. The Key West Extension of Flagler's railroad, often referred to during its construction as "Flagler's Folly," was now being called "The Eighth Wonder of the World."[2]

Flagler's business career had begun during his teenage years, almost seventy years earlier. His personal and business life during those early years was closely connected with the Western Reserve, a large section of northeastern Ohio that had been retained by Connecticut until 1800. The area still had a strong New England flavor into the nineteenth century. A major reason for the continued influence of the eastern section of the nation on the Western Reserve was the transportation link provided by the Erie Canal.³

The Erie Canal was one of the common threads of Flagler's life from his youth through his early career with Standard Oil. Built during the early 1800s, the canal became both an avenue and a symbol of America's penchant for movement. DeWitt Clinton built his political career on the promise of constructing a canal from Buffalo (on Lake Erie) to the Hudson River, thereby uniting the Great Lakes with New York City. Clinton and other New York boosters thought that if the waterway to the plains of the new western states could be built, it would assure the supremacy of New York as the commercial capital of the nation. During his first term as governor, Clinton broke ground for the construction of the canal on July 4, 1817. He was again governor when the canal was completed in 1825. Indeed, the canal became the national thoroughfare uniting the northeast with the midwest. More specifically, an economic union was created between New York and the Lake Erie region.⁴

Members of the Harkness family of the Finger Lakes region of upstate New York made the trek to the Western Reserve region of northeastern Ohio during the early 1820s before the completion of the canal. Since this family was the base for Henry Flagler's rise in the world of business, a close look, both at the family in general and for specific relationships with Flagler, is critical to our understanding of his career.

David Harkness, trained as a physician, was the first person in the family to move from Seneca County, New York, to Ohio's Western Reserve, shortly after the death of his first wife in 1820. He journeyed to Ohio, probably leaving his son, Stephen, behind with a relative in New York. Soon after settling in Milan, he married Elizabeth Caldwell Morrison, a 20-year-old, childless widow. Elizabeth would become the mother of Henry Flagler. During their marriage, David and Elizabeth had a son, Daniel Morrison Harkness, who was born on September 26, 1822.⁵ Both Dan and Stephen played critical roles in the Flagler story of the 1840s and 1850s.

David Harkness's youngest brother, Lamon G. Harkness (Flagler's future father-in-law), followed David both into the field of medicine and to the Western Reserve. Lamon graduated first in his class from Union College in Schenectady, New York, in 1818 at age 17. After four additional years of study, he was licensed to practice medicine in 1821. He initially practiced with another brother in the New York area before going in 1823 to the Ridge, an area in the Lyme Township of Huron County, on the western edge of Ohio's Western Reserve, to set up a practice with a Dr. Stevens. During this period of high mobility, Dr. Lamon Harkness began a solo practice in the York Township the following year. For the remainder of the 1820s, he continued his medical practice in that area.[6]

While Dr. Lamon Harkness was enjoying his medical practice, tragedy struck the family of his brother, David. Dr. David Harkness only briefly enjoyed the opportunity the Reserve offered, for he died in 1825. With the death of her husband, Elizabeth returned to Salem, New York, with her son, Dan, to live with her mother-in-law. More than likely, her stepson, Stephen, lived with other relatives throughout the period following his father's death. By the time Elizabeth remarried, Stephen had moved into the home of his mother's brother in New York.[7]

In 1828, Elizabeth Caldwell Morrison Harkness married the Reverend Isaac Flagler, a local Presbyterian minister in Milton, a small community in Seneca County. Isaac Flagler had come from a German family that had emigrated to America in 1710. The family had fled its home in Franconia, located in the German Palatinate, during the wars of Louis XIV. Isaac Flagler was born in 1789 in Dutchess County, New York. Although he had no formal education, he was self-educated, and at the age of twenty-one, he entered the Presbyterian ministry. Three years later, in 1813, he married his childhood sweetheart, Jane Ward. They had two daughters, Mary Ester, born in 1814, and Jane Augusta, born in 1816. Flagler remained in Dutchess County, on the eastern side of the Hudson River above New York City, until his wife's death in 1820. At that time, it seems that their two daughters were placed with relatives nearby and that Flagler used his freedom from family responsibilities to extend his ministry beyond his native county. He took a pastorate in Milton, New York, where he married Ruth Deyo Smith, one of his congregants, in 1824. They had a daughter, Ann Caroline, called Carrie by the family. Another disruption of Isaac's family occurred when his second wife died in 1827. With a young daughter in his care, Isaac Flagler married Elizabeth Harkness the following year.[8]

Not long after the marriage, Isaac Flagler left his Milton pastorate in Seneca County for another Finger Lakes congregation in Ontario County, settling in the small community of Hopewell. In the pastorium on Mumby Road, Elizabeth settled with her son, Dan, and stepdaughter, Carrie. It was in this house that Henry Flagler was born on January 2, 1830. Henry Morrison Flagler was named after his uncle Henry Flagler and Hugh Morrison, Elizabeth Flagler's first husband. Although the Reverend Flagler attempted to have his only son follow in his footsteps, the lure of the Western Reserve would prove too inviting to the adventurous young Henry.[9]

Isaac Flagler's ministry during Henry's early childhood is lost in obscurity. Henry Flagler would later aptly describe his father as a frontier missionary-pastor. We do know that he served two short terms as the moderator of the Hammondsport presbytery in 1831 and 1832, but the records are more complete for his career in Toledo, Ohio, where he settled in 1837. A vital part of his ministry in Toledo was his work with sailors in that port town. During his brief stay there, Isaac Flagler gained more notoriety for another pastoral function. He officiated at the wedding of a young black man and a white woman, the sister of an Oberlin College student, at a time when mixed marriages were viewed with alarm and horror, even in the free states.[10]

Notoriety was certainly not why the elder Flagler had accepted the Toledo pastorate. A part of his decision was probably based on the family's desire to allow Dan to be near his Harkness relatives. Now fourteen years old, Dan Harkness could visit his Harkness kin who lived in Bellevue and other Western Reserve communities not too far east of Toledo. In fact, shortly after the Flaglers came to Ohio, Dan left the family to live with his Harkness relatives. He first worked at the crossroads store of his Uncle William, who was Lamon and David's brother, at Butternut Ridge, southwest of Bellevue.[11]

The most fortuitous event in the life of the seven-year-old Henry Flagler may have been his family's move to Ohio. Although there is no evidence to indicate that Flagler spent any time with the Harknesses at this point, the stay in Ohio certainly renewed ties between his half-brother and one of the up-and-rising business families on the Ohio frontier. The Harknesses were creating a network of country stores at the western edge of the Western Reserve where Huron County, the westernmost county in the Reserve, and Sandusky County met.

Although Dan Harkness began his mercantile career with his Uncle William, it was Dr. Lamon Harkness who was at the forefront in the Harkness family frontier businesses. In 1832 Dr. Harkness moved his medical practice to Amsden Corners. The following year he gave up his practice and entered a full-time mercantile partnership with Thomas Amsden and Judge Frederick A. Chapman. Probably an important factor in his initial decision to move to the area—and certainly his decision to get into business—was the Ohio legislature's chartering of the Mad River & Lake Erie Railroad Company in January 1832. The line, when completed, would unite Bellevue (Amsden Corners changed its name to Bellevue in honor of the railroad's surveyor) with the port of Sandusky on Lake Erie. Within a year the doctor had given up his medical practice and devoted his full energies to his business interests. He became one of the Bellevue's biggest real estate and railroad promotors. It was Lamon Harkness and his mercantile partners

4

who, along with other local businessmen, quickly formed a real estate venture, dividing a 53½-acre tract in Huron County into town lots. Their development thereby became most of the Huron County half of Bellevue. The other half of the town was in Sandusky County.[12]

With the completion of the Mad River & Lake Erie Railroad in 1839, Bellevue became a thriving frontier commercial center as it served the people not only of western Huron and eastern Sandusky counties, but also of neighboring Seneca County. Communities such as Seneca's Republic and Tiffin became important markets for Bellevue merchants.[13]

As the family business concerns grew, so did the number of Harknesses involved in the various business enterprises. In 1838 Dan left his Uncle William's store to become a clerk for Harkness and Chapman Company in Bellevue. Then when the store owners decided to expand their operation to include a harness shop, Dan immediately contacted his older half-brother, Stephen. In 1833 the brother of Stephen's mother had apprenticed him to a Waterloo, New York, harnessmaker. Six years later, now twenty-one years old, Stephen began work at his Uncle Lamon's store in Bellevue. After just a couple of years at the store, however, he began his own Bellevue general merchandise operation, which included a luncheon counter and a tenpin alley.[14] Stephen later became the major financier, along with Lamon Harkness, for Henry Flagler's entry into the oil industry.

The Flagler-Harkness family mobility continued during the late 1830s and into the 1840s. The Flaglers had returned to New York from Toledo. Isaac Flagler accepted an invitation from a small Presbyterian church nine miles from the Erie Canal town of Medina. Meanwhile, Dan Harkness briefly left Ohio in 1840 for Lansingburg, New York, to apprentice as a printer's helper. He quickly returned to Ohio the following year to manage his Uncle Lamon's new mercantile store, L. G. Harkness & Company, for the community of Republic. With Dan and Stephen now proving themselves in the world of work, fourteen-year-old Henry Flagler convinced his parents to let him leave home to make his way in the world, if only to save his poor country-parson father from the necessity of feeding and clothing a growing teenager.[15]

In 1844, Henry obtained work at Medina as a freight handler on one of the shallow-draft boats being towed along the Erie Canal. When the boat arrived in Buffalo, he continued on to Sandusky, the entry point to the western section of the Western Reserve. (Cleveland, on the twisting Cuyahoga River, was the major port for the eastern portion.) Henry had a brief stay with the Lamon Harknesses in Bellevue since it was about midway in Henry's thirty-mile journey from Sandusky to Dan Harkness's store in

Republic. Henry arrived in Republic with a five-cent piece, four pennies, and a five-franc piece, which often was used as a dollar. He kept the French coin the rest of his life as a reminder of the biblical parable of the talents.[16]

Often during the winter months, Henry and Dan shivered in their sleeping quarters in a rear room of the small mercantile store. With wages of $5 a month, Henry had little choice but to take advantage of the free accommodations. Finally, the two would move to the warmer store area, only to have to add to their thin blankets a covering of wrapping paper from the counter above them. Henry had little time to worry about such discomforts; he was too busy learning the basic principles of American entrepreneurship. His most vivid recollection of the Republic experience dealt with his selling liquor. When a person would order brandy, Henry went to the store's cellar; there he dipped brandy from a keg located underneath the stairs. English immigrants paid $4.00 a gallon for the brandy, Germans paid $1.50, and everyone else paid whatever small amount Henry could extract from them.[17]

The following year, 1845, Chapman and Lamon Harkness invited Dan to join their partnership; they renamed the Bellevue concern Chapman, Harkness & Company. Whether or not they absorbed the Republic store into the new concern is unclear. Flagler's value to Lamon Harkness, however, is beyond question. After just four more years in Republic and still in his teens, Flagler moved to the sales staff at the Bellevue store. With his promotion came an annual salary of $400.[18]

The relationships, both business and social, among Lamon Harkness and his two young protégés became stronger. In 1849, Dan Harkness married Lamon's eldest daughter, Isabella. Three years later, in 1852, Dan bought out Chapman, Harkness & Company, reorganized it as D. M. Harkness & Company, and included Lamon Harkness and Henry Flagler as partners. The social tie among the partners was completed on November 9, 1853, when the youngest of the firm's partners, Henry, married Lamon's second daughter, Mary.[19]

Flagler enjoyed the business atmosphere of Bellevue. Stephen Harkness's 1848 account book of his Bellevue store reveals Flagler having beer and playing tenpins on his visits. On occasion, Flagler and Dan Harkness would visit the establishment together and discuss business over lunch, two meals for six bits. Politics may well have been a topic of lunchtime conversation, for Lamon Harkness was a strong Whig partisan who had cast his first presidential vote on the Ohio frontier for John Quincy Adams in 1824. He had been a delegate to the Ohio Whig nominating convention in 1844.

Flagler in hunting garb, ca. 1850

Dan and Flagler were also partisans of similar persuasion and later became financial backers of Republican causes.[20]

During the 1850s, both the Flaglers and the Dan Harknesses were establishing their own families. The firtborn of Henry and Mary Flagler was Jennie Louise, born on March 18, 1855. Three years later, they had a second child, Carrie, born on June 18, 1858. Meanwhile, Flagler's father had become infirm, and therefore, Isaac and Elizabeth Flagler, along with Henry's half sister, Carrie, came to live in Bellevue. Flagler valued his family time; later he recalled, with evident pride, that he was at the bedside of Mary, his beloved but frail wife, every evening throughout their marriage. Family life for Dan and Bell, as Isabella Harkness was called by family and friends, was marked by tragedy. Of five children born to them during the 1850s, only son William survived to adulthood.[21]

Meanwhile, the young Bellevue merchants were building a thriving business during the decade before the Civil War. The Harkness company continued the business practices of its predecessors, including functioning as the informal banking institution of Bellevue. The company increased its merchandising activities to include the lucrative grain trade, an activity that brought young Flagler into his first contacts with the even more youthful John Rockefeller. Nine years younger than Flagler, Rockefeller had become a broker at the Cleveland grain commission house of Hewitt & Tuttle upon completing a short business course after his high school graduation in 1857. By the Civil War, Flagler had Rockefeller brokering most of the Harkness & Company grain business through his Cleveland commission house.[22]

It was the liquor trade, not grain merchandizing, however, that gave all the Harkness clan, Flagler included, the first taste of real success. The frontier spirit of the Old Northwest was still prevalent in the Ohio of the 1840s and 1850s. Stephen Harkness's 1848 account ledger revealed that beer was selling at $.13 a quart, while a pint of whiskey cost only $.06. As far back as 1836, distilleries are known to have existed in Lyme township. But it was the creation of the sixty-bushel-a-day distillery of Chapman, Harkness & Company in 1849 that called the attention of the public to the tremendous economic possibilities for such an enterprise.[23]

In 1852, as mentioned earlier, Dan Harkness had bought all the Chapman, Harkness & Company properties, including the distillery. He had in turn formed a partnership with Flagler and Lamon Harkness. They immediately increased the capacity of the operation from only sixty bushels of grain per day to six hundred bushels of grain daily. One source stated that this partnership continued the operation intact until 1864, when the part-

Flagler, his wife Mary (standing), and sister-in-law Isabella Harkness, Bellevue
years (early 1850s)

nership was dissolved. Flagler himself later claimed that moral scruples compelled him to sell his interest in the distillery in 1858. When he did sell it, it may have been that his parson father, again living in Ohio, had objected to the activity, and Flagler submitted to the old man's scruples. In any case, Flagler had made a small fortune from his association with whiskey making.[24]

Stephen Harkness's distillery operations fared even better than that of the Bellevue Harknesses. In 1852 Stephen began his first distillery in Caledonia, Ohio. Upon moving back to Monroeville, ten miles east of Bellevue, in 1855 he engaged once again in a distillery business. It was the Civil War and the government's need for tax revenues that gave Stephen Harkness his great windfall. Senator John Sherman of Ohio, from his position on the Senate Finance Committee, passed the word along to his friend in Ohio that Congress would soon pass a tax of $2.00 a gallon on all alcoholic beverages.[25]

Harkness took every dollar he could obtain, including funds from the bank he owned in Monroeville, and bought every barrel of liquor he could find. When anxious farmers came to the bank to have their crop receipts cashed, a paid spokesman of Harkness stood outside the bank to assure them that Steve Harkness would stand behind his debts, so why rush him? When one farmer was not dissuaded, Harkness himself talked with the gentleman long enough for a teller to rush out the back door and borrow the amount needed from another merchant. Congress approved the tax, and Harkness now charged $2.00 a gallon extra for his wine and whiskey— without any taxes due on what he had purchased before enactment of the law. His profits were enormous. Even after he began paying the $2.00-per-gallon taxes, Stephen Harkness continued to reap large profits. His excise tax payments for liquor during 1863 and 1864 were $321,181.89—and that was with the distillery not even running for four months of that period. The wartime profit was reflected in Harkness's income tax statement, which showed his net income for 1864 to have been $120,000, a remarkable sum even in that inflationary year.[26]

Henry Flagler attempted to continue his 1850s lifestyle during the Civil War years. He and Mary had built a home in 1858 on Bellevue's fashionable Southwest Street; the home earned the name of "The Gingerbread House" for its exterior style. In keeping with his position within the Bellevue community, when the Civil War did come, Flagler saw nothing wrong with "buying canteens"—a "patriotic" way of saying he paid a substitute to serve in his place in the war effort. After all, Flagler could easily rationalize his position. His half-brother Dan was the family's representative behind the battle front and Flagler himself had to keep the home front going—with both family and business responsibilities. In reality, he avoided the army in order to do as Stephen Harkness had done: make money. This attitude of indifference toward actual combat was rather common among those who would later rise in the world of business—Rockefeller and Carnegie immediately coming to mind.[27]

As for Dan Harkness, he volunteered for the Quartermaster Corps in the Union cause. He immediately reported to Camp McClellan, located at Norwalk, on September 30, 1861. This was not an all-male affair, however. The wives of officers were indirectly included when the governor requested that they form aid societies for their husbands' units. Such groups could raise money to provide blankets and other necessities for the volunteer units. Bell Harkness's letter from Camp McClellan to her sister Mary Flagler stated that Bell had enlisted their mother to assist in one fund raising effort, reporting that: "I believe we received $113, a very good donation considering the inclement weather."[28]

After his initial training, Dan Harkness and his unit were sent to the western theatre of the war. From his duty station at Ft. Pickering (at Memphis), he acquitted himself well during the Union campaign, which ended in the Battle of Shiloh. His commander, Col. R. P. Buckland, recalled: "No Quartermaster in this Division stands better than Harkness. His ability and energy has [*sic*] contributed largely to the reputation which the 72nd has obtained for promptness in all marches from Shiloh to Memphis. Not in a single instance has his train been behind time." However, during the summer of 1862, the Fremont (Ohio) *Democratic Messenger* printed rumors that charged Flagler's half brother with using his position to enrich himself on the black market. Flagler quickly confronted the Democratic attack, attempting to have the *Messenger* print a letter from members of Dan's unit that cleared him of the charges. When the highly partisan *Messenger* refused, the Fremont *Journal* printed the pro-Harkness story. It then circulated in other area papers. Dan Harkness, with his honor now restored, resigned his commission in early 1863 to return home to run the family business in Bellevue, for Henry Flagler and another son-in-law of Lamon Harkness were entering a new avenue of enterprise, the lucrative salt industry in Saginaw, Michigan.[29]

For Henry Flagler, the Bellevue years of the war were marked by business success—and personal tragedy. He had become one of the most successful merchants on the Western Reserve frontier. On the personal side, however, Flagler grieved with the death of his mother in 1861. Flagler's burden was compounded when three-year-old Carrie died on December

7, 1861. With family relocations occurring throughout the war years, Carrie's death was one of the themes in correspondence between Mary Harkness and her daughters, Mary Flagler and Bell Harkness. Near the first anniversary of Carrie's death, Jennie Flagler was visiting with her Aunt Bell while Henry and Mary Flagler were in Cleveland. The visit brought back a flood of memories, as Bell recalled, "Angel Carrie . . . the gayest of all."[30]

Death and the search for religious meaning in life often seemed to go hand in hand. In the religious world of antebellum America, where death was ever present, the Second Great Awakening had emphasized one's personal relationship with God. In acting on this aspect of evangelical Protestantism during the Civil War, Flagler became a local leader of the Sunday School movement. While Isaac Flagler was superintendent of Bellevue's Congregational Sabbath School in 1862, his son paid for the necessary literature. Then, in January 1863, Flagler succeeded his father as superintendent. Whether or not Flagler could have added to his father's success we do not know, for he resigned his position in April to pursue new business interests.[31]

Henry Flagler and Barney York, soon to become Lamon and Mary Harkness's third son-in-law, had formed a partnership, the Flagler & York Salt Company, in September 1862, in order to start a salt-producing business in Saginaw, Michigan. Probably the original idea for the venture had come from Lamon Harkness, whose investment in the East Saginaw Salt Company was returning handsome profits. On January 8, 1863, Barney York married Julia Harkness. Meanwhile, in preparation for the departure of the Flaglers and Yorks, Dan Harkness had resigned his army commission to return home to run the family businesses. In early February, Dan took over Henry's interest in Flagler & Vail, a warehousing concern in Norwalk. Probably other Flagler businesses were transferred to Dan at the same time. Henry and Mary Flagler sold their home to Dan. With the proceeds from the sale, Flagler bought a home in Saginaw for $2,500 and six lots from Dan in Bellevue, also for $2,500. With matters in Bellevue taken care of and the warm weather, salt-producing season fast approaching, the Flaglers and Yorks moved to Saginaw to make their fortunes.[32]

Henry Flagler and Barney York were entering a field that was already well-known in Michigan. In fact, the salt springs were so prominent that, in admitting Michigan to statehood in 1836, Congress had set aside up to twelve salt springs as part of the state's public domain. Saginaw was at the very center of a major salt basin that stretched fifty miles in every direction.

Salt springs in the area, bubbling to the surface, had provided some persons with their domestic salt needs. Ever since the discovery of salt in the upstate New York area in the 1840s, its price had been steadily rising from its original selling price of $.90 a barrel to $1.40 by 1859. In that year, the *Saginaw Enterprise* declared: "The gold-fields of Kansas possess not half the wealth that lies buried beneath our own feet, and we can have it if we are willing to make the proper efforts to obtain it."[33]

In February 1859 the Michigan legislature passed a salt act that followed the provisions of the bill Saginaw businessmen had submitted to that body. It provided not only a tax exemption for companies engaged in salt manufacture, but also a bounty of $.10 for each bushel of salt produced. Saginaw businessmen immediately capitalized on this enactment, organizing the East Saginaw Salt Manufacturing Company on March 24. Yet the effect of the legislative act on salt production itself was not so readily apparent. In 1860 the state of Michigan produced less than 5,000 bushels of salt. But, with Civil War demand, it produced over 100,000 bushels in 1861 and doubled that amount in 1862.[34]

Flagler and York enthusiastically invested in Saginaw salt. Their initial $20,000 investment as Flagler & York went to purchase a 16½-acre tract of land (in what would later become Salina, just south of East Saginaw) and to construct a brine evaporating operation with two blocks consisting of 100 kettles. They also had a salt well, which they shared with George S. Johnson, another entrepreneur, who owned a lot next to Flagler and York's property.[35]

Flagler & York was not the only Harkness family operation in the area, although it was the first and largest. Stephen Harkness opened a salt company, also in the Salina area, with one block of fifty kettles, representing an initial investment of $16,000. As befitted his exalted station in life, Harkness had a superintendent, Isaac Russell of Mackinaw, Michigan, running his daily operation. The Harkness firm did not operate a well: it simply distilled salt from brine that well owners furnished.[36]

Salt production at the beginning of the Civil War could be a very profitable enterprise. Costs were relatively low: The operation of a block required two skilled workmen at $1.75 a day and one apprentice at $1.25. The barrels usually cost from $.27 to $.28, with nailing and packing the barrels costing $.035 a barrel. Therefore, during the summer months, the production of salt cost the owner $.80 a barrel. By the end of the 1862 season, it cost $1.08 in Saginaw to produce a barrel of salt, while it was costing $1.537 in Syracuse, New York, Saginaw's competition. With the price of

13

salt ranging from two to three times that amount, it is easy to understand why Flagler and York left the security of Bellevue for the opportunities of Saginaw salt.[37]

By the end of 1863, Flagler & York was among the pace-setting salt manufacturers in the valley. With a total output during 1863 of 15,000 barrels, the relatively small operation ranked third in per-kettle output, with each of its kettles accounting for 150 barrels of salt for the year. With such a promising beginning, the young entrepreneurs obtained property located next to their operation, consisting of a salt well and two blocks with 110 kettles, on a five-year lease. The east side of the Saginaw River was booming. Most of the commercial and business class on that side of the river lived in East Saginaw, while workers and the salt operations themselves were located in Salina, just to the south. Also, spread throughout the area, especially just south of the Cass River, were salt wells. Flagler and York owned a major tract along the Cass River, but existing records do not indicate they sunk any wells there.[38]

The Flaglers and Yorks took an active part in their community of East Saginaw. As always, Flagler was very involved in religious activities. In 1858, a group of Presbyterians and Congregationalists, having moved across the river from Saginaw, had established a new church. The small congregation, by a vote of 18 to 4, expressed a desire to organize along Congregational rules of order, thereby becoming the First Congregational Church of East Saginaw. Flagler became active in the affairs of the church. He served as superintendent of the Sabbath School, which met on Sunday afternoons, even though he was not a member of the church at the beginning of his three-year superintendency in 1863. On July 2, 1865, Henry and Mary formally joined the church. Later, Flagler served as one of its trustees.[39]

Flagler became involved in Sabbath School activities beyond the local church level. During one 1865 gathering, the Saginaw Valley Sabbath School Association appointed him as a part of a two-man team to secure speakers for the group. A year later, the association chose him to be a part of a committee formed to raise money to support a missionary. Flagler spent six days of his week in the world's work, but the seventh was fully devoted to his religious roles.[40]

Flagler had other nonbusiness interests during these years. He and other East Saginaw citizens wished to provide the community with at least some cultural activities. The population had grown from 1,712 in 1860 to 5,426 in 1866. The 1866 city directory for the communities in the area indicated that East Saginaw was already 1½ times as large as its parent community of

Saginaw. Flagler took an active interest in the new cultural center, named Irving Hall, which was completed in 1864. As a member of the Young Men's Association, he served on a committee of the association charged with the responsibility of founding a permanent literary society, known as the Lecture Association. The first lecture series at Irving Hall occurred during the winter of 1864–65.[41]

While Flagler had outside religious and cultural interests, Barney York's activities beyond Flagler & York tended to be merely an extension of business affairs. He was active on the Board of Trade. He was also a founder and first president of the Saginaw County Agricultural Society. These positions, however, were of relatively little importance to the business survival of Flagler & York; Barney York's service on what was termed the city enlistment committee in 1865 was another matter. He may have been active in the organization earlier during the Civil War for he had risen to a place of leadership by the last year of the war. The enlistment committee was an organization which, by assessing friends in the business community $20 apiece, attempted to raise money to pay substitutes to meet the city's yearly draft quota of forty-eight men. If the quota was reached, Flagler, York, and other community leaders would not only avoid the draft but also the embarrassment of individually paying substitutes. One might imagine that Flagler gladly contributed $20 for the cause. The other major committee of the Saginaw citizens was the vigilance committee, which had as its responsibility keeping other communities from hiring substitutes from the Saginaw area.[42]

Flagler and York were in Saginaw on a mission to make money, and they were reaping the rewards of their dedication. The Civil War years were good ones for the Flagler & York Salt Company. The best estimate is that Flagler & York made an 1863 profit of $26,850. The young entrepreneurs did not stop with their salt operations. Flagler and York sought to fully utilize all of their Salina property. Since only a small portion of their original 16½-acre tract was necessary for their salt venture, in the spring of 1864, they had a land surveyor plat a portion of their holdings for the Flagler & York Addition of Salina. They divided this property into forty-seven lots, most of which were selling after the Civil War for from $250 to $300 each. Salina had sprung up with the salt wells of the area in late 1862. By the summer of 1864, it had a population of 1,100 in what could only be described as a frontier boomtown. The saws and hammers could be heard throughout the community in May 1864, as two churches, two planing mills, and an academy were under construction. These were in addition to typical structures already on the scene: six saloons, two meat markets, three public houses, seven boarding houses, assorted other establishments required of civilization, and, of course, Salina's reason for existence: twenty salt blocks and sawmills.[43]

There continued to be times of sharing among the Harkness women in spite of the wartime separation. In the summer of 1863, Jennie Flagler sent her Aunt Phena (Tryphene Harkness, Mary Flagler's youngest sister) a cake for her nineteenth birthday. However, the heartache of the great distance separating the family was still evident. Mary Harkness lamented the fact that Jennie and Mary Flagler would not be coming with Julia York for a visit to Bellevue. Although the potential of the Saginaw area continued to attract the business vision of Flagler and York, the end of the Civil War seemed to have had a different meaning in Bellevue. Mary Harkness more than ever seemed to miss her two daughters far away on the Michigan frontier. In the summer of 1865, she wrote Mary about the raspberry and blackberry pickings, and other summertime activities in which they could engage as a family, if only all the family were in Bellevue. She especially pleaded for a visit from her granddaughter Jennie. By December, her letter upon the anniversary of Carrie's death was especially emotional.[44]

The war years were not as kind to the Flagler and Harkness women on the Ohio home front as it had been to the men on the war and business fronts. The deaths of Flagler's mother and daughter in 1861 were a prelude to later tragedies in the family. In December 1863 Phena Harkness died; her death was followed by that of Dan and Bell's eight-year-old daughter, Katie, in February of 1864. Then, on July 5, 1864, Bell died.[45] It had been a tragic Civil War for the Harkness-Flagler family.

The war's end had also altered the economic position of Flagler & York. The lack of wartime demand devastated the overextended salt manufacturers. By October 1865 buyers offered only $1.50 a barrel for Saginaw salt, and the following year the predicament of salt manufacturers became exceedingly desperate. Four companies did not even reopen for business after the normal winter shutdown. Judging from his increasing church commitments in 1865, Flagler was unaware of the negative implications of the war's end on the salt industry. Flagler & York had the dubious honor of being the largest salt company operating in South Saginaw, as Salina was now called; but the position was hardly worth the price. Flagler & York, with four blocks and 208 kettles, produced only 18,000 barrels of salt in 1866, with 3,500 barrels still on hand at year's end. The relatively large number of employees (thirty-four) at Flagler & York intensified the problem.[46]

The movement of salt manufacturers toward monopoly in the late 1860s was a prelude to Standard Oil's more famous business practices in the 1870s. More importantly for our purposes, however, is the effect this movement must have had on Henry Flagler. As his independent, free-entrepreneurial effort at salt manufacture failed after the Civil War, Flagler must have felt his anger give way to grudging admiration as his salt competitors demonstrated the advantages of cooperation over competition. With this in mind, a full account of the movement toward combination in the salt industry is important.

Throughout the Civil War, salt manufacturers had sought ways to halt the "cut-throat competition" occurring in their industry. In the 1862 annual report of the East Saginaw Salt Manufacturing Company, Dr. H. C. Porter, described by the *Saginaw Courier* as one of the more progressive members of the firm, stated his hope that some type of arrangement could be made that would allow someone to oversee the manufacture, transportation, and distribution of Saginaw Valley salt. His ultimate goal was to

secure such union of interest as will place our salt in the hands of common agents and build up a distinctive salt trade for the Saginaw valley *free from competition among ourselves* and enabled by the certainty of a supply and by uniformity in price and quality to acquire and retain a foothold in the markets of the lakes. [emphasis added][47]

Failing to admit that the abnormally high prices had been caused by Civil War demand, some blamed the failure of the Saginaw salt industry after the war on the "want of the proper protection," as the *Saginaw Daily Enterprise* summarized the situation in the bleak month of December 1866. Some Saginaw salt manufacturers did not believe that they could afford to wait on the passage of inspection laws for their "proper protection" to be effected. During January 1867, a headline of the *Saginaw Enterprise* trumpeted the news: "SALT MANUFACTURE. Important Meeting—Proposition for Combination—The Details in Full—Questions of Consolidating the Entire Valley Interests—Another Meeting to be Held."[48]

Much of the impetus for the Saginaw combination meeting had come from the successful salt manufacturing association in Bay County, located on Saginaw Bay just to the north of Saginaw at the mouth of the river. In 1866 the salt manufacturers there had organized the Bay County Salt Association. Although their output was not as great as that of Saginaw, accounting for only about one-third of the production of the valley, the Bay Countians had seen their salt priced at an average of about $.20 to $.30 a barrel more than they could have earned without combination. Saginaw

County quickly followed with a cooperative venture of its own. The Saginaw Salt Company became a clearinghouse, governed by a board, which oversaw everything from regulating wood haulers to the price of the salt. Immediately, two-thirds of the salt companies still operating in Saginaw County signed contracts with the new association. Soon thereafter, the interests in Saginaw and Bay counties resolved their minor differences to form the Bay and Saginaw Salt Company.[49]

By the end of the 1860s, the salt manufacturers of the nation had reached combination, either directly or indirectly. The *Saginaw Weekly Enterprise* had predicted in January 1866 what would be needed for the process to work:

> Something doubtless might be done by an agreement among the salt men to limit and regulate the quantity produced. To make any such arrangement effective, however, it should embrace, not only Saginaw, but the Onondaga manufacturers also. As the Onondaga Salt association have long operated on the principle of limiting their product, there is no doubt they would readily unite with our Salt men in a general arrangement of the kind.

Although there was no formal arrangement to limit supplies, the economic situation had already taken care of that before the combination arrangements were in place. One of the firms to close was the Flagler & York Salt Company.[50]

Henry Flagler watched this process of combination from Cleveland, Ohio. He had left Saginaw in 1866 a failure in business. He did manage to sell his home in Saginaw in March of 1866 at a handsome profit. The Flaglers briefly returned to Bellevue. Now in poverty, Henry, Mary, and Jennie boarded with a family, and he worked at a local dry goods store. Not willing to give up, Flagler, after only a few months in Bellevue, went to Cleveland to rebuild his life. Barney York continued on the scene in Saginaw throughout 1866 and 1867, most surely keeping his partner posted on the events unfolding in Saginaw. Finally, York also moved to Cleveland in the middle of 1867. Although their firm continued to be listed as a salt concern through 1868, Flagler & York produced no salt after 1866. Henry Flagler and Barney York were bankrupt.[51]

In 1871—at a meeting in Cleveland—the salt interests of the nation finally made official what was already a reality: they entered into a national pooling agreement, which took care of the problems caused by what was perceived as too much competition. Flagler & York was never involved in the Saginaw Salt Company scheme to control prices, but Flagler brought the lessons of Saginaw to bear on his later business decisions. In his salt venture, he had been a victim of what he would later term "unbridled competition." He never allowed that to happen again.[52]

In comparing Flagler's early career with that of other post–Civil War business leaders, one is primarily struck with his uniqueness. In some ways, it is true, he did fit the mold. His religious affiliation was within mainline Protestantism, which ranged from Baptist John Rockefeller to Methodist Daniel Drew, a Wall Street speculator. Flagler's education, while not through the secondary level, was beyond rudimentary. What did set Flagler apart were his experiences in the rough-and-tumble entrepreneurial environment of the West, which were at variance with the more exacting— although not necessarily less threatening to competition—business methods being learned in eastern centers such as Philadelphia, Baltimore, and New York. The most striking difference between Flagler and many future millionaires who were his contemporaries was that the latter emerged from the Civil War with a strong start toward their fortunes, whereas Flagler was bankrupt after the Saginaw debacle. Flagler's ability, in his middle thirties, to rebound from his business defeat was a tribute to his infinite faith in his own and the nation's economic future. Later in his career, when asked the secret to his financial success, Flagler responded, "Keep your head above the waters financially and bet on the growth of your country."[53]

During the 1860s, Flagler had bet on the growth of the country—but had failed to keep his head above the waters financially. However, that did not mean that Flagler's early business experience should be dismissed as merely a failure when compared with his tremendous career with Standard Oil. In fact, during the 1840s and 1850s, he had tasted the fruits of economic success in pre–Civil War Ohio. At age thirty-one, on the eve of the Civil War, he seemed well on the way to at least a modest fortune by the standards of the day. He had married a merchant's daughter and become a partner in the family firm. There was a Harkness family network ready to undergird him financially. The Saginaw experience during the war indicated a weakness in Flagler as a businessman: he neither consolidated his gains nor made economic projections as he expanded his business empire. The debacle at Saginaw after the war did not change Flagler's basic goals in life; thereafter, he would continue to seek wealth—but in so doing he would attempt to keep risks to a minimum, usually through "cooperation."

THE STANDARD YEARS

THE 1860s was one of the most economically wrenching decades in American history. The nation was moving from regional economic markets to ones that, thanks to the beginnings of the railroad revolution, were becoming national in scope. Therefore, when considering the rise of Rockefeller and his partners to dominance of the petroleum sector of the nation's economy, it may be more important for us to ask, "How did the Standard organization survive?" rather than merely, "How did Standard crush its competitors?" When John Rockefeller addressed that issue, he asserted that the general economic conditions were crushing his competition—a self-serving statement, but that does not make it any less true. Certainly, as we have just seen, the general economic conditions had devastated the salt manufacturing firm of Flagler & York immediately after the Civil War.

In the post–Civil War "search for order," as historian Robert Weibe so aptly phrased it, many pre–Civil War entrepreneurs involved in both old-line ventures and new get-rich-quick schemes went bankrupt, while others profited from risks associated with the early days of the oil industry. Americans had already begun to use coal oil, a light-oil derivative of coal first manufactured in the early 1850s. Over three-quarters of the country's homes, however, still relied on candles, lard, or whale oil for their lighting. Meanwhile, the only use Americans had found for surface crude oil was as an ingredient in patent medicines, which usually relied on alcohol for their "effectiveness." In fact, John Rockefeller's father had been one of the purveyors of the "medicine."[1]

The petroleum industry radically changed the way Americans and Europeans viewed the slimy product. In the late 1850s, researchers discovered that kerosene, a derivative of the ooze, could be used to light homes and businesses. That led "Colonel" Samuel Drake to sink a well in search of more crude oil. On August 27, 1859, Drake successfully drilled a well at Titusville, Pennsylvania. That area in the northwestern portion of the state, soon to be known as the Oil Regions (or simply the Regions), immediately began pumping out an annual production of 200,000 barrels. By the time the Civil War had ended, over half the production of the nation's refineries was headed to the European market.[2]

During the early days of the oil industry, it was a rough-hewn business frontier. Teamsters originally hauled most of the crude oil from the wells to refineries by wagon, a dangerous task with the highly volatile crude. When the water was high enough, oil barges could be floated down the Allegheny River to Pittsburgh. Early on, however, railroads began to dominate oil transportation. Cleveland's Atlantic & Great Western Railroad moved quickly to claim a portion of the Regions' crude for her refineries. While still being built, the Atlantic had begun in 1862 to connect with short line roads serving the Regions. Then, on November 3, 1863, when the Atlantic opened its through service to New York City, with its connection via the New York Central, a transportation network providing Cleveland with connections with both the crude oil and the export markets was fully in place.[3]

Along the Atlantic's tracks in Cleveland, a number of oil refining operations sprang up to take advantage of this location. John Rockefeller was one of these entrepreneurs. He and his grain merchandising partner Maurice Clark began their investment in Samuel Andrews's refining operation as a secondary venture. When Rockefeller took a greater interest in the oil refinery, the Clark brothers (Rockefeller, Andrews and Maurice Clark having been joined by Clark's brothers James and Richard) would not go along with additional investment in such a risky enterprise. Rockefeller, only twenty-five years old, bought out the Clarks' interest in the oil partnership in 1865 and with Andrews formed the refining firm of Rockefeller & Andrews.[4]

In spite of the statements of persons such as Rockefeller and historian Allan Nevins, it was transportation—and not efficiency and economies of scale—that allowed Rockefeller and his partners to dominate the refining portion of the American oil industry. In the late 1860s, the railroads were leading the way toward the nationalization of the economy. While our textbooks continue to emphasize the exciting story of the development of the transcontinental lines, it was the development of the trunk lines (the Erie, New York Central, Pennsylvania, and Baltimore & Ohio systems) that marked the real revolution in railroading. This process ended many local monopolies (e.g., blacksmith shops and retail grocers) that had earlier been able to make handsome profits because of a lack of outside competition. On the other hand, it created national and international markets for those businessmen willing to work toward such goals. Because the railroads between Chicago and New York overbuilt in the period after the Civil War, they were forced to give excellent rates to large-volume shippers in order to meet fixed-debt costs. Therefore, trunk line officials were much more concerned with consistent shipments by large shippers than they were with being fair. With volume shippers paying off the fixed debt, the railroad officials could then turn to other, smaller shippers for their profits.[5]

One of the industries that took early advantage of the freight-rate situation was the infant petroleum industry. Specifically, we shall see in The Standard Years how Henry Flagler, as the principal rate negotiator first for the partnership and then for Standard, used the American devotion to the ideal of laissez faire as a tool within the transportation realm to allow Standard to become the dominant force in the refining phase of the oil industry. While this approach does emphasize Flagler's role in Standard, it is not meant to eclipse the all-important role of Rockefeller. A good analogy would be that Rockefeller was the architect of Standard policies, while Flagler was the builder of the program in certain areas. Flagler used Standard's power within its sector of the economy to make transportation merely Standard's handmaiden. Transportation competition became the primary means for Standard's horizontal integration (control of refining). That phase was over by the mid-1870s; Standard then moved more and more into direct involvement in transportation during the late 1870s, so totally dominating the oil industry that the creation of the Standard Oil Trust in 1882 became an internal business necessity, not merely a device to thwart state laws.

Rockefeller, Andrews & Flagler

HENRY FLAGLER, the eternal optimist, quickly put the Saginaw disaster behind him. By midsummer 1866, he and his family were in Cleveland. They first boarded at the Russell House. As was their habit, they quickly found a religious home; Henry and Mary Flagler joined the First Presbyterian Church (later known as the Old Stone Church) in April 1867. Flagler had come to Cleveland to take a job with Rockefeller's old grain merchandising firm, reorganized as Clark & Sanford. Not only did this position allow Flagler to build on knowledge gained by his pre–Civil War business experiences, but it also renewed ties with John Rockefeller. Although Rockefeller had left the Clark brothers partnership in the middle of the Civil War to pursue the oil trade full-time as a partner in Rockefeller & Andrews, he was still available to Flagler for advice. In fact, Rockefeller and Flagler had many opportunities to discuss business, for Rockefeller rented Flagler desk space in Rockefeller's own office on the second floor of the Sexton Building.[1]

According to his own account, Flagler met with immediate success. He recalled this period as a grain merchant as a lucrative one. He repaid his father-in-law $100,000, which had been used to erase his Saginaw debts. He also bought out his grain partners and reorganized the firm as H. M. Flagler & Company, with Barney York as his partner. Flagler had earned enough in a year's time to enable him to enter into John Rockefeller's oil partnership. Flagler's recollection, however, seems to be contradictory to the facts. First, although he was undoubtedly in debt at the end of the Saginaw venture, he owed much less than $100,000. Also, it is doubtful that

26

very much, if any, of his initial investment in oil came from his own "fortune."[2]

The exact terms that united Flagler with the Rockefeller concern are not known. From Rockefeller's vantage point, his need for additional capital ironically led to the invitation to the financially recuperating Flagler. Rockefeller's firm expanded as rapidly as his credit line at the local banks would allow. By 1867, he had reached his credit limit and was looking for new sources of capital. From business relationships established during the previous decade and conversations with Flagler, he knew of the immense fortune that Lamon Harkness and his kin, especially Stephen Harkness, had accumulated. More than likely, Stephen or Lamon Harkness loaned Flagler the money to buy into the Rockefeller partnership. Stephen Harkness also came in as a silent partner, with Flagler voting his interest. The partners renamed the firm Rockefeller, Andrews & Flagler. What Rockefeller saw in Flagler was not necessarily Flagler's own capital, but his business genius: a shrewdness in identifying new opportunities and then capitalizing on their potential. Although Flagler could fail in business, as he had done in Saginaw, Rockefeller offered a counterbalance: his own fanatical fascination with wringing a profit from the close control of the day-to-day operations of the business. Samuel Andrews, the third active partner in Cleveland, was in charge of the refining process itself.[3]

The exact details of Flagler's entry into the oil business matter little. What does concern us here is the fact that Flagler quickly became Rockefeller's most trusted adviser and intimate confidant. Their desks were back to back, and they would pass drafts of letters back and forth between one another until the intent and clarity of language satisfied both of them. During the 1870s, when they lived near each other on Euclid Avenue, they would discuss major business decisions while walking to and from work. Such a relationship would later cause Flagler to state, "A friendship founded on business is better than a business founded on friendship." Flagler helped bridge the generation gap between Rockefeller, who was nine years his junior, and the monied interests of Cleveland. Flagler also had developed a keen mind for drawing up contracts and other legal documents. Most importantly, Flagler's Saginaw experience had taught him the great dangers inherent in "ruinous competition"; therefore, he and Rockefeller were as one in their determination to put the Cleveland oil industry on sound footing so that it could be a paying proposition into the future, rather than just a quick-silver venture in speculation.[4]

This is not to say that speculation was not a part of their operating principles. The letter books kept at the New York office of William Rockefeller

& Company reveal that the firm of Rockefeller, Andrews & Flagler constantly played the oil futures market for any advantage that could be gained. During this early period in the history of the oil industry, the difference between success and failure could be determined by just a couple of cents per gallon of refined oil. Rockefeller, Andrews & Flagler had its greatest expense in the purchase of crude oil. In October 1867, of a total expense of $34^1/_7$ cents per gallon in the production of refined oil, 12 cents of it was for crude oil purchases; $5^1/_7$ cents for a federal tax; $5\frac{1}{2}$ cents for barrels; only $4\frac{1}{2}$ cents for the actual refining of the products; and 7 cents for the expenses of the New York office, which included transportation and brokerage fees. John Rockefeller's younger brother, William, managed William Rockefeller & Company in New York City, with the "& Company" understood to be the other RA&F partners.[5]

John Andrews, Samuel's brother, was stationed in Oil City, the most important producing center of the booming Oil Regions of northwestern Pennsylvania. The Cleveland and New York offices would send telegraph messages instructing him how to buy. William Rockefeller kept a close watch on the price quotations coming from Antwerp, Belgium, since most American kerosene during this period was bound for the European markets. RA&F fine-tuned its purchases with its transportation arrangements. In November 1867 William Rockefeller commanded Andrews to buy all the oil required under the old contracts with crude oil producers, but to time his shipments of these purchases in such a way that RA&F would have continuous control of tank cars.[6]

RA&F speculated on both ends of the oil market: buying crude and selling refined. In November 1867 John Rockefeller informed Flagler he was buying all the crude oil he could as it came to market. This was a very risky proposition, for at that time refined oil was selling more cheaply than crude. The Allegheny River was assisting Cleveland refiners during this crisis. The river, flowing from the Oil Regions to Pittsburgh (Cleveland's greatest rival in the refining business) was so low that Pittsburgh was unable to easily obtain crude oil. RA&F anxiously awaited the opening of the Allegheny Valley Railroad, which would finally give its competitors in Pittsburgh a direct rail link with the Oil Regions.[7]

The oil market in the fall of 1867 was extremely erratic. On November 5 John Rockefeller, writing Flagler about the continuing low price of refined oil, suggested that RA&F "*beat* the market & get some cheap oil without selling *any*." Also, Rockefeller indicated that by buying in volume, RA&F could get discounts ranging from $.005 to $.01 a gallon. With this kind of advice, Flagler did buy a 5,000-barrel lot of oil, but at once John Rockefeller, then in New York, reprimanded him for the decision. Rockefeller put the matter bluntly:

> I am very sorry you bought the 5000 barrels oil. There are workings in the market we can judge of better than you and we can know every 5 minutes what Philadelphia is and through a dozen brokers buy any amounts. We ordered a resale *immediately* at 29¢, without any brokerage, the seller *always* pays brokerage but in 3 minutes after broker left office another broker, who was under obligations to us came at top of his speed saying Antwerp 40^2 [40½] & advancing. We expected it, as were privately advised in N.Y. [that brokers] had been buying freely in Antwerp. We countermanded the order to sell at 29¢ hoping to do better in morn on the flurry if one sets in on the report.[8]

This indicates that Flagler, new to the oil business, was unfamiliar with the international marketplace. Grain merchandising and salt manufacturing had prepared him to negotiate with transportation agencies, but not for this type of international speculation.

By the end of November, RA&F had positioned itself well. The New York office wrote Cleveland, "We are filling our contracts as fast as possible, are anxious to get the big differences in our own pockets." Soon thereafter RA&F was again buying as the price of refined oil declined during December. The plan was as it had been earlier: only sell what has been contracted, buy at the lower prices, sell from time to time on the spot market to keep afloat, and hold back all other oil until prices again rise.[9]

When the Cleveland office chastised William Rockefeller for not selling before the sharp fall in prices in late January, he fired back: "We know you *urged* selling, & are also consious [*sic*] of the fact we worked mightily hard *to sell*, & taking everything into consideration think we did *well* & that you ought not to reflect on us for not accomplishing more, it is very much easier to *urge* selling by writing & telegraphing, than it is to talk exporters into buying at the figures you *urge*."[10] Except for this harsh exchange, the selling of RA&F oil was a smooth transaction within the organization.

One of the most critical needs of RA&F continued to be credit. The RA&F partners were rapidly expanding their business during the late 1860s and were always borrowing money to speculate in the oil futures market in New York. They also borrowed money to meet immediate needs, such as payments on current shipments arriving in New York. At times, the debt situation led to a credit crunch. RA&F's financial crisis took on extraordinary proportions in November 1867. When someone attempted to cash some RA&F debt paper at the Ocean Bank in New York, the bank—

to the embarrassment of the RA&F—refused to honor the paper. Upon checking the situation, William Rockefeller discovered that the Cleveland office had allowed the debt paper to be written without informing him. He quickly covered the paper in question, but then advised Cleveland to take up all paper still in circulation to avoid another such incident.[11]

Without a full accounting of RA&F market speculations, it is impossible to state its role in the success of the Cleveland refining firm. However, the attempts by Flagler and the Rockefeller brothers to lessen the risk of spot pricing by broadening the RA&F holdings of oil futures suggest that theirs was a defensive policy of speculation, which allowed them to survive when other refiners were going bankrupt. It was a high-stakes match, refiners in one corner and producers and buyers in other corners—all of them attempting to outwit the market. In August 1867, for instance, buyers were withholding purchases hoping that refiners would be forced to dump warehoused products on the market at the end of the month. As buyers awaited a lowering of August prices, they did indeed tumble.[12]

During 1868 the Cleveland oil industry had the first of what would become many crises over the next decade. It was so severe that some refineries attempted to sell the crude they had on hand. In March 1868 no firm in Cleveland, Pittsburgh, or New York was buying crude. The April instructions from RA&F's Cleveland office to John Andrews commanded him to buy only enough crude to stay a day or two ahead of reduced refining needs. By summer, the crisis had passed, at least for RA&F. The Cleveland office then instructed Andrews to buy all the crude he could on an allowance of approximately $6,000 a week.[13]

A number of oil refiners, including RA&F, continued to engage in speculation. The price of oil was erratic throughout 1868, but tended toward the downward side. During January, Cozzen & Company, another refiner, went bankrupt and took an exporting company down with it. William Rockefeller's assessment of the failure contained words of wisdom for his partners in Cleveland: " 'Cozzen' failure will prove very bad, regular swindle we think. probably will not pay 5¢ on the dollar. Isn't it a warning to *speculators*. I guess we better swear off." Although this may have caused Flagler and Rockefeller some second thoughts, they certainly did not "swear off" their risk-taking ways. William Rockefeller continued to keep his eye on New York, Philadelphia, and Antwerp markets throughout 1868, noting each $.005 change in the market, on both spot and futures. During this period, RA&F was guided by its statement of September 1867 that it would be best for the firm to make a $2.00 profit on each barrel and let others benefit from further speculation. Given the price of refined oil at the time, that reflected a profit margin of 16 percent. If RA&F could continue its $2.00-a-barrel profit margin as the price declined, the profit would be even greater.[14]

One result of the crisis was the congressional decision to reduce, then eliminate, the wartime tax of $.20 a gallon on crude oil for domestic consumption, a change highly beneficial to refiners. In April 1868, the tax fell to $.10 and in June was completely removed. Henry Flagler was the chief RA&F lobbyist in the effort. First, he met with a large group of refining representatives at a Pittsburgh convention in February and then journeyed to Washington to consult with interested parties about the removal of the tax.[15]

During the spring of 1868, Cleveland refiners found the market particularly difficult. The price of crude oil increased while refined held steady. Meanwhile a railroad rate war erupted in Pennsylvania, which resulted in Pittsburgh refiners shipping at $1.225 a barrel rather than $1.575. In spite of this situation, RA&F continued to run its Cleveland refinery at its full capacity of 900 barrels a day. The purpose was to beat an even lower June price for refined, which William was predicting as early as April.[16]

Having become accustomed to the oil market environment of erratic prices, RA&F adopted a new maxim: "Sell when others want to buy, etc. etc." For example, when the market in late April 1868 showed a strong upward tendency from its doldrums, RA&F did sell. Toward the end of the month, however, even RA&F was avoiding its own counsel. The refined market had risen to $.27 a gallon, but RA&F, along with other sellers, held oil off the market and hoped for higher prices. William telegraphed Cleveland: "Have not offered any of your June today. are holding off little. perhaps we are influenced too much by the great bull market, if you think so speak your mind freely tlgm. as we may hold on too long."[17] In spite of such concerns, speculation had allowed RA&F to soften somewhat the general trend of the oil prices in a downward direction.

Transportation arrangements were the key to the survival of RA&F. All participants in the oil industry admitted the superior efficiency of RA&F refineries, but the firm seemed to have a vulnerable geographical situation. The market for most American kerosene was Europe. The source for the product was the Oil Regions of northwestern Pennsylvania. If railroads, in their obligation as common carriers, had continued to charge their customers rates based on standard ton-per-mile calculations, RA&F and other Cleveland refiners would not have survived. New York and Philadelphia refiners would have benefited by being on a direct route between the fields and Europe, and Pittsburgh refiners were near the Oil Regions. Cleveland would have suffered from the fact that companies had to transport crude west for refining in Cleveland, thereby making Cleveland the westernmost point for the movement of refined oil eastward. RA&F always felt it would be competitive with refiners in other areas *provided transportation costs were roughly equal.*[18] RA&F, therefore, began a program in the 1860s that would later be closely associated with the meteoric rise of Standard Oil in the 1870s: seek competitive equality at the eastern seaboard by offsetting RA&F's unfavorable geographic situation with very favorable transportation agreements.

Flagler, as RA&F's chief transportation negotiator, first sought to obtain the best available freight rates. He utilized the Erie Canal as much as possible during the warm weather months. When the waterway was frozen over during the winter, however, railroads would raise rates until the first thaw. Toward the end of each shipping season over the Erie Canal, the canal transport agencies were reluctant to guarantee shipment of oil. As a result, Flagler would stop shipments about mid-November. When canal operators refused RA&F a guarantee of oil in late transit, Flagler threatened to sign exclusive rail contracts, and the canal companies became much more cooperative.[19]

Two major rail lines served Cleveland during the late 1860s, the Atlantic & Great Western and the Lake Shore. In February 1868, as RA&F sought Cleveland-to-New York rate contracts, the New York office thought that there was some collusion in freight rate negotiations between the Atlantic and the Erie, which was the Atlantic's eastern connection at Salamanca, New York. Flagler understood that a contract with the roads would be in two parts, one from October 1 to April 1, and a lower rate from April 1 until the close of navigation on the Erie Canal. Although the summer rail rate was higher than that of the canal, RA&F preferred a rail contract: "We favor very much Rail shipments if they were to give right rate & contract for season. We think it would do the Canal people good for *us* to leave them for one year."[20] At this point, it does not seem to have occurred to the RA&F partners to think in terms of a lower, consistent rail rate year-round that would eliminate use of the canal. Soon enough though, it became Standard Oil policy to use rails exclusively.

Even at this early date, the Atlantic's Robert B. Potter gave RA&F a drawback. While complaining of the Atlantic's $1.93-a-barrel rate— Flagler was attempting to get a $1.75 rate—he was thankful that the Atlantic would continue to give RA&F a drawback. A drawback, given at the end of each month, was a sum of money given by a railroad to one shipper, in this case RA&F, whenever the road transported a competing shipper's product, in this case, for each barrel of refined oil *other* firms shipped via the Atlantic. The advantage to RA&F was obvious; the Atlantic entered into the deal because it swelled its gross revenues, which looked good to the stockholders.[21]

In the early months of 1868, Flagler continued to negotiate for contracts with both canal and rail interests, all the time hoping that rail interests would be RA&F's eventual partner. One reason for this attitude was the high-handed tactics of canal transporters. RA&F had finally filed suit against one canal company for damages to one of its shipments. Hiram Robbins, the owner of the company, had volunteered to give RA&F $.50 on the dollar for the damages. RA&F found this compromise unacceptable, took Robbins to court, and finally won the legal battle.[22]

A second reason for Flagler's preference for rail over canal transport was that some fast freight lines, especially the Empire Transportation Company, began to use tank cars instead of barrels for transporting oil. As noted earlier, RA&F paid more for barrels than the refining process itself. Also, the New York office constantly complained to Cleveland of loose bands, leakage of oil, and poor workmanship in general, which caused some of RA&F's profit to be "lost" in transit. Although RA&F's interoffice complaints reflected a pride in the reputation of its product, these problems would in large part be remedied through the use of tank cars.[23]

The Erie Railroad became a major stumbling block in rate negotiations. Although the relationship would soon become more amicable, Flagler thought, at the beginning of 1868, that the uncooperative attitude of the Erie Railroad would force RA&F to go with a canal rather than a rail contract. When the negotiations with the Erie and its link, the Atlantic, did break down, Flagler switched to negotiations with the Empire, still hoping to avoid a canal contract. The Empire, closely associated with the Pennsylvania Railroad, offered several concessions to RA&F, including delivery to the RA&F yard at no additional cost. RA&F's New York office continued to be noncommittal to the Empire during the negotiations, advising Flagler that it preferred a link with the Erie via the Atlantic. The negotiations dragged on into March, with the Empire being kept waiting while Flagler negotiated with the Erie and the canal companies. His break came on March 6, 1868, when the New York morning papers reported a great rate war caused by the Erie's refusal to sign a rate agreement with the other major rail trunk lines. The RA&F New York office was elated: "[W]e think perhaps something may come as profit for us. Keep your 'eye' on J.M.c. [James

McHenry, guiding force behind the Atlantic]." An RA&F spy in the Erie camp informed Flagler that the Erie was willing to lower its rate for RA&F to $1.58 a barrel.[24]

By the end of March, however, Flagler could wait no longer for a permanent rail contract and began shipping by canal. The rumors spread that the Pennsylvania had already given Pittsburgh refiners reduced rates. In spite of the new canal shipping, probably taking place without long-term contracts, Flagler's negotiations with the Erie and the Atlantic continued. The new problem in negotiations was the crude oil rate. Robert B. Potter, receiver of the Atlantic, threatened to tie the crude oil rate to RA&F's drawback of refined oil. Flagler explained that he did not care what the crude oil rate was, but did expect to receive a drawback on refined. The freight agent of the Erie understood Flagler's position on the matter, and the negotiations once again were proceeding smoothly. By April 18, 1868, the Erie agreed to give RA&F a drawback on refined of $.235 a barrel off its published rate of $1.75.[25]

With a new contract in hand for the summer season, Flagler began a series of critical negotiations with the Erie as the railroad sought to get a contract with RA&F that would extend until January 1, 1869. The immediate response of RA&F's New York office was to accuse the Erie once again of collusion with the Atlantic. Therefore, RA&F continued to use both rail and canal transport for its refined traffic through 1868. The rail contracts got RA&F into some difficult circumstances in New York as it had to keep up deliveries via rail to fulfill volume obligations at a time when refined oil was not selling at a good price.[26]

The spring and summer of 1868 proved to be RA&F's first great step toward its goal of dominating the refining capacity of the country. First, it signed a yearlong contract with the New York Central and its western connection, the Lake Shore, which included a $.175 drawback for refined oil traffic. This did not please the Erie interests, which had counted on the RA&F business. Finally, on June 15, 1868, RA&F also signed a contract with the Erie. This certainly did not end shipping refined via other lines, nor by other means. In fact, a mere two days later, the New York office of RA&F advised John Andrews to make a naphtha shipment by canal in order to beat the market margin by the slower, but cheaper, canal transport.[27]

It was in the transport of crude, however, that Henry Flagler was able to make his greatest gains for RA&F during 1868. That spring, Jay Gould, the master speculator of the era, was maneuvering control of the Erie road into his hands through stock manipulations. At the same time, Gould moved on other fronts to ensure that the Erie would be able to participate in the lucrative oil traffic. The Erie had no direct connections with the Oil Regions, but its western connection, the Atlantic did. Gould first needed to fix the situation so that the crude oil from the Regions found its way to Cleveland via the Atlantic. The Erie would thereby have removed the crude from the Pennsylvania road's territory. If Gould could further manipulate the situation, the Erie might receive at least an equal proportion of the refined traffic with the New York Central.[28]

Gould came up with an ingenious device: he bought the Allegheny Transportation Company from its founder, Henry Harley, who continued as the company's president in name only. In a series of agreements negotiated in the spring and summer of 1868, Gould, operating behind the scenes, closely bound the three major refiners of Cleveland to the Allegheny, and thereby an alliance was indirectly struck with the Erie. The first agreement to be signed was between the Allegheny Transportation Company and the Atlantic road. The Allegheny agreed it would not lay pipage to Franklin, where it could have connected with the Pennsylvania road via the Pennsylvania & Erie; rather, it would build a pipe to Oil City on the Atlantic line. In return, the Atlantic would give the Allegheny its most favorable rates at the Allegheny depots at Corry and Oil City.[29]

Representing RA&F, Flagler joined with the representatives of two other Cleveland refiners in signing an interesting partnership agreement on June 4, 1868. Gould gave Rockefeller, Andrews & Flagler; Clark, Payne & Company; and Westlake, Hutchins & Company a total of one-quarter of the shares of the Allegheny Transportation Company. Not only did the three refiners share one-fourth of the profits of the Allegheny, but they also received a 75 percent rebate on their individual shipments through the Allegheny pipes. In other words, the Allegheny would give RA&F a rebate of 75 percent on RA&F shipments plus its proportion of the one-quarter of the Allegheny profits to which the refiners were entitled.[30]

The day after the agreement was signed between the Allegheny and its refining partners, Flagler became a party to another contract between these refiners and the Atlantic road. In it, the Atlantic established the rate of $.60 a barrel of crude for the Corry-Cleveland and Oil City–Cleveland routes. The Atlantic assured its refining partners that no other Cleveland refining operation would receive a better rate from the road. It would also short bill the three refiners for full cars—with eighty-five–barrel capacity cars billed as though they only had eighty barrels.[31]

Flagler's ability as a negotiator can best be seen in his addendum to the contract, which stated that the contract only related to crude oil used by the refining parties in their own refineries.[32] What Flagler had done with the stroke of his pen was guarantee RA&F equity with its two major competitors in Cleveland. They would be transporting crude to Cleveland at the same rate as RA&F, but they would not be able to form alliances in order to pass along the lower transportation rates on crude to other refiners. Meanwhile, Flagler would be free to negotiate refined rates with any transportation agency, and Rockefeller could continue to expand RA&F's refining capacity in order to take full advantage of the crude oil transportation agreement.

As for Jay Gould, he used the Allegheny leverage to gain control of more oil traffic. By the end of the summer of 1868, Gould was president of the Erie. His next step toward conquest of the west was the establishment of a closer partnership with the Atlantic Road. James McHenry, the principal investor in the Atlantic, agreed to lease the Atlantic to the Erie provided the Atlantic's president Robert B. Potter was fired. The negotations were completed, Potter was fired, and Gould took control of the Atlantic early in 1869.[33]

No sooner had Gould gained control of the Atlantic than he had new competition for the oil traffic from the Oil Regions. Amasa Stone, vice-president of the Cleveland, Columbus & Cincinnati Railroad, president of the Cleveland, Painesville & Ashtabula Railroad, and soon to be a Rockefeller ally, had been leading a group of railroads informally known as the Lake Shore. This loose system was officially recognized with the formation of the Lake Shore and Michigan Southern Railroad on January 1, 1869.[34]

The Lake Shore completed a line to Oil City soon after its incorporation. At about the same time, the RA&F contract with the Atlantic was due to expire. Flagler approached James Devereux, vice-president and general manager of the Lake Shore, concerning the possibility of RA&F shipping crude oil over its line. Devereux offered Flagler a rebate, probably one-third off the usual $.60-a-barrel crude oil rate, in order to capture some of the RA&F business.[35] In all probability, the Atlantic countered with a similar offer. It must also be kept in mind that RA&F was still part owner of the Allegheny Transportation Company.

These activities of Flagler and his RA&F associates occurred during an exciting period of American economic history. During the five years following the Civil War, the American oil industry could only be described as a rapidly growing giant in chaos. By 1870, the annual shipments of refined oil bound for Europe had reached 140 million barrels. The industry was relatively easy to enter; therefore, many companies found themselves bankrupted by fierce competition coupled with poor business decisions.

Paul Giddens, the most noted historian of the Oil Regions of western Pennsylvania, described the entire period from 1868 through 1873 as one of depression for that area. In order to survive, producers developed new strategies. For example, in February 1869 a group of Oil Regions well owners formed the first petroleum producers' association. They attempted to attack certain governmental actions they considered injurious to their businesses, such as taxes on crude oil. The most pressing problem, however, was the number of producers. There were just too many small entrepreneurs sinking wells for anyone to talk in meaningful terms of a limitation on production, which would have been the easiest means of stabilizing prices at maximum rates of return.[36]

Refiners encountered similar, but more complex, problems. For example, RA&F saw its price margin of refined oil over crude oil reduced from an 1865 high of 33 percent steadily down to an 1870 low of 30 percent.[37] But by 1870, RA&F had come up with its solution to the problem: reduce oil freight rates. The market price of crude oil was only one component in the equation which comprised the gap between price and profit. Strangely enough, the greed of the anti-Cleveland Pennsylvania Railroad worked to the advantage of RA&F in this situation.

The Pennsylvania Railroad did not wish to see Pittsburgh become a major refining center. The rationale for this was that it was cheaper and more profitable for the Pennsylvania to carry crude oil to the Atlantic seaboard on a long haul than to carry it a relatively short distance to Pittsburgh, unload it for refining, and then haul the smaller cargo of refined oil to the coast. While the Pennsylvania dominated Pittsburgh, Flagler obtained reduced freight rates by playing the railroads serving Cleveland against one another, with the additional advantage of having the Erie Canal connection as a warm weather threat. RA&F and other Cleveland refiners used the reduced freight rates to their tremendous advantage, making Cleveland, by 1870, the largest refining center in the country.[38]

The great question for Flagler was how to expand the financial base of RA&F without the partners losing control of their company. His solution was for the RA&F partners to change from a partnership to an incorporated stock company. Their plan was to make sure that they retained control of the new corporation, while managing to bring in an infusion of capital. On January 10, 1870, the RA&F partners officially incorporated the Standard Oil Company of Ohio. The capitalization was 10,000 shares of stock at a par value of $100 a share; therefore, Standard Oil was originally incorporated for $1,000,000. The distribution of the shares was as follows: John Rockefeller, 2,667; Stephen Harkness, 1,334; Flagler, William Rockefeller, and Samuel Andrews, 1,333 each; and O. B. Jennings, 1,000. (Jennings was the brother-in-law of William Rockefeller's wife.)[39]

In the reorganization of the company, corporate titles were added, although the responsibilities of each person were already clearly understood. John Rockefeller became president, with the continuing role of general architect of Standard Oil policy and practice. Henry Flagler became secretary and treasurer, which allowed him the freedom to continue to develop his two areas of expertise: transportation arrangements and contractual obligations. William Rockefeller remained in New York in his position as vice-president, overseeing the exporting of oil. The real key to the growth of the company, however, was the one thousand shares of stock retained by John Rockefeller, which he held as a trustee of RA&F. He selectively used this stock to attract new investors into the company, persons with both money *and* influence who could add their expertise to Standard.[40] Rockefeller and his associates would continue to use this tactic in later expansions of Standard.

The first new addition to the company was Amasa Stone, definitely a person of influence. With Stone's purchase of 500 shares of Standard stock, Rockefeller and Flagler had established an important conduit to two businesses critical to the success of Standard: banking and transportation. Stone was not only a leader of the Lake Shore Railroad but also the vice-president of Cleveland's Second National Bank.[41]

Stone did not see a conflict of interest in investing in Standard, an important customer of the Lake Shore. Although some rail leaders of the late 1860s had been rather adamant before legislative investigating committees in stating their opposition to such activity, Stone had been forthright in his attitude. In 1867, during the Ohio senate investigation of fast-freight companies, Stone bluntly told the committee that he did indeed hold ownership in the American Express Company. He argued that since his investment in the express company was no more than 4 percent of his investment in his railroad stock, and since the Cleveland & Erie Railroad, of which he was president, only accounted for approximately one-fortieth of American Express's earnings, there was no ethical conflict in such activity.[42] His Standard Oil purchase, therefore, was only a continuation of his earlier business practices.

Stone saw great potential in the infant Standard. Although Standard began as a relatively small operation, compared with its later size, it already controlled 10 percent of the country's refining capacity by 1870. Its Cleveland operations consisted of two refineries, a barrel-making plant, tank cars, and shipping facilities for the lake traffic out of Cleveland—all of this on a sixty-acre tract of land in Cleveland. It also had facilities in New York, such as warehouses and storage tanks, for its export operations.[43]

As for Flagler, in less than five years, he had risen from bankruptcy to become second in command at Standard Oil, the emerging giant in the oil industry. In a sense, Flagler's success was an indication of John Rockefeller's ability to see administrative talent. On the other hand, with their close working arrangements before Flagler entered into the oil partnership, Rockefeller had had some time to assess Flagler's strengths and weaknesses. Once a part of Rockefeller, Andrews & Flagler, the 37-year-old Flagler made himself an indispensable member of the partnership. He served three principal roles: transportation negotiator, legal expert, and communicator with Rockefeller on new ideas. With the official formation of Standard Oil, Flagler continued to fulfill the three roles effectively.

Cleveland Company, National Business

THE AMERICAN OIL INDUSTRY of the early 1870s was an economic war zone. There were five major areas of economic conflict: among the railroads, among the producers, among the refiners, between refiners and producers, and between refiners and railroads. Throughout the decade, the alliances, level of competition, and degrees of cooperation continually shifted, but the most consistent factors were Standard's steady rise to dominance; the consolidation of railroads into major trunk line systems dominated by the Erie, New York Central, and the Pennsylvania; and the inability of the producers to control the price of crude oil.

The ink had hardly dried on the Standard Oil charter when a railroad freight rate war presented another opportunity to Flagler and Rockefeller. In 1870, the Erie and New York Central, now run by Jay Gould and Cornelius Vanderbilt, respectively, slashed their freight rates by at least 50 percent. Meanwhile, with the threat posed by the Pennsylvania and its refining and producing allies to destroy Cleveland's refiners, Standard took full advantage of the railroad situation. There was a rapid rise in crude oil shipments to Cleveland. With a 60 percent increase in crude oil volume—and a similar increase in refined oil leaving Cleveland—Flagler felt he had a legitimate reason for demanding further rate concessions from the railroads.[1]

Flagler went to James Devereux, vice-president and general manager of the Lake Shore, with a new proposal: Standard would stop its shipments through the Erie Canal if the Lake Shore would reduce its rate for Cleveland oil. He also promised the railroad that Standard would ship sixty carloads of refined to New York *every day of the year.* This type of volume *and* consistency were of great value to the Lake Shore. There was, however, another twist to this well-known agreement. Standard did not have sufficient daily refining capacity to enable Flagler to fulfill his extravagant promise. Instead, Standard had to become the broker for many Cleveland refiners.[2] In other words, at this date—long before the now infamous South Improvement Company pooling scheme of 1872—Standard was already promoting its ideas of cooperation, setting itself as first among "equals."

In exchange for Flagler's concessions, Devereux gave him a substantial reduction in rates. Rather than the regular $2.40 a barrel combination rate from the Oil Regions to Cleveland and thence to the seaboard, the Lake Shore gave Standard a rate of $1.65. Why such a discount? It was not only the volume that Flagler had promised but also its routine delivery—known as "evening"—that attracted Devereux to the proposal. By keeping some trains on a regular schedule to the coast carrying only oil, the Lake Shore used only 600 cars a month for what would ordinarily have required 1,800 cars. The Lake Shore's savings brought about by this relatively simple scheme were phenomenal. Devereux calculated that his railroad saved twenty days' interest on $600,000 worth of rolling stock each month by such an arrangement.[3] Flagler, by using such plans that were advantageous both to the railroad and Standard, proved himself to be a superior negotiator.

News of this contract was bound to leak. When competitors in Cleveland who were not a party to this arrangement heard of it, they rushed to Devereux to demand similar concessions. Devereux calmly but firmly stated his position: if they could supply the Lake Shore with similar volume and conditions, then he would give them the same consideration Standard had received. They could not meet this requirement, and although they lost this battle with Flagler and Rockefeller, Standard's Cleveland competitors renewed their determination to stop Standard if the opportunity ever presented itself.[4]

Standard emerged from railroad rate wars stronger than ever, while the roads found themselves weakened by the experience. For example, the Erie, after losing almost $700,000 on its Atlantic operation in 1870–71, sold that line to a group headed by former Union general George B. McClellan. Meanwhile, in early 1871, Standard declared a dividend of $40 a share, at a time when many oil refiners were going bankrupt.[5]

Not content with an informal system of cooperation, Flagler and Rockefeller, in 1871, set about to formalize Standard's control of Cleveland refineries. In order to guarantee their success, they enticed their strongest competitor first. They thought that such a strategy would result in weaker refiners quickly following suit. The strongest competitor was Clark, Payne & Company, with Colonel Oliver H. Payne and Maurice and James Clark as the active members in the firm. If Payne could be lured into the Standard camp, and if the Clark brothers, former associates of Rockefeller and Flagler in the grain business, could be removed as competitors, Rockefeller and Flagler thought that Standard's position in Cleveland would be unassailable. (They had already consolidated their Cleveland base by bringing two of the officers of the Second National Bank, Stillman Witt and Amasa Stone, into the firm with a 10 percent position.) With his social and political connections in the area, Payne would also serve to enhance Standard's reputation as a sound investment.[6]

On January 1, 1872, Flagler and Rockefeller increased the capitalization of Standard from 10,000 to 25,000 shares at a $100 a share par value. Of the original Standard stockholders, only Rockefeller, with his purchase of 3,000, and Flagler, with 1,400, increased their holdings in Standard beyond their pro rata proportions of 4,000 shares. The remaining 6,600 shares in the new issue were to go to refiners and new shareholders of value to Standard. More than likely, the $440,000 provided by Rockefeller and Flagler in their new purchases was the only cash used in the consolidation effort. The company gave the Clark brothers and Payne a total of 4,000 shares of Standard stock for their properties and goodwill. The Standard leaders also attracted Oliver Payne into active membership on the team.[7]

After appraising other Cleveland refineries, Flagler offered either cash or stock for their properties. Two of the most intriguing deals, however, did not involve Cleveland refineries. Jabez A. Bostwick exchanged shares in his Long Island Oil Company, which had a refinery and terminal at Hunter's Point in New York, for 700 shares of Standard stock. Standard gave 500 shares of the new issue to Peter H. Watson, a Lake Shore railroad official and president of the soon-to-be-infamous South Improvement Company. Watson's entry into Standard gave the company an additional entrée with the Lake Shore and control of the South Improvement scheme. After the distribution of the 15,000 new shares, the original partners of RA&F still dominated Standard with 67 percent of the 25,000 shares of stock. Flagler and Rockefeller now owned 13.8 and 23.3 percent of the company, respectively.[8]

During the negotiations for the Cleveland firms, Flagler and Rockefeller perfected their technique. Charles H. Tucker would later recall one such negotiation between Standard and his firm, Hanna, Baslington & Company. Robert Hanna sent George Baslington and Tucker, then their secretary, to talk with Rockefeller and Flagler concerning any proposal Standard might wish to offer. When the two arrived at a second-story room of the Cushing block that functioned as the office for both Rockefeller and Flagler, they found Rockefeller smoking a pipe containing mullein leaves, which he explained was for his sore throat. As Tucker later reflected on the incident, he was certain that the pipe was a strategic device to allow Flagler and Rockefeller to easily switch the roles of listener and spokesman during the parley. Flagler played the role of the blunt-spoken businessman, arguing that the industry was on the verge of collapse due to ruinous competition. When Rockefeller would philosophically lay his pipe aside, he spoke of the bliss of union with Standard.[9]

Although Cleveland competitors did not accuse Flagler or Rockefeller of making outright threats, other evidence suggests the two employed more subtle methods. When competition complained to the Lake Shore's Peter H. Watson, he (the secret Standard ally) simply stated that his low rates were available to all who could give Standard's guarantee of large volume and dependability. Isaac L. Hewitt, Rockefeller's first employer back in the 1850s and now a partner in the oil firm of Alexander, Scofield & Company, went to New York to complain about the South Improvement Company's activities in the oil industry. William H. Vanderbilt, Cornelius Vanderbilt's fifty-year-old son who was a strong rail leader in his own right, was noncommittal. Peter H. Watson, however, responded to Hewitt, "You better sell—you better get clear—better sell out—no help for it." Alexander, Scofield & Company did sell its property to Standard for $65,000 cash.[10]

It is true that Rockefeller and Flagler approached refiners with an offer of either cash or Standard stock for their properties. From Rockefeller's later recollection of the negotiations, he recalled that Flagler had a special talent in that area: "I can remember [Mr. Flagler's] saying often that when you go into an arrangement you must measure up the rights and priorities of both sides with the same yardstick, and this was the way Henry M. Flagler did." With an industry-wide depression at that time, most chose to take cash instead of Standard Oil stock, either in order to liquidate debts or to begin anew in a less speculative venture than oil refining.[11]

Flagler and Rockefeller proceeded with their original ideas to consolidate the position of Standard in Cleveland, but a railroad scheme, planned in 1871, offered an additional opportunity to promote cooperation and thwart ruinous competition. There had been many efforts to unify the industry, but none so bold and ambitious as that of the Pennsylvania Railroad's South Improvement Company. The Pennsylvania legislature had chartered the company in 1870 at the prompting of Tom Scott, vice-president of the Pennsylvania Railroad. The charter allowed the South Improvement Company to hold the stock of other companies with no restrictions. A group of Philadelphia and Pittsburgh refiners and the Pennsylvania Railroad hatched the idea. The Pennsylvanians bought the charter and incorporated the company on January 2, 1872. It appears that Peter H. Watson first told Rockefeller of the plan on November 30, 1871. Although at first put off by the plan, Rockefeller reported to his wife that "the plan grows on me."[12]

What exactly Rockefeller meant by this is unclear. It is perfectly clear that Standard turned the plan to its own advantage. None of the Standard partners from Cleveland were among the original group incorporating the South Improvement Company on January 2, 1872, but Flagler and Rockefeller allied Peter H. Watson and Jabez Bostwick with Standard through the new issue of Standard stock discussed earlier. So what appeared as a group of persons representative of Pittsburgh, Philadelphia, New York, and Cleveland refiners, with Peter Watson as the railroad referee of the group, was nothing more than another Standard front—unknown to both the public and Standard's partners in the venture. Of the total 2,000-share issue of South Improvement, the Standard group from Cleveland had only 720 shares. Allan Nevins, Rockefeller's biographer, interpreted this to mean that Standard held a minority position in South Improvement Company. With the additional shares owned by secret allies Bostwick and Watson, however, Standard's total jumped to 1,000, one half the shares in the venture.[13]

Standard's role in the South Improvement scheme is intriguing. At first, Flagler and Rockefeller had their own plan for the conquest of the Cleveland refiners, called by Rockefeller "our plan." After Peter H. Watson broached the idea of South Improvement, Rockefeller and Flagler moved slowly, carefully, but surely, into a dominant position. Once they controlled half the stock, they then sought to involve as many refiners as possible in the scheme. Even before the official organization of South Improvement, Watson had convinced William H. Vanderbilt and others of the New York Central system to join in the effort. By the end of January 1872, all the railroads had agreed to the South Improvement plan.[14]

What the incorporators of South Improvement intended to do was to create a double pooling arrangement. The refiners would pool their oil and then function as eveners, assuring each of the railroads involved in the agreements that the previously agreed-upon amount of oil was steadily going to the proper railroad. In return, the railroads would offer to cooperating refiners such attractive concessions that other refiners would be unable to remain in business. During the furor which later broke over these agreements, the parties involved argued that they had just assumed that everyone would be invited into the arrangement and would certainly join. But in defending his Cleveland negotiations, Rockefeller made a telling observation. He stated that he had never even mentioned the South Improvement Company to refiners being pursued by Standard.[15] There is little doubt that he well knew that they were frightened by the specter of South Improvement. In fact, Flagler and Rockefeller used South Improvement in their negotiations as an invisible club to get Cleveland refiners to join Standard, not South Improvement.

The agreement signed by the trunk lines with South Improvement assigned 45 percent of the pool's oil traffic to the Pennsylvania, with the remainder evenly divided between the Erie and New York Central systems. Also, the railroads would raise their rates for all refined oil freight. For example, Flagler's $1.65 a barrel rate for Standard, which he had successfully negotiated in 1870, would now be $2.80. The members of South Improvement agreed to such a rate structure because their competitors would be the only ones paying this higher published rate of $2.80. The railroads would give the Standard and its allies a rebate amounting to $.90 a barrel. [16] This meant Standard would pay only two-thirds of what its non-South Improvement competitors would be charged.

South Improvement was to be the distributor, evener, of all oil traffic among the railroads. For this task, which consisted of keeping exacting records on all oil freight, the railroads would give South Improvement a commission on all non-South Improvement oil traffic equal to the rebate amount to its members, $.90 a barrel. While Flagler and others would later argue that such an amount was a legitimate business charge, others labeled this practice the notorious "drawback."[17] Although the rebate practices could be argued on the principle of efficiency, the drawback policies were nothing more than a thinly disguised means for the railroads to assist South Improvement members in driving their competitors from the field. Not only would the drawback have allowed South Improvement a direct economic advantage, it also would have permitted it to chart every movement by its competitors, enabling South Improvement refiners to move quickly against any outside refiner who threatened their dominance of the refining field.

For the first three weeks of February 1872, the South Improvement veil of secrecy remained intact. Then, on February 21, the *Cleveland Plain Dealer* gave the general public its first glimpse into the South Improvement scheme. Within a week, the Oil Regions' newspapers had pieced the puzzle together and had the producers aroused to a fever pitch. It became apparent that, once the plan was made known, the contracts that bound South Improvement with the railroads were in jeopardy. Even before the month of February was over, George B. McClellan of the Atlantic and Jay Gould of the Erie reneged on their earlier obligations to South Improvement.[18]

Under new, aggressive leadership, the Petroleum Producers' Association met on March 1 at the Oil City opera house to discuss strategy. Two of the forceful leaders of this movement, John Archbold and J. J. Vandergrift, would eventually find themselves in positions of leadership at Standard, but, for now, that was a distant day. They called for a boycott of all railroads and refiners associated with the South Improvement scheme. They also changed the name of their organization to the Petroleum Producers' Union.[19]

Flagler and Rockefeller rushed to combat the countermove and to defend their position as honorable and just. As Rockefeller would later claim, Standard felt that much of the opposition, especially among refiners, stemmed from the fact that they had not been involved in the arrangement. Samuel Downer, a refiner of the period, had once told Flagler on another occasion, "I am opposed to the whole scheme of rebates and drawbacks— without I'm in it!"[20] Flagler and Rockefeller were completing their conquest of Cleveland when the South Improvement scheme failed. With the largest refiners of Cleveland already in the Standard camp, the furor over South Improvement only made the smaller refiners more aware of their uncompetitive position when it came to negotiating with the railroads.

The Cleveland refiners, however, were not the major problem for Flagler and Rockefeller. By March, the two concentrated on placating the Oil Regions' producers. When the producers' meetings erupted during the first week in March, reporters approached Flagler for his reaction. He simply dismissed it as a mass temper tantrum. But as the producers' attacks continued unabated, it became apparent to Flagler, Rockefeller, and others within South Improvement that they had greatly underestimated the uproar.[21]

The aging Cornelius Vanderbilt, soon to be 78, and other railroad leaders sought to keep the plan alive by belatedly inviting the producers to join. In a March 25 meeting between the railroads and producers at the Erie offices, Watson and Rockefeller realized that South Improvement was doomed. A group of producers met with the heads of the three trunk lines. At one point, when the producers threatened violence, Vanderbilt invited Rockefeller and Watson, who had been in an adjoining room, to come in and explain their position. The producers refused to listen to what the

South Improvement leaders had to say and threatened to leave. So, Rockefeller and Watson were the ones to walk out. The trunk line leaders then drew up an agreement with the producers in which a pool would exist in the crude oil traffic.[22] Thus, the South Improvement scheme was broken.

The Producers' Union announced that it would refuse to send crude oil to any known members of the South Improvement clique. At first, it would be assumed that Standard would have been destroyed by the railroads' cancellation of contracts with South Improvement on March 25. Indeed, Standard, which had employed up to 1,200 men in the boom period of 1871, employed only 70 men on March 27, 1872. Whether or not refiners in other cities knew of Standard's takeover of Cleveland is unclear.[23] If Standard kept its refinery purchases a secret, it may well have been that it weathered this outcry by profiting from its newly acquired properties, which had not officially been a part of South Improvement.

Knowing of the fiercely independent nature of the producers, Flagler and Rockefeller realized that if Standard could just persevere, the producers would fall to quarreling among themselves. Rockefeller finally got Fisher Brothers, an Oil City brokerage firm, to sell Standard 20,000 to 25,000 barrels of crude. Once again, Standard had capitalized on the producers' lack of cohesion. At the mass meeting called in Oil City to discipline the Fishers, the independents could not even decide whether the Fishers should be reprimanded, and when it was obvious that no measures would be taken against Fisher Brothers, the Producers' Union attempted to save face. The Union telegraphed Standard a request that Rockefeller and Flagler give the producers assurances that there were no South Improvement contracts with the railroads. On April 8, 1872, Rockefeller, secretly triumphant, telegraphed his reply. Standard Oil, he said, "holds no contract with the railroad companies or any of them, or with the South Improvement Company. I state unqualifiedly that reports that this company, or any member of it, threatened to depress oil, are false."[24] With this simple message, Rockefeller penned the epilogue to the brief career of the Producers' Union as an effective organization. Standard now freely pursued its goal of cooperation without hindrance from a producers' cooperative. There would continue to be periodic railroad rate wars, but never again would the producers effectively challenge Standard.

Although South Improvement Company had technically failed, it had well served Standard's purpose. As a matter of fact, Rockefeller was adamant that the South Improvement scheme intervened at the time that "our plan" was being designed. Rockefeller and Flagler entered the South Improvement plot, technically orchestrated by leaders of the Pennsylvania

Railroad, in order to control it until such time as it had served their purpose: dominance of Cleveland's oil refining capacity. In the aftermath of its successful conquest of Cleveland in the spring of 1872, Standard manufactured 10,000 barrels of refined a day and provided employment for 1,600 men on a weekly payroll of $20,000. Standard emerged as the leading refiner of petroleum in America; its capacity was larger than the total of the refineries in either the Oil Regions or New York and was greater than the total capacity of Baltimore, Philadelphia, and Pittsburgh combined.[25]

Once the Fisher Brothers' action had broken the producers' boycott of Standard, Flagler moved quickly to improve Standard's transportation arrangements. The producers' agreement with the railroads had put the Cleveland refineries in a very poor position with regard to the European market. The rates had favored New York, obviously, since the producers wished to build up the refining capacity there to compete with Cleveland. The producers' boycott also hurt the two railroads serving Cleveland. The Lake Shore and Atlantic saw their combined percentage of the oil traffic plummet to 18 percent, while, conversely, the Pennsylvania's share increased to an astounding 82 percent.[26]

Flagler went to his friends at the Lake Shore and used Standard's large volume and consistent shipments to gain concessions. The Lake Shore reduced its New York rate for Standard from $1.50 to $1.25 a barrel. Flagler guaranteed 4,000 barrels a day to the Lake Shore, and the arrangement held for the remainder of 1872. Another reason for the Lake Shore's willingness to break the pooling and rate agreement was the knowledge that the Pennsylvania had already given its helpmate, the Empire, major rate concessions. Flagler later contended that Standard provided services such as terminal facilities that saved the Lake Shore money; therefore, he simply requested a rate which reflected that savings to the Lake Shore. Flagler also offered his usual rationale for special consideration: "I will say that the railroad companies have expressly reserved the right to give to other parties the same privileges if they furnish the same conveniences."[27]

With the defeat of the South Improvement plan, Flagler and Rockefeller immediately began an attempt to recoup their lost influence in the Regions. In May 1872, they journeyed to Titusville, where they began to talk of a new arrangement to stabilize the oil industry without the negative fallout of the previous agreement. As Flagler and Rockefeller made their rounds in the Regions, area newspapers warned local refiners and dealers not to be taken in by the soft words of proven monopolists. But some of the Regions' leaders, such as John Archbold and J. J. Vandergrift, embraced the new approach. With Rockefeller having returned to Cleveland, Flagler explained Standard's position at public meetings in Titusville on May 15 and 16. Along with William Frew and O. T. Waring of Pittsburgh, Flagler argued that the new plan would allow everyone to participate and would be voluntary. Although this plan, dubbed "The Treaty of Titusville," eventually failed, Flagler and Rockefeller won the confidence of not only Archbold and Vandergrift but also H. H. Rogers and Charles Pratt of New York.[28] These entrepreneurs later proved to be valuable members of the Standard alliance.

In late 1872, Flagler negotiated new transportation arrangements. With the expiration in mid-November of the April rail contract, which had called for $1.25 freight a barrel for refined from Cleveland to New York, Flagler signed another contract with the Lake Shore–New York Central that raised the rate to $1.40 and was to last through March 1873. The new contract required Standard to deliver 4,000 barrels a day over the line. Standard paid the railroad from $50 to $150 a day whenever it failed to meet its quota. Flagler later testified that there were some years in which Standard paid as much as $30,000 in such penalties.[29]

In regard to the November 1872 contract, Flagler discovered that the Pennsylvania charged at least one customer, probably Empire, only $1.05 a barrel. He immediately went to William H. Vanderbilt and stated Standard's position on the matter. He told the New York Central official that if Standard adhered to the contract while others paid less, Standard would be forced to shut down its operations. He reminded Vanderbilt that Standard had been faithful in its quota obligations during the season in which Standard could have used the Erie Canal and asked Vanderbilt to give Standard some consideration.[30]

Flagler continued in his argument to Vanderbilt that he did not think that the Pennsylvania's low charges would survive a rate war. Within a month, Flagler contended, it would be forced to restore its rates to the market level. Flagler indicated that the fight was really a transportation battle, not a refiners' confrontation; therefore, he called upon Vanderbilt to shoulder the entire burden of the rate difference. This Vanderbilt agreed to do; but he did indeed only keep his rates at the $1.05 level for one month, then he returned to the contracted rate. After that, Flagler made sure that Standard delivered only the required amount over the Lake Shore–Central route until the contract expired.[31]

In recounting this rate war to an Ohio legislative committee in 1879, Flagler stated that the railroads never gave Standard special rates—other than concessions owed Standard due to railroad savings brought about by such things as terminal facilities. Flagler did believe that Standard was due every concession he extracted from the railroads, but at the Ohio hearing, he carefully presented contracts that did not contain rebate and drawback clauses.[32]

Although Standard had emerged stronger than ever from the 1872 South Improvement struggle and the subsequent freight rate arrangements, it was within a weakened oil industry. The problems in the industry intensified with the depression that began in 1873. Nationally, there were 100 companies still in the field, with a daily capacity of 47,000 barrels of refined oil, but the daily production was only slightly more than half of capacity. Standard was in line with the industry as a whole, only operating the largest two of its six refineries that year. Its facilities, with a total daily capacity of 12,500 barrels of refined, only produced 6,350. The entire oil industry was in the midst of depression; by December 1873, the price of crude had plummeted to $.70 a barrel.[33]

The depression showed no sign of any letup. In late 1874, crude dropped to less than $.50 a barrel in the Oil Regions. A barrel of water cost more than that. Only transportation could save the industry, but the depression had also devastated the debt-ridden railroads. That worked to Standard's advantage. In 1874 the B&O and the Pennsylvania, desperate for revenues to pay fixed costs, slashed freight rates as a bitter war developed between them for the Pittsburgh traffic. To the north, Standard's April contract with the Erie caused friction between the Erie and the other two northern trunk lines, the Central and Pennsylvania. The latter two roads argued that there was no way the Erie could make a profit with the Standard contract; therefore, they saw the Erie as having gone beyond the bounds of business ethics—even for that era of intense competition.[34]

In July 1874, representatives of the three trunk lines met at Windsor House in Saratoga for a critical conference. They agreed to maintain a standard freight rate—and hinted that fast-freight lines, such as Joseph Potts's Empire, were guilty of excessive rates and other poor business practices. The Empire was especially vulnerable to such an attack. Potts had organized the Empire in 1865, immediately after his service as a Union colonel during the Civil War. It had originally been a subsidiary of the Philadelphia & Erie, but was soon thereafter leased to the Pennsylvania road. Potts led the Empire along an independent course of action, but because of a clause in its contract that allowed the Pennsylvania to buy the Empire at any time it chose, officials of rival roads were convinced that the Empire was merely a creation of the powerful Pennsylvania.[35]

Following the Windsor House conference, follow-up meetings occurred at Long Branch and again at Saratoga. Throughout these meetings, the other lines argued that the Erie had become so greedy that its Standard business was beyond its capacity to carry the traffic—hinting that it was time to share the spoils. The final result of these conferences, commonly referred to as the "Rutter Circular," seems strangely similar to Rockefeller's "our plan." The Pennsylvania, Erie and New York Central were to share the oil freight, the Pennsylvania receiving approximately half, and the other two roads equally sharing the remainder. More importantly for Flagler and Standard, the leading refiners would be the eveners. Finally, Flagler got the concession he had been pushing for years: The rate from the Regions to all refining points and thence to the eastern seaboard would be the same for all points. For example, Standard would pay the same total rate for oil shipped to Cleveland from the Regions and then to New York as would a refiner in Pittsburgh or the Regions itself. The railroads were well pleased with the arrangement for several reasons. First, the refiners would keep the books. Second, the railroads would have a guaranteed traffic at a profitable rate without having costly rate wars.[36]

At the same time, the pipelines of the Regions united in a pooling agreement in September 1874. Standard stood to profit doubly from this arrangement for it owned over one-third of the Regions' pipage. The agreement stated that the refiners would pay $.30 a barrel for piping. Eight cents of that amount would be kept by the company doing the piping, with the other $.22 going into a pool. Standard got 36.5 percent of the pool's profits since it owned that percentage of the gathering pipage in the Regions.[37]

The only weakness in the new freight arrangements was the refusal of the Baltimore & Ohio to enter the pool. This railroad would soon have an entrée into the Regions with a connection via the Columbia Conduit Company, a pipeline concern. If the B&O established an independent outlet for oil through Baltimore, then the northern lines—and Standard—would have a new worry. The Pennsylvania attempted to stop Columbia from reaching the Regions. The railroad contended that its rights of eminent domain allowed it to control its roadbeds; therefore, whenever Columbia laid some pipe under a Pennsylvania trestle, railroad officials sent a destruction crew to dismantle it. After several unsuccessful attempts to cross the Pennsylvania road near Pittsburgh, Columbia attempted to push a new, and better, "free pipe line bill" through the Pennsylvania legislature, but the Pennsylvania road proved to be just as powerful in the legislature as its crews had been in tearing up the Columbia's line.[38]

Standard did not totally depend on transportation for its success. It moved beyond the Cleveland area in its attempt to control the refining stage of the oil industry. In the summer of 1874, Flagler and Rockefeller met with William G. Warden and Charles Lockhart with a proposal that Warden and Lockhart bring their firms into the Standard alliance. The two Pennsylvania refiners reviewed Standard's books, became convinced that such a union would be advantageous to them, and soon thereafter added Warden, Frew & Company and Lockhart, Frew & Company to the Flagler and Rockefeller empire. Things must have been going well for Rockefeller and his organization, for on January 5, 1875, Standard declared a dividend of $115 a share, an amount above the par value of its stock.[39]

During 1874 and 1875, Standard completed the critical alliances that made it a national business in everything but legal status. In October 1874, Standard took over the Philadelphia works of Warden, Frew & Company, the Pittsburgh works of Lockhart, Frew & Company, and the New York works of Charles Pratt & Company. As always, the negotiations were in secret—as were the results. The three refiners continued to operate as though independent of the Rockefeller company. Standard added $1,000,000 to its stock to cover these transactions. Rather than a straight transfer at the $100 a share par value, the owners of these companies paid $265 a share in property and cash for their Standard holdings. In October 1875, the last critical link in Standard's control of the refining of Regions oil fell into place when John Archbold brought in his firm, Porter, Moreland & Company of Titusville. Archbold became president of the Acme Oil Company of New York, which was formed from Porter, Moreland & Company, and Bennett, Warner & Company, the Regions representative in the Standard "alliance."[40]

Technically, the Standard Oil Company of Ohio could not own properties in other states. Rockefeller and Flagler used this legal limitation to its utmost during the takeovers of the mid-1870s. Standard simply let its "allies" absorb other firms into them. One example of this process was the newly acquired Warden, Frew & Company's purchase of the firm of William W. and Norris Harkness in Philadelphia (this Harkness family was not related to Flagler's Harkness clan). With increasing market pressures, such as the inability to get cars for their crude oil, the Harkness brothers sold out to Warden, having no idea that they had actually sold to the much-hated Rockefeller combine. This is only one example of an activity Standard repeated throughout the northeast, especially in Pennsylvania and New York.[41]

While Standard strengthened its transportation and refinery alliances in New York and the Regions, a new transportation threat came from Baltimore. President John Garrett of the B&O wished to include his road in the oil traffic flowing from the Regions. In addition, he had always shown an aversion to rebates, drawbacks, and other arrangements that smacked of rate discrimination. During the mid-1870s, therefore, the B&O was adamant in its independent course. It made its connections with Pittsburgh in early 1875, using the Columbia Conduit Company's pipes where the railroad itself was unable to make linkages. Immediately after its Pittsburgh connection, the B&O saw its oil traffic leap 1,000 percent in less than a month's time.[42] This amount of traffic, coupled with Garrett's righteous attitude and staunch cooperation with small independent refineries, directly threatened Standard's domination of American refining.

If small refineries continued to spring up along the B&O, Standard's northern connections and agreements would be of little value. It was time for a southern strategy. Standard's ally in this maneuver became Johnson Newlon Camden of Parkersburg, West Virginia. Camden, more than any other Standard associate, was a kindred business spirit to the blunt-spoken, hard-negotiating Flagler. The correspondence between Flagler and Camden during the oil wars of the last half of the 1870s furnishes valuable insight into Flagler's behind-the-scenes dealings. Not only do we obtain an intimate account of the war with the B&O, but also, since Flagler would write long letters to his Parkersburg friend after a particular battle, we see Standard's overall strategies stated.[43]

Camden was co-owner, with Col. W. P. Thompson, of Parkersburg's largest refinery. Camden was a well-known Democratic politician, who would later ably serve Standard for a term as a United States Senator. Thompson had been a Confederate officer during the Civil War, and although he was not the same type of business fighter as Camden, the partners worked well together. There is no clear explanation as to how the alliance with Standard originally came about, but there is little doubt that both the parties stood to substantially benefit from the arrangment. On May 19, 1875, J. N. Camden & Company became Camden Consolidated Oil Company. No word was mentioned that the consolidation was with Standard. Camden had gained a powerful ally, and Standard had gained an "independent" who would strike rate deals with the B&O and alliances with refiners along the southern rim of the oil industry.[44]

The opportunity for Standard to dominate its relationships with railroads came in 1875. The 1874 pooling agreement failed when, in 1875, Scott and the Pennsylvania decided on a rate war against the B&O for the Baltimore traffic. Also, the Pennsylvania was again giving the Empire secret rebates. The Erie responded by lowering Standard's rates even below the favorable Rutter Circular of 1874. With the possibility of an all-out rate war, Flagler once again negotiated an agreement among the railroads, this time including Garrett and the B&O. The arrangement was that Standard would be the evener of traffic for a pooling distribution as follows: B&O, 9 percent; Erie, 20; New York Central, 20; and Pennsylvania, 51. For the first time, Flagler would be the only evener, reflecting Standard's control of the refining sector of the industry. But it also marked Standard's movement into a dominant position in the *transportation* aspect of the industry.

Joseph Potts, always aware of his own potential role as the evener of fast-freight traffic, decided that the Empire needed additional concessions from his usual protector, the Pennsylvania. In November 1875, he obtained a special rebate from the Pennsylvania for the building of an Empire pipeline to the Pennsylvania facility at Olean. Also, all the through traffic of Potts's operations went to the Pennsylvania. A second alliance system solidified as the Columbia and B&O struck a similar exclusive agreement. With that, Standard counterattacked with an agreement to send half its *crude* oil along the Erie with the other half going with the Central. Although the letter of the new refined-oil pool—similar to the Rutter Circular—was followed by all parties, they had broken the spirit of the recent arrangement. Scott and Potts made their agreement because they feared that if Standard completely dominated the refining portion of the industry, it would dictate to both producers *and* transportation organizations what rates and prices would be acceptable to it.[46]

Early in 1877, Standard and some of its allies formed the United Pipe Lines, capitalized at $3,000,000. The firm combined the old UPL with some of the properties of the American Transfer Company and other smaller lines. This became Standard's first major entry into the transportation sector. Although Standard held the overwhelming majority of stock, old transportation friends Amasa Stone and William H. Vanderbilt also held 1,000 shares each in the company. The combination put Standard into direct competition with Joseph Potts's Empire Transportation Company and its pipeline holdings in the regions. The only other pipeline company of any consequence was the Columbia Conduit Company, which was allied with the B&O.[47]

By bending state laws to meet their demands as a national business, in a single decade Rockefeller and Flagler had created a powerful national alliance system from the humble origins of Rockefeller, Andrews & Flagler, a small oil refining partnership headquartered in a second-floor office located in Cleveland, away from the seaboard centers of economic power. Now Flagler and Rockefeller stood ready to challenge the Pennsylvania, the world's largest railroad. The three alliances for the coming transportation battle had been drawn: (1) the United Pipe Lines, Erie, Central, and Standard; (2) the Pennsylvania and Empire; and (3) the Columbia and B&O. The stage was now set for the great battle, as Standard sought to dominate oil transportation as it had already dominated oil refining.

The Supreme Evener
of Oil Transport

IN THE SUMMER of 1876, the nation's Centennial Exhibition was held in Philadelphia. During the event, local businesses took advantage of the situation to advertise their various wares. One pamphlet circulating among the throng predicted a new American revolution—this time in the transportation realm. Joseph Potts, in this Empire Transportation Company publication, promised that the Empire would stabilize the freight rate structure of the northeast. In what must have sent shivers through Flagler and Rockefeller, Potts suggested this would be accomplished by abolishing "unjust distinctions between competitive and noncompetitive localities."[1] The Empire plan, which called for doing away with volume rebates and long-versus-short-haul discriminations, would completely destroy the advantages Standard had built up over the first half of the 1870s.

During the 1870s, the lines between activities that were strictly transportational and those that were needed adjuncts to transportation began to blur. For example, we have already seen how Standard became more and more involved in pipeline-gathering activities. While Flagler and Rockefeller led Standard into these areas, Potts involved his Empire Transportation Company in oil-refining arrangements. This was not a sudden departure on the part of transportation agencies. The Pennsylvania itself had already bought coal fields in the early 1870s and had even invested heavily in the Pennsylvania Steel Works Company as a means of ensuring a steady supply of steel rails. The Pennsylvania took these actions as a defensive measure to guarantee access to materials it would need in its transportation of goods. So when Potts of the Empire bought a refinery in New York in

1876, it was in keeping with this type of activity. What he wished to do was assure for his fast-freight line an oil traffic independent of Standard. But it was also obvious that Potts's goals went beyond mere defensive activities. With his 1876 Centennial Exhibition pamphlet, Potts clearly stated his intentions to Standard leaders.[2]

Flagler began to look for an opportunity to take "a principled position" for a fight with Potts, who obviously desired to become the sole evener of oil transport among the railroads. Potts provided Flagler with an ideal issue. In 1877, with the cooperation of the Pennsylvania, Potts wholeheartedly entered the field of refining. In January, Potts and Tom Scott of the Pennsylvania made a pact: Potts would finance the purchase and building of refineries from the treasury of the Empire—the Pennsylvania would not have to provide any investment monies. For its part, the Pennsylvania could—as had always been the case—buy all the properties of the Empire at any time it chose. This arrangement would include both the Empire's transportation and refining ventures.[3]

Potts had made the Empire into a transportation force in its own right. Before 1872, it had been the handmaiden of the Pennsylvania, acting as its fast-freight agency. Since officers of the Pennsylvania privately held much of the stock in the Empire, the road seemed to give the Empire special rates—and its stockholders exorbitant profits. In 1872, Potts began buying into the gathering pipes of the Regions. By 1877, the Empire had over 5,000 cars, 1,500 of them tank cars used in the oil traffic, 18 steamships plying the Great Lakes, and 520 miles of Regions pipe lines.[4]

With this power directly at his disposal, plus the support of the Pennsylvania, Potts moved directly against Standard in 1877 by buying Sone & Fleming (a concern with refineries in New York City) and the Philadelphia Refining Company. Together they were capable of producing 4,000 barrels of refined a day. Potts hoped to keep these early purchases quiet. The plan might have worked except for the fact that Standard allies Henry H. Rogers and Charles Lockhart were also busy buying refineries in New York and Philadelphia, respectively. When they discovered that their bids for these concerns were countered by Potts, they immediately notified Standard officials in Cleveland. Although Rockefeller and Flagler knew that the Pennsylvania was the most powerful corporation in the United States, the railroad's favorite offspring, the Empire, was a direct threat to the very existence of Standard.[5] Therefore, Flagler, Rockefeller, and their Standard allies reacted with the utmost speed.

Flagler realized that he could count on officials of the other trunk lines to support Standard in a battle with the Pennsylvania. They had always considered the Empire to be at best an untrustworthy ally, and at worst, merely a pawn of the Pennsylvania officials. None of them thought that Potts could ever be truly neutral in the evening of the oil traffic among the competing transportation interests. When Flagler and Rockefeller strode into the offices of the Pennsylvania's Tom Scott in early 1877, they did so with the full knowledge that the Central, Erie, and B&O would fully support Standard's position, even in a full-scale rate war.[6]

The argument Flagler and Rockefeller made to Scott was that the Empire, a common carrier, had violated its public trust by investing in refining, thereby failing to maintain an attitude of strict neutrality with regard to the oil traffic. Everyone knew that principle was not at issue. As indicated earlier, the Pennsylvania had already been involved in mining and steel manufacture. Standard itself was becoming more and more a common carrier with its crude oil gathering pipes in the Regions.[7] Although Standard appealed to principle, it would adhere to power in this battle. The Empire and Standard became involved in an epic struggle for the role of evener within the oil industry.

Knowing the great cost of a rate war, the Pennsylvania's competitors approached Scott, requesting that he get Potts to sell the Empire's refining properties to Standard, thereby avoiding a confrontation over the issue. Potts's counterargument to Scott was that the Pennsylvania could ill afford to let Standard become a monopoly in the area of refining. If Standard completely controlled refining, it would begin issuing the inevitable ultimatums with regard to acceptable freight rates. The goals of both major parties in the struggle were obvious: Standard wished to crush non-Cleveland refining; the Pennsylvania, the largest freight carrier in the world, was not about to have any sector of its traffic controlled by a single shipper.[8]

Early in the fray, Potts had alerted Standard by his purchases. Standard was therefore already doing battle when Potts increased his refining capacity in Philadelphia. What Potts had hoped to do was to have his new refinery in place when the rate war occurred. The normally cooperative Standard officials, however, were prepared for battle. They broke their contracts with the Pennsylvania. Flagler notified allies in Pittsburgh that no refined oil was to leave that city under the Standard label until arrangements were made with the B&O. Potts' agents went into the Regions, buying all the crude oil available in an attempt to dry up the market for Standard's refineries. As for refined, Standard sold its kerosene at rock-bottom prices.[9]

The war was on. The Pennsylvania cut its oil rates. The Erie and Central did likewise. The Pennsylvania again cut. A. J. Cassatt, third vice-president of the Pennsylvania in charge of its freight arrangements, would confess years later that, in light of rebates and drawbacks, the Pennsylvania was actually *paying shippers* to carry their oil. Meanwhile, Potts attempted to buy out refineries associated with the Columbia Conduit Company, but he was unable to do this as William Brough and other Columbia officials kept J. N. Camden informed. Camden, in turn, communicated Potts's every move on the southern front to command headquarters in Cleveland.[10]

By summer's end, Flagler and his forces were in control. Two factors had contributed to this result. First, Potts had hoped to bring the producers into the Empire camp for the battle. He thought their natural enmity toward Standard, dating back to the South Improvement war, would make them the Empire's natural ally. But the producers, independent as ever, saw the fight as strictly one between transportation companies, and therefore the crude oil traffic was going to the highest bidder—which was usually Standard. Second, the Great Railroad Strike, which swept the country in 1877, severely injured Potts and the Pennsylvania. Although the Pennsylvania previously had experienced good labor-management relations, especially when compared with other railroads, it had followed the pattern of other roads during the 1870s depression by cutting wages in 1877. The strike was costly to the world's largest freight carrier, not only in terms of lost revenue, but also in the destruction of rail property by strikers. With the combination of the oil battle and the strike, the value of Pennsylvania stock dropped by almost 50 percent during the first half of 1877.[11]

The troubles of 1877 affected Standard and the Pennsylvania in different ways. Standard had benefited by the "sweat," as Flagler was so fond of saying, it had imposed on the Pennsylvania. Standard declared quarterly dividends in April and July—in the midst of the battle—totaling $50 a share. The Erie and the Central sent most of the oil traffic to New York; Philadelphia, the principal port of the Pennsylvania, saw its oil export traffic decline to only one-eighth of the total amount. By the end of July, Tom Scott and his Pennsylvania officials sued for peace with Standard.[12]

During the month of August, A. J. Cassatt twice traveled to Cleveland to negotiate with Flagler and Rockefeller concerning the terms of surrender. Meanwhile, Potts feverishly attempted to place his trump card on the negotiating table. Payne wrote Flagler and Rockefeller a coded message from New York that Potts was on the verge of refining crude at the Empire's new Philadelphia facility. Payne feared that if Potts's refinery did begin operation it would undercut Standard's bargaining position. Not only was Potts a direct threat to Standard, but with the rates his Empire was offering New York refiners, he also represented a threat to Standard's transportation allies.[13]

In later testimony concerning the Standard-Pennsylvania transactions, both Standard and Pennsylvania officials stated that Standard first offered to buy the Empire's refining capacity, with the Pennsylvania buying the remainder of Potts's operation (cars, pipe lines, and the like). According to this version—which Allan Nevins and other historians have accepted at face value—Tom Scott was not willing for the Pennsylvania to spend so large an amount of money in an arrangement that would essentially help Standard. His alleged counterproposal was that Standard buy everything in the Empire operation. The fact was that Standard was really interested in the transportation arrangements, and it was the Pennsylvania that forced the sale of Sone & Fleming and other refining operations on Standard. The reason that Flagler wished to gain the Empire's transportation facilities was that he was also negotiating for the purchase of Columbia Conduit Company. If Standard succeeded in both deals, it would be able to control not only most of the refining capacity of the nation but also the gathering pipes in the Regions and the new Bradford oil field of northcentral Pennsylvania. The railroads depended on these pipes almost exclusively to get crude from the wellhead to railroad terminals.[14]

By mid-September, Pennsylvania officials and Flagler had negotiated the basic agreement. On September 17, the Pennsylvania directors agreed in principle to Tom Scott's purchase of the Empire. Standard provided the monies for the revolving-door purchase, because the Pennsylvania was simply a middleman in the arrangment. For his part, Potts took comfort in the fact that the purchase price, estimated to be in excess of $3 million, would require a large amount of ready capital, and he did not believe that Flagler and Rockefeller could come up with such a large amount in a short period of time. Knowing by mid-September what the purchase price would be, William Rockefeller requested Oliver Payne to begin transferring money to New York. The New York office was running a positive balance as of September 18 of $1.5 million.[15]

By mid-October, Standard's New York office had made most of the important financial arrangements. On October 15, William Rockefeller wrote his brother, estimating for him the costs resulting from Flagler's negotiations. Standard would pay $3,500,000 for all the properties. In addition to the original agreement for Standard to buy the Empire itself for $2,500,000, Flagler had arranged Standard's purchase of Sone & Fleming for $600,000 and the other Empire refineries at $400,000. Contrary to pre-

vious interpretations, this accounting would suggest that Flagler negotiated the purchase of the refining properties *after* the tentative proposal to
buy the main Empire transportation properties. In any case, rather than
cash in some of Standard's holdings in government bonds, which at the
time were selling below par, William Rockefeller and Flagler decided to
have John Rockefeller take short-term loans from Cleveland banks. By
October 17, Standard's New York office already had on hand $1,250,000
for the purchase and depended on the Cleveland office to provide it with an
additional $350,000 from its own coffers. That would leave $1,750,000 to
be borrowed. Since the Empire officials had given Standard such a difficult
time, Flagler wanted the cash to be readily available for the purchase.[16]

That evening, Flagler headed the Standard delegation, which met at
Potts's office. Tom Scott handed Potts a Standard-backed certified check
of almost $3.4 million for the Empire. This represented $1,094,805.56 for
the Empire's pipe lines, $501,652.78 for Sone & Fleming, $900,000 for the
Empire's portion of the Oil Tank Car Trust, and the remainder for the
Empire's other refining facilities and oil stocks on hand. On that same date,
Standard officially paid another $1,050,000 for the Columbia Conduit
Company.[17]

Once the properties were in the Standard empire, its auditors gave their
own valuation to these new acquisitions. The Standard Oil Company of
New York legally owned the Empire properties, and their value was placed
at $3,100,000. In addition, Sone & Fleming's crude and refined oil on hand
was valued at $300,000.[18] The Standard auditors placed the value of the
various properties as follows.

Sone & Fleming Manufacturing Company and Philadelphia Refining Company	$1,100,000
Empire Pipe Company	1,100,000
Tank Car Trust of Philadelphia	900,000
	$3,100,000

If a historian had to give a precise date for Standard's complete domination of the oil industry, it would be October 17, 1877. Not only did Standard obtain both the Empire and the Columbia Conduit Company, but
there was also a third transaction on that date. Following upon a new October 1 rate structure, Standard signed another pooling agreement on October 17 with the railroads. Although similar to the arrangement that had
been destroyed in the recent war over the Empire, the victors took the
spoils: the Erie and Central saw their percentage of the traffic increased to

21 percent each, while the B&O stood at 11 percent, and the Pennsylvania suffered a decline to 47 percent. Not only did the rails get a pooling agreement, but Standard also guaranteed them a minimum volume of traffic.[19]

In exchange for these concessions, Standard became the sole evener of all oil traffic bound for Europe, with a 10 percent commission on its own freight and other oil under its control. In order to avoid possible embarrassment, Flagler did not request a drawback on the trifling traffic outside Standard's realm, but the contract did specify that only refiners providing equal or greater traffic for the roads could demand the commission rate—a physical impossibility since Standard controlled over 90 percent of the refining capacity in the country. Flagler was so confident of Standard's position that he did not demand any concessions on its pipage fees. This was a moot point since Standard now *owned* the overwhelming majority of stock in the pipage volume of the country.[20] One way or the other, Standard was going to get the profits from the piping of oil.

Now that the basic transportation arrangements had been put into place, Flagler began consolidating the new acquisitions. With regard to the Empire Pipe Company, he had one share of stock issued to each of the five officers of the company, and he held the remaining 29,985 shares in trust as Standard's part of the 30,000 issue. He began uniting the Standard pipelines into a single system. This included the new Bradford, Pennsylvania, field, which was gushing with crude oil. He issued United Pipe Lines certificates for all crude the Standard organization took in, no matter where it was produced, in an attempt to stabilize the price of the Bradford oil.[21]

While Flagler was working on these new matters, he continued to have problems with the transition. Former Empire officials would not release documents for Flagler's perusal. He reassured them that he cared nothing for papers of a "private nature," but did wish to see those which would require Standard "to perpetuate their legal existence." As these materials finally began to trickle in, Flagler was shocked at the Pennsylvania's insistence on keeping one Empire concession. The Empire had an 1875 contract with the Buffalo, New York & Philadelphia Railroad that had given the Empire a drawback on all Olean Petroleum pipeline crude shipped to the Pennsylvania terminal at New York. What made this situation rather unique was that the Pennsylvania had given one of its subsidiaries, the Empire, this concession over another of its subsidiaries, the Olean Petroleum Company.[22]

Upon investigation, Flagler was shocked to discover that the Pennsylvania had not given Standard the same concession as the Empire, even though Standard was now carrying out the provisions of the old contract. A. J. Cassatt argued that, as the legal successor of the Empire Transportation Company, the Pennsylvania was entitled to keep the drawback. Flagler responded that an agreement of such nature could not be transferred from the fast freight company to the railroad company. He implied that the Pennsylvania should allow the Standard subsidiary, as a pipeline entity, to continue to receive the drawback. Although the American Transfer Company would have been the natural Standard subsidiary for the inheritance of this drawback, when Flagler did finally win his argument with the Pennsylvania, he saw it otherwise: "It [the Olean Petroleum] is one of those peculiar accounts such as Mr. D. O'Day [Standard's "manager" of pipeline arrangements] has been in the habit of collecting, and which I have no doubt he would like to include in the business of the American Transfer Co. but I see no necessity for swelling the fictitious profits of that company."[23] Flagler's position indicated that he was not going to have anyone outside Standard, even its American Transfer partners, sharing 10 percent of such lucrative arrangements.

Flagler had to convince others that Standard had not taken advantage of its inheritance of the Empire contract with the Buffalo road. In a confidential letter to the Pennsylvania's Cassatt, Flagler stated that Standard's United Pipe Lines partners were not jealous of Standard's special arrangement with the Buffalo road. He must have been effective, for there was no response from either the Pennsylvania or the Buffalo road.[24] As later events were to show, the Buffalo road never became a party to Flagler's attempts to dominate transportation arrangements.

Although Flagler insisted on some advantageous agreements being continued, there were other agreements he wished to cancel. He instructed George Chester, a lawyer on Standard's retainer, that the contract between Columbia Conduit and the B&O was not to pass to United Pipe Lines. Flagler continued by giving Chester specific instructions as to how to accomplish that end. There were two reasons Flagler did not wish to have the contract continued: Since Standard was only one of several interested parties in the United Pipe Lines arrangement, if the contract continued, the other partners would be getting the same concessions as Standard. Also, Flagler in no way wished for pipeline arrangements to interfere with Standard's good relations with the railroads. He called upon Camden for advice on the subject: "You have such a happy way of thinking out knotty subjects." Flagler was straightforward in his rationale to Camden. The scenario Flagler presented to Camden was for the Standard alliance to present

Garrett with a Standard contract that would require the B&O to break the Columbia agreement. Flagler stated that Garrett "can't 'keep his cherries and eat them.' "[25]

For the remainder of 1877, Flagler's time was consumed by details growing out of the Empire purchase. He especially worked on the consolidation of pipeline activities. His natural grasp of legal technicalities was reflected in a letter written to George Chester, one of Standard's lawyers, with regard to the merger of the American Transfer Company into the United. "Of course I am bound to believe you know what you are talking about," Flagler wrote to Chester, "and I assume that the statute makes these steps necessary; but I have looked through the special act incorporating the company and fail to find anything requiring either of these things to be done. Am I right in supposing that they come under the general law governing corporations?"[26]

Even though the formal mergers into the United Pipe Lines occurred on November 13, 1877, the entire process was not completed until later. For example, the United Pipe Lines had to lease the pipage of the Empire until mid-January 1878, when the legalities of the situation would allow a formal purchase of the property. One of those legal hurdles was that stockholders' meetings had to take place to validate the purchases. Since certain charters of the merging companies required the stockholder meetings to occur in a specific place at a specific time, Flagler had to do some complex maneuvering. By the use of devices such as "present by proxy" and meeting adjournments, three of the directors of the companies (Flagler, William Brough, and George H. Vilas) would be able to fulfill the legal obligations of the charters by crisscrossing Pennsylvania in a matter of days.[27] When Flagler and Rockefeller later organized the Standard Oil Trust, they did so in part to avoid such problems.

At the same time Flagler supervised the pipeline transition, he oversaw a new agreement between the trunk lines and Standard. Even before the pooling agreement previously mentioned, the railroad executives, meeting with Flagler at Saratoga's Windsor House on September 20, had agreed to new oil freight rates, which would go into effect October 1. Under the new agreement, due to the 10 percent commission on all shipments, Standard and its allies moved refined to the ports more cheaply than competitors could move crude.[28]

One of the historical debates concerning Standard's relationship with the trunk lines has centered on Flagler's 10 percent drawback/commission arrangement. Flagler detractors, such as his contemporary journalist/critic Ida Tarbell, stated that this was a devious means which allowed Standard to snuff out its independent competition. Flagler's argument, presented before investigating committees, was that Standard was paid a commission as the evener of the oil traffic among the roads. It is true that Standard did not dictate to the roads their arrangements. For example, Flagler assured Cassatt just before the October 17, 1877, pooling agreement that Standard merely stood ready to do its distributing "in good faith to all parties." If the 10 percent was a true commission for the bookkeeping involved, surely the office of Standard auditor George Vail in Cleveland would get the proceeds on its books. But on at least one occasion, Flagler told Vail that Standard allies in New York, such as Bostwick, were to get their proportion of the 10 percent commission. This arrangement completely undercuts Flagler's testimony about the rationale for the "commission." Indeed, he confided to a railroad official with regard to rebates, "The fact is the whole system of reaching the net rate is substantially an arbitrary one."[29] Rebates, commissions, drawbacks, crude allowances, and other statistical devices were simply means of getting to the net rate in an honorable fashion.

Flagler designed the fall 1877 rate agreement to squeeze the independent Pittsburgh refiners into submission or extinction. Although Standard's freight payments did go up, by adhering to the new rate structure, Flagler gave Standard an even greater advantage over its refining competitors. The trunk lines gave additional aid and comfort to Standard by allowing refined already contracted for delivery before the September 20 agreement date to continue to come forward under the old $.60 net rate, even after October 1.[30]

In at least one case, that involving the Erie, the road brought all of Standard's October refined oil to the seaboard at the old $.60 rate, and then settled with Standard at the end of the month. When George Vail brought this to Flagler's attention, Flagler gave the auditor a brief lesson in business: "If Mr. Vilas [general freight agent of the Erie] is willing to let more oil come forward at the 60¢ rate than they stipulated for, that is his business. We, of course, holding ourselves in readiness to pay an additional sum, when he presents his bills, but not before. It is not our province to inquire into his motives for doing the thing in this way." Flagler made clear to his fellow conspirators that the old rate overrun into October was to be kept secret. As he stated to J. H. Rutter, "You will of course keep this information as strictly confidential, as if known in the market it would work injury to our interests."[31]

The October overrun was not an isolated practice on the part of Flagler. He capitalized on any advantage Standard could achieve. When a short line road's billing was $.30 a barrel in Standard's favor, he informed Vail, "I have no conscientious scruples about availing ourselves of any errors of omission on their part. It will be time enough to correct the matter when they discover it." Flagler did not allow sentiment to becloud his business judgment. When the Atlantic road, now in receivership, sought to collect a $2,000 debt the Standard owed it, Flagler notified Vail as to his position on the matter. Since the Atlantic owed Standard much more than that amount, Flagler reasoned, "It seems to me, that if this old Atlantic organization is too far gone to pay, it is also too far gone to receive any moneys. It is a poor rule that won't work both ways."[32]

Flagler showed a truly remarkable ability to keep the traffic among the trunk lines even. Admittedly, his work on their behalf in this regard would have easily been worth Standard's 10 percent commission on their oil freight revenues. As Flagler carefully watched the movements of refining competitors, his diligence continued to be worth much more to Standard than a mere monetary amount. On one occasion Flagler noticed that the Central had loaned tank cars to the firm of Barnsdall & Company ("must be some little affair recently sprung up," Flagler said). J. H. Rutter of the Central explained to Flagler that the only reason the Central had assisted Barnsdall was that the firm had been unable to get tank cars from Standard. The Barnsdall firm had stated to Rutter that Standard had been unwilling—hinting that the empty cars were available—to lease them to the firm for a reasonable amount. Flagler retorted that if the facts as presented were true, then the Central might have had a proper excuse for its action. But Flagler issued a strong warning: "In view of the fact, that we have spent an enormous sum of money, and have provided facilities, not only ample, but largely in excess of the business that can be done over your road, I feel it is not treating us fairly, to encourage competition against us by the course your road is pursuing in this matter, and would be very glad to have your views on the subject."[33]

Being a business diplomat, Flagler did not let Rutter think ill of him for long. The next day Flagler reassured Rutter that the reason the Erie was currently getting more Standard traffic than the Central was because Standard was behind on its Erie commitment. Flagler stated, "We have not 'gone over to the enemy bodily' or *spiritually.*" But it was not long before Flagler again admonished Rutter for assisting independent refiners. Flagler complained of the Central's policy that allowed a small railroad to use not only Central docks but also its trucks (frames on wheels) upon which to mount independent refiners' tanks. The crude involved in that traffic went from Titusville to Buffalo, and then by canal to New York. Flagler pointedly advised Rutter to state that if the short line road's traffic hurt the Central—and by implication Standard—then the Central would take an uncooperative attitude. The Central was only to assist the short line in its local traffic.[34]

Just as Flagler got the October 1 rate structure operational, new circumstances called for a quick revision. The new Bradford field, located east of the Regions in northcentral Pennsylvania, began gushing in late 1877. It immediately accounted for a larger proportion of the oil production than anticipated. Flagler noted that the western railroads, the Atlantic and Lake Shore, were not even involved in the Bradford traffic. He then argued with the Central and Erie for a rate differential between the old Regions area and the Bradford District. The new rate structure, instituted to take effect on December 1, provided that the roads would carry crude from the Regions (now known as "the lower district") to New York for $1.40 a barrel, while the rate from Bradford to New York was to be $1.15. The railroads took advantage of this opportunity to advance the published rates for refined to $1.90. In all cases Standard got its 10 percent commission.[35]

The situation on the southern rim of the Standard empire did not go as well as the Standard relations with the three northern trunk lines. Camden constantly complained to Flagler about the treatment he was receiving from the B&O. In October 1877, Camden began a billing dispute with the B&O. Although it was a relatively minor business matter, Flagler's actions during the controversy give us insight into his business attitudes and manner. Flagler encouraged Camden in this battle with Garrett and the B&O: "If you think the perspiration don't roll off freely enough, pile the blankets on him. I would rather lose a great deal of money than to yield a pint to him at this time. The slightest concession now, will cost us a great many thousand dollars in our business intercourse hereafter, and never was a better time for us to test our strength with him."[36]

As the battle between Camden and the B&O became more heated, Flagler confided in Hugh J. Jewett, receiver of the Erie, that Garrett "has treated us as alien enemies instead of allies and friends. His talk about 'Monopoly' is childish." Flagler was disappointed that Garrett failed to see the situation as the Standard did: rate reductions and pooling agreements were mutually beneficial to all cooperating parties. Flagler advised Jewett that Garrett would probably be in New York trying to convince Jewett and Vanderbilt that the trunk lines could do better than they were doing with the Standard arrangements. Flagler continued, "I think you know enough of the real situation to convince you that he can do no such thing." One thing Flagler was sure of: "We certainly do not propose to become, 'hewers of wood and drawers of water' for the B. and O.R.R." Flagler even advised

Garrett himself that to impose an immediate increase in oil freight rates by a trunk line agreement in mid-November would be a dangerous precedent. Flagler suggested delaying the increase until December 1 and having it at an even higher rate at that time.[37]

Meanwhile, Flagler enjoyed the dispute between Camden and Garrett. Camden reported to Flagler a letter he had written Garrett regarding the disputed billing, in which Camden had stated to Garrett how he had conducted an interview with another B&O official. Flagler was elated at Camden's tone, "You have *beaten* the old gentleman at his own game. . . . I don't see how you can compromise any claim you have against the road, without compromising your character as a gentleman." Throughout November, Flagler continued to advise Camden. As for compromise, Flagler would not even entertain such a thought: "I am in favor of leaving him [Garrett] and his road entirely, until he reaches a correct view of the whole situation and is willing to do what is right."[38]

When the B&O formally requested payment of its claim against Camden, Flagler continued to advise Camden to fight the claim. Flagler himself sat down with Andrew Anderson, Garrett's assistant, to present Camden's position. Flagler described the interview to Camden as a "spicy session." Flagler pointedly told Anderson that Standard backed Camden fully in the dispute. Anderson returned to Flagler's office the following day with a proposal that the parties gather at the Breevort House for a conference on the matter, to which Flagler agreed.[39]

Flagler took Anderson's second interview as an opportunity to impress upon him the gravity with which Standard was approaching the matter. While maintaining a serious demeanor in his delivery, Flagler realized that he had given a command performance before Anderson. "I stated to him," Flagler reported to Camden,

> that a conviction was fastening itself upon my mind, that our relation to the transportation of oil was not as well appreciated by the roads as it ought to be or else we were overestimating our services, and that I was coming more and more to the feeling, that we would stand better in the eyes of the producers and of the world generally if we had no alliances with the railroads, that we were popularly accredited with receiving from the roads large [concessions], which he of his own knowledge knew to be untrue, and that in consequence of this a hostility existed toward us which had no foundation in fact; and that I was not certain but that all the roads had better put us on the same footing with other shippers, and then we [would] be [free] from all obligations to the roads. I said this with a great deal of earnestness and apparent sincerity, and I saw that it was a bombshell.

Flagler was rather self-congratulatory. He told Camden he had made a similar pitch to Cassatt, "and if I hear any more nonsense on this subject on the part of [trunk line] managers or see any disposition on their part to squirm whenever sentiment seems to be against us, I shall take occasion to repeat what I have said to these two gentlemen, to others."[40]

The B&O crisis which Flagler had feared never came. On December 20, Flagler reached an agreement with the B&O. Once again, practical business sense won over principle. Flagler, in order to win B&O concessions on other points, agreed that Camden would pay half the disputed bill to the B&O. In response to Flagler's report, Camden was more upset with the concession Flagler had made on the river traffic from Pittsburgh to Parkersburg. Flagler had agreed to send all oil traffic to Parkersburg by the more expensive B&O route.[41]

Flagler continued to press B&O officials on Camden's behalf. By the end of January, Flagler cleared up one matter of concern to Camden. Flagler took up the issue of B&O's guarantee to an independent refiner of the lowest rates the B&O would provide any shipper. Flagler reported to Camden that the agreement "was prior to our having 'buried the hatchet,' and that Mr. Garrett fully understands, that we are to have protection as against every shipper and [Anderson] assures me positively that Mr. Garrett is doing nothing and will do nothing prejudicial to our interests."[42] This was the type of cooperative attitude Flagler always sought from the trunk lines.

As for his commitment, Flagler, the evener in trunk line agreements, kept exacting records. On one occasion, he devoted a lengthy letter to Standard auditor Vail discussing a year-old drawback from the Central on Eclipse Lubricating Oil to New England, although the entire amount at issue was only $171.98 for 376 barrels. One reason for this close attention to detail was that it was rather easy for errors to occur in the world of rebates, drawbacks, and other "private concessions." On one such occasion, the Pennsylvania mistakenly charged Standard $.70 a barrel on shipments of over 150,000 barrels, when the charge should have been $.465 a barrel. This single error, if undetected, would have cost Standard over $35,000.[43]

With the Bradford District producing so rapidly, Flagler attempted to keep all transportation parties satisfied. In January 1878, Standard had its Acme, Imperial, and Keystone refineries running at full capacity to meet the Lake Shore–Central requirement of 5,000 barrels a day, which Flagler had earlier negotiated. He had to juggle both shipments from the individual refineries and shipments among the railroads to make sure that all the parts of shipment schedules fit together.[44]

69

Although Flagler sought to keep the railroads contented, he would not sacrifice Standard profits for peace with the rails. Due to the depressed European oil market, primarily caused by the Bradford glut, Flagler got rate concessions from the Central and Erie with little difficulty. Finally, on February 1, the Pennsylvania's Cassatt agreed to a $.25-a-barrel reduction in the contracted rate for refined to New York, but not to its other ports. Even though Flagler guaranteed the Pennsylvania 240,000 barrels of oil over a two-month period in exchange for the agreement, Cassatt was not pleased with the reduction: "I am sorry to have to make this concession, as we were in hopes of being able to maintain the present rates strictly."[45]

The railroads, for their part, served Flagler well—if at times grudgingly—in his wars against Cleveland's refining rivals. By the end of April 1878, he boasted that Pittsburgh had been "cleaned up" of major independent refinery threats, and he began to work on New York. When Andrew Anderson of the B&O complained of a lack of traffic from Standard, Flagler assured him that it was a temporary problem brought about by the difficulty in getting ships to go from New York to Baltimore before returning to Europe. In explaining this situation, Flagler indicated to Anderson Baltimore's weak trade position, hinting that the B&O would be well served by treating Standard with respect. Flagler noted complaints of New York refiners with regard to the difficulty of obtaining shipments of crude. They had said, according to what Flagler had heard, that the Standard was out to "kill New York, by refusing to sell New York delivery." "This of course is not literally true," Flagler noted to Garrett's young associate, "but it's pretty near it."[46] The strong intimation was that Flagler would not appreciate the B&O's shipping of crude oil to Baltimore.

While Flagler played this game of cat-and-mouse with the B&O, he had a more serious matter to discuss with the Central. With the Bradford District producing oil at such a rapid rate, William H. Vanderbilt and other Central shareholders bought into a new railroad venture, the Rochester and State Line road, and built that line to Bradford. Toward the end of February, Flagler pressed Vanderbilt for a commitment to allow a Standard pipeline to serve the State Line road in the Bradford District. Vanderbilt, being rather cagey in his negotiations with Flagler, first indicated that the Central had no authority over the State Line officials. He argued that although the Central would be hauling some of the State Line oil, the "independent" line reserved the right to make contracts with other roads as it saw fit. When Flagler proved unwilling to accept this ploy, Vanderbilt asserted that the State Line could not legally sign any contracts for transportation arrangements until the building contractor officially turned it over to the railroad officials.[47]

Flagler did not allow Vanderbilt to dissuade him. Flagler encouraged Standard contractors to rapidly build a pipeline loading rack at Bradford for an anticipated tie in with the State Line road. A delay would hurt Standard's ability to control the flow of oil from the Bradford area. By February 26, Flagler had reached an agreement with J. H. Rutter, the general freight agent of the Central. Standard's United Pipe Lines would go ahead with construction of pipes to the Bradford connection with the State Line, with the understanding that the State Line would give a $.20-a-barrel rebate to the United for all oil shipped over the State Line. Flagler had an ulterior motive for such vigilance: "I want to give them a very large amount of business in the start, in order that they may feel that we are the parties with whom it will be to their interest to work."[48]

The victory over the Pennsylvania in the battle for the Empire, coupled with the resulting consolidations, was the pinnacle of Flagler's successes in transportation battles. However, success created the need for Flagler to move permanently to New York City. From that center of commerce, he could more easily oversee Standard's far-flung empire. While Rockefeller remained behind at company headquarters in Cleveland, Flagler moved to New York in the fall of 1877.[49]

The Cleveland years had been a period of both business and family growth for Henry Flagler. He had continued his church work by becoming the superintendent of First Presbyterian's Sabbath School. With the birth of his only son, Harry Harkness, on December 2, 1870, less than a year after the creation of the Standard Oil Company, Flagler built a home on fashionable Euclid Avenue. The Flaglers enjoyed the social scene in Cleveland, even more than Rockefeller, who seemed to be content with church work alone.[50]

During the 1870s, Flagler's personal life changed dramatically. There were times of rejoicing. Of course, the birth of son Harry in 1870 had been a proud moment. Also, daughter Jennie's marriage to John Arthur Hinckley on April 26, 1876, was a joyous occasion. After her marriage, Jennie and John made their home in New York. Although Hinckley had begun his career back in the 1860s as a cashier for one of the western railroads headquartered in Chicago, Flagler quickly incorporated his new son-in-law into the Standard organization.[51]

When Henry, Mary, and Harry moved to New York, they lived at the Buckingham Hotel while their home at 509 Fifth Avenue was being constructed during late 1877 and early 1878. Of course, Flagler himself closely watched the progress. In a New Year's Eve, 1877, letter to D. D. Tompkins, his contractor out of Greenwich, Connecticut, Flagler advised him on a minor matter. A week and a half later, Flagler wrote Tompkins again:

> Yours of the 9th at hand and carefully noted. Sorry they are not making better progress on the house. Do all in your power to crowd them. We'll see Mr Hatch about the plumber and furnace man. The fire-brick and fire-clay was shipped yesterday. I sent you an invoice which when received check and return. Don't think I will be able to get up this week. If you want money better come down. How are you getting along with the slating, are they nearly through with it? Will not require any insurance on the home at the moment. Did the party with whom you figured for lightening rods propose putting the twisted copper cable? If I put up any kind it will be that. Has Mr Thomas got the wall foundation in yet? Are you going ahead with the grading? Does the man expect to get the other trees right away[?] Supposing you look around a little and see if you could find near our house 20 or 30 acres of nice land. If you could find such nicely situated, under good state of cultivation, high ground, at a reasonable price, think would buy it. You might make inquiries about 20, 30, 40, or even 50 acres. George can probably tell you where you would find such a piece. Would not object to having part of it woodland.[52]

Flagler's concern for detail and planning was evident throughout his correspondence with Tompkins.

Late 1877 and throughout 1878 were times of transition for the Flaglers. They wasted little time after the New York move in getting settled in the new city. They attended the West Presbyterian Church, and its pastor and future president of Union Seminary, Thomas S. Hastings, became Flagler's lifelong friend. Meanwhile, Flagler attempted to sell or trade his Cleveland home for some Cleveland investment property. By the summer of 1878, the house had not sold and Flagler, along with Rockefeller, sent his trotting horses to Cleveland and stayed there for the summer.[53]

Neither Henry nor Mary Flagler could afford to wait until the summer for a needed rest. Mary's health had always been poor and Flagler himself was exhausted. In early 1878, he planned a long Florida vacation, to begin the latter part of February and last into April. With the problems Standard had with various railroad matters, Flagler did not leave until February 27, after having settled the State Line railroad question. He instructed Daniel O'Day to "keep me closely advised in regard to current matters."[54]

Although Flagler did need a vacation, the Florida trip was primarily for Mary. She had always been in poor health, but always active too, at least in their early years before the Civil War when she traveled with Flagler on his Bellevue to Cleveland business trips. It was evident after the birth of Harry in 1870, however, that her condition was getting worse. Her bronchial problems continued; the doctors diagnosed it as consumption, today known as tuberculosis. Both her doctor and Flagler wanted her to go to Florida for the worst of the winter season, but she had refused to go without him.[55]

The first time Flagler went to Florida, he, Mary, and Harry went only to Jacksonville. There were probably several reasons for stopping there. First, a railroad did not even cross the St. Johns River. Second, Florida had a well-deserved reputation for poor transportation arrangements south of Jacksonville. For example, the best way to get to St. Augustine in 1878 was to take a river steamer from Jacksonville to Tocoi, and then the remaining fifteen miles to the coastal town would be on the St. John's Railway, which ran on wooden rails. The Flaglers stayed at Jacksonville's St. James Hotel. As indicated in his letter to O'Day, Flagler did not intend to forget about what was going on at the Standard office in New York. Consequently, the Flaglers did not stay in Jacksonville until mid-April. Flagler returned to New York about March 17, for Standard was being challenged by a new transportation revolution. Mary, of course, would not stay in Florida without him.[56]

The Great Pipeline Battle

AT THE BEGINNING of 1878, Flagler concentrated on consolidating the Empire gains and cooperating with the trunk lines in freight rate arrangements, but a new tempest appeared on the horizon. On January 4, 1878, J. N. Camden wrote Flagler, "I see a good deal said in the newspapers in relation to sea-board pipe line. I hope we have no cause to be disturbed by it." The reason for Camden's concern was that if alternative means of transportation became available, especially with the glut of oil at the time, Flagler might not control transportation to the benefit of Standard. Indeed, it could mean the demise of Cleveland as a refining center, since pipes would provide much cheaper transport to the seaboard than rails. In his reply to Camden, Flagler was lighthearted, but aware of the threat: "I note your reference to the Seaboard Pipe Line, and as it is a pretty long subject, (upwards of 200 miles) I dare not attempt to discuss it in the limits of a letter. It is however one of those things we need to watch, and to be ready for. I trust however if we keep our heads level, it will not result to our injury, and I doubt whether it will be built right away."[1]

Flagler had cause for concern. The leaders of the proposed pipeline project were men who had formerly been associated with the Columbia Conduit—including Byron Benson, David McKelvy, and Robert Hopkins. Their new plan was to run a pipe from Brady's Bend, on the Allegheny River near Pittsburgh, to Baltimore. They met with the Petroleum Producers' Union council, discussed their plan, and gained the support of the producers. Seaboard and other pipeline companies also attempted to push through the legislatures of New York, Pennsylvania, and Maryland "free pipeline" bills, which would give pipeline companies the same rights of eminent domain as those held by railroads.[2]

Flagler reacted by calling upon the Standard network of partners and transportation allies for assistance. On January 22, with an article on the free-pipeline subject from *Railroad World* enclosed, Flagler wrote Daniel O'Day, assuring him that actions were being taken in both New York and Pennsylvania to squash the movement: "I saw Mr. Vanderbilt on the subject yesterday morning, and no effort will be spared to defeat all these things at Albany. I think you had better not mention my name in connection with any Legislative interference. We are watching these things pretty closely at Harrisburg also, and hope that everything will come out all right. Keep me closely advised."[3]

By the time Flagler reacted to the Maryland situation, the legislature had already passed a pipeline charter. It seemed that a Mr. Barclay was behind the scheme and was in the process of selling the charter to the highest bidder. What Flagler feared was that, even if Camden did obtain the charter from Barclay, there was nothing to prevent Barclay from doing the same thing all over again. Flagler thought that as long as the forces of the Pennsylvania road could keep Pennsylvania free-pipeline legislation off the books, Seaboard would find little use for the Maryland charter, especially considering Barclay's $25,000 asking price. Flagler simply did not believe the Seaboard group had the funds to buy the Maryland charter and the necessary right-of-way without an assurance that the Pennsylvania bill would become law. He also had faith enough in the Pennsylvania Railroad's lobbyists that such an eventuality would not occur.[4]

Less than a week later, Flagler was less confident concerning the Maryland matter. Still uncertain as to the course of action, he advised Camden to buy the charter should an immediate decision be thrust upon him: "You know your man, and whether the matter is safe as you have left it, if not, I think it would be well for you if possible to try and get it shaped up, so the Benson party [Seaboard Pipeline Company] cannot steal a march on us." Camden's delay became potentially costly for Standard. By mid-February, Barclay had increased his asking price for the Maryland charter to at least $30,000. Although Flagler hoped Camden could buy it for only $30,000, even $35,000 was "too small a sum to allow the trade to be broken off." Flagler comforted himself with the thought that if Standard could make it through the legislative halls of Annapolis for a couple more weeks without another pipeline charter, it would be safe until 1880, the next regular session of the Maryland legislature.[5]

With regard to seaboard pipeline threats, Flagler was willing to buy charters and bribe legislators. "The Standard Oil Co. has now a charter, under which it can build pipelines anywhere in the State of Pennsylvania," Flagler stated in a December 1877 letter to James Devereux,

> and as it has no ambition to build railroads, and as we have spent a large sum of money to squelch Seaboard Pipe Line Charters, we have about made up our minds, that if any danger is likely to occur from Seaboard Pipes, the Trunk Lines may hereafter furnish the money necessary to take care of such charters . . . at the moment I feel reluctant to invest any more money in controlling Pipe Line Enterprises to the Seaboard. When the Trunk Lines will come up and *put down* as much money as we have for this purpose, we might feel more inclined to take another step forward.

Nothing had really changed by the spring of 1878 insofar as pipeline threats were concerned. Flagler did not insist, however, on railroad contributions for the stopping of seaboard pipes, even though he continued to be willing to buy up charters.[6] This is clear evidence that the construction of seaboard pipelines carrying crude to refineries in New York, Philadelphia, and Baltimore would most harm Standard, not the railroads.

Although Standard bore the brunt of the seaboard fight during the winter and spring of 1878, Flagler was still confident of the railroads' support. He had the Pennsylvania road do Standard's bidding in Harrisburg. "With the money recently invested at Harrisburg." Flagler wrote Oliver Payne on February 7, "my own feeling is, to go slow on much or all of this sort of thing [buying Maryland charters]." Even the B&O was supportive of Standard in the pipeline battles. In discussing the Seaboard situation with Andrew Anderson, Flagler became aware that John Garrett had already fully apprised Anderson as to the threat that Seaboard posed to the B&O. Flagler even overcame his natural dislike of Garrett on this particular occasion: "While I have not changed my opinion in respect to Mr. Garrett's unfortunate manner, yet, when I divest myself of the prejudice I have entertained toward him, I cannot resist the conviction, that Mr. Garrett is a deep thinker, and perhaps sees this question more clearly than any other gentleman connected with the Trunk Lines."[7] On that point Flagler would later be sorely disappointed.

Flagler returned from his Florida vacation in ill health, unable to attend to day-to-day business until March 28. Upon his return to the office, Flagler had to first protect *Standard's* pipeline activities. Standard was in the process of buying rights-of-way so that gathering pipes could connect with the B&O between the Allegheny and Monongahela rivers. Flagler immediately sent a note to Andrew Anderson of the B&O warning of the need for secrecy with regard to Standard's Pittsburgh pipeline.[8]

Standard also moved to buy up another pipeline's right-of-way contracts on the Buffalo route. Rockefeller wrote Hugh Jewett, the receiver of the Erie, on March 30 that a Dr. Shamburg of Titusville had obtained right-of-way rights over the Buffalo and Jamestown Railway, but that Standard officials thought they could buy out the contract for only $2,500: "it would probably be better to give this than allow the pipe to be laid. I feel a hesitancy about speaking definitely regarding this last feature, as Mr. Flagler has had the whole matter in charge, and I am not familiar with it."[9]

The Central lobbyists in Albany had failed in their efforts to thwart the pipeline; now it was time for Flagler to apply his Standard solution. In order to gain concessions from the railroads, Flagler told Oliver Payne he intended to have a meeting with the trunk line presidents: "My feeling is to say to these gentlemen as this seems to be a scramble, each one for the most, that perhaps it would be better for the Standard Oil Co. not to have any further alliances with the Trunk Lines." Flagler thought that such threats, which he had already administered to Tom Scott and Hugh Jewett with success, would bring William H. Vanderbilt into line on the matter.[10]

In pressing the Pennsylvania's Cassatt for rate relief, Flagler was rather blunt in giving his reasons for the need for a change. In the fall 1877 agreement with the trunk lines, Flagler had negotiated relatively high rates for refined oil to the seaboard, "Our motive was apparent when I say to you, that at that time our great competition was in Pittsburgh. Now Pittsburgh is cleaned up and about all there is left is here in New York." With that in mind, Flagler now asked for a "private reduction" on refined oil from the trunk lines. For his part, Flagler promised to set the rate so that the roads would net $1.00 a barrel on the traffic. He would also make contracts for future delivery in such a way as to keep all the traffic for Standard and the roads. Another plum for the roads was that there would be no change on the crude rates at that time, and Flagler would hold off on any request for a crude oil reduction "until it becomes *absolutely* necessary." Within two days, the trunk lines had informally approved a $.25-a-barrel private reduction from the interior refining points to the seaboard.[11]

The trunk lines had acquiesced in the rate reduction with relative ease, especially the three northern roads, because of the threat of independent competition. New York refiners had already signed contracts with the Buffalo, New York, & Philadelphia road for transport of crude to Buffalo. Cassatt, hoping for some new Standard business, suggested that Flagler build a pipe over to the Pittsburgh & Erie road, a subsidiary of the Pennsylvania. Flagler had already discussed such an alternative with his Standard allies, but he did not reveal this to Cassatt.[12]

Cassatt did not have to wait long to talk with Flagler in person, for on April 23, Flagler requested an immediate meeting with leaders of the trunk lines concerning his rate reduction proposal. The meeting took place on Friday, April 26, at the Windsor Hotel in New York City. The railroad representatives agreed to rates Flagler had earlier proposed. The net rate to New York was $1.00, $.865 to Philadelphia and Baltimore, and there was no change in the refined rates to New England and local points or in crude oil rates.[13]

Flagler was very pleased, not only with the results of the Friday meeting but also with the way the roads reacted to the Standard proposal. The Erie and the Pennsylvania, as well as the Central's William K. Vanderbilt, stood solidly with Standard. William K. Vanderbilt, the 28-year-old son of William H., had argued in the meeting that, if it had not been for Standard's cooperative attitude during the mid-1870s, it would have been impossible for the roads to have better rates from non-oil traffic. The younger Vanderbilt urged that it was now time for the roads to assist Standard. Anderson had argued, unsuccessfully, for a crude rate reduction. Flagler understood his objections, for the B&O would suffer most from Flagler's squeeze of seaboard refiners. Flagler wrote Camden, "Poor Anderson was really in a very tight place and it did not require any special effort on my part to make it exceedingly warm for him. I really pitied him." All the representatives gave their respective road's consent to the reduction except Anderson of the B&O. Anderson promised Flagler at the end of the Friday meeting he would attempt to have an answer the next day. Flagler spent all day Saturday with Anderson discussing the B&O predicament, but Anderson again left without giving Flagler a definite decision.[14]

Flagler gave Camden his assessment of his meeting with the trunk line officials. Standard had solid support from the Erie, Pennsylvania, and Central, but would continue to have trouble from the B&O. In fact, even before the meeting had taken place, President Garrett of the B&O had telegraphed Flagler at his home with a list of complaints. Garrett had also sent William H. Vanderbilt a four-page message arguing against the reduction. Flagler became unyielding. He informed Camden:

Had Mr. Garrett met this question even half-way on the deficiency which may appear May 1st in excess of the deficiency which existed Jan'y 1st or even December 1st, on the ground that the November business by the other roads was all done below prices, less even than rates to take effect after May 1st, but he acted so badly in this matter I now propose to say to him that he cannot expect from us any different guarantees than those we give to the other Trunk Lines, which are in substance this: that we undertake at the end of each year to secure to each road the percentage of the business allotted to each, and that having paid the existing rate during the winter on the surplus to the other roads we are not willing to pay it the second time on his shipments, etc. etc.[15]

The B&O finally acquiesced to the May 1 change in rates, but Flagler was well aware that there would be a continuing struggle with the line. He probably shared his friend J. N. Camden's assessment of Garrett. Camden wrote Flagler advising him to remain tough in his negotiating posture with Garrett: "He is a perfect Jew in his nature, and it matters not how well you were to treat him, or how much disposition you would show to conciliate him, it would only incline him to press his advances and ask for more." In spite of this unfortunately phrased assessment, Camden predicted that Garrett would abide by the rate structure of the trunk line agreement. As for the question of the old rates, Camden agreed with Flagler's position on the matter: "Your views in reference to [not] making up deficiencies at the old rates I think are wise and just."[16]

Meanwhile, Flagler continued his campaign against free-pipeline bills. He had the Standard auditor open a Seaboard Pipe account. Upon his return from his Florida vacation, Flagler apologized to Cassatt for not keeping the Pennsylvania road vice-president apprised of railroad matters: "Since my return sickness has prevented me from usual attention to business, besides that I have had these infernal pipe-line matters occupying every moment of my time, so much so, that I have been unable to make any suitable response to the several communications received from you by wire." The next day, Flagler was more at ease in writing Cassatt. He thanked the Pennsylvania officer for overseeing the pipeline matters in the Pennsylvania legislature. He also assured Cassatt that he felt that he had worked on the New York matter enough since his return from Florida that Standard and its railroad allies "will be able to defeat all pipeline legislation at Albany."[17]

Cassatt sent Flagler a copy of the Pennsylvania free-pipeline bill as it stood in its committee draft, asking what Flagler wished the Pennsylvania Railroad lobbyists to do with it. Flagler sent it to William Brough for his suggestions. Brough recommended to Cassatt and Flagler that the pipeline bill be amended rather than killed outright. This strategy would also open up new avenues of exploration for Daniel O'Day. Since the pipeline bill would give all pipeline companies access to powers of eminent domain, the

United could capitalize on the matter for its projected connection with the B&O in the Pittsburgh area and later projects. Cassatt assured Flagler that things were going well in the matters in Harrisburg. Therefore, Flagler confidently wrote Brough that "we shall secure the passage of the bill as amended."[18]

The situation in the New York legislature was quite another matter. Flagler confided to Cassatt, "Upon my return from the South, I found that matters had gone so far, that it would be almost impossible to defeat the Free Pipe Line Bill in the Assembly at Albany." In spite of his pessimism, Flagler had the Central lobbyists in Albany attach amendments in the assembly. He was confident of the outcome: "It now goes back to the Senate for that body to act on the amendments, and we have every reason to believe that it will be properly taken care of there."[19]

The Central failed Flagler in the Albany effort. The senate passed the amended assembly version intact. Flagler was in the office of Chauncey Depew, the Central's lobbyist and future New York governor, when the telegram containing the bad news arrived in New York: "Mr. Depew seemed very much cut up about it and I really cannot understand it." Upon further reflection, Flagler became increasingly suspicious of William H. Vanderbilt's role in the affair. Flagler thought that Vanderbilt was in the process of switching his allegiance from trunk line arrangements with the Standard to a Central agreement with the refiners and pipeline owners of western New York.[20]

Flagler immediately informed his railroad allies of the New York situation. He wrote Cassatt, "My suspicions [regarding W. H. Vanderbilt] are confirmed by the action of the Senate at Albany, and while I have good reason to believe that the Governor will veto the pipeline bill, I think it very important you should be advised of matters as they appear to us." Flagler also sought a more dependable New York ally. He went to see the Erie's Hugh Jewett, recently elected as president of the reorganized road, and arranged for Gorman B. Eaton, an Erie lawyer, to prepare a brief for presentation to New York's governor. Eaton, as a ghostwriter for the New York attorney general, argued that the pipeline bill was unconstitutional. The attorney general then made the formal presentation to the governor.[21]

In preparing for his attack on the pipeline bill in New York, Flagler wrote George R. Blanchard, Jewett's assistant, that the railroads should argue before the governor that legislative rumors had twisted the relationship that Standard had with the railroads. Flagler thought these rumors of Standard's power over the roads had been in large part responsible for the pipeline bill's passage. Blanchard was to argue that the railroads had met, without Standard's urging, and adopted a system of gross rates that was fair to railroads in allowing them to make a profit by putting all manufacturing points on terms of equality. Flagler then advised Blanchard to assure the governor that most of the refining interests in the country were in favor of this method. Since Flagler well knew Standard's overwhelming dominance of refining in America, he encouraged Blanchard to submit Flagler's version of the refiners' reaction to the railroad agreement: "I believe I am justified in asserting that 95% of the refining interest[s] of this country are entirely satisfied with the system by which freight rates are made, and that the complaints and denunciations of the Trunk Lines and the Standard Oil Co. come from a class of people who have comparatively small or insignificant interests at stake."[22]

The seaboard pipeline question continued to be a major problem for Flagler. The governor of New York refused to veto the free-pipeline bill, in spite of Flagler's earlier confidence that such an eventuality would occur if needed. Rather than the Central, Flagler now used the Erie as his agent. Smith M. Weed, an attorney and lobbyist for the Erie, was Flagler's new contact with the proper authorities. Weed was to pay someone—and it is unclear whom—a goodly sum to derail the pipeline. Flagler assured Weed, "If you will undertake this matter at once it will be greatly obliged, and you may rely upon our furnishing the necessary *backing*." Flagler was willing to pay up to $60,000 for the "buy," but Jewett seemed to indicate that it could be had for only $15,000. In any case, Flagler sent the first $10,000 cash installment to Jewett on April 25.[23]

The ploy did not work. The following Monday, Flagler found himself fighting the first proposed charter to come under the new pipeline bill. Plans called for the pipeline to be built along the Genesee Valley Canal. Flagler met with the Central's Chauncey Depew in order to plot strategy against the Genesee charter. Flagler's first line of attack was to delay passage of the bill until less than ten days before the end of the legislative session. This would allow the governor to kill the bill by simply not signing it into law. Flagler wrote Blanchard of the Erie: "Don't spare one moment of time or any effort on your part to secure the necessary delay in the passage of the [Genesee] Bill for I assume that it will pass and that the Governor will not veto the Free Bill." Flagler feared the Genesee pipeline charter because, as a result of the route it would take, it stood the best chance of actually being built of any of the seaboard proposals he had heard. He was even more certain of his assessment because the same day he wrote Blanchard that he had received word that the Benson interest had abandoned its Baltimore pipeline.[24] As we shall later see, this was only a temporary truce in the battle between Flagler and the "Benson party."

The seaboards were not the only pipelines Flagler feared. In lieu of the free-pipeline legislation, Pennsylvania had passed a law, with the assistance of Flagler and Cassatt, that supposedly strengthened the state's regulation of pipelines. Flagler requested his Philadelphia ally W. G. Warden to work through Cassatt to have the governor, in his selection of examiners, "not appoint men wholly inimical to the interests of the Company."[25] Flagler was concerned that, if gathering pipelines found their way to canals or uncooperative independent railroads, he could have just as much trouble controlling transportation arrangements as the seaboard pipes would have threatened.

Meanwhile, Flagler had to create a "new" pipeline company. Because of loose talk, it was widely known in the Pittsburgh area that Standard was behind the pipeline-B&O connection. The Pennsylvania, for example, had not allowed the Standard pipes to cross its rights of way. That created an especially delicate situation for Flagler. At the same time that he attempted to get the Pennsylvania road to go along with Standard's pipeline project, he joined the trunk lines in the courts of New York to argue the unconstitutionality of the legislature's free-pipeline law. He took a behind-the-scenes role in the new pipeline company, letting Daniel O'Day negotiate the details of the new venture.[26]

Toward the end of April, Flagler notified Cassatt that the pipeline concern attempting a connection at Williamsport was negotiating with the Reading road. Pipeline manufacturers, quite naturally, had already announced their support of the venture. Flagler feared that if the Reading did indeed sign contracts with the pipeline concern, then the pipeline entrepreneurs, based on the Reading commitment, would be able to borrow capital for the building of the line.[27]

As for possible transportation competition, of greater concern to Flagler than what appeared to be a futuristic Williamsport pipe was the possibility of the Buffalo, New York & Philadelphia road providing a link between the Regions and the Erie Canal at Buffalo. This problem had been lingering for several months. Finally Flagler's manipulation of the BNY&P road through contracts with the trunk lines paid its dividend. Flagler had given the Buffalo officials specific instructions regarding their response if approached by producers wishing to send crude along the Erie Canal: "They [the BNY&P] would not make their railroad a connection or caudal appendage to the Erie Canal, that they had a valuable oil traffic which could only be continued to them by their cooperating with the Trunk Lines, and they were unwilling to supply crude oil for shipment via the Erie Canal." Just in case the BNY&P position was not dissuasive enough, Flagler called upon J. H. Rutter of the Central to have Chauncey Depew write an article for distribution to Buffalo-area newspapers. Depew's article was to indicate how dangerous it would be to carry the volatile crude oil along the canal. Such an article, Flagler prophesied, "could create a sentiment among canal boat owners and shippers very prejudicial to the movement of bulk crude on the canal." A couple of weeks later, Flagler and Cassatt again met with the president and general freight agent of the BNY&P. After a lengthy conversation, the BNY&P officials agreed to stand firm in their refusal to carry crude oil bound for the Erie Canal.[28]

As soon as Flagler took care of one such situation, another emerged. He learned of a new move by the crude oil shippers: They were hoping to use General McKee's coal road, located only a short distance from the BNY&P, as their canal connection. Flagler encouraged J. H. Rutter to crush that movement by encouraging McKee to charge an outrageous $10 fee per tank car for his cost. Although McKee did have a very short road, Flagler argued, "it involves a great deal of switching, in fact, all there is to it is switching."[29]

Possibly believing that such activity on his part warranted a show of appreciation, Flagler pressed his railroad allies for additional concessions to the May 1 rate reduction. Garrett of the B&O was not about to suffer the further rate reduction. He first sent his son Robert to talk with Flagler. To the arguments of the younger Garrett, Flagler responded by indicating there were several disadvantages the Standard operation in Cleveland had to overcome with regard to seaboard refiners. Flagler's final, bottom-line argument was that Standard was actually *losing* $.40 a barrel for the "privilege" of shipping refined over the B&O. Flagler also noted that he was forced to make New York and Philadelphia shipments when he was unable to make European connections at the Baltimore harbor. He admitted to Camden that the arguments made no impact on Garrett. Flagler became frustrated at his inability to convince the younger Garrett of the superior business arrangements which cooperation with the Standard could bring.[30]

President Garrett, now convinced that he could not compromise with Flagler, called a meeting of the executive committee of the trunk lines. Garrett wished to have a pact among the presidents that no action by any of their subordinates would be accepted as being final until the presidents themselves had approved the action. Flagler carefully noted the first reactions of the presidents to this call, for he knew that Garrett's ulterior motive for the meeting was to pressure the other presidents to adhere to the May 1 rates, rather than have further reductions. When Garrett telegraphed Tom Scott on the matter, Scott seemed to respond positively to the proposal—a disappointment to Flagler. Scott forwarded the message for a call to William K. Vanderbilt, but the younger Vanderbilt refused to meet on the matter.[31]

Flagler knew that Standard needed the united support of the trunk lines. He told John Rockefeller, "So far as companies are concerned we are pushing things to an extremity and I am greatly impressed with a fear lest there will come a wave of public opinion so strong against us that the roads will be compelled to desert us." On at least one question, that of the further rate reduction, they did. Vanderbilt was the only one of the parties who refused to vote on the matter, stating that he did not agree with the decision to return to the May 1 rates. When Garrett reminded him that the B&O president had grudgingly gone along with the majority on the May 1 decision, Vanderbilt acquiesced. The united front by trunk line officials delayed, at least temporarily, Flagler's attempt at further concessions.[32]

The relationship between Flagler and the trunk lines was an uneasy one. Both he and the railroad officials realized that Standard and the trunk lines needed one another, especially in light of the new pipeline threats. On the other hand, since the trunk lines were competitors in freight matters, Flagler continued to exploit their weaknesses. At times, he would calm fears concerning their individual situations. For example, because of the Erie's support of the May 1 agreement and its refusal to promote a crude outlet to Buffalo, the directors of the line from western New York were threatening to remove Jewett as head of the road. Flagler reassured him that the Standard would use all its influence to prevent such an eventuality.[33]

When creating suspicions among the railroad leaders, Flagler was at his best. The usual result of this gambit was that the presidents came to trust only Flagler, the evener, with their allotment of oil shipments. In one such incident in the summer of 1878, Flagler got his revenge on Garrett. Flagler met with William K. Vanderbilt on June 3, warning the younger Vanderbilt that Robert Garrett was stalling a trunk lines decision on a rate matter until John Garrett could return from a European trip. Flagler asserted that he was positive that John Garrett would then attempt to turn William H. Vanderbilt against Standard. In order to convince the younger Vanderbilt of the Central's real enemy in the war, Flagler "confidentially" showed him a letter Camden had sent Flagler. In that letter, Camden had given a vivid description of a meeting he had had with John Garrett. In that conversation, Garrett had complained of the B&O's position with regard to the oil traffic. Garrett was so unhappy about it that he told Camden he would even support a pipeline to Baltimore before he would continue to be hemmed in by Standard's trunk line agreements.[34]

Vanderbilt's reaction to that letter was just as Flagler had intended. Flagler confidently reported to Rockefeller, "Of course I made all the capital out of this letter I could. I cannot explain within the limits of a letter the points made by me in my interview with W. K. I am satisfied however, have spiked Garrett's gun in that direction." Flagler felt that henceforth William K. Vanderbilt would be sure that he himself was the messenger between his father and the B&O. As for "confidentiality," the following day, Flagler fully explained to Hugh Jewett of the Erie his conversation with Vanderbilt. Flagler also indicated to Jewett that Standard was ready to break with the B&O. Jewett responded that he felt Flagler was fully justified in his position, and, as for himself, Jewett would refuse to attend any meeting Garrett might propose on the matter.[35]

Although Flagler had problems with Garrett and the B&O, he continued a cordial relationship with the other trunk lines' officials. The May 1 agreement had left several areas of the oil traffic at loose ends. By the end of the month, Flagler negotiated with the northern roads a trunk line agreement for New England traffic. He was most conciliatory in this agreement. He even allowed the Central to drop the special tank car rate it had given Standard for its New York traffic. All this was in order to obtain his long-term goal. As a result of the negotiations on the New England trade, Flagler reported to Rockefeller, "we have largely succeeded in establishing the principle, namely commission and pipe charges on all shipments."[36]

Flagler increased the pressure on shippers of both crude and refined who were not in the Standard camp, especially seaboard refiners. During this time Norris and William W. Harkness of Philadelphia had difficulty locating available tank cars for crude shipments to their refining facility. The reason was that Flagler had secured the Pennsylvania's cooperation with Standard in making "cars very scarce for the other parties." He had the same understanding with both the Erie and Central officials. As for the other remaining competition, the Erie Canal traffic, Flagler stated to Rockefeller, "It really looks as though we had got the canal shippers by the throat." Flagler had solid evidence for this assertion since he had paid a spy to keep him abreast of developments among the canal shippers in Buffalo.[37]

At the same time that Flagler squeezed competing shippers and refiners, he had difficulty fulfilling Standard's traffic commitments to the trunk lines. By June 3, he was 60,000 barrels behind on Standard's quota for the

Central. Although he had cornered the broad-gauge tank cars needed for refined oil, he still searched for narrow-gauge cars to get the oil from the Regions and Bradford District to the refineries. The glutted oil market created a transportation crisis that Flagler and the railroads could not overcome. The oversupply of oil was about to burst the transportation bottleneck that Flagler had so zealously guarded during the 1870s.[38]

Within such a competitive environment, the seaboard pipeline was too efficient a form of transportation to be permanently stopped. In the spring of 1878, Flagler had done everything humanly possible to stop the progress of the seaboard pipeline. He had bought charters and legislators and had used the influence of the Erie, Central, and Pennsylvania in the legislative halls and executive offices at Albany and Harrisburg. On November 22, 1878, Benson, Hopkins, and McKelvey once again threatened Flagler's control over transportation with their formation of Tidewater Pipe Company, Ltd. They organized as a limited partnership, rather than attempting a charter, thereby avoiding the Pennsylvania legislature. Now it became clear why they had abandoned the Seaboard project through Maryland. Long-distance pipelines, as was the 250-mile line to Baltimore, were still crude, risky experiments. Tidewater's plans offered its owners more flexibility and opportunity for funding. By connecting with the Reading Railroad at Williamsport, Tidewater would assure itself both financial support and an opportunity to prove its value as a long-distance transporter of oil before a final push to the seaboard. In exchange for the Reading's providing half the needed $500,000 to build the pipeline the 100 miles from Corryville to Williamsport, Tidewater officials promised that they would not extend their line to the coast for at least eight years.[39]

As the spring thaw of 1879 began, Tidewater moved quickly to get its pipes laid. On February 22, its first thirty-four sections were laid—in an almost straight line between Corryville and Williamsport—without the benefit of eminent domain. By the end of April, laying pipe at the rate of two miles a day, the builders had completed two-thirds of the line. The Pennsylvania and Tidewater attempted to outwit one another in both the field and the courts, with Tidewater winning the important battles with regard to right of way. On Wednesday, May 28, 1879, Byron Benson, president of Tidewater, started the pump at Corryville which sent the crude coursing through the pipes toward the heights of the Alleghenies. The next morning, the first of the oil peaked the mountains and headed downward to Williamsport.[40] With the success of pipeline venture, Flagler and his Standard associates had to plot a strategy against this new competitor.

Flagler's immediate reaction was to turn to the railroads to seek protection from the pipeline. Rockefeller had foreseen the battle in a May 13 letter to Flagler: "I see the seaboard pipe is proclaiming itself ready for business. I suppose this will create a stir in freight matters East." Believing that they could best control the oil traffic via railroad transport, Flagler, Rockefeller, and their Standard allies convinced themselves of a need to maintain their ties with the trunk lines. While Flagler was negotiating new rates with the railroads, Rockefeller was attempting to buy Benson's interest in Tidewater for $300,000. Benson, feeling a flush of victory, refused such an offer from Standard's empire builder. Rockefeller then attempted to make an arrangement with Tidewater whereby Standard would contract to purchase all the oil coming through Tidewater; again, this proposal was unsuccessful.[41]

In early June, Flagler opened negotiations with the trunk lines at Saratoga. He met with Cassatt, Jewett, and William H. Vanderbilt on June 5. By this time Standard's relations with the B&O had reached an impasse, and the B&O did not participate in pooling agreements with the other trunk lines on oil freight. Flagler would later testify that he attempted to get the trunk line officials to agree to a compromise with Tidewater. They would not hear of such talk. Flagler finally agreed to remain with the trunk lines in their rate wars with Tidewater in exchange for *major* rate concessions. The trunk lines first agreed to haul Standard's oil at the rate of $.20 a barrel. With later agreements, the rate finally fell to only $.10 a barrel.[42]

This was to be a full-scale war. Not only did the trunk lines give Standard concessions, but also the open rate to the seaboard immediately fell to $.25 a barrel, eventually declining even further. With the actual costs of carrying the oil by rail being from $.35 to $.40 a barrel, while the pipeline cost was about $.05 a barrel, the railroads were doomed to fail in this particular rate war. Amid rumors that Standard was preparing to build its own pipeline to the seaboard, the railroads began to realize the futility of their struggle. On February 12, 1880, the trunk lines and Tidewater entered into a pooling agreement. Tidewater and its rail ally, the Jersey Central road, got one-sixth of the oil traffic.[43] Although Standard was not directly involved in this negotiation, its officials attempted to regain control of the oil traffic process.

Rockefeller and Flagler negotiated with the railroads on a combined rail-pipeline rate that would continue to give Standard protection from independent refinery movements. The final agreement called for the trunk lines to haul crude from the Regions to New York for $.51, with a $.41 rate to apply to the Philadelphia and Baltimore traffic. Although Cleveland enjoyed a most-favored-shipper status with its two-way rate only $.50 a barrel, Standard seemed to have lost, on the surface at least, its enviable status as the evener of oil traffic.[44]

Standard officials were not idle during 1879 and 1880 while transportation agencies apparently controlled the field. Standard redoubled its efforts, beginning in the spring of 1879, to control as much of the oil-refining capacity of the nation as possible. Transporting crude oil would be of no use to the trunk lines and pipelines if there was no party willing to buy it; thereby, Standard was attempting to fix the market in such a way that the transportation agencies would have to come to Standard's terms or have no oil traffic at all—with huge investments in rolling stock to pay off. This activity would have in itself caused Benson alarm, for he had to depend on refineries to buy the crude passing through his pipes. It was Standard's movement into the seaboard pipeline field, however, that most disturbed him.[45]

As early as 1878, J. N. Camden had advised Flagler that the best way for Standard to continue to control transportation would be to build its own pipeline facilities and then strike pooling agreements with its rail allies. According to Camden, that would create peace in the transportation field with *Standard giving its trunk line allies a drawback* on oil it shipped more cheaply through its pipelines. Other officials, such as William Brough in the spring of 1879, offered similar advice. By the fall of 1879, Standard was busy gaining rights-of-way between the Regions and Cleveland. Throughout this buying and building activity, Standard continued to be cooperative with its rail allies, even going so far as to get right-of-way concessions from them. In one such instance, Rockefeller paid $50,000 to the Erie for such an arrangement. As Rockefeller indicated to the Erie's Jewett, the oil traffic was now so great that the pipes would merely supplement, rather than replace, the business Standard already gave the trunk lines. As soon as Standard completed the pipeline to Cleveland around the end of January 1880, Rockefeller began building a line to New York from the Bradford District.[46]

On March 10, 1880, Byron Benson approached Daniel O'Day with his olive branch. Standard's activities over the past year had indicated to the president of Tidewater that Standard would do whatever it thought necessary to continue to dominate the oil industry—and that included crushing Tidewater if necessary. Rockefeller did enter into negotiations with Benson, but nothing came of these 1880 conversations. Standard offered to guarantee Tidewater a 6,000-barrel-a-day proportion of the oil traffic, but Benson and his associates thought that was too small an amount.[47]

The situation remained at this impasse until events began to increasingly favor Standard. First, Tidewater's ally, the Reading, went into receivership in 1880. As a result of stockholder dissatisfaction, President Franklin B. Gowen resigned his office. He counterattacked by stating that his enemies among the stockholders were really pawns of the Pennsylvania. Such assertions helped Gowen to return to the presidency in 1882. Nonetheless, because of this and other troubles, the Reading was never again a dependable ally for Tidewater. This mattered little, for the pipeline by 1882 had extended to a connecting point with the Jersey Central. The construction costs strained the financial resources of the Benson party. Tidewater stockholders not associated with the Benson group, controlling $200,000 of the company's stock, became disenchanted. H. L. Taylor and John Satterfield, the leaders of this group, felt they deserved a more important role in the management of the company.[48]

While the internal bickering simmered, Standard continued to thwart Tidewater whenever and wherever possible. Standard monopolized tank cars—even going to the point of overordering from manufacturers in order to keep cars away from Tidewater. Standard also bought and consolidated all non-Tidewater pipelines in the Pennsylvania area. Standard even brought Joseph Potts and his National Storage Company into the fray by buying that concern. Although Potts was by this time inactive in day-to-day business matters, he was now a Standard ally. The new Standard company that absorbed all these new properties was the $30 million National Transit Company, consisting of Standard's pipelines and storage facilities.[49]

Although Standard was never able to crush Tidewater, the two did finally come to an agreement. On October 8, 1883, Standard signed an agreement whereby Tidewater would receive 11.5 percent of the pipeline traffic to the seaboard, with Standard subsidiaries carrying the remainder. This compromise may well have been the result of a free-pipeline bill that had passed the Democratic-dominated Pennsylvania legislature earlier that year.[50] In any case, Standard had accomplished what it always sought—cooperation.

The great pipeline battle was Flagler's last crucial transportation fight as a member of Standard. Although he continued in active management of Standard even after his initial investment in Florida, it was in a planning and policy-making role rather than in active, daily decisions concerning rail and pipeline activities.[51] In the pipeline confrontation, he had waged a strong fight as he and the trunk lines sought to run a new interloper from the field. Times had changed, however. No longer were the New York Central and the Pennsylvania able to rule over the legislatures of their respective states. The pipeline was just too efficient and popular to be stopped by those seeking merely their own economic gain. With that new reality, Flagler and Rockefeller were forced to compromise with Tidewater.

After the settlement of the pipeline war, Flagler began to spend more of his time and effort on his Florida venture. At first, that seemed justified. The new pipeline arrangements did not call for a person with superior negotiating skills and an ability to manipulate contracts and officials. Also, even though Standard continued to use the rails heavily, the wars of the 1870s were over; therefore, Flagler's talents were not even needed with the rails—or so it was initially thought. Standard soon discovered a need to have someone on the scene to monitor the transport of oil. Therefore, in 1886, Howard Page was brought from Standard's Kentucky office to oversee freight arrangements. That move was almost prophetic, for in 1887, with the passage of the Interstate Commerce Act and with Flagler not in the office on a consistent basis, Page's skills were needed more than ever to arrange efficient transportation while keeping Standard within the letter of the law.[52] As for Flagler, he did find another area of Standard where his skills would continue to be needed.

Standard's "Lawyer"

BY 1882 the entire nation was becoming aware of the power of the Standard Oil Company. Early that year its stockholders had organized the Standard Oil Trust. That fall a committee of the United States Senate held hearings on the trust at New York's Metropolitan Hotel. When Henry Flagler appeared before the committee, he was an uncooperative witness. He supplied little information that was new, and he and the committee sparred aggressively. At one point during Flagler's testimony, the committee's lawyer requested that Flagler stop evading questions and provide specific answers. Flagler retorted, "It suits me to go elsewhere for advice, particularly as I am not paying you for it." The lawyer, seeking to present the inquiry as a fight between the public interest and robber barons, responded, "I am not paying you to rob the community, I am trying to expose your robbery."[1] Flagler himself had been perfecting his legal sparring techniques for some years, both behind the scenes and before state legislative committees.

As Flagler's crucial role in transportation lessened during the pipeline revolution, his knowledge of law and governmental relations became more critical to Standard. Beginning in 1878, lawsuits, both civil and criminal, and legislative investigations, on state and national levels, occupied more and more of his time. He had become well prepared for the position of legalist within the Standard organization because of his role as the draftsman and enforcer of contracts.

Flagler's general attitude toward contracts was to draw them carefully and then abide by the letter—but not always the spirit—of the document.

An example of this philosophy is reflected in his advice to Charles Lockhart in 1878. At that time, Lockhart was in the process of buying the Dale Oil Works for Standard. Flagler wrote the contract and then called Lockhart's attention to the fact that Flagler required the Dale party to sign two contracts. Flagler appreciated both the legal and "ethical" implications of such a combination of contracts. "I am in the habit of making two covenants," Flagler advised Lockhart,

> one broad enough to cover the World (which I understand is illegal but has a moral effect) but which might be violated with impunity by the signers to the paper, such violation, however, would not affect their obligations under the limited covenant, whereas, if we should say in the County of Allegheny or at any other place or places whatever, it would destroy the legal obligation in the County of Allegheny, and I have assumed that the law of your commonwealth [Pennsylvania] is about the same as in Ohio, at any rate, it does no harm and is safer put in this way than if embodied merely in one convenant.

Whenever Standard exceeded its obligations under a contract, Flagler quickly indicated such activity to the other parties to the contract so that he could use it later to show Standard's goodwill. On most occasions, Flagler supported a strict interpretation of contracts, especially agreements with railroads on oil rates.[2]

In February 1878, the Regions refining firm of Satterfield & Taylor, which had earlier been an ally, brought suit against Standard. Satterfield & Taylor claimed that Standard had violated an agreement with the Regions concern. Flagler immediately acted to lessen any damage that might occur to Standard from the suit. He tried to halt the litigation, but the Butler County court allowed Satterfield & Taylor to continue its attempt to dissolve its partnership with Standard and gain $2.5 million in damages. Flagler instructed A. J. Cassatt to use the influence of the Pennsylvania Railroad to get the case transferred to the state supreme court. That would require a special legislative act, which Flagler felt the Pennsylvania road was capable of obtaining.[3] It was not.

As the spring progressed, Flagler became increasingly concerned about Standard's position in the suit. He requested the aid of Rufus P. Ranney of Cleveland, commonly referred to as "Judge Ranney," to assist Standard's Pittsburgh attorneys in the Butler County case. Meanwhile, Flagler advised the Pittsburgh attorneys to refuse to even appear in the Butler County court, arguing that it was not the proper place for such a case. A United States District Court judge, however, ruled against that Flagler interpretation.[4]

By June, Flagler admitted to Rockefeller that Standard's Pittsburgh attorneys had done poorly against the Satterfield & Taylor lawyers, who were led by Samuel C. T. Dodd. Dodd's team pushed for an out-of-court settlement, which Flagler initially opposed, fearing that Satterfield & Taylor would use such a compromise in the Regions to demonstrate that Standard could be defeated. By August, Flagler, having given up hope that Judge Ranney would become involved in the case, settled it out of court. Flagler was impressed with Dodd, who, as principal architect of the settlement, had represented both parties. This was Dodd's first friendly relationship with Standard in what became a lifelong association with the concern. He had attracted the attention of Flagler and other Standard executives because of his ability to understand the increasing legal tangles that were being hurled Standard's way.[5]

On February 4, 1878, shortly after the Satterfield & Taylor suit had originally been filed, J. F. Temple, the auditor-general of Pennsylvania, wrote Flagler, addressing the letter to "J. H. Flagger, Tres of SOC." Temple stated that if Standard did not furnish a report of the financial condition of the company to the State of Pennsylvania for the purpose of taxation, Standard would be subject to a 50 percent penalty on taxes owed. Flagler realized that this communication by the Pennsylvania auditor-general was dangerous, in both its financial and legal implications. He immediately contacted Rockefeller, who then requested the Cleveland office to send to New York a set of the original incorporation papers of the Standard Oil Company of Ohio. Flagler needed the papers to prove that Standard was a "foreign" company, with no connection to Pennsylvania.[6]

In researching his formal answer, Flagler discovered that Pennsylvania had a law that allowed for the taxation of all corporations even "foreign"—that did business within the state. Within the month, Flagler instructed W. G. Warden to transfer all Pennsylvania properties of Standard Oil of Ohio into the Standard Oil Company of Pennsylvania, thereby avoiding any question as to whether or not Standard Oil of Ohio was engaged in business within Pennsylvania. Flagler then noted in his formal reply to Temple that the Standard Oil Company of Ohio was only involved in Pennsylvania to the extent that it purchased oil for the purpose of doing business elsewhere. Flagler closed his letter on a firm but conciliatory note: "There is much current talk as to the action of the Standard Oil Co in the State of Penna," Flagler wrote, "applicable to parties, corporations, etc. interested in producing, transporting, and refining petroleum, with whom we have intimate business relations. I suppose this is a necessary result of the prominence our company has in the oil trade and in its widely extended connections, and I think has undoubtedly misled you in respect to our obligations to your Commonwealth." The response satisfied Temple, but others were still in search of monopolies within Pennsylvania. In August, the state indicted the Pennsylvania Railroad for discriminatory practices. In other actions striking more directly at Flagler's realm, Pennsylvania also brought suit against Standard's United Pipe Lines, calling for a revocation of its charter since it had violated its duties as a common carrier.[7]

William McCandless, the Pennsylvania Commissioner of Internal Affairs, sent an investigator to Titusville to determine the factual basis for the charges against these and other carriers. McCandless issued a report in mid-October 1878 that stated that none of the charges against the carriers were strong enough to warrant governmental action. This report, along with the trunk line agreement of the summer of 1878, sent the Regions into riot. The Regions leaders accused McCandless of taking a $20,000 Standard bribe; they burned McCandless in effigy, and a Regions letter writer requested of the New York *Sun*: "Send a reporter to the oil regions if you have one who cannot be bought like Buck McC."[8]

The public pressure in Pennsylvania did lead to further investigation of rate practices. During hearings concerning the Pennsylvania road and other transportation agencies, the state gleaned enough testimony, especially from Cassatt, for a grand jury investigation of Standard. Standard officials encouraged one another to take trips, vacations, or any other activity that would keep them clear of Titusville subpoenas. Flagler even requested that Judge Ranney and other Standard associates journey from Cleveland to New York for strategy sessions so Flagler and other defendants could avoid traveling through Pennsylvania. John Archbold encouraged T. O. Barstow, a Standard official in Titusville, to make "your contemplated visit to Cleveland, so as not to embarrass the proceedings at Titusville with your presence." These actions may have hampered the grand jury, but they did not stop the eventual indictments. On April 29, 1879, the Titusville grand jury handed down eight conspiracy counts against Flagler, Rockefeller, and other high-ranking Standard officials. O'Day, Warden, Lockhart, and Vandergrift, residents of Pennsylvania, immediately surrendered and gave bail. Other Standard officials avoided prosecution by staying out of Pennsylvania. Standard had A. J. Cassatt bring pressure on the governor of Pennsylvania not to issue extradition papers. Meanwhile, Chauncey Depew encouraged New York's governor not to honor any extradition papers. This was not necessary since Cassatt and his forces in Pennsylvania were successful.[9]

While the United Pipe Lines testimony was being taken, Pennsylvania's governor gave Standard officials behind-the-scenes assurances that the questioning of Captain Vandergrift would not go into "private" corporate matters, but would only deal with pipage rates and related matters. Flagler told Rockefeller that if the courts pursued this narrow path, Vandergrift could easily, and legally, state that United had no connection with the Standard Oil Company of Ohio. Flagler continued, "As to discrimination in rates made by the United Pipe Line, he [Vandergrift] knows there never have been any." As for railroad discriminations, Flagler did not think that Vandergrift would have to answer any questions on those points.[10]

Standard's lawyers succeeded in arguing, after the testimony had been heard in the United Pipe Lines suit, that the courts should not allow the action against United to go forward until the Clarion County criminal indictment in Titusville was ruled upon; otherwise, possible self-incrimination could occur. As for the Clarion case, Standard's lawyers delayed it for several months. That time could be well spent, Standard officials soon discovered, on the several state legislative investigations of freight rates, which were touching both directly and indirectly on Standard's practices.[11]

While Flagler and the group of Standard lawyers used various means to keep the Clarion County suit from going to trial, the legislatures of Ohio and New York held hearings that included Standard. On the day the Clarion County indictments were handed down, Oliver Payne advised J. N. Camden's Parkersburg partner W. P. Thompson to take his planned European trip. Payne's advice to Thompson was not to avoid a Clarion subpoena, but rather the investigation of the Ohio senate: "I hardly think it will be desirable to have you testify at Columbus. Everything is as favorable there as can be expected. Later should anything develop that would make it desirable to have you subpoenaed it can be easily arranged. In the meantime, would keep out of the way of any subpoenas."[12]

Flagler was the Standard official who led the Columbus offensive. He voluntarily journeyed to Columbus to testify so that he could present the best Standard version of the issues before the Ohio senate committee. He was rather pleased with his performance. He assured the committee that Standard had no contracts with railroads that provided for discriminations or rebates in any form. After questions posed by the committee chairman, other committee members had no further questions for Flagler. Before he left the room, he stayed long enough to hear the reassuring words that, with no further witnesses, the chairman would only reconvene the committee to vote on the final report.[13]

With various legal issues coming to the fore, Flagler, Rockefeller, and their Standard associates came to rely more and more on the expertise of

95

Samuel C. T. Dodd. Oliver Payne had been unable to contact Judge Ranney since the judge had gone to a resort for his health. Although Ranney was technically directing the Standard trial team in the *Commonwealth of Pennsylvania* v. *Pennsylvania Railroad* case, Dodd assumed the day-to-day decisions in the case. The job of the Standard lawyers in the Pennsylvania case was twofold: they were to protect Standard and, at the same time, not harm the Pennsylvania Railroad.[14]

As if these state activities were not enough for Standard, rumors circulated that George Rice, the producer responsible for launching the Ohio investigation of oil freight rates, had gained commitments from James Garfield that the United States House of Representatives would begin its own investigation. Rockefeller immediately dispatched J. N. Camden to Washington to check on the rumors. Although Camden found them to be without foundation, it was not before the exasperated Rockefeller had lashed out at "that iniquitous proceeding of getting the United States out with a drag-net for the Standard Oil Co. It is hard enough to have each of the three or four States at that business."[15] Indeed, it was New York's "Hepburn Committee" that would do the greatest damage to Standard's reputation.

The New York investigation into unfair railroad practices began when Alonzo Barton Hepburn, a young legislator with both an empathy for the underdog and a command of voter psychology, saw what was happening with the Pennsylvania investigation of Pennsylvania Railroad practices. Of course, with the Central and Erie primarily operating within New York, Hepburn thought legislative inquiries into those two organizations would yield similar results.[16]

As Hepburn's committee continued its work, it changed the direction of its inquiry. It moved away from an investigation limited to railroad abuses, in spite of railroad admissions that they gave special rates on at least 50 percent of their traffic, and moved toward Standard's role in the transportation realm. Beginning in Albany in July 1879, the committee moved throughout the state over the next six months gathering incriminating material on Standard's methods. During the proceedings, Standard kept to Rockefeller's dictum of silence while the press emphasized the high-handed responses of Standard officials on the witness stand. For example, when John Archbold was asked what exactly was his role as a director of the Standard, he responded, "I am a clamorer for dividends. That is the only function I have in connection with the Standard Oil Company." Throughout the proceedings, Standard officials used the pending Clarion County criminal case as a means of refusing to testify because of possible self-incrimination.[17]

Standard's uncooperative attitude did not prevent evidence from accumulating. The hearings enlightened the public about railroad rebates given to Standard and its pipeline subsidiaries, showed how Standard used its pipelines against its competition, and demonstrated how Standard tied up tank cars in order to obstruct the shipment of crude by independents. By the end of the investigation, Hepburn described Standard as "a mysterious organization whose business and transactions are of such a character that its members decline giving its history lest their testimony be used to convict them of crime." As for results, Hepburn eventually had his suggestions written into New York law. The legislation provided for a railroad commission that regulated railway rates and accounts.[18] Unaware of the importance of public image, Standard leaders did not understand the long-term damage that had been done. They were more concerned with other, immediate legal threats.

The last major hurdle Standard had toward the end of 1879 was the lingering suits, both criminal and civil, that B. B. Campbell and the Producers' Union had originated in Clarion County, Pennsylvania. Finally, Flagler and Rockefeller met with Campbell and Roger Sherman, attorney for the producers. In a six-week series of meetings at New York's Fifth Avenue Hotel, they reached an out-of-court settlement on the Clarion County criminal suit and several other suits that had been brought by the producers, including the one against the United Pipe Lines. Not only did the Standard directors approve the settlement between the company and the Campbell party, but they also agreed to shoulder the responsibility, including a large payment, in dismissing the H. C. Ohlen suit against the Pennsylvania Railroad.[19]

At a producers' meeting on February 20, 1880, Campbell and Sherman announced the results of their negotiations with Standard. Rockefeller and Flagler stated that Standard would no longer sign any rebate, drawback, or secret rate agreements with the railroads. As for the pipelines, there would be no discrimination toward any producer and a 30-day advance notice would be given for any increase in rates. Regarding storage, so long as the producers kept their production at 65,000 barrels a day or less, Standard pipelines would store the oil, provided producers never sold immediate shipment oil to others at rates less than those Standard paid. On the surface, Flagler and Rockefeller seemed to have given in to all of the producers' demands, but within the agreement was the usual Standard loophole: the Pennsylvania Railroad was to give all firms shipping *like quantity* the same rates. In other words, nothing had really changed from the earlier Standard arrangements. Had Campbell and Sherman been deceived by

97

Flagler and Rockefeller? Maybe the fact that the Standard officials agreed to pay the $40,000 legal fees the Producers' Union owed Sherman influenced their attitude. In any case, by 1880 the Producers' Union was so weak that any agreement would have been accepted by—although not necessarily acceptable to—the producers.[20] As for Standard, the events of 1879, both in the field and in the courtrooms and legislative halls of the country, had convinced officials of a need for a cohesive organization, one that could avoid conspiracy suits.

From the very beginning of Standard, at its incorporation in 1870, Flagler and Rockefeller had created an organization in which major decisions could be made quickly by a small group. A prime example of such an arrangement was the Executive Committee: Rockefeller and Flagler, the only members of the initial Executive Committee, were in charge of Standard's overall policies and long-range planning. Although other members were added during the 1870s, Rockefeller and Flagler remained the core decision-makers at Standard.[21]

In its organizational structure Standard was a bridge between the old partnership concept and new management concepts, as seen in the railroads of the 1870s and 1880s with their line-and-staff arrangements. Rockefeller and his partners have often been seen, therefore, as representing an antiquated business arrangement. To some degree that was true, but one must remember that Standard was a tightly held company—having only 41 stockholders when the Standard Oil Trust was formed in 1882. In that relatively small alliance system, a committee form of management could work for Standard when it would have collapsed in other business environments. As new organizational problems were found, Rockefeller and Flagler would create a new committee to provide structure and seek answers. Since Standard was basically an enlarged partnership, each member was placed on a committee or committees where his expertise could best assist the organization. For example, Flagler headed the transportation committee until its dissolution in 1888. At the top of that committee system was the Executive Committee, with Rockefeller and Flagler in charge. Although the Executive Committee met almost daily at Standard's New York office, by the late 1870s, few members could consistently attend. Because the members were now located throughout the East, only four members of the committee were required to be present in order to conduct business.[22]

It does sound trite, but it was true: Standard was an organization founded on trust. At no time in the history of Standard did John Rockefeller own more than 30 percent of its stock, and his ownership percentage tended to hover around 25 percent. Without a person with a majority of stock, Standard depended on consensus in its major activities. Various agency and trust arrangements were evident throughout the 1870s. With the incorporation of Standard in 1870, Rockefeller had held 1,000 shares as the agent for the partnership of Rockefeller, Andrews & Flagler. In the 1872 expansion of the corporation, Rockefeller was once again an agent, this time holding 1,200 shares for the company itself. The first formal trust arrangement seems to have been in 1872 when Standard stockholders appointed Flagler trustee of the Long Island Oil Company when Standard purchased it. The reason for this was that Standard could not legally own Long Island Oil, so Flagler merely held its stock in trust for the *stockholders* of Standard.[23]

Flagler was Standard's usual trustee during various trust arrangements of the 1870s. He held the Standard stock certificates of all nonresidents of Ohio in a trust account until 1879. By the later years of that decade, Standard officials began to realize a major defect of such arrangements. Although it cannot be proved, it was probably Samuel C. T. Dodd, or Dodd in concert with Flagler, who first detected the problems. If Flagler or another trustee of some Standard arrangement had died, the resulting legal questions could have been a nightmare. Also, it would have been possible for a trustee to break with the organization, thereby causing major legal difficulties. With these things in mind, on April 8, 1879—in the midst of the court activities and legislative investigations—Standard assigned three staff employees as the trustees of all non-Ohio properties held by Standard stockholders.[24] At that particular juncture, it seemed to be merely a legal device to allow Standard officials to technically deny any Standard connection with companies outside Ohio's jurisdiction.

Within a year or two, Samuel C. T. Dodd, Rockefeller, and Flagler weighed the options available to Standard, seeking a means of legally providing for a more centralized operation. One option they discussed would have created a central corporation. In a letter to Flagler on July 23, 1881, Dodd outlined the disadvantages of such a plan: (1) the incorporating legislature would have too much power over the organization; (2) other states might balk at giving such a powerful company entrée into their territory; and (3) some major questions would be raised as to the proper means of taxation by the states. A second option was the creation of a copartnership arrangement among the Standard stockholders. This presented so many legal difficulties as to be unworkable. A third plan, the one eventually adopted, called for a Standard company to be created in each state, with a trust agreement uniting all of the companies under a single management

Flagler, ca. 1882, the year the Standard Oil Trust was formed

umbrella. In following the plan, the stockholders formed the Standard Oil Trust on January 2, 1882. Flagler was one of the original nine trustees. The stockholders also approved the creation of Standard companies in various states as needed, with Flagler becoming president of the newly created Standard Oil Company of New Jersey.[25]

While Flagler usually enjoyed a good transportation fight with railroads, he had always promoted a cooperative atmosphere within Standard. During the 1870s he attempted to quell a series of confrontations between Standard partners John Rockefeller and Amasa Stone. Rockefeller would recall years later that Flagler greatly admired Stone, whereas Rockefeller himself would simply not defer to the aging railroad entrepreneur. On one occasion Stone and Rockefeller had violently disagreed on a matter of Standard policy. Stone finally announced that he was willing to have the matter resolved, selecting Henry B. Payne and Stillman Witt as the arbitrators. Rockefeller agreed to this arrangement. On their way home from work that day, Flagler stated to Rockefeller that he felt that Rockefeller should not confront Stone in such a bold manner. Rockefeller responded that he did so simply because his own position on the question was sound. Indeed, after hearing both Stone and Rockefeller state their cases, Witt and Payne ruled in Rockefeller's favor.[26]

There were other occasions on which Stone and Rockefeller disagreed. Rockefeller, as a patient warrior, bided his time until he found an opening. Once, he denied Stone additional Standard shares because the old man had failed to exercise an option before it expired. Rockefeller delighted in telling that story years later, especially noting that Flagler had been intimidated enough by Stone to be willing to go ahead and honor the option, even though it had technically expired. Finally, Stone sold his holdings in Standard.[27]

In reviewing the Rockefeller-Stone battle, it seems that once Standard had used Stone's Lake Shore—New York Central connections to its advantage, Rockefeller did not want Stone blocking the future progress of Standard and sought ways of driving Stone out of the concern. If Ida Tarbell accurately presented her 1902 interview with Flagler, it may well have been Flagler's recollection of the Rockefeller-Stone confrontations that led to the following remarks: "[Flagler], for instance, did not conceal his distrust of John Rockefeller, 'He would do me out of a dollar today,' he cried, off his guard, and with an excited smash of his fist on the table; and then, catching himself and with a remarkable change of tone: 'That is, if he could do it honestly, Miss Tarbell, if he could do it honestly.' "[28]

Tarbell's anecdote is not indicative of the relationship Flagler had with Rockefeller, especially in their active years together during the 1870s and early 1880s. A more representative illustration is Flagler's role in a complicated stock transaction. It seemed that some stock had been given to Rockefeller which caused Standard's outstanding holdings to be above the amount chartered, thereby making the transaction technically illegal.

Flagler belatedly discovered the error. He then painstakingly explained the situation to the other Standard stockholders and convinced them to give up a portion of their own shares to Rockefeller so that he would not suffer financially. Flagler and Rockefeller remained close friends throughout the remainder of Flagler's life. In fact, Rockefeller had hoped to retire at an early age as Flagler did, but the Panic of 1893 caused him to remain active with Standard until about 1897.[29]

After the formation of the trust, the public belatedly became aware of Flagler as one of the leaders of Standard. From time to time when investigating committees came calling, he testified as to his role during Standard's early years. In 1888 he had his greatest challenge when he came before the United States House of Representatives committee on manufacturing. Flagler was evasive on important points, while reminding committee members of Standard's progress—which had not only helped the company itself but the national economy as well.[30]

During the 1888 House investigation, Flagler had a worthy opponent as his legal sparsman, Franklin B. Gowen, the committee's attorney. Gowen already enjoyed a national reputation as having been the prosecutor to originally expose the operation of the Molly Maguires, a radical group of Irish-American laborers in the Pennsylvania coal district in the late-1860s and early-1870s. Eventually, after Pinkerton detectives successfully broke an 1875 strike, the state hanged twenty of the Molly Maguires for their activities.[31] Gowen also had a personal reason for pursuing the investigation of Standard Oil. He had been president of the Reading Railroad during Standard's pipeline battle of the late-1870s, in which the Reading had allied with the Tidewater Pipeline.

Flagler was thoroughly prepared to meet Gowen's challenge. Several exchanges between Flagler and Gowen indicate both Flagler's ability to avoid an issue and the public's (as represented by Gowen's) lack of faith in Standard. On the question of pipeline rates, the following exchange occurred:

QUESTIONER: Won't you be able to ship oil cheaper by the pipe line than by any of the railroads?

FLAGLER: We think so.

QUESTIONER: So you expect by that means to get control of that whole oil product to go through your lines?

FLAGLER: I do not think that is a correct inference at all. It is much fairer to say that we expect, by the instrumentality of this pipe line, to deliver oil to the consumer at the lowest possible figure.

QUESTIONER: And that same factor will bring the oil to your pipe line?

FLAGLER: Is there any crime in that?

QUESTIONER: There is no crime at all; I only want to get you down on record.[32]

The subject of rebates was an important part of the 1888 investigation. A "misunderstanding" of the difference between a commission and a rebate touched off another heated exchange between Gowen and Flager:

QUESTIONER: By a commission thrown off and by this rebate?

FLAGLER: A commission thrown off for services rendered that no other gentleman in this room would have rendered for the price.

QUESTIONER: I want to get the facts from you, and we will discuss it afterwards.

FLAGLER: I don't object to stating any fact, only I say it is not fair treatment of the case to call it a preferential rate. If I give a dollar for a dollar's worth of flour, that is not a preferential rate. I say it is not fair construction of words to call a commission rate for a valuable service rendered preferential rates.

Flagler continued by explaining the vast amount of paperwork involved in monthly balancing of accounts owed each railroad. He also indicated that in order to balance shipments, thousands of dollars were lost per month running unproductive refineries in order to meet proper allocations.[33]

Flagler served on Standard's crucial decision-making Executive Committee throughout the 1880s. In fact, on one occasion in 1885 Rockefeller became irate with him when Flagler would not support the Rockefeller brothers in their quest to buy a large lot of oil at $.80 a barrel. Flagler confessed, "I don't believe I was cut out for a big operator." After the opportunity had passed, Rockefeller reminded Flagler that if Flagler had voted with the two Rockefellers, money which was only earning 3 percent per annum in an account would have resulted in a sizeable short-term profit for Standard. On this occasion, Rockefeller was the partner willing to take a risk: "We happen to be very large manufacturers of the oil and whether we were cut out for big operators or not we have to do business on a very large scale in the buying of crude oil as in many other things." Rockefeller, on the "active side" of this particular question, continued, "I can readily understand if we had bought two millions more of crude at 80 we could have been about $250,000 better off this morning."[34]

During the 1890s, opponents increased their attacks on Standard, both in the courts and the press. In 1892 the Ohio supreme court decreed that the Standard Oil Trust be dismantled. Flagler, one of the trustees of the organization throughout its existence—in fact, as its secretary, he kept its complicated transactions in order—now became one of the dissolution trustees. During that period, 1892 to 1899, Flagler was also a director and president of Standard Oil of New Jersey. This position allowed him to re-create the company as Standard Oil (New Jersey), a holding company arrangement completed in 1899. That had been Flagler's goal since his first discussions on the subject with Dodd in 1881, and now New Jersey law would allow one company to hold *other* companies. As of 1895, Flagler also held director-ships in four Standard pipeline companies and three other state-chartered Standards, those of New York, Indiana, and Kentucky. With the reorgani-zation of Standard (New Jersey) completed in 1899, he became its vice-president, with Rockefeller at the helm as president.[35]

Two years after the Ohio court order, Henry Demarest Lloyd published his *Wealth against Commonwealth.* This was the first of many journalistic attacks on Standard during the 1890s and the first decade of the twentieth century. Lloyd pursued a rather interesting literary device in his attack on Standard—he never referred to Rockefeller by name, it was always "the president of the company." As for Flagler, he was not even mentioned in Lloyd's scathing attack on Standard.[36] What Lloyd did accomplish was the popularization of an attitude toward Standard and its officials already shared by many politicians.

Efforts by politicians to halt monopolistic practices in general and Standard's in particular were occurring on both the state and national lev-els in the 1890s. Standard's business practices of the 1870s and 1880s had, for the most part, been legal at the time, but the legislatures began to list such practices when drawing up lists of prohibited abuses. The first state antitrust laws were not passed until 1889. A year later, Congress passed the weak Sherman Antitrust Act—without a dissenting vote. In 1895, the United States Supreme Court decision in the *E. C. Knight* case, which exempted manufacturing from interstate commerce and thereby the Sher-man Act, weakened the law to the point that only interstate transportation itself would be covered under the act. Also, after the 1890 Sherman Act's provision outlawing *trusts,* more and more companies followed the new path Standard had taken in its reorganization into Standard Oil (New Jer-sey) as they converted their legal arrangements from trusts to holding com-panies.[37] By the turn of the century, persons wishing to halt this process of combination were beginning to wonder if anyone could make the nation fully aware of the disturbing problem of monopoly. A woman from the Regions focused the attention of the nation on the rise of Standard.

Ida Minerva Tarbell emerged from the Progressive period as Standard's strongest critic. A native of Pennsylvania, Tarbell was born in Erie County in 1857. Her family had moved to Titusville when she was a child, and both her father and brother had been in the oil industry. In spite of such a background, she seemed a most unlikely candidate to take up Lloyd's cause. She had received her education near home, gaining both her B.A. and M.A. degress from Allegheny College. After teaching for a time and editing the *Chautauquan* for eight years, Tarbell went to Paris to pursue a feminist outlook she had acquired from her mother; Tarbell was in France to research the role of women during the period of the French Revolution.[38]

It was while she was in France that she was approached by S. S. McClure about the possibility of writing for his publications. She at first pursued biographical topics, writing for McClure a life of Napoleon which was serialized in *McClure's* before it came out in book form. Then she wrote her *Life of Madam Roland,* published in 1896.[39]

With the Sherman Antitrust Act of 1890 on the books but monopolies still arising, McClure determined that his organization needed to do a major piece on one of the emerging trusts. When Ray Stannard Baker wrote him that oil had been discovered in California, McClure quickly changed his plans. With such an oil find, surely the public would wish to know if that would mean renewed competition in that industry. McClure first offered the writing assignment on Standard to Baker. It was only when Baker turned down the project that McClure selected Ida Tarbell to research and write it.[40]

Tarbell had enjoyed her reading of Lloyd's *Wealth against Commonwealth,* but her view was a much more optimistic assessment of American capitalism. She received a copy of Lloyd's work while still in Europe in 1894. Her recollection of her initial reaction is worth retelling:

> I had been hearing about the book from home, but the first copy was brought me by my English friend H. Wickham Steed, who, fresh from two years' contact with German socialism, took the work with great seriousness. Was not this a conclusive proof that capitalism was necessarily inconsistent with fair and just economic life? Was not socialism the only way out, as Lloyd thought?
> I was more simple-minded about it. As I saw it, it was not capitalism but an open disregard of decent ethical business practices by capitalists which lay at the bottom of the story Mr. Lloyd told so dramatically.[41]

With this ethical point of view, Tarbell began her research in 1901 and continued the research after the series began appearing in *McClure's* in 1902. In view of the positive reception of Tarbell's *McClure's* series, which ran from November 1902 through 1904, and *The History of the Standard*

Oil Company, appearing in the latter year, Standard officials soon changed their long-standing policy of silence. Her attack had been so thorough, and the public acceptance of her view so complete, that Standard brought J. I. C. Clark into its legal department to begin a publicity campaign. As a part of the efforts, Rockefeller penned his *Random Reminiscences of Men and Events.* Flagler contributed directly by submitting to the only lengthy interview of his long life. However, this was still not enough to calm the public. Finally, in 1917, John Rockefeller, Jr. convinced his father to undergo a series of interviews by William O. Inglis, so that Rockefeller's side of the story could be fully told for the first time. Although the Inglis study never got into print, the interviews have offered historians valuable insights into Rockefeller's perceptions of events.[42]

In the longer view, historians have praised Tarbell's factual accuracy while finding fault with her interpretive framework. Allan Nevins, in *Study in Power,* spent several pages citing what he considered to be Tarbell's shortcomings. However, he was well aware of her immediate impact on the American public. As he noted: "The time, the magazine, and the writer combined to make this serialized book the most spectacular success of the muckraking school of journalism, and its most enduring achievement." David Chalmers, in his introduction to the abridged edition of Tarbell's history of Standard, was even more perceptive. Tarbell, according to Chalmers, was the captive of her own belief in the role of competition, Oil Regions-style, in the continuing development of the American economy. Therefore, rather than realizing that the only way the Regions producers could have combated Standard would have been by giving up some of their own independence in favor of a competing combination, Tarbell laid all the blame for Standard's ascent on unethical business practices.[43]

Tarbell failed to realize that in the changing competition within the American economy during the post–Civil War era, there was no clear-cut definition of "ethical business practices." Flagler and his fellow Standard officers saw the economy as a war zone: anything that was legal was ethical. Even if technically illegal, a protective act—such as paying a committee chairman to pigeonhole a bill—was defensible if it was the only way to preserve the organization. During the period of Standard's rise to power, American business had outgrown state boundaries. Because the states lacked the ability and Congress lacked the will to control these businesses, Standard and other large business combinations emerged.

The federal government reacted forcefully against Standard in 1906. The attorney general filed a civil suit against the officers of Standard, including Flagler, charging Standard with restraint of trade. As that suit moved through the courts, Charles Bonaparte, the new attorney general, threatened criminal action. Toward the end of 1907, the mere threat of criminal action caused Standard to attempt to settle all accounts out of court. Standard even offered the government $100,000 to help defray the expenses of an investigation. Although nothing came of this offer, the Roosevelt administration failed to follow through on any type of criminal indictment. During the remainder of the Roosevelt administration, the whole matter was shelved in spite of the president's continuing antitrust rhetoric.[44]

In 1909 the federal government finally presented its civil case against Standard in the St. Louis circuit court. In November of that year, the court decided in favor of the government's position. The government's suggestion for dissolution, however, would have perpetuated the control of all Standard entities by the eight persons, including Flagler, who together held a majority of the concern's stock. All the federal prosecutors asked for in the dissolution portion of their case was that the companies of the Standard organization be broken into their component parts, with each stockholder in Standard (New Jersey) being given a pro rata portion of the stock of each component company of that holding company.[45]

Standard appealed the circuit court decision, but in 1911, the United States Supreme Court upheld the lower court's verdict. Standard moved immediately to follow the Court's directive—primarily because, although Standard's holding company scheme would be legally dissolved, the control of all companies would remain in the hands of the few families who had always controlled it. Thereby, nothing changed but the legal technicality that allowed Rockefeller and his associates to state that each company was now separate from the other companies in the portfolio. The courts had ruled in favor of property rights over the commonweal. The only thing the dissolution process really did was show that Standard was even richer and more powerful than the general public could have imagined. Less than a year after the Supreme Court decision, the "broken pieces" of Standard were worth $222 million more than the $663 million that Standard Oil (New Jersey) was worth at the time of the dissolution.[46]

During the years of 1881 and 1882, Henry Flagler made major changes in the direction of his personal and business lives. His beloved wife, Mary, had died on May 18, 1881, leaving him with a ten-year-old son. Flagler brought his sister, Carrie, into his household to take care of Harry. Also, his daughter Jennie helped give a sense of family by visiting often. Mary's death caused Flagler to reassess his priorities.[47] He had spent the better part of his life attempting to become wealthy. He had attained the goal, and the creation of the Trust in 1882 seemed to indicate that Standard would indefinitely continue as a stable institution issuing generous quarterly dividends. Now, he could relax and enjoy his family and leisure time.

As if to give emphasis to his new life of leisure, Flagler rented Leonard Jacob's estate, Satan's Toe, located on Long Island Sound at Mamaroneck, New York, for the 1881 summer season. James Fenimore Cooper had named the point when he had first observed it. The year after Flagler first rented Satan's Toe, he paid Jacob $125,000 for the property. Satan's Toe, which Flagler quickly changed to Satanstoe, was a forty-room summer home located on a thirty-two-acre estate. The property was on a narrow peninsula which extended out into the sound. Over the next several years, Flagler spent over $330,000 on improvements, including a complete renovation and the construction of a sea wall around most of the estate. He later brought in sand to create a man-made beach and renamed the estate Lawn Beach.[48]

Beginning with the formation of the Standard Oil Trust in 1882, Flagler began to spend less and less time at Standard's New York offices. This, however, did not mean he abruptly ended his commitment to Standard. In fact, as the secretary of the Standard Oil Trust, he moved his office to 40 Broadway and employed William H. Beardsley as his private secretary. Flagler had hired the thirty-year-old stenographer from the Richmond and Danville Railroad's New York office. Beardsley would serve as the head of Flagler's New York office for the rest of Flagler's life and would serve the businesses of Flagler beyond that time.[49]

In spite of his lessening role with the organization, Flagler continued to perform critical tasks for the Standard when necessary. A prime example of such activity occurred in 1895 when Standard, under the leadership of John Archbold, was pursuing a program to dominate not only the refining but also the marketing of petroleum products throughout the nation. Flagler was on hand in New York as Archbold negotiated an agreement with John H. Galey for Standard's Missouri operation to ally with Galey's Kansas concern, thereby putting a Standard operation in Kansas for the first time.[50] We do not know how often Flagler performed such tasks, but he was certainly more active in the Standard organization during these years than Standard historians Ida Tarbell and Allan Nevins had earlier indicated.

As with his detachment from day-do-day operations, Flagler slowly eased out of Standard's boardroom. Over the years, he gradually assigned his committee responsibilities and offices to those whom he had been training for years. In 1908 he resigned his position as vice-president of Standard (New Jersey), although he maintained his last official position with Standard, his directorship in the holding company, until its dissolution by the Supreme Court in 1911.[51]

As various governmental bodies inquired into Standard's activities, Flagler found his lessening involvement with the giant company—and his corresponding increasing interest in Florida developments—a convenient excuse for claiming no knowledge of what was currently occurring at 26 Broadway, Standard's headquarters. Indeed, with his increasing commitment to Florida, beginning in 1885, had gone a decreasing interest in Standard. Flagler's holding of Standard stock declined in relative terms over the years. The stock expansion back in 1872 had marked the height of his financial power with Standard. At that time, with 13.77 percent of Standard's stock, Flagler was second only to Rockefeller as a Standard investor. By 1879 his relative holdings had declined to 8.5 percent of the company. In the early twentieth century, Flagler had only 30,000 shares of the Standard Oil (New Jersey) holding company, out of over 972,500 outstanding shares. In spite of the financial pressures of his Florida empire, which especially burdened him during the building of the Key West Extension, Flagler's shares in Standard (New Jersey) remained constant until the time of the holding company's dissolution in 1911.[52]

In assessing Flagler's motivation for turning from Standard and to Florida, one must not lose sight of his penchant for activity. Flagler's career with Standard had been filled with adventure that only pioneers in business enterprise could experience. That type of entrepreneurship could not be duplicated in the boardroom atmosphere of the Standard giant that had been created by the 1882 trust. Within four years of that date, Flagler turned his vast reservoir of energy toward Florida. Although he did not enter Florida with the intent of a second, full career, his activism predisposed him in that direction. Retirement—from Standard or to Florida— was not a term with which Flagler would ever become familiar. Many people complained, then and now, about how he built, but there was no denying that Flagler was always in the process of building something.

THE FLORIDA YEARS

"THE SUNSHINE STATE". That designation is one used by Florida tourist officials nowadays to lure vacationing Americans to one of the nation's most populous states; but it was a far different place, both in time and image, in the 1880s. When Henry Flagler came to Florida, he was entering a new venture on the southern frontier. Although located east of the Mississippi River and having a town, St. Augustine, which enjoyed the designation of the oldest city in the United States, Florida had been and remained until well after the Civil War the last frontier area east of the great river. In spite of its lengthy history, Florida had been in American hands only since 1821. In that year, the Spanish officially turned over control of the area to President James Monroe's territorial governor, Andrew Jackson. Jackson's ventures in Florida, which had begun during the late 1810s, marked the beginning of a major change for the area. As a result of his victories during the First Seminole War, Jackson cleared the way for a wave of white settlement into the area. Although two European powers, Spain and—for a brief period—Britain, had controlled the area, no large settler colonies had developed. The port towns of Pensacola, Jacksonville, and Tampa existed, but isolated Key West remained Florida's largest city throughout the pre–Civil War era.[1]

With no European cultural traditions in the way, Americans quickly changed the landscape. By 1825 there were 13,500 non-Indians living in Florida. The white migration into the area continued: 34,730 (1830), 87,445 (1850), and 140,000 (1860). In spite of this rapid growth, Florida's popula-

113

tion was still next to last among the fifteen southern states at the time of the Civil War.[2]

Floridians were convinced that a good transportation network would change the state. Entrepreneurs began building short lines in 1836. By the Civil War, there were two cross-state railroads, one uniting Jacksonville and Tallahassee and the Florida Railroad, which connected Fernandina, north of Jacksonville, with Cedar Key, a fishing village north of Tampa Bay.[3]

Without a strong population base as an economic lure, Florida used its public lands as inducement for development. When Florida entered the Union as a state in 1845, the federal government gave it over 500,000 acres of public lands. Five years later, the federal government granted ten million acres to Florida as part of a general "swamp and overflowed" lands act. The state was to have these lands drained and made productive. The Florida legislature created the Internal Improvements Board in 1851 to administer its new domain. With railroad builders such as former United States Senator David L. Yulee of the Florida Railroad on the board, it was no surprise that in 1854 politicians and developers bent the original intent of the federal act. The board agreed that the public domain might be used as an inducement to railroad builders. In addition to railroads, the board also proposed a canal to connect the St. Johns and Indian rivers. The board at this time could only make these suggestions; it did not yet have the power to make public land grants to transportation companies.[4]

To resolve this problem, the legislature in 1855 passed a comprehensive land act. It created the Internal Improvements Fund (IIF) with a board of trustees to replace the Internal Improvements Board. This act also gave great power to the trustees. In addition to a 200-foot right-of-way, they could grant railroad companies alternate square miles on either side of the railroad, equivalent to 3,840 acres for each mile of constructed road. The entire process took on the nature of a government-subsidized project since the trustees could also guarantee bonds issued by the transportation companies. Once a company had completed its roadbed and had laid crossties, the trustees could authorize it to issue bonds for up to $10,000 for each mile of road constructed. Additional bonds could be sold for more expensive bridge and trestle work. The companies were to use proceeds from the bond sales to purchase rails and rolling stock. In some transactions, manufacturers accepted the bonds rather than cash. After all, the law allowed the future sales of remaining Florida public lands as a guarantee for the bonds.[5]

This process collapsed during the post–Civil War era. Railroads went bankrupt, leaving the trustees of the IIF liable for the bonded indebtedness of the defunct roads. One of the bondholders was Francis Vose, a manufacturer of railroad iron who had accepted Florida Railroad bonds in lieu of cash. In 1870 he requested, and received, a court order barring Florida from accepting anything but United States currency for land sales. During the late 1860s, Florida had been selling lands at very low rates, even at times taking depreciated greenbacks and bank notes in payment. In spite of the court order Vose had obtained, sales continued. Finally, Vose and others had the public lands of Florida placed in receivership. Thereafter, the receiver could sell IIF lands only with the approval of the railroad bondholders.[6]

Although some land was sold by this process, the IIF was going further into debt due to high interest rates and legal costs. In the spring of 1881, Governor William D. Bloxham solved this problem by arranging the sale of four million acres to Hamilton A. Disston, a Philadelphia steel manufacturer, for $1 million. The money from the sale allowed the IIF to clear its debt and to begin full-scale promotion and sale of public lands.[7]

At one time, almost 60 percent of the state had been in the public domain. During the years after 1876, the politicians of Florida granted millions of acres to encourage railroad and canal companies to provide the sparsely settled areas of the state with transportation facilities. Prior to 1881, the state had disposed of only 1,700,000 acres of Florida public land. During the next year, 1881–82, this increased to 12,200,000 acres.[8]

After that opening of Florida for economic exploitation, it would seem to follow that Flagler would immediately seize the opportunity for economic gain. Such was not the case. If Flagler originally entered Florida with the idea of building up its east coast—and along the way gaining vast amounts of the public domain—he certainly kept such counsel to himself. The record strongly suggests that Flagler entered Florida with the original intent of dabbling in St. Augustine business ventures. However, that would have gone against every principle of business he had adopted during his Standard career. He *had* to control his destiny by dominating his environment. He would not leave anything to chance.

St. Augustine: "Newport of the South"

"MY THOUGHT WAS to make King St. the 5th Ave. of St. Augustine," Henry Flagler wrote a close friend in St. Augustine, Florida, in November 1885. Flagler continued, "I believe . . . we can make St. Augustine the Newport of the South."[1] These were certainly grand sentiments for a seacoast town mired in its past. But Flagler, probably wishing for a business legacy independent of his Standard Oil contribution, entered his second full-fledged career with enthusiasm.

Newport, Rhode Island, was indeed the most famous of American resorts. One Newporter claimed that it had been a retreat for wealthy Americans as early as 1729, but it became firmly established as a leisure center during what Cleveland Amory, the chronicler of American "high society," termed "the Southern Planter era." With the decline of Newport as a trade center after the American Revolution, rich cotton planters flocked there during the hot summer months. Many stayed until fall, after their crops had been harvested.[2] After Reconstruction, Henry Flagler and other entrepreneurs sought to bring the leisure aspect of the Gilded Age to Florida. He began transforming St. Augustine into a fashionable vacation area by building the Ponce de Leon, one of the country's great luxury hotels.

Flagler first visited St. Augustine on a Florida trip with his second wife, Ida Alice Shourds, in December 1883. Alice had been Mary Flagler's companion during her final illness. Flagler and Alice were married on June 5, 1883; the bride was thirty-four and the groom, fifty-five. Carrie Flagler, who had been living with Flagler, decided that her obligation for the care of her half-brother's son was fulfilled, so she moved to an apartment in another part of New York City. Young Harry did not like Alice replacing Carrie in the household; he felt that although his father did love Alice, he had married beneath his social standing.[3]

On their trip to Florida, the Flaglers stayed until March 1, 1884, which gave them ample opportunity to see St. Augustine and its culture. St. Augustine, established in 1565, was the United States' oldest permanent settlement; people commonly referred to it as the "ancient city." Among its tourist attractions were Fort Marion (the Spanish Fort of San Marco), the old city gate, the seawall, the Catholic cathedral, which was built in 1793, and the Huguenot cemetery.[4]

St. Augustine's history was also its curse. People tended to think of it as a coastal town where time stood still. In his 1883 description of winter resorts for a railway brochure, John Temple Graves, a southern newspaperman, stated, "Now put on thy musty garments, Oh. ST. AUGUSTINE! Gather the cobwebs around thy ancient ruins. Lay out the speaking emblems of thy antiquity; for the time of the year is come when the people gather from afar to see the patriarch of cities with a Ponce de Leon flowing in its heart!" Less than a decade later the image had changed, and Henry Flagler was primarily responsible for the transformation of St. Augustine. The subtitle of the 1892 edition of *Health Resorts of the South* described St. Augustine as presenting "the most desirable resorts of the southern states."[5]

Flagler knew that St. Augustine had long been a winter mecca for the infirm, and he saw its pleasant climate as an inducement for the wealthy as well. In 1875 Joseph W. Howe had written *Winter Homes for Invalids* in which he advised invalids and their families that the city had a pleasant winter temperature, but that it had more humidity than inland Florida towns. Howe told his readers to select a private residence, if possible, for "the old hotels in the town generally lack all the requisites of a healthy residence, and, unless they are improved, they should be shunned under all circumstances." During Flagler's first trip to St. Augustine, the accommodations available in the town were meager. The most attractive characteristic of St. Augustine was its average yearly temperature of seventy degrees, with the average winter temperature a mild sixty degrees.[6]

Even before leaving St. Augustine, Flagler made plans to return to the city, and he and Alice did that on February 17, 1885. They stayed at the recently constructed San Marco Hotel, located near the old city gate, where he met the hotel's builder, James A. McGuire, and manager, Osborn D. Seavey. Both these men played important roles in Flagler's St. Augustine venture, but Flagler's most important business contact in St. Augustine was Dr. Andrew Anderson (unrelated to the Baltimore & Ohio Railroad's

Andrew Anderson mentioned in "The Standard Years"). Dr. Anderson agreed to become Flagler's agent in St. Augustine. A native of the city, Anderson received his undergraduate education at Princeton, completed his medical training at the College of Physicians and Surgeons in New York City in 1865, and returned to Florida. Being a large landowner in St. Augustine, Anderson was naturally interested in Flagler's plans. Flagler had been inspired by a celebration St. Augustine had held in honor of the landing of Ponce de Leon. At Anderson's home, probably toward the end of March, he disclosed his idea for a luxury hotel to be called the Ponce de Leon.[7]

Flagler originally proposed to Franklin W. Smith, a Boston capitalist and amateur architect, that Flagler would pay three-quarters of the $200,000 needed to build a hotel and entertainment center. Flagler wished to remain a silent partner, with Smith as his main associate in the venture. Smith could not provide the needed capital, and when no one else came forward with the additional $50,000, Flagler financed the operation alone. This first scheme thus unexpectedly demanded not only large amounts of Flagler's wealth but also his personal supervision. If Flagler had merely wished to dabble in St. Augustine affairs, by October 1885 he was fully committed. In a letter to Smith, Flagler stated, "Thus, you see, the scheme has outgrown my original ideas."[8]

Several property transactions were necessary for Flagler to fulfill his ambitious Ponce de Leon plans. In 1885, he purchased Sunnyside, a small hotel on the western edge of St. Augustine. He had the hotel removed and the site became the southeastern portion of the Ponce de Leon. He obtained several other lots, but the hotel plans were beclouded when Anderson's three half sisters and their families brought suit against him to block the sale of the family property to Flagler. This property, located west and north of Sunnyside, was crucial for the Ponce de Leon site. Insisting that he could no longer delay, Flagler entered into an agreement with the contestants in September 1885. He paid the three families three-quarters of the purchase price of $14,670, Anderson receiving the remainder. According to Flagler, "The motive that prompted Dr. A to give up three quarters of the hotel purchase money, was his great desire to see the work commenced at once." Flagler gave a more forthright account of the deal to Franklin Smith: "As already advised, the Dr. and I have met the Northrups and Crafts, and have either captured them, or been 'gobbled' by them, I don't know which."[9]

The Ball estate, located to the north of the Anderson property, was an important part of Flagler's plans. It provided the additional acreage needed for the full realization of the hotel structure. Flagler, asking Anderson to instruct Flagler's St. Augustine lawyer to draw up a deed for the Ball holdings, further stated, "I see no reason why it should be delayed, and the money is *rusting* in my possession."[10]

Flagler's first year of business in St. Augustine had been far from tranquil. He wrote a Standard Oil associate about the scavengers in St. Augustine, warning him not to "forget that those St. Augustinians think they have a bonanza" in the new venture, "and they are working it for all it is worth." Flagler was dissatisfied with St. Augustine businessmen who wished to increase their stake in his business venture, but who failed on their original commitment.[11]

Since many St. Augustinians either imagined handsome profits when negotiating with a millionnaire or felt anxious in selling to an outsider, Flagler often requested that one of his associates act on his behalf. In one case, Flagler asked a St. Augustine lawyer to act as his agent in buying marsh land north of the city and a lot on King Street. As early as the spring of 1885, Flagler tried to buy what was known as the George Atwood lot, which constituted part of the Maria Sanchez marsh along Bridge Street. After an unsuccessful attempt by Flagler to buy the lot, Smith and St. Augustine Mayor John G. Long became involved. Atwood had previously offered his property to Long for $1,600. Knowing that it was best to defer to Flagler, Long wrote: "I will not, however, stand in your way, as I would prefer you to have it; besides, you are doing too much for St. Augustine for any of her people to offer an obstacle or stand in the way; we appreciate too highly the advantages to result from your investments there." Long obtained the Atwood lot for Flagler for only $1,500.[12]

During the latter part of 1885 and early 1886, as real estate speculation in St. Augustine continued to boom, Flagler slowed down his purchases. He only bought land for which he had a definite plan. Others, however, tried to reap great profits by selling in an inflated market. A newspaper article in August 1886 reported that property which sold for $30,000 in St. Augustine had an assessment of only $6,000 on the St. Johns County books.[13]

Flagler's problems in real estate dealings are illustrated in his attempt to procure two federal lots (the dragoon barracks and the powder house) which adjoined his properties. He persuaded the War Department to agree to a public auction of these government parcels. He was negotiating with Secretary of Interior L. Q. C. Lamar when United States Senator Wilkinson Call of Florida unwittingly intervened. Call presented a bill that would have given the city of St. Augustine any unneeded federal property within its boundaries.[14]

John Flagg, a lobbyist for Flagler in Washington, asked Call to withdraw the dragoon barracks lot from his list of property to be deeded to St. Augustine. The senator agreed, provided the original petitioners would consent. Flagler confided to Anderson, "I don't believe there is a 'ghost of a chance' of passing Call's bill, but (as I stated in my former letter) I don't want to antagonize any of the citizens of St. A." Flagler was willing to allow passage of the bill provided the petitioners would compromise, but "if they will not, I must *try* to defeat it." Flagler offered to give the city needed property elsewhere if it would not interfere with his business interests there. He made it clear that if Call would withdraw his bill, he would reward St. Augustine liberally. By February 1886, Anderson had obtained most of the original petitioners' signatures requesting Call to withdraw the bill.[15]

The Treasury Department transferred the dragoon barracks lot to the Interior Department. However, the property was for sale only through the War Department with the Interior having no right to lease it. This bureaucratic process prompted Flagler to explode, "Under the present beautiful democratic administration, business matters at Washington are in a dreadful condition." Flagler received a tract known as the powder house lot on March 28, 1901.[16] There is no record of Flagler obtaining a deed to the dragoon barracks property.

The St. Augustine experiment called for a considerable amount of innovation; Flagler had to establish a Gilded Age resort image. He later explained the situation: "How to build a hotel to meet the requirements of nineteenth-century America and have it in keeping with the character of the place—that was my hardest problem." He chose for the task two relatively inexperienced New York City architects from the renowned firm of McKim, Meade and White. Both these young architects, John Carrère and Thomas Hastings, had received training in French Renaissance architecture at the Ecole des Beaux-Arts in Paris. Flagler's decision may not have been based entirely on professional credentials since Hastings's father was his New York pastor and a close friend.[17]

Flagler's choice of construction methods earned him a place in the history of American architecture. As late as May 1885, he had not reached a decision on whether to use brick or concrete as the major construction material. If brick were used, Flagler would have had to transport it long distances, making the cost prohibitive. Franklin Smith persuasively argued for the use of concrete as the basic building material. During an 1882 European tour, Smith had noticed the use of concrete in the building of a chateau on Lake of Geneva. Returning to Boston, he experimented with different ratios of concrete. The tests resulted in the building of the Villa Zorayda, his private home in St. Augustine modeled after one of the buildings of the Alhambra. Although the house was not as large as Flagler's envisioned Ponce de Leon, Smith had used two building materials that were available at St. Augustine—sand and coquina shell. These two ingredients Flagler also used in his concrete mixture. The Ponce de Leon, when completed, became the largest concrete structure in the world.[18]

Having decided to use concrete, Flagler's next problem was obtaining coquina. He hoped to take it from the public lands on Anastasia, a barrier island located on the Atlantic Ocean, across the Matanzas River from St. Augustine. Mr. Sanchez, a coquina property owner on the island who wished to sell to Flagler some of his quarry property, had raised the chief argument against Flagler's procuring coquina from public lands. When President Cleveland's Secretary of War William Endicott then blocked Flagler's proposal, Flagler asked Franklin Smith to investigate the possibility of buying a private quarry on the island. Flagler's Washington representative was to determine which of the Anastasia lands were private property. Sanchez then offered Flagler some of his quarry property for $20,000. Flagler saw this as an exorbitant amount for what he termed a "white elephant." He made a counteroffer of $10,000 with a veiled threat: "Mr. Sanchez can make more money out of me by being friendly, and not interfering with the removal of the shell." Instead of continuing to deal with Sanchez, Flagler's builder James McGuire bought a neighboring quarry.[19]

If Flagler's plans for the Ponce de Leon were to materialize, he had to control diseases common to the area. He requested that Anderson use his own discretion on how to best avoid an outbreak of malaria: "it would be very unfortunate if sickness should be caused by our excavations, as it would give other hotels a good opportunity to promulgate theories adverse to the locality, which might be hard to suppress." Flagler instructed his builders that the site was to show no trace of once having been a marsh.[20]

Although a wealthy man, Flagler wished to avoid unnecessary costs. The expensive formula he used for the concrete foundation was only three parts coquina for each part of sand and cement. He hoped this would not be the proportion needed once the foundation was completed, since using too much cement would make construction prohibitively expensive. Finally, willing to pay the price for a lasting monument, he confided to Smith, "I think it more likely I am spending an unnecessary amount of money in the foundation walls, but I comfort myself with the reflection that a hundred years hence it will be all the same to me, and the building better, because of my extravagance." Construction did not proceed as rapidly as Flagler had hoped. By early 1886, he realized that the hotel would not be ready until the 1888 winter season, a year after his initial target date.[21]

The Ponce de Leon was in the eclectic style of the day. Bernard Maybeck, an architect for Carrère and Hastings (and later well-known for his work in California), combined Moorish and Renaissance influences within a Spanish motif for the building's exterior. Flagler's workers had literally cast the hotel—pouring concrete and ramming it in sections three feet in height. The contractors used bricks in arches, corner joints, and window jambs; terra-cotta for the corbels, balconies, and ornaments; and Spanish tile for the roof. The loggia surrounding the interior courtyard contained woodwork reminiscent of some of the older St. Augustine buildings.[22]

The Ponce de Leon was an open structure to take advantage of the sun's warmth during the winter months. The main building was 380 by 520 feet, with a large courtyard located just within the grand entrance. The structure occupied four and one-half acres, with another one and one-half acres for the dining hall and other buildings. Rooms for the white members of the hotel staff were located to the rear of the kitchen. Black staff members lived in separate quarters some distance from the hotel. At the back of the Ponce de Leon lot, Flagler's builders constructed studios for the local artist colony. Each of the two towers rising above the main structure contained four terra-cotta balconies weighing five tons each. Arched windows opening onto these balconies were reminiscent of the Moorish influence on Spanish architecture. In addition to their aesthetic beauty, the towers housed 16,000 gallons of water for fire protection.[23]

The interior was much more personal in character than the massive exterior of the hotel. The lobby area contained a rotunda three stories high. Corridors opened toward the center from the second and third stories. To the left of the lobby was the grand parlor. With the aid of arches, portieres, and screens, the room was effectively divided into five areas. From the grand parlor, the guest could walk through the lobby, up the stairs, to either the men's bar or ladies' saloon area, both located next to the dining room.[24]

The hotel came equipped with all the appointments essential for a luxury hotel of its day. It included a writing room, barber shop, and ladies' billiard room. The hotel had electric power throughout. Artesian wells provided the hotel with sulfur water. Although the water had to be aerated through a series of fountains on the grounds, many doctors of the time claimed its sulfur content had medicinal value. The Ponce de Leon kept pace with the changing standards for luxury hotels. When it was first built, the only pri-

Hotel Ponce de Leon, the first of Flagler's Florida hotels, which opened in St. Augustine in 1888

vate bathroom in the hotel was in the Flagler suite. But soon afterward, Flagler added private baths in other areas of the hotel.[25]

The Ponce de Leon opened on January 10, 1888. There were no special ceremonies or even a ball. Flagler hired Joyce's New York Military Band and a twenty-one–piece orchestra for the first season. Early in January, a special train arrived from New York with the seasonal employees. The first vestibule train (which had vestibules at the end of each car to protect passengers from the weather as they moved from car to car) ever to reach St. Augustine brought the Ponce de Leon's first guests.[26]

Osborn D. Seavey, the manager of the Ponce de Leon, had first come to Florida to operate Isaac S. Cruft's winter hotel, the Magnolia, located at Magnolia Springs. As was the custom of many hotel personnel during the Gilded Age, Seavey had overseen the Magnolia during the winter and Cruft's Maplewood Hotel in Bethlehem, New Hampshire, during the summer. Seavey served the Ponce de Leon from its opening until the end of the 1895 season. During this time, he was also associated with the Hotel Champlain on Lake Champlain during the summer season.[27]

Flagler found himself competing with his former business associate, Franklin Smith. By the latter part of 1885, Flagler had sought to end his real estate venture with Smith. Earlier, Flagler had offered his partner an interest in the Ball estate. Although Flagler expressed willingness to go through with this deal, his intentions were otherwise. He exchanged property located on the south side of King Street for Smith's interest in the Ball property. In addition, Flagler agreed to move the Sunnyside Hotel from the Ponce de Leon site to the new Smith property and prepare it for business. Smith, however, planned a luxury hotel for the new location. In the early days of 1886, Flagler advised Smith that "the property, as you will soon have it, will pay quite as good, if not better, return on the money, than if you erect 'Casa-Monica.' "[28]

Although Smith did build his Casa Monica, he operated it only one season. In April 1888, he sold the hotel to Flagler for $325,000. Flagler renamed the structure the Cordova before its opening for the 1889 season. Although built on the edge of the old Spanish section, the hotel left the area undisturbed. It had more recognizable Moorish influences than the Flagler-built hotels. The distinguishing features of the exterior of the hotel were the kneeling balconies, influenced by the architecture of Moorish Seville. It offered first-class accommodations and cuisine in an open-air environment. It had 200 rooms for its guests. The Plaza del Sol, the glass-covered interior patio on the first floor, was its most innovative design.[29]

From the beginning of his St. Augustine venture, Flagler had planned a casino. It was to be a recreation and amusement area (quite unlike the gambling casinos of today) located across from the Ponce de Leon. Flagler did not advertise the nature of the venture, fearing local opposition. George Atwood, who had sold Flagler part of the proposed site, stated that people would be more likely to sell to Flagler if they were under the impression that the area would be used for a park.[30]

The Alcazar, as the casino was called, opened for the 1889 season. Although primarily serving as the entertainment center for the Ponce de Leon, it also functioned as a separate hotel—Flagler termed it his "two-dollar-a-day" hotel. In spite of being less pretentious than the Ponce de Leon, the Alcazar became a very popular hostelry. As the St. Augustine *Tatler,* the society paper during the winter season, described it, "The people of St. Augustine are proud of the Ponce de Leon, but they love the Alcazar." The hotel included a first-floor shopping arcade, 300 guest rooms, and a restaurant. Unlike the Ponce de Leon, the Alcazar operated on the less-expensive European meal plan after 1890.[31]

The casino, located to the rear of the hotel portion of the Alcazar, provided guests a variety of recreational and entertainment activities, including dancing, plays and musicals, water polo, swimming matches, cakewalks, jubilee concerts, bowling, and tennis. There were both a large pool with artesian water and a saltwater pool with a bandstand suspended over it. Guests could choose among Roman, Russian, or Turkish baths. In addition to hotels, Flagler built cottages for winter patrons. By 1903 his fourteen St. Augustine cottages had become an important part of his resort holdings.[32]

Flagler used every means available to convert the image of the St. Augustine hotels and community into that of a fashionable resort for the wealthy. In 1890, a brochure campaign began in the summer, with Flagler sending 2,000 folders to Seavey for distribution at the Hotel Champlain. Northern hotels and advertisers had distributed 25,000 brochures before the winter season began. Flagler used other means to advertise his hotels: A cigar manufacturer in Jacksonville used a picture of the Ponce de Leon on his cigar boxes. Flagler allowed another cigar firm the use of the trademark "Ponce de Leon." An 1891 guide to the city prominently featured the Ponce de Leon and other Flagler structures.[33]

Although Flagler's Florida venture was doing well, the death of his daughter, Jennie, in 1889, was a major blow to him. During the early 1880s, she had divorced John Hinckley and shortly thereafter married Frederick H. Benedict. The Benedicts lost their first child at birth, and then Jennie suffered from childbirth complications. Her doctors recommended a trip to Florida for rest and recuperation. The family felt that a cruise would be less taxing on her health than travel by rail. E. C. Benedict, her father-in-law, made his yacht *Oneida* available for the trip. But before it could even get to Charleston, its first port of call, Jennie died, on March 25, 1889.[34]

Flagler had a new building constructed for St. Augustine's First Presbyterian congregation, and they renamed their church the Memorial Presbyterian Church in Jennie's memory. Within the church was a mausoleum for the Flagler family. Although it was designed and built rapidly, it was the most beautiful of the Flagler buildings in the city. The exterior was an eclectic composition of Romanesque, Byzantine, and Italian Renaissance motifs; the interior was in the classical Renaissance style, with the sanctuary in the form of a Latin cross. The floors were of imported Siena tile in a Venetian pattern.[35]

The dedication of the Memorial Presbyterian Church on March 16, 1890, attracted national attention. Present were Mrs. Benjamin Harrison, wife of the president of the United States; Vice-President and Mrs. Levi Morton; and members of the John Wanamaker family of Philadelphia. Dr. John R. Paxton, Flagler's pastor at the West Presbyterian Church in New York, brought his choir and preached the first sermon in the new building.

Jennie Louise Flagler Benedict, Flagler's daughter, ca. 1880. She died in 1889, and Flagler built the Memorial Presbyterian Church in St. Augustine in her memory.

St. Augustine Memorial Presbyterian Church, where Flagler and his first wife
Mary are buried

The Reverend E. K. Mitchell, pastor of the local congregation, gave the invocation. The Flagler pew was occupied by Flagler, his wife Alice, Harry, and Frederick H. Benedict, husband of the deceased Jennie.[36]

The Presbyterian congregation was not the only one to receive Flagler's attention. Shortly after his arrival, he indicated his desire to be on good terms with the Methodists, since they wielded a major influence in the community. He donated land for a church building and parsonage in exchange for their meeting site, which became part of the Alcazar property. Flagler built the Grace Methodist Episcopal Church on the new site from materials similar to the ones used on the Ponce de Leon. He told his contractors that the church was not to have the same careful attention as the hotel: "I see that you are wheeling the muck into the church lot. Country sand is good enough for them."[37]

Thus, Presbyterians, more than any other religious group in St. Augustine, received Flagler's personal attention, including advice on possible choices for church personnel. In 1890 the church hired the Reverend S. D. Paine as a one-year temporary replacement. At the end of his term, however, Paine accused Flagler of trying to run the church by terminating his contract. Flagler retorted: "The *facts* are, that you were first invited to fill the pulpit of the Memorial Church for one year,—afterwards, until the first Sunday of next month. Now, You claim that 'simple justice' requires your *RE ELECTION FOR ANOTHER YEAR THAT YOU MAY GET DURING THE SUMMER ANOTHER PULPIT.* It seems to me very clear, that what you call 'simple justice' is nothing but selfishness."[38]

Flagler was not usually so undiplomatic. For instance, he realized St. Augustine's need for public buildings. On October 3, 1889, the city council approved a plan in which Flagler would build a new city market that would also house the city offices and jail. In 1889 the city leased the building for a twenty-year period with the option to buy. The first floor contained market stalls, a fire engine room, and government offices, including those of mayor and city clerk. The second floor contained the council chambers, municipal courtroom, and the city jail. Flagler also exchanged lots with the county and built a new county jail under similar financial arrangements.[39]

Control was a major consideration in Flagler's business operations. Rather than just managing the business of his hotels and cottages, he moved into other sectors of St. Augustine's economy. Through an August 1890 lease with Captain E. E. Vaill, Flagler got control of what was known as the Vaill block, a group of business buildings on the north side of the old slave market. On October 28, 1895, Vaill deeded the block to Flagler. Flagler had other profitable rental properties. In 1890 a tenant paid $850 a year for the use of the round tower in the Cordova. When George Myers and Company wished to locate in a building near the city market, Flagler advised his St. Augustine agent to rent it: "While I do not hold this concern in very high respect, I recall the fact that they paid their rent promptly when in the little building on the corner of King and Ribiera Sts., and 'business is business,' I see no reason why you should not take them as tenants, provided you can get a *good* rental out of them and prompt pay."[40]

Because Flagler wished to create his own transportation system in St. Augustine, he attempted to stop the building of an electric railway. In 1889 he deeded a right-of-way to the city that had been taken by the widening of Cordova, Ribiera, and other streets. The deed stipulated, however, that the city had to get Flagler's permission for the construction of any transportation or communication facilities on this property. In reviewing the matter, the city council committee on streets noted that the contract did not give the city clear title, but was rather a restrictive covenant.[41]

St. Augustine officials soon found a loophole in Flagler's opposition to the needed street railway. In a legal opinion, the city attorney stated that, although Flagler could block a street railway on that portion of King Street that had been widened by him onto his property, the old portion was, and had been, a public street. Since the first railway ordinance had lapsed, the St. Augustine city council passed another in 1895 that gave the franchise owners a ninety-nine-year franchise for the construction and operation of a street railway. On first glance, this seemed to be a setback for Flagler, but the last provision of the ordinance was a concession to him. It required the franchise owners to receive Flagler's permission to operate on Malaga and King streets.[42]

Flagler's philanthropic activities reflected his own—at times unique—brand of community assistance. He assisted St. Joseph's Academy, a Catholic school, in 1886. When the academy requested an interest-free loan, Flagler rejected the proposal as poor business practice, but then volunteered to contribute the amount needed to defray the cost of its building project. Flagler assisted another of his favorite charities by constructing the St. Augustine Young Men's Christian Association building at a cost of over $50,000. He provided funds for the "colored school" to be built and for the rebuilding of the Catholic cathedral after a fire had destroyed it.[43]

Toward business, Flagler took a more laissez-faire attitude. When John T. Dismukes, a local businessman and banker, attempted to interest Flagler in his St. Augustine National Bank stock, Flagler replied that he could find better buys on Wall Street. In 1895 Dismukes persuaded Flagler to rent a building to a cigar company for a factory. Flagler agreed to reduce the annual rental rate by $200, with St. Augustine businessmen providing another $300. Dismukes renewed this liberal lease agreement with Mr. Caraba, the cigar company owner, at the end of the original five-year period. Flagler was irritated: "I do not know Mr. Caraba, but I cannot resist the conviction that he is playing upon the fears of the St. Augustine people. I understand that he is a man of means, and not an object of charity. . . . He can have the building for five years at $800, if he wants it, and if he doesn't, let him vacate it *immediately*. I would rather shut it up and lose the rental than be imposed upon."[44]

The Flaglers thoroughly enjoyed St. Augustine. They attended many of the events during the winter season and often hosted social affairs of their own. In the early 1890s they decided to build a home in the resort. Kirkside, begun in 1892, was completed in the spring of 1893. It was a two-story frame structure of colonial style. Only two blocks from the Ponce de Leon, the fifteen-room home was comfortable, but unpretentious. The landscaped grounds were surrounded by a four-foot wall.[45]

Alice Flagler entertained often during the season. Most of the social events she sponsored, such as the "Hermitage Ball" honoring Andrew Jackson's contribution to Florida, took place at the Ponce de Leon. Smaller parties and teas were held at Kirkside. Alice always wore beautiful gowns on these formal occasions. During the 1893 season, The *Tatler,* the local society paper, was so taken with a necklace Alice wore at a social occasion that it dubbed the event the "pearl dance."[46]

During the St. Augustine years, Henry Flagler's relationship with his son, Harry, deteriorated to the point of a permanent estrangement. In 1894, when his father asked him to supervise the St. Augustine interests, Harry Flagler was only twenty-three years old. Reluctantly accepting the responsibility, he oversaw preparations for the opening of the 1895 winter season: repairing the cottages, painting the Ponce de Leon exterior, and replastering the bedrooms in the Alcazar. These preparations were important, but Harry had a greater interest in the Alcazar casino. Attendance at the casino improved during the early 1895 season since Harry granted patrons free admission—charging them only when they used the bath area; he kept the bowling and billiard rooms closed until there were enough patrons to guarantee a profit. Disturbed by the casino musicians' lack of uniform dress, he ordered that they wear black cutaways and gray trousers. A Hungarian band proved to be both popular and profitable, with double-daily concert receipts ranging from $15 to $20. Harry worked only one season for his father. Harry's failure to work closely with Flagler in fulfilling the Florida vision led to the estrangement.[47]

Ida Alice Shourds Flagler, Flagler's second wife, 1885

Harry returned to New York and soon thereafter married a daughter of the rich and powerful Lamont family. He also returned to Columbia to complete his education, graduating in 1897 with a Phi Beta Kappa key. He devoted his life to philanthropic causes, primarily musical interests, and became involved in the activities of the New York Symphony. He later founded and served as the principal benefactor of the New York Philharmonic Orchestra.[48]

131

Harry Harkness Flagler, Henry's only son, as a young man, 1894. Harry later founded the New York Philharmonic Orchestra.

St. Augustine's pretentions as a southern Newport were short-lived. In terms of number of guests, the first season of the Ponce de Leon was its best. In 1895 Flagler closed the Cordova except the guests rooms. Eight years later, he connected the Cordova and Alcazar with an overhead walk and renamed the Cordova the Alcazar Annex.[49] Flagler's building of other hotels on Florida's lower east coast was indicative of St. Augustine's poor standing, but not its cause. Indeed, the reason for Flagler's building south of St. Augustine was his hope in a "guaranteed" mild winter stay for his hotel guests.

Even before the construction of the Ponce de Leon, nature had sent Flagler an ominous warning. On January 11, 1886, New York papers reported the temperature in St. Augustine had dropped to twenty-two degrees, a reading only six degrees higher than that of New York. Flagler chose to regard the matter as an unusual occurrence. He jokingly asked his friend Anderson, "Would it not be a good plan to mix a little 'Old Granada' with the water in your pitcher, and thus prevent freezing?" A yellow fever epidemic in the late summer and fall of 1888 caused the St. Augustine hotels to have a poor 1889 season. The record freezes of the 1894–1895 winter sealed St. Augustine's fate. When Henry James wrote *The American Scene* in 1907, St. Augustine had relinquished the title "Newport of the South" to Palm Beach. However, James would not deny the magnificent Ponce de Leon an accolade. "The Ponce de Leon . . . comes as near producing, all by itself, the illusion of romance as a highly modern, a most cleverly-constructed and smoothly-administered great caravansery can come. . . . [It] is, in all sorts of ways and in the highest sense of the word, the most "amusing" of hotels. It did for me, at St. Augustine I was well aware, everything that an hotel could do."[50]

St. Augustine provided Flagler with a perfect outlet for his creative talents. His business genius was his ability to turn a vision into reality. He did not allow either local entrepreneurs or national bureaucrats to thwart him. Flagler captured the Gilded Age tastes and imagination. He dealt with local churches, government, and businesses in whatever manner necessary to transform St. Augustine from a town mired in the past into a Gilded Age resort.

Since it would have been impossible for the "retired" Flagler to have made a full business commitment to the Florida east coast in 1885, St. Augustine provided him with an excellent entrée into Florida development. By the end of the 1880s, however, Flagler was feeling his business energies restricted by partnerships. He broke rather early with his hotel partner Franklin Smith. He then pushed his railroad partners for concessions that would allow him to move farther down Florida's undeveloped east coast. As during his Standard Oil career, Flagler wished for cooperation only if others were willing to recognize his organization as "first among equals."

7

Railroads:
From Short Lines
to East Coast Lines

AS THE FIFTY-SIX-YEAR-OLD Henry Flagler supervised the planning of the Ponce de Leon in 1886, he was already looking for future projects. The president of the St. John's Railway proposed to Flagler a temporary working arrangement between their two roads. Flagler replied, "What would you think of some more permanent arrangement for operating your road under our management?"[1] This was the first indication of Flagler's plans for a major expansion effort beyond his St. Augustine activities. But, of course, it was so typical of this visionary as businessman.

With his total commitment to St. Augustine, Flagler realized that he would also have to do something about the city's poor transportation arrangements. While much of the eastern area of the United States became laced with rails, Florida remained a frontier region. From 1881 to 1885, Florida railroad mileage increased 776 miles, giving the state a total of only 1,313 miles. Just two states east of the Mississippi River, small Rhode Island and Delaware, had less trackage than Florida. St. Augustine's status as a rail center was in keeping with Florida's poor position. Only two roads served it in 1885, the St. John's Railway and the Jacksonville, St. Augustine and Halifax River Railway.[2]

The St. John's Railway, a fifteen-mile line from Tocoi on the St. Johns River to St. Augustine, had been chartered in 1856. First constructed with wooden rails in 1874, two years later the St. John's ran on iron rails. William Astor of New York City was the principal owner of the road, with Richard McLaughlin and John Stockton of Jacksonville serving as president and treasurer, respectively. Although the Astor road had only two locomotives, it was a financial success. Its 1883 net earnings were an astonishing 63 percent of its revenue.[3]

In 1881 the Florida legislature chartered the Jacksonville, St. Augustine and Halifax River Railway (hereinafter, the Jacksonville Railway) for a line from South Jacksonville, located across the St. Johns River from Jacksonville, through St. Augustine to the Halifax River. In June 1883, the Jacksonville Railway opened its South Jacksonville to St. Augustine division, a distance of thirty-six miles. When Flagler began his St. Augustine venture, this was the only portion of the road completed. Charles Green of Utica, New York, was principal owner and president of the road, and W. L. Crawford, later to be Flagler's general freight agent, served as treasurer and general manager. This road had more traffic than the Tocoi–St. Augustine connection, but its net earnings for the year ending February 1, 1885, were only 34 percent of the gross revenues, indicating an inefficient operation.[4]

Jacksonville Railway officials courted Flagler's favor. They gave him an annual pass that entitled him to free travel over the line, and on December 10, 1885, named him to the railway's board of directors. From the beginning of his Florida venture, however, Flagler had been dissatisfied with the railway, realizing that this crucial transportation link for northern passengers to St. Augustine suffered because of its poor facilities, especially the lack of a good passenger depot. He confided to his hotel builders, "Unless there is an early improvement in the condition of affairs, I shall take decided measures to correct the evils complained of."[5]

Flagler's first attempt at improving the Jacksonville Railway was to purchase a locomotive and tender for $200,000. He promised that if the railway officials would place an additional locomotive on the line, he would allow the road to take over filling operations at the Ponce de Leon building site. Flagler warned the railway's general manager to be cautious about the use of annual passes since free transportation did not contain dividend potential. This interest in the Jacksonville Railway was not altogether altruistic. Flagler indicated in November 1885 his desire to own an interest in the company, and on December 31, 1885, he bought Green's portion for $300,000. Flagler immediately arranged a directors' meeting for the reorganization of the company and had himself elected president.[6]

Rumors of a "Flagler syndicate" circulated throughout the St. Augustine area. In a confidential letter to a Daytona resident, Flagler gave him the facts of the matter: " 'The Flagler syndicate' consists of H. M. Flagler. In the Railroad matter, however, I joined with some personal friends, who are interested in the 'J.T.&K.W.R.R.' [Jacksonville, Tampa & Key West Railroad]. They put in 1/2 of the money, as I did not want to bother with the administration of the road. While it is true that my interest preponderates very largely, it is equally true that I have so many irons in the fire, I would rather sink the property than take it into my care." Flagler's first official act as president of the Jacksonville Railway was to have Anderson appointed to the board of directors. In a display of dry wit, Flagler wrote Anderson concerning his ceremonial position, "I suggest that you look over your largest file of red feathers, & select one which you think will be best adapted to this new degree to be conferred upon you." Anderson was to act as Flagler's personal Florida representative in official railway business.[7]

Flagler's first St. Augustine railroad project was a depot south of the San Sebastian River causeway. Before his coming, no railroad crossed the river into St. Augustine. The 1885 plan called for a building 250 feet from the river with docks and warehouse facilities. Construction began in 1888 when McGuire & McDonald, Flagler's contracting firm, filled in thirty acres of marsh land. They then completed a gravel road extension of King Street to the two-story depot. The first story, with its thirteen-foot-wide verandas, contained a waiting room, restrooms and the ticket office. Administrative offices were on the second floor. Flagler's builders then widened and asphalted Valencia and Mill streets to provide thoroughfares from the depot to the hotels.[8]

Maybe Flagler had first come to St. Augustine just to fulfill a millionaire's fantasy; but it was not within his personality to allow others to dictate his business options and decisions. When his St. Augustine investments became viable business ventures, he sought to dominate that city. By the beginning of the 1890s, he had accomplished that task. With the vastness of the Florida east coast south of St. Augustine still undeveloped, Flagler next set out to rid himself of his railroad partners and then to control the development of the Florida east coast.

Since Flagler's associates had interests in two railroads, they determined which would be allowed to expand. During their early association, Flagler was not disturbed that his partners chose to expand the Jacksonville, Tampa & Key West (JT&KW) road rather than his. The JT&KW Railway had begun operations between Jacksonville and Palatka in the spring of 1884, and an extension of the line in 1885 brought it to Sanford. Charles C. Deming was the treasurer of both this road and Flagler's road. Persons associated with the JT&KW who were directors of the Flagler road were Deming, Robert H. Coleman, and Mason Young. Dr. Andrew Anderson and Flagler were the only directors of the Flagler road independent of the larger concern.[9]

Robert H. Coleman, JT&KW's major stockholder, wrote Flagler a letter

136

in 1888 regarding rumors that Flagler planned to purchase the St. Johns and Halifax River Railway independently of the JT&KW System. Coleman had been under the impression that it would become a JT&KW property and that Flagler had no interest in the matter whatsoever. On the other hand, Coleman was one of Flagler's allies within the JT&KW organization; therefore, he emphasized his desire to have Flagler's approval of the JT&KW purchase of the property. Coleman outlined his reasoning: (1) The JT&KW would offer the most direct route from Jacksonville to the Halifax River. (2) If Flagler's road did indeed take over the new property, then there would be more conflict between the JT&KW and Flagler's road than in the past, due to the fact that there now would be more direct competition. (3) Even if Flagler purchased the St. Johns and Halifax River Railway, he would not have a direct connection with it, being forced to use William Astor's St. John's Railway as his link.[10]

Coleman was correct on the first two points, but Flagler quickly moved to solve his problems related to the third. He first bought both railways in the area that were owned by William Astor: the St. John's Railway, connecting Tocoi with St. Augustine, and the St. Augustine and Palatka Railway, a spur line, which connected Tocoi Junction with East Palatka. With Flagler's purchase of a third property, the St. Johns and Halifax River Railway, he offered service by the spring of 1889 from Jacksonville to Daytona, via St. Augustine and East Palatka.[11]

With the expansion of his railroad venture into the Daytona area, Flagler bought the Hotel Ormond interest of S. V. White, former owner of the St. Johns and Halifax River Railway. In 1876, John Anderson of Maine and Joseph D. Price of Kentucky had constructed the hotel, located a few miles above Daytona on the Halifax River. White had financially assisted them in the project, in the area then known as New Britain. After Flagler took over White's interest in 1890, he doubled the capacity of the hotel from 75 to 150 rooms. Later he bought out Anderson and Price, although they remained the managers until their deaths in 1911. In 1899, Flagler again doubled the capacity of the Ormond. With this addition, the hotel completely lost its country look: Flagler's workers destroyed the natural wilderness surrounding the hotel, replacing the native pines with palmettos.[12]

Ormond became famous for both its automobile races on the hard-packed beach and its golf course. Stating that "automobilists are a lot of cranks," Flagler nevertheless lowered the rates charged by his railroad for hauling automobiles to Ormond. He also gave attention to his Ormond garage, which serviced the world's first automobile racers. Golf, a major sport of America's wealthy, was closer to his understanding of recreation. With additions and improvements, the value of the Ormond golf course increased from $1,000 in 1898 to $95,167 in 1913.[13]

The main line from South Jacksonville to Daytona underwent major reconstruction in 1889 when Flagler changed it to standard gauge and purchased new rolling stock. In addition, two secondhand locomotives and four cars came with Flagler's purchase of the St. Augustine and Palatka Railway. Reconstruction costs were high, but the changes were beneficial. Flagler and his associates had created a network of standard-gauge rails under the general title of the East Coast Lines (ECL). Flagler used this name even though the old corporations legally operated under the Jacksonville Railway organization, with the old roads simply becoming divisions of that road. The ECL enjoyed excellent connections along the St. Johns River. Due to the charter for the Jacksonville Railway, Flagler had an exclusive ferry franchise across the St. Johns River at Jacksonville. In addition, the ECL built a bridge joining Jacksonville with South Jacksonville, which opened in July 1890. Other river connections included the railway at Tocoi and the bridge at Palatka.[14] These new links gave travelers easy access to St. Augustine and Ormond.

While Flagler was busy along the east coast, other sections of Florida were being developed. Henry Bradley Plant, Flagler's counterpart on the Florida west coast and in the interior of the peninsula, was a Connecticut native who had come south during the 1850s as a northern express-company representative. He remained during the Civil War and continued to operate his express business. In 1879, he purchased a large block of the Atlantic and Gulf Railroad of Georgia and later organized the Savannah, Florida and Western Railroad. This latter road served, along with Plant's Charleston and Savannah Railroad, as an important northern connection for the ECL.[15]

In coordinating his expanding rail empire, Plant organized the Plant Investment Company in 1882. The company entered the railway business in peninsular Florida with the purchase of the South Florida Railroad in 1885. By 1895, with the additions of the Florida Southern Railway from the JT&KW and the Sanford and St. Petersburg Railroad, Plant had a network of rails with corners at Montgomery, Alabama, Charleston, South Carolina, and Tampa. To connect with the trade of the Caribbean, Plant created the Plant Steamship Line in 1886. In addition to his transportation ventures, Plant, like Flagler, lured northerners to visit Florida, most notably with his magnificent Tampa Bay Hotel.[16]

While Plant seemed to easily control his empire, the financial status of the ECL during Flagler's association with his JT&KW partners is unclear. During the first couple of years of independent operation under Flagler, the ECL showed increases in net earnings. The ECL gave no report of operations in the 1889 volume of *Poor's Manual of Railroads,* and in late 1890, Flagler instructed Charles C. Deming, the ECL treasurer, to provide as little information to *Poor's* as possible. ECL officials did issue to Flagler weekly and monthly reports, comparing the period with the corresponding period of the preceding year. The reports available indicate that 1890 was not as good a year as 1889. Flagler was at a loss for a remedy to the situation; as he wrote his general freight agent, "I am discouraged with the results of 1890, but I don't know what to recommend, except the exercise of constant daily vigilance, to secure a revenue."[17]

Flagler began to have trouble with his ECL partners. The Jacksonville Railway had a $1 million mortgage against it. As owner of half the stock, it was Flagler's duty to provide $15,000 each six months to cover half the interest due. Since Flagler owned $300,000 of the mortgage bonds and held another $100,000 in trust for his half brother Dan Harkness, Flagler received most of his own interest payment. His associates in the ECL venture failed to fulfill their financial obligations: not only were they refusing to pay their portion of ECL debts, but as officials of the JT&KW, they also were pressing the ECL for the payment of its debts to their line. Flagler was incredulous. The ECL owed the other road less than $25,000, while his partners had defaulted on their portion of the bond interest due in mid-1890. Flagler had already advanced the ECL approximately $283,000. He firmly told Mason Young, a director of the ECL and vice-president of the JT&KW, "I must ask you to wait on the J.St.A.&H.R.R.'y Co. until it is more convenient for that Company to pay the debt."[18]

In late July 1890, Flagler invited Mason Young, Joseph R. Parrott (the general counsel of both the ECL and JT&KW), and Deming to a meeting aboard the new Flagler yacht, *Alicia,* anchored at New York. The purpose of the meeting was to discuss the relationship of the two roads. The parties decided that the ECL would get the Ormond-Daytona-Titusville business, but that the Indian River Steamboat Company would operate between Titusville and points south of it. Flagler could not negotiate with other navigation companies for this traffic, but Young assured him that the steamboat company would give satisfactory service.[19]

Robert H. Coleman was discontented with the actions of Mason Young. Coleman, still in his thirties, had inherited a fortune, which by 1890, was estimated to be $30 million, larger than those of many Gilded Age business leaders. He had invested $2 million of this fortune in Florida ventures such as the JT&KW and the Florida Construction Company. He had early become an ally of Flagler in JT&KW infighting. In 1889, when Flagler had hinted that he would like someone to relieve John Rockefeller of the burden of carrying so much of the Jacksonville Railway bonded debt, Coleman had purchased $300,000 worth of the bonds from Rockefeller.[20]

Close cooperation between Flagler and Coleman began in 1890 as Flagler moved to separate himself from the power of the JT&KW. Coleman's problems paralleled those of Flagler. In late 1890, he complained to Flagler that Young had been uncooperative. Coleman threatened to wreck the JT&KW rather than let Young neglect his financial obligations. In December 1890, Coleman suggested that Flagler might wish to avoid becoming embroiled in the coming battle by buying the JT&KW interest in the ECL for the sum of $1. Although Flagler did not take Coleman's offer at that time, relations between Flagler and the JT&KW continued to deteriorate.[21]

Coleman had interest payment troubles with his JT&KW partners similar to those Flagler had encountered. In 1891, Flagler agreed to pay Coleman's portion of the ECL debt, with Coleman reimbursing him from future earnings of the JT&KW. Coleman's financial problem was that Mason Young continued to refuse to pay his portion of the JT&KW interest. As owner of approximately half the JT&KW stock, Coleman did not mind at all paying his portion of the interest payment, but the interest incident indicated that relations between him and Young were disintegrating.[22]

In 1892, Flagler's final break with the JT&KW occurred. He incorporated the Florida Coast and Gulf Railway Company on May 28, 1892. This allowed him to extend his railroad vision beyond the restrictions of his JT&KW partners. Less than a month after the incorporation of his new company, Flagler ordered construction to begin on an extension from Daytona to New Smyrna. As one newspaper indicated, "This will give Mr. Flagler full control on the Florida east coast, as he will put a line of steamers on the Indian River to operate with his railway terminus at Rock Ledge for the Lake Worth trade." Four months after the new incorporation, Flagler announced the resignation of Deming as vice-president and secretary of the Jacksonville Railway. Joseph Parrott, former general counsel for the JT&KW, replaced Deming as vice-president. One of Flagler's Standard secretaries, J. C. Salter, became secretary. Flagler moved the headquarters from Deming's 10 Wall Street office to his Standard offices at 26 Broadway.[23] Flagler had achieved control of his railroad.

The new directors of Flagler's railroad were Flagler, his son Harry, Anderson, Parrott, and James E. Ingraham, head of the ECL land operations.

There was no longer any overlap between JT&KW and Flagler railroad officers. Flagler increased his locomotives and passenger cars by over 50 percent in 1894. During this period, Flagler's secretary wrote to *Poor's Manual of Railroads*, "As no one but Mr. Flagler is interested in the J., St.A.&I.R.Ry. Co., he does not desire to give publicity to the affairs of the road til its completion."[24]

Joseph R. Parrott was an important addition to Flagler's management team. He was born in 1858, the son of a Maine woolen manufacturer. After graduating from Phillips Exeter, Parrott attended Yale University, where he was a "gentleman C" student, graduating 68th in his class of 149. Although he may have absorbed some conservative economic positions in his political economy course taught by William Graham Sumner, Parrott spent most of his undergraduate time in social activities, such as those of Skull and Bones, a secretive men's association, and sports, including the class intramural football and rowing teams. After completing undergraduate school, Parrott entered Yale Law School, graduating cum laude in 1885. He was on the university crew throughout his six years at Yale, and on the varsity the last three years.[25]

Upon graduation from Yale Law, Parrott returned to Maine, but only practiced law there for about a year. He then entered practice in Jacksonville with the law firm headed by Duncan U. Fletcher, who would later become the city's mayor and a United States Senator. The firm represented the Jacksonville, Tampa & Key West Railroad. Parrott's knowledge of the JT&KW business activities led to his appointment as receiver of that road when it went bankrupt.[26]

In 1893, the Florida legislature passed a new law granting any railroad 8,000, rather than the customary 3,840, acres of the public domain for each mile of rail constructed south of Daytona. Flagler—with his new-found freedom—immediately created the Jacksonville, St. Augustine and Indian River Railway Company to include the provisions of the new law and legally bring all his rail operations under one corporate umbrella. Flagler wrote his general freight agent in September 1893, "The Jacksonville, St. Augustine & Indian River Ry. and the trade mark of pineapple and East Coast Line and the St. Augustine Route we hope to adopt as our standard." It was under the new Indian River name that Flagler built the New Smyrna-to-Lake Worth extension of 175 miles.[27]

South Floridians greeted the announcement of the extension of the ECL to the Lake Worth area with great enthusiasm. Guy I. Metcalf, editor of the Juno *Tropical Sun*, predicted that the ECL would be at the head of Lake Worth by the 1893–94 winter season. He had a personal interest in the project since he had the contract for a stage line from Lake Worth to Ft. Dallas, on the Miami River. Metcalf dreamed of even greater accomplishments by the Flagler organization: "This year a hack line will serve the purpose, next year or the one after, Mr. Flagler may see fit to go Metcalf 'one better' and put an iron horse on the route."[28]

The ECL extension steadily moved south. The contractors completed the railroad to New Smyrna on November 2, 1892. Three months later it arrived at Titusville and Rock Ledge. The right-of-way contractor worked on the road from Rock Ledge to Eau Gaillie in the spring of 1893. In addition to the extension, Flagler acquired the thirty-mile Atlantic and Western Railroad, which connected New Smyrna with Blue Spring, located on the St. Johns River.[29]

In less than a decade, Flagler had transformed the rails of the Florida east coast from a few short, almost bankrupt, affairs to a system which served the east coast from Jacksonville to the Lake Worth region. He had always negotiated with the railroad leaders of the age during his Standard Oil years, now he was a minor player in that drama; but in Florida he was, along with Henry B. Plant on the west coast of the peninsula, the dominant force in railroading and resort building.

Palm Beach: "Queen of Winter Resorts"

IN 1885 FLAGLER had declared his intentions of making St. Augustine the Newport of the South; but, as we have seen, the freezes of the era had made that eventuality difficult. In reality, as each mile of the ECL was constructed, it was getting that much nearer what would become the real "Newport of the South," the Lake Worth region—specifically, Palm Beach.

The Lake Worth area had a legendary history before Flagler's 1893 arrival. According to local lore, during the Civil War a deserter named Lang hid on the island of Palm Beach in a wooded area between the lake and ocean. Charles Moore, a fugitive from Chicago later joined him. During their stay Moore and Lang supposedly discovered a shipwreck's trunk containing $8,000. Fearing capture for desertion, Lang stayed on the island. Moore went to Jacksonville but lost his part of the fortune during a drunken spree.[1]

A second, less legendary, discovery of Lake Worth occurred during an 1867 expedition up the Florida east coast. Michael Sears, a local explorer from Ft. Dallas, and his son George located an inlet leading into Lake Worth. A colony of southern Michigan families originally settled at the future site of Palm Beach in 1876. When a storm in 1879 wrecked the *Providencia* (a cargo ship traveling from Trinidad to Spain) in the general vicinity of Palm Beach, the residents gathered approximately 20,000 coconuts from the wreckage, planting over two-thirds of them on the island.[2]

The area was first known as Lake Worth, that being the name of the post office serving the region in 1880. The Post Office Department changed its name in March 1886 to Palm Beach. The area's reputation as a winter resort began that same year with the arrival of Robert R. McCormick, a railroad entrepreneur from Denver. McCormick, unable to resist the lures of the region, bought property and built a cottage on the east side of the lake. Others were also becoming involved in resort activities. Captain E. N. Dimick, one of the original settlers, added rooms onto his home in 1884, naming it the Cocoanut Grove House. Just before Flagler's arrival, Dimick sold his fifty-room hotel to C. T. Clark, a Pittsburgh millionaire. Flagler rented the hotel from Clark in 1893, using it as his headquarters during construction of his first Palm Beach hotel.[3]

When Flagler announced his plans to build a railroad into the Lake Worth area in 1893, West Palm Beach did not exist. In discussing his plans for this new community, according to the recollections of Lake Worth residents, Flagler pointed across Lake Worth from Palm Beach to an untouched wilderness and predicted: "In a few years there'll be a town over there as big as Jacksonville, and St. Augustine will be a way station for it." Flagler's agent purchased a $45,000 piece of real estate on the west side of Lake Worth, which became the site for West Palm Beach. Although prices for other property in the area quickly accelerated, Flagler continued a nonspeculative land policy that he had begun in St. Augustine. He stated some years later, "I have not bought any land at Palm Beach with the expectation or desire to sell it again. . . . As to a matter of profit, I think I can make more in one week in Wall Street than I can make in one year in real-estate in Florida."[4]

West Palm Beach was literally Flagler's creation. As the building of his railroad progressed southward from the Indian River, his employees laid out the 200-acre town site along a one-half-mile frontage on Lake Worth. James Ingraham, in charge of Flagler's land development projects, platted the town in the typical gridiron pattern of the day, alphabetically naming the streets after various plants common to the area. On March 22, 1894, the ECL completed its road into the infant town.[5]

Flagler not only created West Palm Beach but also provided it with essential services. At the inland Clear Water Lake, he placed a pumping station to provide fresh water to his hotels. J. A. McGuire built the $45,000 station, which also provided fire protection for West Palm Beach through a system of hydrants. Later, the East Coast Hotel Waterworks Company provided water to the community. In 1904 the company expanded its facilities by developing a one-acre park at Clear Water Lake. The much-admired centerpieces of the park were its fountain and aquarium.[6]

Flagler's philanthropic activities in West Palm Beach were numerous.

His builders constructed the city hall, a fire station, and a courthouse (when Palm Beach County was created in 1909). Flagler contributed the funds for a hospital and a Catholic church, but did not react positively to all financial appeals. When the Holy Trinity Church asked for money to build its rectory, Flagler replied, "I realize very well that we all have our preferences, but with so much real suffering in the world, there comes home to me this one thought—Ought I to give money for an ecclesiastical luxury, and in doing so deprive worthy persons of the necessities of life?" On the other hand, after the St. Louis Benevolent Educational Society had completed a church and school, Flagler deeded the property to it in accordance with an earlier agreement.[7]

As the founder of West Palm Beach, Flagler occasionally projected his will over the community. For instance, he instructed an associate to persuade George Zapf, a local saloon operator, to stop using his establishment as a house of prostitution. On another occasion, Flagler used his influence to block a proposed road along Lake Worth in West Palm Beach.[8]

Although Flagler kept abreast of happenings in West Palm Beach, his primary interests in the area were his hotel enterprises on Palm Beach Lake Worth, twenty-two miles in length, separated West Palm Beach from the narrow coral island of Palm Beach. When Flagler first arrived in the Lake Worth area, thirty to forty cottages, two stores, and a couple of hotels were the only structures scattered around the lake. The editor of the Juno *Tropical Sun* enthusiastically speculated that Flagler might spend a year's worth of earnings, which the editor estimated to be from $2 million to $3 million, developing the area.[9]

The paper announced in April 1893 that Flagler's hotel would be called The Royal Poinciana. Flagler had bought the Robert R. McCormick property the previous winter for $75,000; this acquisition included the McCormick cottage, the interior of which was solid mahogany acquired from logs that had washed ashore. When Flagler began construction of the Poinciana, he had the cottage moved to another location rather than destroy it. Meanwhile, he bought other properties, spending a total of $300,000 for the 100-acre hotel site. The groundbreaking for the Poinciana took place in May 1893, and it opened the following February. Henry W. Merrill, the manager, had formerly been associated with the Hotel Raymond of Pasadena, California, and the Crawford House in the White Mountains of New Hampshire. His assistants came from New York's Waldorf and the White Mountains' Twin Mountain House.[10]

The Poinciana was a six-story colonial-style wooden building. It faced Lake Worth, with rear wings for dining rooms, kitchens, servants' rooms,

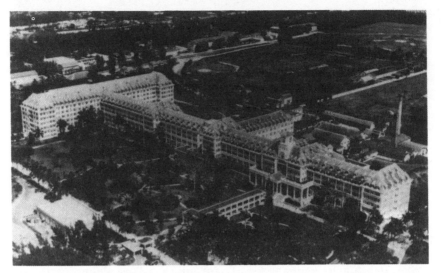

The Royal Poinciana, Flagler's first Palm Beach hotel. First opened in 1894, after the additions leading to the above depiction, it was not only the world's largest hotel but also the largest wooden structure in the world.

and a large ballroom. Corridors from the rotunda were intersected by the north and south wings. The hotel contained 125 private baths and was electric throughout, including its three elevators. There were several additions to the building from 1900 to 1905. Upon final completion, the Poinciana became the world's largest hotel. Its valuation increased from less than $1 million in 1898 to almost $2 million in 1913.[11]

The hotel grounds were beautiful, particularly the coconut palms, which gave the area its tropical character. Flagler provided pavilions and bathhouses on the ocean side and the local yacht club and a music pavilion on the lake side of the island. In March 1896, the first train arrived on Palm Beach on the recently completed spur from the main line of the Flagler road. Its passengers were among the "Four Hundred," the most exclusive set in American high society. Prominent within this entourage were members of the Vanderbilt family.[12]

The Poinciana was an immediate success. Flagler enthusiastically reported after its 1895 opening that his new hotel had more guests than any other Florida establishment. At the time of his initial investment in Palm Beach, it had been rumored that Flagler might build another hotel on the ocean side. Indeed, he did begin the hotel, the Palm Beach Inn, during the summer of 1895, and it opened for the following winter season. Although not as large or pretentious as the Poinciana, the Inn had a sizable following. Flagler therefore doubled its size before the 1901 season, renaming it the Breakers.[13]

The spirited rivalry between the two Flagler hotels came to a temporary halt when fire destroyed the Breakers on June 9, 1903. With the Breakers only insured for $100,000, Flagler estimated his financial loss to be $400,000. Although there had been some apprehension that the structure would not be replaced, Flagler announced two weeks later that he would rebuild the hotel. It was completed in time for the 1904 season, even though it required rapid building and added expense. Flagler promised: "We are going to try to make a feature of the Breakers, and if possible, make it better than the Poinciana."[14]

An important part of his formula for success was that Flagler always sought the best personnel for his hotels. Fred Sterry was the first manager of the Palm Beach Inn and for a time oversaw both the Inn and Royal Poinciana when Henry W. Merrill was sent to another Flagler hotel. By 1907, in addition to the Palm Beach operation, Sterry was associated with the Homestead at Hot Springs, Virginia. Flagler hired as superintendent of the Palm Beach Casino George E. Andrews of Philadelphia, a yachtsman who had also played twelve years of baseball in the National League. Since his retirement from baseball, Andrews had become a prominent coach and trainer of some of the nation's most outstanding athletes.[15]

In addition to the hotels, Flagler had a number of cottages built along the lake and ocean fronts for some of the winter residents. In time the cottage community emerged as the leading social segment of the winter resort. Cottagers included Joseph Jefferson, the actor and comedian noted for his portrayal of Rip Van Winkle; Wayne MacVeagh, James A. Garfield's attorney general; and the Henry Phipps family of Pittsburgh. By 1907, there were seven cottages alongside the Breakers.[16]

At the same time that Flagler's public reputation as the builder of the Florida east coast was increasing, his personal life was in turmoil. Alice Flagler lost her mental competence during the 1890s. At first her behavior was not noticeably different from many around her. She did seem to be unusually sensitive and emotional. She also tended to exaggerate things. There was no doubt she was self-centered, always most interested in her social position and personal appearance. As the 1890s progressed, however, she became obsessed with things. Flagler had built Kirkside as their St. Augustine home, but he could not control her deteriorating mental condition.[17]

Dr. George Shelton, the Flagler family physician since the mid-1880s, noticed in a visit to the Flagler home at Mamaroneck, New York, in 1895 that Alice was having unusual delusions. She began to tell Shelton all sorts of stories, even saying that she knew one lady of social prominence who was the illegitimate daughter of European nobility. On the same occasion, she brought to Shelton three pebbles that she claimed had an image of Jesus on them. This type of behavior became even more pronounced. She attempted to send some jewelry to the Russian czar, which was intercepted, and she also believed herself to be the czarina.[18]

Flagler placed Alice at the "House of Dr. Choate," a late-nineteenth century form of institutionalizing the mentally ill of the upper class, on October 24, 1895. She was released from the Pleasantville, New York, facility in June 1896, but Flagler had to return her to Pleasantville the spring of 1897. Dr. Carlos MacDonald, now in charge of the facility, found Alice's condition had changed for the worse. Alice told MacDonald that Henry Flagler was in Florida constructing a Nicaraguan canal that would reduce the travel time from New York to London by two days. She continued to do unexplainable things, such as write a check in the amount of one million roses, rather than dollars.[19]

Alice's condition, however, was a part of a larger picture of turmoil in the personal life of Henry Flagler during the 1890s. A major reason for Flagler's problems was that his marriage was complicated by his relationship with Mary Lily Kenan. Her father, William Rand Kenan, Sr., was from a prominent North Carolina family with his family "place," Kenansville, near Wilmington. Born just after the Civil War, on June 14, 1867, Mary Lily Kenan was the eldest of four children. Her siblings were sisters Jessie and Sarah, and William Rand Kenan, Jr., the youngest child. As befit a southern belle of her standing, she became an accomplished vocalist and pianist with study at the Peace Institute in Raleigh, North Carolina. She then entered the southern society set, with its rounds of parties and social connections.[20]

It seems that Flagler first met Mary Lily in 1891, probably at some social function. As the story goes, the thirty-four-year-old spinster Mary Lily Kenan was living in the attic of her wealthy relative Pembroke Jones's mansion in Newport, Rhode Island. She had sewn a button on Flagler's coat, and, thus, it was love! Although it is true that the Joneses were close friends of Mary Lily and may have indeed first introduced her to Flagler, the romantic aspect of the Henry Flagler-Mary Lily Kenan relationship was much more complicated than that.[21]

As the years passed, Flagler's relationship with Mary Lily developed into a romantic attachment—and a major social scandal. Beginning at least as early as Alice's final confinement in 1896, Flagler was often seen in the company of his cousin, Eliza Ashley, and her good friend, Mary Lily Kenan. Finally, in 1899, Mr. Kenan talked with Flagler concerning his true intentions toward Kenan's eldest daughter. The Kenans' second daughter, Jessie, had married J. Cilsy Wise, who left her and their infant daughter shortly after Louise Wise's birth on June 28, 1895. Kenan did not wish for Mary Lily also to be betrayed. On April 3, 1899, Flagler's secretary, W. H. Beardsley, informed Mr. Kenan that 1,000 shares of Flagler's Standard Oil stock had been transferred to Mary Lily Kenan. In addition, members of the Kenan family recount that at that time Flagler gave Mary Lily gifts, including a strand of Oriental pearls held together with a 12-carat diamond clasp, and a diamond bracelet; the jewelry itself was said to have been worth $1 million.[22] At any rate, the major problem was now not desire, but the fact that Henry Flagler was still a married man.

After this April agreement with the Kenans, Flagler petitioned the New York Supreme Court to have his wife Alice declared insane and incompetent. After hearing testimony from several doctors, a court-appointed commission ruled her to be insane. She then became a permanent resident of "Dr. McDonalds's house." The court appointed Flagler as Alice Flagler's guardian. After the hearing, Flagler wrote Dr. Carlos MacDonald:

I am in receipt of your favor of yesterday's date and thank you for the information it affords. As you say I trust there will be nothing more in the newspapers.

I have just received a bill from Dr. Talcott [one of the witnesses at the hearing], $1000 for his visit to Pleasantville on the 29th ult. [June], and testimony as expert witness on the 20th inst. [July][23]

A political and social controversy exploded in Florida when Flagler sought to change the Florida divorce law in 1901. In order to marry Mary Lily, he had to secure a divorce from Alice. Both New York and Florida only allowed divorce on the grounds of adultery. Therefore, Flagler, thinking he could more easily change the Florida law, first established his legal residence as Florida and then had a bill submitted to the state legislature in 1901 that would allow divorce in that state on grounds of insanity as well as adultery. The bill, introduced on April 9, 1901, passed the house by a margin of 42 to 19 and the senate by 24 to 8.[24]

Rumors circulated that Flagler had bribed some of the legislators to get the bill passed. Persons on both sides of the issue pressured Governor William Sherman Jennings when the bill reached his desk. Antidivorce forces

Mary Lily Kenan Flagler, Flagler's third wife, 1904

encouraged him not to bow to the monied interests of the state. Frank Clark, a newspaperman and congressman from Ocala, urged Jennings's father-in-law to encourage the governor to veto the measure. Clark stated that such an action would endear Jennings to the majority of the electorate. On the other hand, Duncan U. Fletcher, now mayor of Jacksonville, stated that the bill should be signed. If Jennings was inclined to veto the measure, Fletcher expressed a desire to talk with him to dissuade it. Apparently this was not necessary; Jennings signed the bill into law on April 25. On August 13, 1901, Flagler's divorce was official. He paid former Governor Francis P. Fleming $15,000 for representing his insane wife in the divorce proceedings. George P. Raney, a member of the Florida legislature from Leon County, charged Flagler $14,500 for his services as Flagler's attorney.[25] These large sums were obviously payment for the lobbying effort in the legislature on behalf of the divorce law in addition to the divorce itself.

The marriage of the seventy-one-year-old Henry Flagler and the thirty-four-year-old Mary Lily Kenan took place at Liberty Hall, her family's home at Kenansville, near Wilmington, North Carolina, on August 24, 1901. Flagler built Whitehall for his bride, possibly presenting its deed to her on their wedding day. Some eight months before the wedding, Carrère and Hastings had completed the initial plans for the $2.5 million home for the Flaglers, which was to be built next to the Poinciana on Palm Beach. Pottier and Stymus Company of New York, the interior furnishers of the Flagler hotels, provided the interior decor. In addition to the main building, there was a separate laundry building, which also contained dormitories for black servants on its second floor. As construction proceeded on Whitehall, Flagler made suggestions for changes. A ballroom was added to the west of the courtyard and offices, and service areas were moved into twin west wings flanking a piazza. Flagler had the architects modify the design of the roof gable from its Spanish look to a traditional colonial design. The basic design, with the two-storied white columns on the front of Whitehall, remained intact.[26]

Passing through the double bronze doors into the great white marble entry hall, the visitor to Whitehall saw dual staircases leading to the second-floor guest rooms. To the left of the main hall, along the south side of the courtyard, were the music and billiard rooms and the library. The southwest corner contained the offices of Flagler and his secretaries. A magnificent ballroom was to the west of the courtyard. Decorated in gold and white, it was reminiscent of the great ballrooms of the Louis XV period. The north side of the first floor contained the kitchen, breakfast and dining rooms, and a parlor.[27]

While Whitehall's exterior and first floor exuded a public presence, the upper floors provided comfort, rest, and privacy for the Flaglers, their servants, and guests. There were thirteen servants' rooms on the second floor and another five on the third. The second floor, however, was primarily for the Flaglers and their guests. It had an intimate morning room. There were fourteen guest rooms, each with a distinctive decor, private bath, and large walk-in closet. On the southeast corner of the second floor was the Flagler bedroom, complete with a dressing room and sunken bathtub. In an allegorical word picture of Palm Beach, Henry James recreated Whitehall on the pages of his *American Scene:*

> The palace rears itself, behind its own high gates and gilded, transparent barriers, at a few minutes' walk from the great caravanseries; it sits there, in its admirable garden, amid its statues and fountains, the hugeness of its more or less antique vases and sarcophagi—costliest reproductions all—as if to put to shame those remembered villas of the Lake of Como, of the Borromean Islands, the type, the climate, the horticultural elegance, the contained curiosities, luxuries, treasures, of which invokes only to surpass them at every point . . . those who have conformed with due earnestness to the hotel-spirit, and for a sufficiently long probation, may hope eventually to penetrate or perhaps actually retire.

If a person were not familiar with Henry James's prose, this portrait could be interpreted as honoring Whitehall. But his allusions to the unreal nature of the house and the conformity of Palm Beach society belied his true feelings. Upon his return to Cambridge, Massachusetts, James remarked, "Florida is a fearful fraud."[28]

With the completion of Whitehall in early 1902, it became a center of Palm Beach social activity. Even before the Flaglers moved into their home on February 6, there had been a couple of musicales performed at Whitehall. The Flaglers entertained lavishly on such occasions as Christmas and New Year's. Russell T. Joy, formerly of the Memorial Church in St. Augustine, was the first Whitehall organist. During most of the season the Flaglers invited only their closest friends and relatives as house guests. Among those were Mary Lily's parents, her brother, William Rand Kenan, Jr., her sisters, Sarah Kenan and Jessie Kenan Wise, Mrs. Wise's daughter and Mrs. Flagler's only niece, Louise Wise, and a favorite cousin of Mary Lily, Owen Kenan. J. N. Camden, Standard Oil ally and former United States senator from West Virginia, was a frequent guest, along with Flagler's closest Florida friend, Dr. Andrew Anderson, and Flagler's second cousin, and close friend of Mary Lily, Eliza Ashley and her husband Eugene. At times, however, Flagler would avoid the frequent gaiety of

Whitehall by retiring early, using a concealed stairway that enabled him to move unnoticed from the first to the second floor of the mansion.[29]

Henry and Mary Lily Flagler especially enjoyed having Mary Lily's sister, Jessie, and her daughter, Louise, visit Whitehall. Not only did Louise bring the vitality of the young to the place, but she was also the only member of the W. R. Kenan, Sr., family of her generation. The following is a typical letter from Flagler to Louise:

Aug. 2'11.

My dear Baby,

The letter you wrote me Monday came this morning, and I can only repeat what I have said a good many times before,—that I am always very glad to hear from you.

That red hot weather we had a while ago has disappeared, and now it is warm, but endurable.

Your experience diving through the surf ought to impress you with the necessity of looking out for strange men before you start. I hope your neck is better by this time.

Delos [his dog] is a darling. I don't know how to describe him.

You want me to ask Aunt Mary Lily when she is ready for you and mother to come to Mamaroneck; I am not going to ask her, but to tell you that we are ready any time, and I hope it won't be long before you will come.

Aunt Mary Lily had a letter from her mother yesterday, in which she said that Uncle Tom is much better than she expected to find him. Uncle Owen is back. He went to Chicago or rather to a neighborhood about 60 miles from Chicago to visit some friends there, but a phone message this morning says he is back and is coming out to Mamaroneck this afternoon.

With dearest love, believe me,

Your affectionate

[signed] Uncle Henry

Miss Louise C. Wise
Wrightsville Beach, N.C.[30]

Arthur Spalding, the second organist at Whitehall, gave rare insight into the life of the Flagler home through his almost daily letters to his mother in Lowell, Massachusetts. Born in 1877, Spalding had graduated with a major in musicology from Harvard College in 1899. Three years later he obtained a law degree from Harvard. Most probably, the Reverend George Ward had recommended Spalding for the organist position since Spalding had been the organist for Ward's Kirk Street Church in Lowell. In any case, Spalding was the resident organist at Whitehall from the 1907 through the

Whitehall, the home Flagler built for his wife Mary Lily Kenan as a wedding gift. This is a depiction during the later phase of construction in 1901–2.

1911 seasons. After leaving Whitehall, Spalding entered full-time law practice with his brother George in Lowell.[31]

When Spalding arrived at Whitehall in January 1907, his first impression of Flagler was one of awe. Flagler was "seated in one of the big gold arm chairs like a king on his throne with six or eight people about him like loyal subjects." Spalding found both Henry and Mary Lily Flagler to be unpretentious and cordial. As for Spalding's organ arrangments, Mrs. Flagler enjoyed a wide range of music, but Flagler himself liked *loud* arrangements, since he was becoming increasingly deaf. Flagler's demeanor struck Spalding as that of an elderly gentleman appreciative of gestures of friendship: "As we came out of church this noon, a little girl ran up and kissed him, then walked along part way with us, holding on to his hand. He is just that grandfatherly sort of man, and he and his wife seem devoted to each other." Spalding constantly heard of various Flagler accomplishments on Florida's east coast, and seemed vicariously to enjoy the experience: "As Mrs. Flagler says, he wouldn't be happy if he wasn't working and accomplishing unusual things. To be sure most of the improvements are carried out in the name of the East Coast R.R. but he is the whole thing and almost sole owner of it—the one man who instigates every improvement. Yet, he's the most modest appearing man about the place."[32]

Palm Beach became the great winter mecca for the status conscious of America—or as Henry James would have it, the epitome of the "hotel-spirit." The Breakers opened in December and closed in early April; the Poinciana welcomed guests in mid-January and remained open until about the middle of April. The Poinciana and Breakers in 1903 could accommodate 1,500 and 500 guests, respectively. Three post offices operated on Palm Beach at the height of each season. The Poinciana required $3,500 a day for provisioning the kitchen, and twenty-five tons of coal a day to operate its electric power plant.[33]

The new capitalists of the age, both great and small, led the migration to Palm Beach. New York and New Jersey usually provided from 40 to 50 percent of the clientele at the Poinciana and the Breakers. The old commercial states of New England were poorly represented; the migration was predominately an urban movement. Cities such as New York, Chicago, Pittsburgh, and Philadelphia were the permanent residences of most of the Palm Beach set. Even in rural states such as Wisconsin and Nebraska, the number of migrants from outside the major cities was negligible. Palm Beach attracted not only wealthy individuals but also many middle-class businessmen and their families who desired higher social status.[34]

The "high season" of the winter resort was marked by the Washington's Birthday Ball, which was the crowning event of each year. In recounting his impressions of the 1907 ball, Spalding was pleased to note that the guests were limited to those staying in the Flagler hotels or living in the cottages. Spalding had heard that the 1906 affair had been spoiled by the West Palm Beach "rabble" and persons who had come from some of the smaller hotels about the area. In keeping with the patriotism of the occasion, red, white, and blue lights sparkled among the greenery at the Poinciana. Although Spalding was a bit disappointed by the decorations, the main purpose of the event was not lost on him: "Palm Beach society was there with the goods, and if I could have the money that I suppose was represented by the gowns and jewelry, I should probably be handing out bills for tips instead of dimes and quarters."[35]

During "high season," the Poinciana employed 320 waiters for its dining area. Although both hotels were at full capacity from mid-February through March, the staffs made special provisions for the Rockefeller family and other Standard Oil friends. Flagler took full credit for what *Palm Beach Life*, the local society paper, termed the "Queen of Winter Resorts." Flagler noted to a correspondent in 1903, "While I agree with you in the belief that Palm Beach 'has come to stay,' it is I think an undisputed fact that my investments have given it its permanence as a winter resort."[36]

In keeping with his attitude toward what he had done for Palm Beach, Flagler tended to exercise more control over it than any other resort he had created. He closed his casinos and other amusements on Sundays. As for objections to his policy, Flagler stated, "If they do not like it they need not come. I am not asking their opinion in this any more than I consult them about my other affairs. Sunday is to be kept at Palm Beach. Its observance is one of the features of the place." On at least one occasion George Ward reined in Flagler when the businessman told the minister that the Royal Poinciana Chapel was part of the East Coast System. Ward immediately challenged, "I thought, Mr. Flagler, it was the Church of Almighty God. As such it cannot be a part of any human system." Flagler responded, "You are right, and if it has ever been in any way dependent it never shall be again."[37]

During the winter season, Palm Beach was a world unto itself. Daily activities included bridge and dinner parties, luncheons and teas. Several events during the winter season gained special attention. The annual charity bazaar of the Women's Guild of Bethesda-by-the-Sea, the Palm Beach Episcopal Church, served both a charitable and social purpose. The prominent social position of Mrs. Frederick Robert was emphasized by the *Palm Beach Life*'s capitalization of her weekly tea, simply referred to as "Tuesday Morning." At one such occasion, Mrs. Mary Lily Flagler entertained the guests by singing two Negro dialect songs, "Little Alabama Coon" and "I Want You My Honey."[38]

The typical Palm Beach day began with breakfast and a trip to the Breakers' beach. Black swim suits covered the women from neck to ankle because strict dress codes did not allow them to reveal much of their bodies. The beach was almost deserted by one in the afternoon as hotel guests partook of an eight-course lunch.[39]

The afternoons at Palm Beach afforded guests opportunities to wander about the area. One activity that was both utilitarian and fun was the mule car. When Flagler built Whitehall, he did not like the idea of the railroad passengers disembarking just outside his home; therefore, he had the main railroad spur moved north of the Poinciana. The island portion of the old spur became an easy mule-car conveyance to the Breakers side of the island. For a nickel ride, one could witness a mule so obstinate that he had to be whipped to start, and was almost as difficult to stop. In order to warn persons along the way to beware, the driver would merely tickle the beast, causing the mule to bray. As Spalding noted, this was much more effective than a mechanical device. The other favorite form of transportation on the island was what were commonly referred to as "Afromobiles," enlarged tricycle vehicles usually pedaled by black hotel employees seated behind the patron or patrons. The Poinciana had some 200 such vehicles. Often guests would merely take a bicycle ride along the jungle trail to observe the semitropical vegetation, ranging from various palm trees—both domestic and imported—to the banyan tree. Others, looking for more exotic entertainment, would visit Joe Frazier's alligator farm a few miles south of Palm Beach. It consisted of alligators, sea lions, turtles, and other unfamiliar animals. For the less adventurous, an afternoon of dancing could be enjoyed.[40]

Guests could go to the baseball field to watch black hotel employees of the Poinciana and Breakers' teams. These were no ordinary hotel employees. Although they did hold positions such as waiters or porters, that was only incidental; Flagler hired them for their baseball talents. Many of the athletes spent their summer months playing for the Cuban Giants. Much of the spectators' enjoyment of the activity, however, came from the stereotypical behavior of the players. Spalding said of one of the 1907 games, "The third baseman on the Poinciana team was a wonderful ball-player and kept the whole crowd roaring with his horseplay and cakewalks up and down the sidelines."[41]

The Cocoanut Grove, an arbor of coconut palms located next to the Poinciana, was the focal point of the late-afternoon and evening social scene. At five o'clock, waiters served tea and coconut cakes among the palms. Dancing ended before eight, allowing the guests an opportunity to change into dinner attire. Although there were after-dinner activities every night, Saturday evening in the Grove was a special occasion. It marked the weekly cakewalk of the hotels' black employees. They performed a dance, similar to the twentieth century tap dance, with a cake as a prize. Audience applause determined the winning couple. Although many songs were used to accompany the dancers, the dialect song "De Cake Walk Queen" was an audience favorite:

> Dar's a meeting of all de high society,
> To decide what dancers has most variety,
> And a prize they offer with all propriety,

And de winner shall be de cake walk queen!
Come you children dar's a priety.
Der gal dat wins it shall be de cake walk queen![42]

Witnessing a cakewalk held in the dining room of the Breakers, Spalding noted that there were three judges, selected from among the hotel's guests. They sat behind a table that had upon it a huge cake, built in terraced layers and adorned with a small American flag. In his final assessment of the affair, Spalding stated, "Some of them were mightly clever and graceful, especially the prize-winners who I am told took the cake at about every cake-walk last season, and at the close the couples were all lined up facing the judges and the cake presented to the winners, who pranced triumphantly out of the room holding the cake aloft."[43]

There were also many Palm Beach activities for the sportsman. In the area between the two hotels was an elaborately designed eighteen-hole golf course. The local paper noted, "Golf has always held a prominent place among the sports at Palm Beach and has attracted such interest that New York papers give the daily events as much prominence as those of large northern clubs." During the 1907 season, Arthur Fenn, the senior professional golfer in America, served as the manager of the Palm Beach links. The golf schedule at Palm Beach was hectic. There were eight tournaments between mid-January and the end of February 1907. The Annual East Coast Tournament in March climaxed the season. The Golf Ball at the Breakers coincided with this event. The Breakers staff converted the large dining room into a ballroom for the occasion. This gala ranked second only to Washington's Birthday as the social event of the season.[44]

Another Palm Beach activity that Flagler supported was boating. Flagler owned four yachts in what was sometimes called his Lake Worth Fleet, with his superintendent of hotels serving as general superintendent of the vessels. Flagler helped organize the Lake Worth Yacht Club and provided a building for its use. He also served as president of the Motorboat and Carnival Association, which in 1905 began to sponsor an annual regatta on Lake Worth. William K. Vanderbilt, Jr., served as first vicepresident. In 1911, the seventh annual regatta, with Flagler still president, offered $2,500 in gold as the grand prize.[45]

One Palm Beach social activity that flourished in spite of Flagler's opposition was the Bradley Beach Club, supposedly a restaurant, but actually a gambling establishment. Edward R. Bradley built the club, located a short distance north of the Poinciana, prior to the 1899 winter season. It was a two-story frame house located along Lake Worth. Bradley offered club members every comfort imaginable, with Turkish carpeting and Persian rugs covering the floors. The former caterer of the Bacchus Club of St. Augustine served guests in private dining facilities on the second floor. The telegraph office relayed daily stock market quotations to the Beach Club. One local paper stated, "The Beach Club is one of the most popular and famous places of resort for the best class of our winter visitors in Palm Beach." Flagler attempted to have Captain E. N. Dimick, owner of the property, break the lease, but was unsuccessful. Bradley's Beach Club became famous partly because of the honesty of its proprietor and also as a result of the large stakes wagered on its tables.[46]

Although Spalding had earlier in 1907 assured his mother that he had no desire to visit the Beach Club, he made it a point to visit before the end of the season. The gambling room was octagonal, furnished in green, and brightly lighted. Although gambling was illegal, Spalding noted that the best of the Flagler hotels' clientele were present and that none of the trappings of illegality were apparent: no barricades or secrecy about the place. There were two gaming tables and six or seven roulette tables in the room. The stakes were rather high; therefore, the appearance of $100 bills on the tables was no cause for surprise. Spalding's final assessment of the Beach Club, however, was much as Flagler's would have been. "There's such an air of indifference about the whole thing," Spalding wrote his mother, "that your first impression is no different from what it would be if you were looking at a game played with beans. But when you stay there the whole evening there's something shocking about the whole thing. The amount of money made there during the season is appalling and the lowest estimate I've heard as to their net profits is $200,000."[47]

Palm Beach emerged by World War I as the leading winter resort in the United States. Although there were many summer resorts in the northeastern United States competing for the "conspicuous leisure" market, Palm Beach and other Flagler resorts were almost alone in the winter market.[48] California could offer some competition, but the rapid transportation network that Flagler had established with the eastern seaboard and the midwest contributed to the success of Palm Beach. In Palm Beach, Flagler offered his visitors an opportunity to escape from the ordinary daily activities of home to the fanciful winter world of southern Florida. The hotels, with their many diversions, provided an idyllic environment set apart from reality. Not even Flagler's desire to impose his morality could prevent his guests from escaping the normal constraints of life.

Miami and Nassau: "American Riviera"

DURING THE FLORIDA FREEZES of 1894–95, the area around the Miami River remained unaffected while most of the state was devastated. Mrs. Julia Tuttle, owner of land on the Miami River, sent Henry Flagler a bouquet of flowers to symbolize her area's escape from the tragedy. This incident has become for many the only explanation for Henry Flagler's decision to extend his railway to Miami.[1] In fact, the background and the decision itself were much more complex.

When Flagler created West Palm Beach, the future site of Miami was called Ft. Dallas, a small trading post sixty miles to the south. Its two most prominent citizens were Mrs. Mary Brickell and Mrs. Julia Tuttle. Mrs. Brickell, a native of Yorkshire, England, had moved to Australia as a child. While there, she had married William Barnwell Brickell, a Cleveland, Ohio, businessman and adventurer. Seeking new opportunity after the Civil War, Brickell had traveled to the Biscayne Bay country of Florida with Ephraim Tanner Sturtevant in 1870. The following year the Brickells and Sturtevants moved to the Ft. Dallas area. They homesteaded land on the south side of the Miami River, and Sturtevant was elected to the state legislature. Although Mrs. Brickell had seven children, she found time to help her husband with his trading business and managed it herself after his death.[2]

Mrs. Tuttle, Ephraim Sturtevant's daughter, visited her parents often during the 1870s. She loved the region so much that she bought a 640-acre tract of property on the north side of the Miami River. With the death of her husband in February 1886, Julia Tuttle increased her interest in Florida. She turned to John D. Rockefeller for assistance. This was not unusual at all, for the two had been fellow members of the Euclid Baptist Church in Cleveland during the 1860s and 1870s. Also, Mrs. Tuttle's father-in-law had been Rockefeller's first employer at Hewitt & Tuttle back in the late 1850s.[3]

Mrs. Tuttle requested that Rockefeller recommend her to his Standard Oil partner Henry Flagler for the position of housekeeper at the Ponce de Leon, which was being built at the time. Although Rockefeller did make the request, she did not obtain the position. That did not dissuade Mrs. Tuttle from other Florida plans. In 1889, she decided to sell her Cleveland home and holdings and move to the Miami area permanently, partially out of concern for her daughter's health.[4]

By 1891, Mrs. Tuttle, having firmly established herself at Ft. Dallas, hoped to influence Flagler to build his railroad into the area. With his announcement that the railroad would be built into the Lake Worth region, she set about to convince Flagler to extend the railroad even farther south. She realized that she needed convenient transportation facilities to entice guests to her newly built Hotel Miami. She visited Flagler at St. Augustine in 1893. This visit and a series of letters failed to convince him of a need to extend his railroad south of West Palm Beach. He tried to dissuade her gently in a letter to her of April 27 that his assistance was not needed: "With the waterway completed to Lake Worth, and a line of steamers to Miami, do you not think that your object would be accomplished as well as if the railroad was built?" As for her proposal to give him land if he would build his railroad to Miami: "I should certainly build it as soon as the development of the country will justify it, but with all my present undertakings, I dare not make the positive promise, no matter what inducement is offered." Flagler saw the Palm Beach and Lake Worth area as a semitropical paradise with great potential as a winter resort. He believed that additional enterprises in Miami would be a duplication of effort.[5]

James E. Ingraham, Flagler's principal land agent, saw the potential of Ft. Dallas long before Flagler. Part of Ingraham's enthusiasm for the Miami area went back to his relationship with Julia Tuttle. He had first met her at a dinner at her home in Cleveland in 1890. She had told him at that time that she intended to settle permanently in the Miami area. She had said that she would be willing to give a railroad one-half her property holdings in exchange for a transportation link to the north. At the time of that conversation, Ingraham was the president of Henry B. Plant's South Florida Railroad. Ingraham kept in touch with Mrs. Tuttle during two surveying expeditions he made through the Everglades in 1892, checking for possible South Florida Railroad routes. It was in the fall of that year that Flagler hired Ingraham as his land developer.[6]

The disastrous freezes of 1894–95 made Flagler aware of a possible need to extend his railway to the southern portion of the state. When the freezes occurred, he sent Ingraham to Ft. Dallas to investigate the situation there. Ingraham was at Julia Tuttle's side when she sent Flagler the bouquet of flowers. Tuttle's bouquet was a fitting symbol, but something more lasting was needed to convince Flagler. In the spring of 1895, J. R. Parrott asked officials of the Florida East Coast Canal and Transportation Company how much they were willing to give Flagler to have him build south of Lake Worth. Parrott stated that the decision to construct this extension rested with the large landowners of Dade and Monroe counties—intimating that land grants to Flagler were in order. The canal company responded with a pledge of 1,500 acres for each mile of the proposed seventy-mile extension from West Palm Beach to Miami. Following the canal company's lead, the Boston and Florida Atlantic Coast Land Company promised 10,000 acres for the Miami extension.[7]

As for Julia Tuttle, her final agreement with Flagler was beneficial to both parties. Although she did make substantial land concessions, she realized that the coming of the railroad assured the profitability of real estate remaining in her possession. She gave Flagler 100 acres for a hotel site, railroad terminal, and several business blocks. She and Flagler equally divided in alternating strips her 540 remaining acres. Flagler agreed to survey and clear the town site for streets and to provide a waterworks. In keeping with the expanded size of his railroad, Flagler changed the name of his railroad enterprises to the Florida East Coast Railway Company (FEC). The state approved the new company in September 1895, with the extension to Miami opening for public traffic on April 21, 1896.[8]

Mrs. Brickell gave Flagler one-half of her 640 acres on the south side of the Miami River. One of Flagler's lawyers, who was also editor of the *Miami Metropolis*, warned Parrott that the Brickell family expected equal treatment with the Tuttles. During the early stages of development, clearing operations had progressed more rapidly on the Tuttle side of the river, therefore threatening the potential of the Brickell's land sales.[9]

Flagler's relationship with the Tuttles was stormy. During her lifetime, Mrs. Tuttle borrowed heavily from Flagler in order to make improvements in her Miami property holdings. After several letters in which he gently encouraged her to pay off debts—many of which Flagler stood behind—in late 1896, he pointedly advised her to clear up her unsecured short-term debt. He did loan Mrs. Tuttle $22,000 against a mortgage on her Hotel

Miami. To protect his loan, he bought a $30,000 insurance policy on the hotel. This policy proved to be a wise investment because the structure burned in 1899, the year following Mrs. Tuttle's death. On the other hand, what dominated the relationship between Flagler and Mrs. Tuttle's estate was a debate over a purported antisaloon agreement. The deeds for Flagler lots stipulated that no liquor establishments were to be housed on the property. Flagler himself drank in moderation, but did not trust the lower classes with ardent spirits. Flagler contended that Mrs. Tuttle had agreed that the antiliquor provision would be written into her deeds. Since the Hotel Miami was not a part of the land agreement, it had been permitted to serve alcohol. As late as 1900, Flagler was uncompromising in his stand; but by 1902, although his principles had not changed, he gave up the antisaloon fight in Miami.[10]

Flagler's primary business activity in Miami, other than his railroad enterprise, was the expansion of his hotel interests. When Joseph Freeling, later to become secretary to Flagler's Miami hotel manager, visited Miami in 1890, an Indian mound occupied the future site of Flagler's Royal Palm Hotel. The fifteen-acre site was on the north side of the Miami River at Biscayne Bay. John Sewell, future mayor of Miami, conducted the March 1896 groundbreaking. Flagler's work force of 500 to 600 men completed construction of the Royal Palm in time for the 1897 winter season. Henry W. Merrill came from the Poinciana as the first manager of the Royal Palm. Although it did not formally open until January 1897, the first guest registered during the Christmas season of 1896. This special guest was John Jacob Astor, great-grandson and namesake of the original founder of the Astor fortune and himself the builder of the Astoria section of New York's Waldorf-Astoria Hotel.[11]

The Royal Palm, although smaller in size, was similar to the Poinciana. Its exterior was of a colonial design, painted in yellow with white trim. A sixteen-foot veranda was on the Biscayne Bay side of the hotel. Ionic and Corinthian columns supported the structure. One hundred of the 450 guest rooms had private baths. For entertainment, the hotel offered a billiard room, casino, and swimming pool. The Royal Palm was electric throughout, powered by its basement plant. In 1898, Flagler bought an additional seventy-five acres from the Tuttle estate, developing the Royal Palm golf links on this property, located one and one-quarter miles west of Miami.[12]

The Royal Palm became a popular hotel. The highlight of the social season, as elsewhere in the Flagler empire, was the Washington's Birthday Ball. The 1898 ball, attracting 1,000 socialites, was a benefit for the new Miami hospital. To accommodate his increasing clientele, Flagler spent

Hotel Royal Palm (1901), Flagler's resort hotel which opened in Miami in 1896

over $300,000 on additions to its physical plant between 1904 and 1907. For a quarter of a century, the hotel was the center of Miami's winter society.[13]

In addition to the Royal Palm, the Flagler hotel company operated the Hotel Biscayne. Joseph A. McDonald owned this hotel, which he had constructed in 1896. The hotel cost $23,000 to build and an additional $1,000 to furnish. H. E. Bemis, who supervised the Lake Mohawk (New York) Mountain House in the summer, became the hotel's first manager. The Flagler association with the Biscayne was short-lived for McDonald sold it before the 1899 winter season.[14]

In order to create demand for his other Miami land holdings, Flagler organized the Fort Dallas Land Company (FDLC) in 1895. Technically, he paid $8,000 for 80 percent of the stock issued in the company. The other 20 percent was divided equally between Joseph R. Parrott and James E. Ingraham, who became officers of the concern. The FDLC sold Miami lots for prices ranging from $50 to $1,000. Flagler permitted buyers to pay one-quarter of their purchase amount in cash, with the balance to be paid in three annual installments at 8 percent annual interest. The land company also built houses for permanent residents, using three basic designs with an average cost of $1,500 each.[15]

James E. Ingraham, with responsibility over the FDLC, sought various means to sell Miami lots. The FDLC had a slow beginning. During its first three years, the company sold only $10,827.21 in Miami lots; but by 1899, land sales were booming. In the autumn of 1902, Ingraham requested that Flagler give cash customers of Miami lots 10 to 15 percent discounts. Flagler denied this request, but did allow purchasers a sixty-day period for payment in full without any interest or penalties. Ingraham's request came at a time when Miami suffered a housing shortage. While on the one hand he sought discounts, on the other he requested that Flagler build more houses to relieve the shortage, but Flagler stated he did not have the ready cash for such a project.[16]

Persons associated with Flagler enterprises were heavily involved in the politics of early Miami. Joseph A. McDonald served as the community's mayor before it was incorporated on July 28, 1896. John B. Reilly, who had been McDonald's bookkeeper, became the first mayor of Miami after incorporation. Reilly was also an agent for the FDLC during his term in office. Frederick S. Morse, FDLC agent, and Walter S. Graham, Flagler attorney, joined McDonald on the first Miami city council. John Sewell, who served as mayor of Miami from 1903 to 1907, had been a foreman of a Flagler work gang that had cleared the Miami site in 1896. During that same year, Sewell had begun his clothing business in the town.[17]

Flagler financially assisted Miami during its infancy as he had earlier done for St. Augustine and West Palm Beach. R. E. McDonald opened the first public school in 1895 in an empty store building. Due to a lack of facilities, he had to turn away many children. Flagler gave $1,000 and donated three lots for a larger public school building. He also spent $8,000 to establish a hospital in 1898. True to his promise to Mrs. Tuttle, Flagler established a waterworks system for the city. He also created the Miami Electric Light and Power Company, which received its electricity from the power plant of the Royal Palm.[18]

In a May 1898 election, Dade County voters approved the removal of the county seat from Juno to Miami. Flagler, wishing to see the town take advantage of the opportunity, was dismayed when the county commissioners only appropriated $5,000 for a courthouse the following summer. He stated, "I have a great desire that Dade should become the banner county outside of Duval." During the general election of that year, the voters did approve a $10,000 bond issue for the construction of a courthouse. In spite of such efforts, some persons still resented Flagler. The *Florida East Coast Homeseeker,* Flagler's promotional publication based in Miami, criticized Flagler's detractors in the town: "We [Miami] are growing in spite of the little '8x10s' who stand in the street corners and talk of the 'good old times,' and inveigh mightily against monopolies, etc. What a great thing it will be when such monopolies as ours get control of the whole State, opening up the now worthless thousands upon thousands of acres of land, building railroads, towns, paying good wages, taxes, and making things 'get' generally."[19]

During its formative years, Miami had to counter its image as a disease-ridden area. A yellow fever epidemic swept the community in 1899. The first threats surfaced in late September. At first, it seemed the fever was under control, but by the latter part of October officials of the United States Surgeon General's office refused to permit passengers on FEC trains south of Fort Lauderdale. Flagler gave Miami $1,000 for a temporary hospital to assist in the fight. In addition, he loaned almost $4,000 to the Florida state board of health, which had already spent its 1899 allocation. By February 1900, the Surgeon General's office removed the quarantine and Miami returned to normal.[20]

The epidemic slowed, but did not halt Miami's growth. With yellow fever controlled, Miami's climate once again became a positive force in its development. Miami doubled in size during the decade preceding 1913. With a population of 10,875, in 1913, it ranked as Florida's fifth largest city. The migration of wealthy northerners swelled Miami during the winter months. In addition to Flagler's hotel, there were eight others in the community. During the 1910 winter season, the hotels provided accommodations for over 100,000 guests.[21]

Flagler directed most of his philanthropic activities in Miami toward its religious organizations. Many denominations were available for white Miamians, and there were three black congregations in the town by 1899. Flagler thought there were too many churches. When one layman proposed a union church for Miami, Flagler enthusiastically agreed with the theory: "For a great many years, I have felt that when people want to indulge in denominational prejudices, the time for them is when they can put their hands in their own pockets and pay for the luxury." There was a gap between Flagler's parsimonious theory and magnanimous practice. He made donations and gifts to several Miami religious groups, but he assisted his Presbyterian brethren most, having a building constructed for them. Although the Miami church was not on the same scale as the Memorial Church in St. Augustine, Flagler's obsessive attention to detail was still apparent. He personally negotiated the buying of hymn books and seat cushions. The furnishers of his hotels, New York's Pottier and Stymus, decorated the church's interior.[22]

Realizing the importance and power of the press, Flagler also concerned himself with the newspaper situation in Miami. Miami's first newspaper was the *Miami Metropolis*, which began in 1897. Walter S. Graham, its first editor, had been not only editor of the *Indian River Advocate* but also a Flagler lawyer in Titusville. Flagler donated property to Graham for the *Metropolis* building. The next year, Flagler loaned B. B. Tatum the necessary capital to buy the paper from Graham. The situation was a good one for Flagler until Joel and S. Bobo Dean, publishers of the *Palm Beach News*, secured a one-half interest in the *Metropolis* in 1905.[23]

Although Tatum remained president during the transition period, the newspaper became anti-Flagler under the Deans. In 1909, Flagler pronounced the tabloid to be " 'incurable.' The policy of the paper has been opposition to the F.E.C. Ry Co." Flagler even compiled a list of fifty-five prominent Miamians and compared it with the *Metropolis* advertisers. He happily reported to Parrott that none of the persons on the list bought advertising space in the newspaper. When one of its owners made an overture that Flagler interpreted as a blackmail attempt, he actively sought to counter the *Metropolis*. Rather than completely subsidize the *Morning News-Record*, the newspaper's competitor, Flagler sought to enlist the "monied co-operation of the merchants and business men of Miami." But in 1910, after the indirect effort failed, he bought the *Metropolis* and converted it into the *Miami Herald*.[24]

Miami served as the American link to Flagler's first foreign venture. In the latter 1890s, Flagler took his concept of an "American Riviera" to Nassau. In 1897, the *Nassau Guardian* announced Flagler's intention to expand into the British-controlled Bahamas. Flagler proposed the building of a one-half-million-dollar hotel with a pier at Nassau, a one-quarter-million-dollar steamship service, and the improvement of the Royal Victoria Hotel, then owned by the British government.[25]

The *Guardian* was elated at the prospects of America's winter resort king investing in Nassau. The newspaper noted that the government had built the Royal Victoria at an initial cost of £25,000. The annual interest payments on the hotel had been £1,250, while the government had leased it for only £400 per season. The authorities had also given a £6,000 annual steamship subsidy for twice-monthly New York service. In an address to the general assembly in December 1897, the Bahamian governor outlined Flagler's steamship service proposal. Flagler would provide the service once a week during the off-season. He would schedule two trips weekly during January and April with an additional weekly trip during February and March. The combined fare for a passenger traveling from New York to Miami by rail and thence to Nassau by ship could not exceed the current New York to Nassau steamship fare. The Bahamian government would provide an annual subsidy of £6,700 to Flagler's steamship company.[26]

The Bahamian government entertained Flagler and his party in January 1898 after passage of the bill that allowed him to begin steamship service. Both Flagler and the government had reason for celebration. The bill provided Flagler with an annual subsidy of £8,500 for ten years. There was no tariff on Flagler's building materials or meats imported for use by the hotels. Flagler bought the Victoria for £10,000. In exchange for these concessions, he was to build a new hotel with no less than 340 guest rooms. It was to be open at least ten weeks per year. He would give the government £2,500 for the building of a new barracks area to replace the one it had deeded to him. He promised to maintain fast and frequent mail and passenger service between Nassau and Miami.[27]

Flagler acquired private property next to these government lands in Nassau. He bought the Carthagena, a privately owned hotel, for £5,000 and another lot for £2,500. These purchases consolidated his control over the tourist industry of the island. His purchase of the Victoria and the Carthagena, which he renamed the Victoria Annex, were probably prompted in part to protect the revenue of his planned hotel. The Victoria remained open for several seasons. When it failed to attract guests, Flagler ordered it closed and its furniture moved to another of his hotels. Ever the legalist, Flagler noted in a 1901 reading of his agreement with the Bahamian government that it only required him to keep his *new* hotel in operation, but said nothing about the Victoria. The older hotel did not open after the 1901 season, although it was advertised for several years afterward in Flagler promotional material.[28]

The construction of the Colonial, Flagler's new Nassau hotel, began in the spring of 1898, with Joseph A. McDonald in charge of the project. McDonald built the hotel on a slope on the south side of the harbor. The side facing the harbor consisted of seven stories, with five on the landward side. McDonald also built an electric power plant, waterworks, and an ice plant to serve the hotels. The Colonial had many of the amenities that had come to be expected of a Flagler hotel, including a 2,500-yard, nine-hole golf course developed around an old fort; twelve golf ranges from one tee area; tennis courts; and a swimming pool.[29]

The Colonial provided its guests with a busy social season. An orchestra performed three times daily. There were weekly "hops," Saturday night formal dances and informal dances on Wednesday evening. Without a hint of irony, the highlight of the winter social season in the British possession was the Washington's Birthday Ball. Flagler would not have regarded this as odd, for his Nassau properties were an integral part of *his* empire. He wrote Sir William Van Horn, owner of the Canadian Pacific and Cuba railways, "I am sending you specimens of our East Coast literature for the coming winter. One you will observe is devoted to the Bahamas. It shows how we 'take in' our foreign possession. Something of this kind I think could be done to our mutual benefit for Cuba another year."[30]

After Cuba gained its independence from Spain in 1898, Flagler took an interest in the island's potential. There is no evidence that he ever campaigned for American involvement in the Spanish-American War. Once independence was achieved, however, he sought to invest in Cuba's economic future. He had large investments in Van Horn's Cuba Company, owner of the Cuba Railway. In March 1902, Flagler made the final payment of his $250,000 stock subscription in the company. He also held $75,000 of Cuba Company bonds.[31]

Due to his Florida experience, Flagler knew that Van Horn would be overwhelmed with many schemes promising economic gain. In 1902, he wrote Van Horn, "I have no doubt but that you have been offered the whole of Havana by this time." For his part, Flagler aided both himself and Van Horn by selling tickets for Cuba Railway destinations through the FEC. In 1909, an owner of Cuban land offered Flagler twenty-five acres of Havana if he would build a hotel on the site.[32] Flagler refused this opportunity for direct investment in Cuba.

To connect the mainland and island portions of his empire, Flagler created the Florida East Coast Steamship Company. In 1897, he signed a contract for the construction of its first new ship. Parrott wrote to Flagler on August 23, 1897, "Replying to your favor of the 20th inst. in regard to name 'Miami' for the new ship. I think the name is very pretty and would help us from an advertising standpoint." The *Miami* consisted of three decks and two tiers of staterooms. These staterooms were of white mahogany paneling, each containing running water. The Cramps yards of Philadelphia built the all-electric *Miami*. The twin-screwed vessel was capable of seventeen knots an hour. It began its schedule to Nassau after a banquet and ball in Miami on January 17, 1898. It achieved its most notable service when it brought Theodore Roosevelt and his Rough Riders home to New York at the end of the Spanish-American War.[33]

The Florida East Coast Steamship Company had three ships in operation by the 1899 winter season. The company switched the *Miami* to the Havana schedule. The newly purchased *Southern Cross*, with a 300-passenger capacity, plied the waters between Miami and Nassau. The ladies' saloon apartments of the *Southern Cross* had carved cherry berth fronts and mahogany wash stands. The main saloon had a white and gold color scheme with a finish of quartered oak. Triple expansion engines powered the twin-screwed vessel. The *City of Key West* connected Miami with the American island city. Unlike Flagler's deep-water vessels, it was a light-draft, side-wheel craft. The 900-ton ship contained seventy first-class staterooms. The *City of Key West* made the Miami-to-Key West run in ten hours. Other Flagler ships, such as the *Miami* and *Cocoa*, made the Miami-to-Havana run in fifteen hours. An 1899 incident involving the *Miami* indicated that Flagler rarely missed an economic opportunity. During the off-season, it was in a Philadelphia dry dock. Before the *Miami* returned south, Flagler used it as a tourist vessel during the International Yacht Races and earned $7,000 from the venture.[34]

When Flagler initially invested in Miami, it lacked facilities for ocean-going ships. In 1897, he began to deepen Biscayne Bay to create an adequate harbor for the city. In announcing Flagler's intentions, the *Miami Metropolis* emphasized the importance of the project to the area's future. Flagler brought in a dredge that deepened Biscayne Bay at the rate of 6,000 cubic yards every twenty-four hours. When he first began the project, he did so without federal assistance; but he quickly remedied that situation. A Standard Oil lobbyist got congressmen and senators appointed to the Rivers and Harbors Committee of each house who would act favorably on the Miami project. The lobbying effort was successful: an 1899 Senate committee placed the Biscayne Bay project on the continuous contract list with an initial appropriation of $100,000. The *Miami Metropolis* estimated that the federal grants would eventually top $10 million with a 200-foot channel 18 feet deep leading to Norris' Cut, which would cost an additional $3 million to dredge.[35]

Flagler sought more aid from the federal government after the initial $100,000. He asked Parrott to press the War Department for payments due since "The calls made upon me for money are simply overwhelming, and I am feeling poorer than Lazarus." E. M. Ashley, Flagler's friend and business associate, went to Washington in 1900 to lobby for additional Biscayne Bay appropriations. These efforts were also successful, for by the spring of 1902, Congress had committed a total of $300,000 to the project to deepen the bay to sixteen feet. At the same time Flagler began considering an eighteen-foot depth, which would require additional federal money. Senator Stephen Elkins of West Virginia, James McMillan of Michigan, and James Taliaferro of Florida were instrumental in obtaining additional legislation in 1902. The resulting appropriation of $300,000 allowed the final dimensions of the harbor at Miami to be 1,200 yards by 300 yards with a depth of 18 feet. In addition, the Florida East Coast Railway provided docking and warehouse facilities. These improvements led to the designation of Miami as an official port of entry for the United States.[36]

During his Standard Oil years, Flagler had learned the value of "cooperation." His uniting of the Florida East Coast Steamship Company with the Plant Steamship Company to form the Peninsular and Occidental Steamship Company (P&O) on July 1, 1900, was merely a continuation of this policy. Flagler had the greatest influence in the P&O, even though he and the Plant Investment Company held equal shares in the new company. He served as the first president, and upon his resignation in 1901, Joseph R. Parrott served as his figurehead president. During the early P&O years, Flagler showed a marked preference for the old Florida East Coast Steamship routes and ships. The partnership did give him some power over competition originating from Port Tampa, which had served as the home port of the Plant Steamship Company. Due to a change in Plant ownership, the Flagler-Plant Investment Company partnership in the P&O lasted less than two years.[37]

In 1902, the Plant Investment Company sold its interest in the P&O to the Atlantic Coast Line Railway as part of its general consolidation into the larger road. At the time, the P&O owned four of the old Florida East Coast Steamship Company ships valued at more than $400,000 and $135,000 of Key West terminal property. The Atlantic Coast Line bought the Plant interest in the P&O for about $400,000. Plant personnel failed to obtain Flagler's permission for the sale, but Flagler noted to Parrott, "I don't object to it [the sale] at all. I think it is better for me."[38]

Flagler continued to be protective of Miami's part of the P&O traffic. Parrott had understood that the Havana service of the P&O was to be from Port Tampa. But Flagler did not agree, "It may be all right to make it that way, but it seems to me that we should have a contract between Miami and Havana." In his statistical diary, Flagler kept a comparative record of the Port Tampa–Havana service. A Miami-Havana connection was made, and one December 1908 one-way trip of the *Miami* to Havana earned over $900. Flagler was still not satisfied: in 1909, he noted that the P&O received more from a passenger traveling from the Florida east coast to Havana than the Flagler railway received for the same passenger traveling from Jacksonville to the embarkation point. Flagler suggested that the railroad skirt government regulations and hide a rate increase in the wharfage.[39]

Whenever possible, Flagler made sure the P&O did not infringe on the profitability of his own empire: cooperation did have limits. Functioning as part of Flagler's system, the steamship company had to assume its proper fiscal responsibilities. When the P&O missed several trips to Nassau in 1909, Flagler instructed the company treasurer to make certain that the penalty came out of the steamship company's £3,500 annual subsidy rather than from the Colonial Hotel's £1,500 stipend.[40]

After the successes of his foreign investments, Flagler decided to include southerners as customers for a summer resort clientele. Instead of appealing to northerners during the winter months as he did with his south Florida hotels, he hoped to attract wealthy southerners to the seacoast of north Florida during the summer. In the fall of 1900, Flagler commissioned J. A. McGuire to begin plans for a hotel at Atlantic Beach, located two miles north of Pablo Beach and fifteen miles east of Jacksonville. Named the Continental, the hotel was to be the traditional Flagler System yellow with white trim. McGuire shingled the exterior of the upper two stories and the center section of the hotel. He built the hotel parallel to the beach and had it ready for its June 1, 1901, opening.[41]

All the amenities of the Flagler winter resorts were also present at his summer hotel. Flagler's railroad offered excellent parlor and sleeping car connections to the Continental. The hotel had a pier 800 feet long and 20 feet wide and a beach with hard-packed sand, making an excellent speedway for automobiles and bicycles.[42]

Despite these measures, the Continental did not become a "summer Palm Beach." Although the hotel was a heavy loser its first season, Flagler remained optimistic about its potential. In fact, when one business acquaintance suggested that another hotel north of Florida's Atlantic Beach be named "South Atlantic Beach," Flagler discouraged it on the grounds that his resort might someday rival the better-known Atlantic Beach of New Jersey. But this did not occur. During its first five years of operation, the Continental suffered a net loss of over $50,000. Flagler blamed its failure on the lack of wealth and population in the South. He bitterly noted to Parrott, "there is *a possibility* that before the building rots down, we may be able to make some money out of it, but I must confess that the prospect seems rather remote." The Continental suffered an embarrassing end. First, Flagler changed its name to the Atlantic Beach Hotel in 1907. In 1909, he sought to rid himself of its operating expenses by renting it to another party. Finally, in 1919, a fire destroyed the structure.[43]

In spite of the failure of the Continental venture, Florida's east coast was the American counterpart of the European Riviera by World War I. Miami and Nassau are examples of Flagler's ability to improve the image of an area. Mrs. Julia Tuttle realized that without the Flagler railway Miami would be unable to become a resort center. The Bahamian government in

Nassau also discovered what a millionaire could do for the island. Both Miami entrepreneurs and Nassau officials were willing to grant concessions to Flagler. With land and subsidies, he was able to control not only his integrated system of transportation and hotels but also the general economy of these areas, especially Miami. In that city, he directly exercised power over the electric and water services and, to some degree, the churches, politicians, and newspapers.

The Cuban investment and the merger of Flagler's steamship line with the Plant line to form the Peninsular and Occidental Steamship Company demonstrated Flagler's business flexibility. In the first situation, he sought to capitalize on the economic opportunity that the independence of the island offered. In the steamship merger, he was able to control potential competition. To this list of accomplishments must be added a failure. In the building of the Continental at Atlantic Beach, Flagler failed to realize, until it was too late, the poor economic condition of the South. Southern resorts existed on revenue produced by a northern leisure class. The American Riviera was in—but not of—the South.

10

Land Baron

ACCORDING TO THE Jacksonville *Florida Times-Union*, Flagler's role in an 1893 canal venture was that of a charitable businessman: "The people along the east coast should bear in mind that Mr. Henry Flagler is at the head of the Florida East Coast Canal and Transportation Company, and everyone knows that he is not after the lands; and they must know, that when he does complete the project, the lands are not likely to bring a paying price during his lifetime." At least one of Flagler's associates in the canal project was not as kind as the *Times-Union*. George F. Miles, acting as an intermediary between Flagler and Albert P. Sawyer, the head of a cooperating land development company, warned Sawyer of the pitfalls of an alliance with Flagler: "I am glad you referred the matter to me as the East Coast officials are somewhat 'foxy' and they are not bashful about asking favors." Much of the east coast of Florida had been part of the state's public domain before Henry Flagler appeared on the scene. How Flagler obtained and distributed his land holdings was a debatable subject, even while the process was occurring. There is no doubt that the transfer from public to private ownership of vast amounts of land along the Florida east coast occurred within a context of intrigue, manipulation, and political chicanery. However, Flagler speeded the process of settlement in that area through the land promotion activities of his railroad. As Florida Governor Francis P. Fleming noted in 1889, "It has been the history of railroad construction in our State that it has usually preceded the demand for transportation."[1]

It was apparent why Florida's governing officials would become interested in a wealthy man like Flagler. He had the financial capacity to build a railroad system; all he needed was incentive. The state at first promised Flagler the standard 3,840 acres of public land for each mile of road built. His four original lines obtained over half of the public lands that the state originally promised them. By 1892, the state had deeded Flagler's railroad companies 251,000 acres, all in the northern part of Florida.[2] With this kind of beginning, the ability of Flagler's railroads to get land grants seemed favorable indeed. The Florida politicians of the late nineteenth century believed that their liberal land policies toward railroads and other transportation agencies would be both the most inexpensive and most rapid means of developing unsettled areas of the state.

Florida politicians gave Flagler preferential treatment. An example was the incorporation of the Jacksonville, St. Augustine and Indian River Railway in 1892, and the land grant the legislature gave the company the following year. Although pre–Civil War legislation was still in effect, the legislature passed a special land grant law to encourage Flagler's activities south of Daytona Beach. For each mile of constructed road, the state would transfer to Flagler's road 8,000 acres, rather than the standard 3,840 acres. Problems immediately arose because not enough public land was available. The administration of President Grover Cleveland, a conservative Democrat, proved not to be as cooperative as Florida state officials. In 1885, the federal government, amid rumors that lands other than swamp areas were being given as land grants, stopped its donations to Florida. The federal action did not initially affect Flagler's relationship with Florida. For its part, the state reserved for Flagler anticipated federal land transfers at the tip of southern Florida.[3] The reservation, of course, rested on the ability of the state to obtain the land from the federal government.

A worsening in the relationship between Flagler and Florida officials complicated the land grant situation. William Sherman Jennings became governor of Florida in 1901. Unlike his predecessors, he interpreted his role to be that of keeper of the public domain, rather than its distributor. In spite of the fact that the federal government had finally granted three million acres to Florida in April 1903, the Internal Improvement Fund of Florida (IIF) trustees supported Jennings in a series of decisions announced in 1904. When Florida East Coast officials applied for land grants "alleged to have been earned by it and its predecessor, the Jacksonville, St. Augustine, and Indian River Railway Co., amounting to 2,040,000," the request was denied.[4] This decision reflected a new philosophy that included reforming the loose public land grant policy begun by conservative Florida politicians during the late nineteenth century. The Progressives of the early twentieth century were convinced that government could do a better and less exploitive job of development than private interests. They thought that Flagler and other developers had taken advantage of the state. Due to the delayed federal grants to Florida, the Progressives could attempt to stop the land transfers to at least some of the railroads.

In rejecting the FEC application, Governor Jennings noted that the 1850 federal land grant to Florida related specifically to the reclamation of swamp lands. He sought to nullify a series of legislative acts that had authorized grants to canal and railroad companies, insisting that they did not meet the original intent of the law. In December 1904, the trustees revoked the 1882 resolution granting the Jacksonville, St. Augustine and Halifax River Railway alternate sections of land in townships adjoining the railroad. The new political leaders in Florida continued their Progressive attitude toward Flagler's company and other railroads by repeatedly denying the roads' petitions for land.[5]

When Napoleon Bonaparte Broward became governor in 1905, he appointed Jennings as general counsel for the IIF trustees. Jennings was still not satisfied with the effect of earlier directives aimed at the FEC. He argued that Flagler's original roads could not transfer their land grant rights to the FEC. James E. Ingraham, the FEC vice-president in charge of Flagler's land development, objected to this point of view and questioned its legality. In a letter to the Jacksonville *Florida Times-Union*, Ingraham reviewed the entire public land debate from the FEC's perspective. According to him, the railroads that Flagler had originally bought during the 1880s were eligible for a total of 472,473 acres of public land, but had received only 251,000 acres. The state had failed to deed any of the property offered under the 1893 special land grant that was designed to encourage the building of a railroad south of Daytona.[6]

Flagler's efforts to obtain Florida public lands were more effective after Broward left office in 1909. The new governor, Albert Gilchrist, met with Ingraham, who then informed Flagler that the chief executive seemed receptive to the FEC's position concerning land grants. Jennings had not been successful in blocking all land transfers; on at least one occasion even he agreed that Flagler's claims should be honored. This situation arose when Ingraham asked State Attorney General Park Trammell for a ruling on the validity of a land grant that the state had made to the Palatka and Indian River Railway Company. Although Flagler had never owned this line, he bought a one-half interest in its land grant through the Florida Commercial Company. Trammell ruled that the 134,000-acre grant was legally binding on the IIF and that the FEC was entitled to one-half this amount under a quitclaim deed. With Jennings concurring in this opinion, the IIF trustees ordered 67,000 acres deeded to the FEC in 1910.[7]

This action by the state did not end its legal difficulties with Flagler. It was only the beginning of further company quests. The FEC brought two suits against the IIF for additional land claims. The company agreed to drop the action and to relinquish all claims to public lands, however, if the IIF would agree to a deed of approximately 210,000 acres. The IIF accepted this arrangement. Some of the land, such as a seventy-four-square-mile tract in the area southwest of West Palm Beach, was valuable to the Flagler enterprises. However, the bulk of the grant was in the swampy southwestern tip of Florida near Cape Sable.[8] Although this compromise was less than 10 percent of the land Flagler had claimed, it was a practical victory for him. He now had clear title to important agricultural acreage in south Florida. Considering his previous battles with state officials, this compromise was as much as he could have expected. In the final analysis, Flagler's development of the Florida east coast was a financial bargain for the state. He had built his railroad under the assumption that he would be gaining vast amounts of land for development. With the decisions and compromises of the Progressive era, Flagler built his railroad south of Daytona at practically no cost to Florida's public domain.

There were indirect avenues open for Flagler to tap the Florida public lands. He had more success acquiring property from large Florida land-owners than he had with the IIF. These corporations received their original holdings either directly or indirectly from the IIF, as had Flagler. Two of these companies proved to be especially good sources of land for Flagler. One, the Florida Coast Line Canal and Transportation Company, organized in 1881, developed an inland waterway along Florida's east coast. The IIF was to give the canal company 3,840 acres of public lands for each mile of canal constructed. By the time it completed the route from St. Augustine to Biscayne Bay, the state had granted it 516,480 acres. In order to develop settlement and thus increase the value of its holdings, the canal company sold large amounts of acreage to the Boston and Florida Atlantic Coast Land Company. Albert P. Sawyer, the principal owner of the Domestic Electrical Manufacturing Company of Boston, was also president of the Boston Company. In 1891 alone, he purchased 100,000 acres from the canal company.[9]

Finding itself in financial difficulty in 1892, the canal company requested assistance from Flagler. George F. Miles, one of its directors and general manager of its Florida properties, negotiated an arrangement whereby Flagler gave the company $100,000. In return, the canal company gave

177

Flagler bonds and a note for the difference in the two amounts. Flagler became the figurehead president of the company, although he did not own any large block of its stock. The arrangement allowed the canal company to resume dredging with new equipment. The owners were elated at the prospects. Not only had Flagler improved their financial position, but the possibility of his building a railroad into the area of their grant increased the opportunity for immense profits from land sales.[10]

In his dealings with the canal and Boston companies, Flagler effectively used his best weapon, the potential availability of transportation. For the extension of the railroad from Daytona to Lake Worth, the canal company promised Flagler a donation of 76,500 acres. The canal company responded with a pledge of 1,500 acres for each completed mile of the proposed seventy-mile extension from West Palm Beach to Miami. Following the canal company's lead, the Boston company originally offered Flagler 10,000 acres for the Miami extension. But rather than a straight gift of this amount, George F. Miles suggested to Sawyer that Flagler take a one-half interest in the Boston company's planned immigrant communities in the area. This would profit both Flagler and Sawyer, Miles argued. The completion of the FEC would increase the value of the remaining Boston company properties before sales occurred. Of course, Flagler would benefit from the sales of the large amount of acreage he was receiving. Miles also had something else in mind. As he noted to Sawyer, the Boston company owners would be able "to prevent our lands from being discriminated against by such a powerful organization as the RR Company would be if they [*sic*] decided to offer advantages to settlers which we are not in a position to parallel."[11]

The Boston company and the FEC began this joint venture in 1896. Early that year, Ingraham informed Miles that the Flagler organization had an opportunity to locate 400 Danish families in a colony in south Dade County to be called Modelo, a site twenty miles above Miami near the railroad. Ingraham had contacted a group of Danes in the Chicago area. The Chicago organizers of the venture obtained 2,000 acres of the proposed colony, thereby giving them management control of Modelo. At first, the venture moved along well. By the fall of 1896, Miles had platted the colonies of Modelo and Hallandale, a Swedish cooperative agricultural colony nearby, and lots were ready for sale. Ingraham's concept of the ideal colonist remained consistent throughout the period: "the understanding is the Agents are to get purchasers who have money, and are able to make their payments and improve the lands, so that the prospects are very good for getting two first class colonies in these two locations."[12]

Problems, especially in the Hallandale colony, developed. Miles reported to Sawyer in January 1897 that sales were moving slowly, partly because of the poor location of the colony. Otto Zetterlund, general manager of the Halland Land Company, complained that the possibilities of freezes and yellow fever made the selling of Florida land more difficult than land in the West and Southwest. There may have been, however, a much more human cause for the troubles. The Reverend F. Jacobson, pastor of the Swedish Evangelical Lutheran Bethlehem Church in New York City, reviewed some of the complaints of potential Swedish immigrants to Hallandale. He recommended that the pre-December 1896 prices remain in effect until June 1897 in order to encourage potential settlers. Although he thought most of the Hallandale operation was beneficial for the colonists, he was outraged at the freight rates being charged by the FEC. He stated that owners of first-quality furniture costing only $37.00 were being charged $20.00 freight to ship it from Jacksonville to Hallandale—"The same goods could have been sent to Kansas City and back again for less than $20.00."[13]

Railway officials were unimpressed with this type of plea. Ingraham's solution for the settlement problem was to bypass the Halland Land Company and send his own agent directly to Sweden. During four months of 1897, FEC agent John A. Bostrom visited Stockholm to recruit potential residents for south Florida colonies. Although the Swedish government opposed the colonization effort, which would take part of the labor force from the homeland, Bostrom was successful in his advertising effort. He promoted the colonies in the Swedish press and he issued a pamphlet in Swedish. He also obtained permission from the Swedish consul's office to serve as a permanent representative of his Florida employers in directing Swedes to the state.[14]

Jacobson's ire and Ingraham's response raises the question of who was benefiting most from the settlement of south Florida. One area newspaper claimed that the railroad would greatly profit from the settler's presence but more from high freight rates than from the selling of land. During a family's first year in the Miami area, the newspaper predicted, the FEC would earn at least $400 in freight charges. This would include $25 to $100 for lumber and other necessities needed to build a house, $25 for fertilizer and crates delivered for the tomato farmer, and $300 for 1,000 crates of vegetables shipped north during the harvest season.[15]

Sawyer and his associates were well aware of the kind of partner they had in Flagler. He and his employees had often demonstrated their power and shrewdness. In discussing a right-of-way matter, Frederick Morse, a

Flagler land agent, warned Sawyer to cooperate with the railroad if he wished to profit from his speculative land venture. If Sawyer ever forgot about Flagler's power, Miles, now doubling as the Florida agent for the Boston company in addition to his canal company duties, reminded him. Miles became paranoid concerning the railroad's power. In 1902, he strongly suspected that Flagler had suppressed the canal company financially in order to prevent a waterway along the east coast that would compete with the FEC. Although there is no evidence of such a scheme, Miles still urged Albert Sawyer's son Haydn not to appoint land agents jointly with the railroad.[16]

At times Miles negotiated well from a relatively weak position. In 1898, he persuaded Flagler to accept canal company lands in southern Dade County at the rate of $6.00 an acre in exchange for Flagler's interest in the canal company. Miles was also confident that a group of businessmen from Jacksonville could pressure Flagler into cooperating with a West Palm Beach drainage operation. Meanwhile, Miles advised W. I. Metcalf, Dade County Commission lawyer, not to implement the state charter, which allowed the county to perform drainage operations in the interior. In order to obtain Metcalf's cooperation, Miles promised him that a private operation would be forthcoming.[17]

While Miles was at work, Flagler moved independently in a similar direction. In late 1903, the FEC officials publicly criticized the Dade County Commission drainage contract. J. R. Parrott stated that the tax would be an unbearable $60,000 burden on the FEC, and he expressed fears that other communities might begin the same type of tax if a precedent were set. Flagler officials also argued that their poorly located land would be assessed, and therefore taxed, at the same rate as other property located near public roads.[18]

Flagler stopped both Miles and the Dade County Commission. As a substitute for the county commission plan, a private venture did indeed emerge, but under the direction of Flagler rather than Miles. Flagler, under the 1906 plan, agreed to cooperate with the Boston and canal companies in reclaiming 8,000 acres west of Lake Worth. In addition to reclamation, a wagon road several miles long would be built. The entire operation was to cost $50,000.[19]

The financial burden of development did not rest entirely with Flagler and his large land company allies. West Palm Beach merchants, wishing to attract settlers, pledged to purchase 1,000 acres of the drainage area at $25.00 an acre. At first the FEC, Boston company, and canal company jointly held the Lake Worth property, as Miles preferred. Ingraham began negotiating the purchase of all the property in the proposed drainage area. By the end of November, Flagler had bought his partners' interests in the area for $40,000.[20]

Immediately following the purchase, Flagler increased the scope of the drainage operation. The FEC announced a one-year reclamation project consisting of twelve miles of dikes to be three feet higher than Lake Clark, the inland lake near Lake Worth. The FEC spent $20,000 for wagon roads. The main drainage canal from Lake Clark to Lake Worth was to have a lock at the inland lake sixteen feet above sea level. The total cost, including the land purchased, was $120,000. When the project was completed, the FEC offered the land at the rate of $25.00 an acre.[21] Once Flagler had the entire operation in his own hands, he made major improvements. He was willing to take risks—if he clearly saw future profits; however, he wanted control and did not wish to see others easily profiting from his money and risk taking.

In order to protect Flagler's land interests from politicians in Tallahassee, Ingraham led an effort in 1906 that supposedly was an immigration association of the large land companies of the state. The five original companies in the association owned a total of six million acres in Florida. Ingraham then invited the Boston and canal companies to join. The assessment was to be six mills per acre for promotion and development work. The real purpose of the association was to block the land policies of Governor Broward's administration, especially a proposed $.10-per-acre drainage tax. According to Miles, action before the May Democratic primary was necessary in order to elect conservatives to the legislature. The association would act as a lobbying agent to keep land company holdings "from practical confiscation by irresponsible politicians." Defeat of the drainage tax did not need the help of the immigration association lobbyists since Flagler and the Boston company were successful in a court suit against the state over the drainage matter.[22]

There are really two stories concerning Henry Flagler and the public domain of Florida. One has Flagler attempting to obtain land directly from the Internal Improvement Fund of Florida. In this area he was constantly thwarted, first by the federal government's freeze on donations in 1885, and then by Progressives within the Florida Democratic Party during the early years of the twentieth century. The other story is the intriguing account of Flagler's indirect methods of securing land through other corporations, most importantly the Florida Coast Line Canal and Transportation Company and the Boston and Florida Atlantic Coast Land Company. Flagler's relations with these two companies provide an excellent view of land speculation and promotion. While owners of the canal company obtained their public land with relative ease, their lack of money caused them to turn to Flagler for the actual development of their speculative ventures.

The land, without exploitation, was of little use to Flagler or anyone else. He began to combine the sales of his land acquisitions into his comprehensive plan for development of the Florida east coast. In November 1892, he hired James E. Ingraham as general manager of the Jacksonville, St. Augustine and Indian River Railway, and placed him in charge of its land department. Ingraham brought to his new job a thorough understanding of Florida. The son of an Episcopal minister, Ingraham had been born in Wisconsin in 1850. His father's frequent moves throughout the Midwest honed Ingraham's outgoing nature, enabling him to make friends easily.

Ingraham first entered Florida railroading in 1876 as an employee of Henry S. Sanford. Sanford invested in Florida real estate and railroads after a career in government service, which included a period as United States ambassador to Belgium. Unlike Flagler, Sanford was primarily an absentee landlord, with infrequent visits to Florida. Ingraham first built the South Florida Railroad from Sanford to Kissimmee, becoming its president in 1879. The following year, Ingraham convinced Henry Plant to buy 60 percent of the enterprise from Sanford. Ingraham, now a part of the Plant System team, continued as president of the road. It was in this capacity that he attracted Flagler's attention with his survey of the Everglades for a possible South Florida Railway route.[23]

The extroverted Ingraham served the FEC well in his new public relations position. When he returned from a trip to the Everglades shortly after Flagler's announcement of his appointment, the Juno *Tropical Sun* had the highest praise for the decision: "If Mr. Flagler had used a search-light of a million candle power—he could not have found a more able or affable gentleman to represent his business interests in Florida."[24]

As Flagler organized each of his land companies, he appointed Ingraham to its presidency. The first of these was the Model Land Company (MLC). Although Flagler first created it as his colonizing agency for Modelo and other colonies in south Florida, it eventually became the primary land company in the Flagler System. Flagler began the company in 1896, giving himself a paper stock issue of twenty-eight shares. He issued Parrott and Ingraham one share each and appointed them as MLC officers. The MLC immediately assumed the debts due Flagler personally through the land

department of the railway. He later had two other stock subscriptions totaling 4,970 shares issued to himself. Each of these shares held a paper value of
$1,000, thereby erasing an almost $5 million debt the land company technically owed Flagler.[25]

In 1902, Flagler's auditor began transferring title of FEC lands to the
MLC. By crediting the transfer to the FEC, the financial position of the
railway appeared stronger for purposes of borrowing on bond markets. By
the end of 1909, the MLC had a negative balance of $1,022,449.62. That
year, Flagler ordered his auditor to put all nonrailway lands in the MLC
account.[26]

From time to time, Flagler formed other sales units under the FEC land
department. He created the Perrine Grant Land Company, Chuluota Land
Company, Okeechobee Company, and the Fort Dallas Land Company to
sell lands in specific territories as indicated in their respective titles. The
Fort Dallas company, responsible for sales in Miami and its vicinity, was
the most important of these subordinate units. The Chuluota venture was
not successful. The MLC set aside 11,000 acres for an agricultural colony at
Chuluota, but the land company could not sell it.[27]

Of the agricultural operations, Flagler and his associates concentrated
on the Perrine Grant Land Company. The Perrine grant was located along
Biscayne Bay eighteen miles south of Miami, and it extended six miles west
of the bay. The federal government granted it to Dr. Henry Perrine in 1838
for the introduction and cultivation of tropical trees and plants. Indians
killed Perrine at Indian Key in 1840, and his work ceased. In the 1890s,
Perrine heirs and their associates began colonizing the area, planting exotic
food and medicinal plants. This venture met with mixed success. In 1896,
Flagler had S. H. Richmond, a practical civil engineer from Boston, survey
the Perrine grant. Richmond reported that the tract contained excellent
land, both of the pine and muck variety: "There are no less than a thousand
acres of good orange land in the center of the grant, a small amount—of
fine hammock—a good water front . . . and of course acres of worthless
rock."[28]

By the latter part of 1898, Flagler's land department entered into a partnership with the Perrine heirs, organizing the Perrine company with
Flagler owning a one-half interest. In 1902, he bought another one-ninth
interest, for which the railway paid $9,000. During that year, Flagler
loaned the land company $20,000. He considered the impact on the Perrine
company when making decisions about the area: "I have hoped . . . that
the extension of the Railroad would bring those lands [the Perrine Grant]

into the market, and that they would bring a profit to the owners. I do not want to speculate with the holdings of our associates in this company. If it turns out profitably, I would much rather they would share the success."[29]

Although land sales created some operating capital, Flagler used them primarily to provide his railway with a permanent clientele. He realized that if his colonization schemes were successful, income would naturally come from the freight fees paid by the settlers to transport goods to and from the market. He and his associates used a variety of devices to create demand for their land. The *Florida East Coast Homeseeker*, begun in 1899 by the land department of the FEC, distributed information to potential settlers. E. V. Blackman, editor of this monthly journal, usually featured a story of a Florida east coast community, and included weather reports, short news items, and real estate advertising. Many of the *Homeseeker* articles dealt with agriculture, with Blackman often referring to profitable citrus crops. The *Homeseeker* sounded a constant, positive note for migration to all of Florida. Parrott insisted that the *Homeseeker* make no unkind public remarks about Flagler's competition on the west coast of Florida.[30]

Flagler System personnel recognized public relations as an important function. The best way to accomplish its ends was to bond the Flagler enterprises with local people and organizations. When the Swedish Evangelical Lutheran Bethlehem Church of Brooklyn began colonization efforts in Flagler System territory, Flagler donated a parcel of Florida land to it. In thanking Ingraham, the pastor recognized the temporal value of the donation: "The object of the donation is to advertise land to other churches." Flagler also gave northern newspaper editors free trips to the state. He even recognized the value of the United States Weather Bureau, donating property in Miami for a weather station so that Miami's pleasant winter climate could become known nationwide.[31]

Without neglecting his hotels, Flagler concentrated his main advertising efforts on attracting permanent residents. Many of his public relations ventures were major undertakings. The Travellers' Information Company promoted the system in thirteen northern cities. Its task was primarily to attract settlers to Florida. During the 1890s, the Flagler road designed a special car named Florida On Wheels, which toured throughout the Midwest, with a special stop at Chicago's 1892 Columbian Exposition.[32]

Flagler insisted that advertising had to show results. When the St. Augustine *Church Register* asked that the land company renew an advertisement, Ingraham refused. Attached to a cutout of the old advertisement was a note in longhand that stated, "Don't think this has brought any business." Flagler opposed direct financial support of east coast institutions whenever possible: "I note what you [Ingraham] say about the series of Farmers Institutes along the East Coast, and that you hope 'without responsibility on our part,' to teach the farmer, etc., etc. I sincerely hope that it will not only be without responsibility, *but without expense* to us. I fully endorse your views of economy in the conduct of your Department, for it seems to me that the East Coast is now so well known that we ought to stop all expensive advertising."[33]

As with so many other aspects of his Florida enterprises, Flagler turned to his transportation agency for special inducements. The FEC offered inexpensive transportation for potential investors: FEC special excursion rates for homeseekers and even lower rates for settlers. Ingraham aided the homeseeker at both ends of the line. On one occasion, in 1900, the Detroit office of the Travellers' Information Company informed Ingraham of 140 homeseekers who were planning an excursion to Florida. At the receiving end, Ingraham arranged for representatives to greet the travelers at Fort Pierce, West Palm Beach, Fort Lauderdale, Dania, and Miami. When a person came to Florida as a homeseeker and decided to settle, the Flagler System offered special rates: one-half the regular one-way second-class ticket plus $2.00. The settler rates were much lower than normal fares, especially for purchasers of FEC lands. The railway's land department granted freight rebates of 50 percent to new settlers buying Flagler property, with heads of households receiving free transportation.[34]

The FEC land department on occasion played an active role in assisting immigrant groups. In fact, Flagler helped the Danish colony of White City become established when its founder, Louis Pio, died. Flagler set up an "Immigrant House" in the colony to aid the destitute. By 1897, the colony, which had struggled at its 1893 beginning, was a permanent, ongoing operation. During the early years of the twentieth century, the FEC cooperated with the Yamato Colony Association in establishing a Japanese colony dedicated to pineapple cultivation at Yamato, near present-day Boca Raton.[35]

Although the FEC had helped the Japanese settle, those colonists were unhappy with other Flagler policies. Flagler's P&O Steamship Company relied heavily on the Cuban pineapple traffic for its freight revenue with the island. To encourage this business, Flagler offered reduced rates for Cuban pineapple shipments on his railroad. While Florida growers were being charged over $1.00 a crate for pineapples shipped to Chicago, the railway was charging the Cuban shipper only $.34 a crate from Havana to Chicago. Florida pineapple growers angrily protested against this policy, which had begun as early as 1905. Flagler attempted to combat this protest by indicat ing that the FEC shipped less than 10 percent of the 1909 Cuban pineapple crop. The Florida grower was concerned only with the Cuban grower and FEC rates, not Flagler's transport competitors. Finally Flagler admitted his public relations error to his general freight agent, "I am greatly surprised and disappointed at the showing [of the Cuban pineapple shipments] . . . I doubt if we have made enough out of it to compensate for the ill-feeling engendered among our local growers." More was endangered than goodwill. In 1909, Florida pineapple prices fell to $1.50 for a two-bushel crate. Market forces had destroyed the Florida pineapple industry by 1911. In that year, the Japanese at Yamato only grew fifty acres of pineapples.[36]

The pineapple incident was an unusual error in Flagler's business judgment. Since the primary interest of most potential Florida settlers was farming, Flagler sought to make the agricultural production of permanent residents as high as possible. High production would fill northbound trains with citrus and vegetables. As a means of determining what agricultural products could be grown on the east coast, Flagler set up a series of experimental farms, each dedicated to different products. The first was the Prairie Garden farm in St. Johns County, under the management of Flagler's cousin, Thomas H. Hastings. This area, named after Hastings, became famous for its potatoes and other vegetables. By 1902, Prairie Garden, or Hastings Farm as it came to be called, consisted of a cottage, a gardener's cottage, barn, warehouse, and three tenements. In 1909, its produce grossed $1 million, primarily in Irish potatoes.[37]

Flagler founded experimental farms all along the Florida east coast. His farm at San Mateo was to determine if tobacco could be grown in St. Johns County. From January 1897 to February 1899, Flagler subsidized the farm on an average monthly rate of $200. The San Mateo cigar factory slowly began using Flagler farm tobacco in place of Cuban tobacco in its cigars. The *Homeseeker* asserted that the Florida tobacco was better quality than the best Cuban brand. Although one doubts that, the success of the farm indicated that the growing of tobacco was a profitable business. The yearly cost of shading, fertilizer, labor, and curing of an acre of tobacco on the San Mateo farm was $465. This produced 450 pounds of tobacco, which sold for $750, that being $285 over operating costs. Farther south, Flagler farms experimented with citrus production. Pineapples were the specialty of the Riviera Pinery, located north of West Palm Beach. Flagler also operated several experimental orange groves in Dade County.[38]

Agricultural scientists and the Flagler System cooperated in some experiments. In 1902, when George Washington Carver asked for coconuts for experimental purposes, Flagler ordered his Palm Beach gardener to forward them immediately. Professor H. E. Stockbridge of the Florida Agricultural College at Lake City was an important source of information about Florida's agricultural possibilities. He assured Ingraham that celery could be grown in certain east coast areas. He also provided information on fertilizers to improve the soil near Boca Raton to enable it to grow citrus. Ingraham passed this data on to the *Homeseeker* for publication.[39]

Flagler assisted agricultural promotion efforts at both the local and national levels. As early as 1890, he helped defray the expenses of the St. Johns County Fair. He consistently supported the Dade County Agricultural and Horticultural Fair. In 1899, the FEC awarded prizes at the fair for the best oranges, grapefruit, and lemons displayed. Flagler kept a close watch on the fair developments. In 1901, he avoided subsidizing the fair since the Dade County commissioners and the merchants of Miami contributed $500. He urged that the 1902 fair be held in West Palm Beach not only because it had outgrown the Miami facilities, but also to keep the fair from becoming a local institution. The reputation of the superior citrus culture of the east coast was not confined to Florida. The Louisiana Purchase Exposition, held in St. Louis in 1905, awarded the FEC a gold medal for its display of Florida citrus and pineapples.[40]

The shipping of citrus, especially oranges, played an important part in the freight traffic of the Flagler railway. During any winter season, a freeze could send the revenues from this traffic plummeting. During the 1890s, not only the growers but also the railway suffered with each freeze. Cold weather caused the number of boxes of oranges shipped via the Flagler road to decline from 29,860 in 1890 to 13,685 the following year. The number increased the next several seasons, reaching 167,790 boxes for the 1893–94 season. A series of cold snaps during the 1892–93 winter failed to affect the orange crop or the resulting freight activity.[41]

Then in December 1894, the worst freeze in Florida history occurred, surpassing even that of January 12, 1886. The 1894 freeze destroyed more than two million boxes of citrus. The temperature dropped to fourteen degrees in Jacksonville and eighteen in Titusville and Tampa. The various Florida railroads estimated their losses at $500,000. Not only did the freeze damage the remainder of the 1894 crop, but it decreased the 1895 crop by over one million boxes. Only the southernmost part of the state escaped the freeze. In spite of Flagler's own financial problems, he ordered railway personnel to help the embattled citrus growers in any way they could. Then in early February 1895, another freeze enveloped the entire South. New Orleans reported snow, and the temperature dropped twenty-five degrees in two hours at Jacksonville. The next winter marked an even lower point for the railway. Its total citrus freight revenue for the last week in December 1895 and the first three weeks of January 1896 totaled $77.80.[42]

When another freeze hit in 1899, Flagler quickly acted to implement his program of aid to the suffering east coast. He ordered Ingraham to distribute $100,000 in loans to the growers. He instructed Ingraham to "err on the side of generosity" in his distribution of the funds. There was little doubt as to Flagler's intent; Ingraham stated: "It will be done in the name of the Ry. Co. to strengthen the bond between the grower and the company." In 1909, Flagler changed his lending policy. He informed Ingraham: "I only have this to say: that we *must stop* making loans; on the other hand, we must undertake to collect all or as much of the indebtedness due the Model Land Co. as possible, and keep on at it until we have worked the thing out."[43] In spite of the policy reversal, Flagler's good deed had already been done: his aid during the crises of the previous fifteen years had assisted many Florida citrus growers.

Flagler had a major impact on the settlement of the east coast. Not only was the region advertised through his land companies and various publications, but he had made inexpensive passenger rates available to settlers who purchased property from his concerns. During the period of Flagler's railway building, the region realized a higher percentage of population growth than any other section of the state. The decade in which the railroad entered a county and the decade of the county's highest rate of population increase showed a direct relationship. During the 1880s, Brevard and Volusia counties more than doubled, while St. Johns increased over 90 percent. Dade County grew almost 500 percent during the 1890s. The legislature created several new counties in the area that had been so sparsely populated. Dade County, for example, had a total population in 1870 of only eighty-five. In 1909, the state created Palm Beach County from the northern portion of Dade, and in 1915, the legislature carved Broward from these two counties. St. Lucie County, established in 1905, came from a part of Brevard. Flagler County, formed in 1917, consisted of former parts of St. Johns and Volusia counties.[44]

Not only had the number of people increased, but also the value of east coast property rose significantly. In 1888, the total property assessment for Dade County was $309,484; its value increased eightfold by 1899. The state comptroller stated that in 1900 east coast counties were paying one-quarter of the state's taxes. The agricultural richness, combined with the intensive farming of the area, was responsible for this prosperity. For example, the *Homeseeker* in 1898 reported that the vegetable farmers in Dade County were working tracts averaging ten acres and less.[45]

The lower east coast was still a true frontier region in the late 1890s. The *Homeseeker* in 1898 described Melbourne as "a village of handsome cottages." It noted that Fort Lauderdale consisted of a post office, a hotel, and a store. West Palm Beach had a population of only 1,500. The area did attract foreign-born Americans. In 1900, 7 percent of Brevard and 12 percent of Dade County were foreign born, while the state average was less than 5 percent. In a letter to Ingraham in 1902, Flagler made clear his intentions with regard to the settlement of the east coast: "While I feel the necessity of getting as large a price as possible for our lands, I would not favor establishing a rate high enough to check the development of the country. What we want for some little time to come is more settlers, more cultivation and more freights."[46]

Flagler achieved his goals of settlement, cultivation, and freight. He had transformed the Florida east coast from an eastern version of the unpopulated West in the 1880s into the most viable economic area of Florida by the time of his death in 1913. For example, the density of Dade County increased from 1.12 persons per square mile in 1900 to 15.04 in 1910.[47]

If one uses what economists term "social cost" to determine Flagler's impact on Florida, the state benefited greatly from his activities along the east coast, for indeed the evidence is that Flagler's Florida venture was unprofitable during his lifetime. On the other hand, the control he exercised during the process of land distribution and settlement is disturbing. In the final analysis, Flagler deserves the credit for encouraging the rapid settlement of the Florida east coast. He did not take the quickest route to profits by simply selling to speculators. Rather, he and his FEC personnel encouraged the development of communities of small farmers and landowners. Of course, there was the business motive of freight profits. But even there, as the following chapter indicates, Flagler would be found wanting if one merely looks at the business side of the ledger sheet.

11

"My Domain"

DURING THE WINTER SEASON of 1898, Flagler invited President William McKinley to visit him in Florida. Aware of his own position in Florida, Flagler boasted, "My domain begins at Jacksonville." He added that even "if the East Coast of Florida belonged to anyone else I should venture to say that it possesses very great attractions."[1] The indirect control that Flagler exercised through his railway and hotel holdings was similar in many ways to a medieval fiefdom. In referring to his various business interests, Flagler referred to his overall organization as the Flagler System. Within it, his major source of power was his railroad.

The expansion of the Flagler road did not end with its extension to Miami. Flagler bought the Titusville–Enterprise Junction branch of the Jacksonville, Tampa and Key West road and the Pablo Beach Railroad in 1899. The latter connected Flagler's Continental hotel with Jacksonville. In 1904, Flagler extended the FEC south from Miami to Homestead in order to carry the area's agricultural produce north. Six years later, the FEC began a 135-mile extension from a point ten miles west of Titusville to the northern edge of Lake Okeechobee.[2] The greatest feat of the Flagler railroad would be the construction of the Key West Extension during the first decade of the twentieth century (to be discussed in the next chapter).

Flagler constantly emphasized efficiency and economy. In 1898, he began investigations into the relative efficiency and cost of wood- versus coal-burning locomotives. The FEC had found it increasingly difficult to obtain wood in Florida. Flagler ordered a study, the results of which showed that FEC locomotives traveled 56.7 miles per cord of wood at a cost of $2.26, while the locomotives of the Georgia Southern and Florida Railway achieved 40.12 miles per ton of coal at a cost of $1.74. Although the study indicated wood to be slightly cheaper, Flagler decided to switch to the more reliable source, coal. In the ten-year period beginning in 1904, the FEC annually spent over $100,000 for the purchase of coal-burning locomotives.[3]

During the first years of the twentieth century, the FEC lowered rates in spite of the fact that its costs were rising. In late 1904, J. R. Parrott suggested to Flagler that passenger rates be reduced. Although Flagler thought northern roads' wage increases would eventually result in the FEC having to increase payroll expenses, he did lower the passenger rate. In order to avoid wage increases, he suggested that a sharing with employees of the net revenue of the road might be in order; however, he never seriously entertained the idea. The FEC lowered its freight rates in 1909. Flagler suggested that, within the new rate structure, the FEC charge lower rates on southbound necessities. He gave his principle regarding the burdens of the consumer: "I have always been a believer in the doctrine that the consumer pays the freight, and for that reason I do not see how it is any advantage to the [Florida] consumer to reduce freights on citrus fruits and vegetables, but if the principle is correct, then the consumer is burdened with an excessive rate on commodities, and I suggest whether this would not be a good time to take into consideration and (perhaps) put into effect a reduction on staple goods."[4]

Passenger trains were an important component of the Flagler System. Parlor cars, named after Florida governors and St. Augustine hotels, provided good publicity, albeit not sizable revenues. The FEC at first owned its parlor cars. In 1895, for instance, it paid the Pullman Company $16,000 for two parlor cars. Pullman delivered seven elegantly furnished cars in 1899, with the interiors finished in white mahogany with silk curtains and green plush seats. In 1908, Flagler sold his company's parlor and sleeping cars to Pullman, and thereafter, Pullman operated these cars along Flagler's road. Under an 1908 agreement, Flagler paid Pullman the first $7,750 of earnings from each of these cars, revenue in excess of this amount being divided equally between Pullman and the FEC. Flagler also placed Pullman dining cars, at first not included in the arrangement, on his road in September 1909 at a rental rate of $350 a month. The FEC, however, shared with Pullman any losses in the dining operation.[5]

The number of passengers on vestibule trains was an indicator of the success of the Flagler road's passenger traffic during the winter season. Other roads allowed the Flagler road to use their vestibule cars. Although passengers from the east, originating in New York, accounted for 60 percent of the FEC's traffic during the first decade of the twentieth century, this traffic suffered a steady decline. From a high of 20,251 southbound passengers for the 1904–5 season, the rate declined to 17,603 in 1905–6; 17,108 in 1907–8; and 13,084 in 1908–9.[6]

Flagler depended on the good faith of other railroads for directing passengers toward the Florida east coast. During his early Florida experience, he worked closely with Henry Plant, whose Savannah, Florida and Western road was an important FEC connection with the North. Although they were competitors, Flagler and Plant enjoyed a friendly business relationship. They closely cooperated on ventures of mutual value, such as their northern railroad connections and steamship lines. On the other hand, their hotel competition has been the subject of much legend. One story, according to the Plant interpretation, had Flagler asking about the location of the Tampa Bay Hotel when it was first built. Plant's alleged reply was that Flagler could best find the hostelry by following the crowds. The two developers' subordinates, however, did not always show a high regard for one another. When FEC personnel complained about derogatory advertising by the Plant interests, J. R. Parrott ordered them not to react in kind. In private, however, Flagler was fond of favorably comparing the earnings of his road with those of the Plant System. One such monthly comparison showed the FEC with a 20 percent higher net revenue per mile of road operated.[7]

One example of Flagler's cooperation with his fellow railroad owners was the establishment of terminal facilities. Plant, Flagler, and H. R. Duval of the Florida Central and Peninsular road cooperated in the building of the Jacksonville Terminal, and rented additional space in the terminal to the Jacksonville, Tampa and Key West road. When the Plant Investment Company purchased this latter road in 1899, Flagler wanted Plant to pay a higher rate to the Jacksonville Terminal Company for the additional use of the facilities by Plant's enlarged company.[8]

An era of cooperation ended with the death of Plant in 1899—and a new one began. In 1902, his son, Morton F. Plant, sold the Plant Investment Company properties to the Southern Railway and the Atlantic Coast Line. Flagler formed an alliance with the Atlantic Coast Line by cooperating in the formation of the Atlantic and East Coast Terminal Company. This company, organized in 1905, provided freight facilities in Jacksonville for the two railroads. The Atlantic Coast Line and Flagler owned equal shares of its $25,000 stock issue. With this arrangement, Flagler controlled half the shares of Atlantic and East Coast Terminal Company stock in addition to his one-third interest in the Jacksonville Terminal Company.[9]

The trains of other roads provided additional service to the FEC during the winter season. Six trains arrived daily in Jacksonville from points north: the New York and Florida Special, Chicago and Florida Special, Chicago and Florida Limited, Southern Palm Limited, Seaboard Air Line Limited, and the Florida Limited. When the Seaboard Air Line and the Atlantic Coast Line opposed through service to the FEC in 1909, Flagler expressed his displeasure: "The average passenger will take a through car ninety five times out of a hundred, in preference to making a change. My advice is to stick to the through car, and if possible, get one car next Winter from Boston to Knights Key, located on the FEC's Key West extension. This I think, would be a good 'ad' for us." That winter the Florida and West Indian Limited did indeed run along the tracks of the Pennsylvania, Atlantic Coast Line, and the FEC from New York to Knights Key for a distance of 1,475 miles—"The longest Sleeping Car Line in the United States East of the Mississippi River."[10]

Arrangements between the FEC and other lines for these trains into Jacksonville were crucial to Flagler's hotel interests. The railroads made agreements regarding Pullman sleeper rates and other special payments. At times, other roads placed the Flagler road in an awkward position when they failed to be on time at Jacksonville. When an incoming train was late, the Flagler road sometimes ran a special catch-up train from Jacksonville to St. Augustine. At other times, it was Flagler who was on the receiving end of the criticism. In 1894, the Florida Central and Peninsular accused the Flagler road of discriminating against its Florida Special from Chicago. Since it arrived in Jacksonville at 6:30 A.M. and the Atlantic Coast Line's Florida Special from New York did not arrive until after 8:00 A.M., the FEC forced its passengers to wait an hour and a half before continuing their southbound journey.[11]

Although there were occasional problems with business associates, for the most part Flagler enjoyed congenial relations with other businessmen. Because of his position as a railroad president, Flagler had many privileges. Telegraph companies allowed him to use their wires for railroad business. He had an additional franking privilege with Western Union because of his position on that company's board of directors. The Adams Express Company and the Southern Express Company allowed him free use of their facilities for the sending of packages that did not exceed 150 pounds. Flagler also cooperated with business associates in providing services on his road. William H. Beardsley, his personal secretary at Standard Oil's Broadway office, helped arrange Florida vacations for Standard Oil personnel. Flagler exchanged passes with officials of other railroads. In 1901, he even received the traditional annual pass from the Southern Pacific. In addition, the western railroad sent him a pass that would have allowed his private car and its passengers free use of Southern Pacific facilities. That same year, August Belmont sent Flagler a pass for the Louisville and Nashville Railroad. Flagler reciprocated.[12]

Luxurious private cars regularly traveled across the South to the winter haven of America's economic aristocracy on Florida's east coast. The FEC's round trip rate from Jacksonville to Palm Beach for private cars was $342. The FEC hauled notable private cars, including T. B. Wannamaker's Oceanic, W. C. Whitney's Pilgrim, and the New York Central private cars of William Rockefeller and F. W. Vanderbilt. Because of the many favors provided by the Pennsylvania Railroad, the FEC did not charge its executives for hauling private cars. In 1902, this practice stopped because of a rule adopted by many of the roads that prevented their executives from requesting passes beyond the limits of their own lines.[13]

Florida also passed new rules governing railroads during Flagler's Florida career. Flagler humorously warned Parrott in 1899 about the excessive freight rate the FEC was charging for oil, "It looks as though you need a Rail Road Commission." In fact, the Florida legislature had first created a railroad commission in 1887. The reason for such action during a period when Florida needed expanded railroad mileage was that over one-third of the state's mileage was in receivership, and the 1887 constitutional convention delegates believed a commission was needed to assist in railway stability. The legislature implemented this constitutional suggestion in April 1887. The railroads did not oppose the legislation, but rather made it ineffective. The weak law that emerged provided for an appointive commission of three members. The commission had the power to receive copies of all agreements and contracts between railroads, hold hearings, and initiate suits. Fines could range from $100 to $4,000 if railroads failed to follow commission regulations.[14]

The commission proved to be unsatisfactory. Citizens of the undeveloped southern sections of Florida thought the commission hindered progress of their areas. In 1890, the legislature passed a bill abolishing the commission. The reason for the repeal lay in the unusual opposition of both railway interests *and* the Farmers' Alliance to the commission. When Governor Francis P. Fleming proposed to appoint his prorailroad secretary E. J. Triay to the commission, Alliancemen vowed that they would rather have no commission than have a weak one. Therefore, the Alliance-men cooperated with the railroads in abolishing it.[15] (Triay will become important later in the Key West Extension story.)

The Interstate Commerce Commission (ICC) also regulated Flagler's road. Although Flagler could have attempted exemption from national regulation due to the intrastate nature of his road, he did not choose to do so. His inaction may have been prompted by a fear of being without recourse should interstate carriers violate agreements with his road. As for the ICC, it considered the FEC to be engaged in interstate commerce. In any case, the ICC conducted periodic safety inspections and audits, and required yearly reports of the financial condition of the road.[16]

Floridians took a renewed interest in a state railroad commission in 1897 because of the abuses practiced by many of the railroads. The charges were: (1) Interstate railroads were using high rates within the state to compensate for low charges on regulated interstate commerce. (2) Rates charged were not based on the service rendered, but on the changing value of the produce shipped. (3) As would be expected, competitive routes had lower rates than noncompetitive ones. (4) Growers had no opportunity for appeal against roads that failed to provide needed services.[17]

Flagler offered justifications for the high freight rates charged by his railroad. In 1890, when public criticism mounted regarding the rate for citrus products shipped out of Florida, a newspaper interviewed one of the Flagler freight agents. In congratulating his freight agent on the answers, Flagler gave his own view of the situation: "The reasonable and truthful answer, I believe is this,—that there is nothing that competes with Fla. oranges but Fla. oranges,—that an advance in rates *always* comes out of the pocket of the consumer,—that the low rates into Fla. are made by the railroads for the benefit of the Fla. consumer,—that the comparatively higher rates *out* of Fla. are also paid by the [non-Florida] consumer." Flagler encouraged his agent to obtain another interview to get this point across—without mentioning Flagler's name.[18] Such an argument may have worked in 1890, the year the first Florida railroad commission was abolished, but farmers and legislators were not accepting Flagler's logic in 1897.

The railroad commission bill passed the state senate 24 to 2 on April 14, 1897, eleven days after its introduction. The house subsequently passed the measure 58 to 3. Conservative Governor William D. Bloxham, recognizing the futility of attempting to stop this reform legislation, allowed the bill to become law without his signature. Initially, the governor would appoint the three commissioners, but then the voters would select them beginning in 1898. Candidates could not hold railroad stock or bonds. The commission could set and adjust freight and passenger rates, establish regular passenger and freight depots, prevent rate discrimination, and regulate associated enterprises (storage, wharfage, and the like). The law instructed commissioners to cooperate with the ICC in all matters dealing with interstate rates.[19]

Prorailroad newspapers expressed their strong opposition to this second Florida railroad commission. The New York *Post* saw the legislation as a slap in the face of developers who had been responsible for the growth of Florida during the post-Reconstruction era. The Jacksonville *Florida Times-Union*, owned by Flagler and other railroad interests, added its own editorial lament to its reprinting of the *Post* article: "It is possible to right the wrong that may be done an individual by a railroad company without turning its property over to three men empowered to bankrupt the owners at their pleasure." The *Railroad Age* warned that probably only one-fifth of the projected 1,700 miles of new railroad construction would take place in Florida due to such legislation as the railroad commission law.[20]

These threats did not deter the reform movement in the legislature. Another 1897 law forbade railroad involvement in politics in any way, ranging from campaign funds to politicians or political parties to influencing legislation. Two years later, the legislature passed a law requiring railroads to begin fencing their rights-of-way within sixty days, this process to be completed within two years. If a road failed to comply, it became responsible for full payment for any cattle killed by its trains. The railroad commission moved rapidly to adopt regulations. Straight mileage became the only basis for freight and passenger rates, therefore removing the opportunity for roads to charge customers higher rates on noncompetitive routes. The commission reduced cabbage rates by $.03 a box and oranges by $.04. This rate change saved growers a total of $30,000 to $40,000 during the first year of the 1897 railroad commission's operation. The commission kept passenger rates at $.04 mile, but railroads had to make available one-thousand-mile pass books at a $.025 rate.[21]

At first railroads did not believe that the 1897 railroad commission had any more power than the commission of 1887. The first show of strength came in a case involving the FEC. In 1899, Flagler supported a proposal to allow the Atlantic, Valdosta and Western railroad to use the Jacksonville Terminal, knowing that if he did not, the railroad commission would order it opened. His terminal associates opposed such a move since the other road competed with them. Flagler countered that they should pay the Jacksonville Terminal Company for business lost if the railroad was kept out of the depot. Under the authority of the railroad commission, the Atlantic,

Valdosta and Western sued the terminal company. Meanwhile, one of Morton Plant's officers agreed with Flagler that the Plant Investment Company and the Florida Central and Peninsular Railroad should pay for the defense of the terminal company since they, and not the Flagler road, were benefiting from the exclusion of the road. The state supreme court upheld the railroad commission; thereby allowing the road, by now owned by the Southern Railway, to enter the terminal in 1902. Even with this negative decision, the roads had obtained a compromise in another matter. The railroad commission agreed to continue the $.04-a-mile passenger rate rather than implement the proposed $.03 rate, provided that one-thousand-mile $.03 books were available for passengers to purchase.[22]

When the railroad commission challenged the amount of capitalization of the FEC, hinting that the figure was inflated, J. R. Parrott issued a report that gave some indication of the financial condition of the road. He assured the commissioners that the listed $7,200,000 figure was the actual amount of cash Flagler had put into the road. He further stated that Flagler had been willing to decrease the bond interest owed Flagler for a period of five years in an effort to help the FEC meet its obligations. The interest due on the bonded indebtedness was $186,000 per year with an additional $13,000 interest on the 5 percent floating debt. The road paid $48,000 in taxes in the 1898 fiscal year. Parrott claimed that by strict economy measures, the FEC had built its road for $10,000 a mile. Attempting to dissuade the commission from implementing its proposed $.03-a-mile passenger rate, Parrott stated that 70 percent of the FEC's passenger business was from outside Flordia.[23]

The pressure by the commission seemed to have had its effect on the FEC. In December 1902, it voluntarily announced a reduction in its passenger rate to $.03 a mile. Since the FEC failed in some cases to follow its own directive, the commission officially ordered the $.03 rate in June 1906. The road reacted by gaining a temporary injunction against the order in United States Circuit Court in Jacksonville. The commission then ordered the books of the road audited to determine if the FEC's defense was correct. Flagler, as the sole holder of FEC bonds, had the Colonial Trust Company sue the commission in 1907 to block the new rate. The trust company contended that the proposed $.03-a-mile passenger rate was excessive interference in a debt-ridden company. When the United States District Court of Miami dismissed the Colonial suit in 1909, the commission immediately reinstated its 1906 rate order.[24]

The commission also challenged FEC freight rates. The Fruit and Vegetable Growers' Association, organized in Miami during January 1901, lobbied the commission for a reduction of FEC freight rates. At the request of this organization, the commission held hearings in Fort Lauderdale in the fall of 1901. When the FEC presented its case on December 12, it argued that the association's position was a minority opinion of the growers. According to Parrott, most growers were willing to pay higher rates for faster service. In spite of this argument, Flagler finally agreed to a reduction. With the highest new rate being Miami's $.05 a box, the rates went into effect with the fall crop of 1902. During 1911, the commission again persuaded the FEC to reduce shipping charges for fruits and vegetables by an average of 15 to 16 percent. The ICC also forced the FEC, along with the Seaboard Air Line and the Atlantic Coast Line, to reduce its vegetable and fruit charges from producing points to base points within Florida.[25]

Financial records of the FEC are not available for most of the 1895–1901 period. The statements that were reported to *Poor's Manual of Railroads* indicate that the railway was in debt. Although it had a net revenue in both 1895 and 1896 that indicated no losses, after deductions for taxes and bonded indebtedness, the balance was approximately $100,000 and $400,000 in debt for each year, respectively. Flagler did not blame the poor financial condition of his road on revenue, which he felt was adequate, but upon inefficient management of the FEC. Expenses did not necessarily decrease when there was a decrease in revenue. Efficiency of operation, however, did not always improve when earnings increased.[26]

In 1902, it appeared that the FEC had improved its efficiency. Its net balance for 1902 was $149,693. But after that year, the road's financial position declined once again. By 1908, it was more than $400,000 in debt. With a new bond issue, the FEC was able to show a net profit from 1909 through 1912. Yet, Flagler continued to be concerned with inefficient management. In 1909 he wrote to J. P. Beckwith, the head of FEC operations: "Our operating expenses are, to my judgement, the place where we must look for a decided reform, which I trust you will lose no time in accomplishing." Admonitions such as this may have been effective. The FEC had an increase in its gross revenue of over $17,000 during October 1909 as compared with the same month the previous year. More importantly to Flagler, he noted a decrease of over $17,000 in operating expenses between the two periods being compared.[27]

Financing the FEC required the wise use of all the resources at Flagler's disposal. He borrowed money from his Standard Oil account for short periods. He used revenues not only from the railway but also from the hotel system to pay the interest due on railway mortgages. To improve the accounting balance of the railway, Flagler took notes against railway debts owed him, usually in $100,000 increments. Until the building of the Key West Extension, Flagler was able to remain the sole owner of all FEC stock and bonds.[28]

The building of the Extension, however, put tremendous pressures on Flagler's financial resources. In fact, for a time he even allowed collateral trust notes to be sold to others. In 1908, however, Flagler halted negotiations with the Guaranty Trust Company when he learned that the company was considering a public sale of the bond issue. In 1909, earlier mortgages of $7,259,000 and $8,741,000, issued to Flagler in 1897 and 1902, respectively, were cancelled and a new bonding of the FEC took place. Flagler approved a private bond issue of $40 million. He used the first $10 million, purchaed by J. P. Morgan Company, to pay off the floating indebtedness of the road to himself. He used $18 million more for immediate expenses. The remaining $12 million was used for consolidated mortgage bonds, $2 million of that amount being reserved for future sales, to be sold in $400,000 or $500,000 yearly increments. In 1911, Flagler requested that the United States Mortgage and Trust Company, as his trustee of an earlier $20 million issue of 5 percent gold bonds, should accept for the 1911 fiscal year an interest rate of 4 rather than 5 percent from the FEC.[29] He did not wish to damage his reputation by selling bonds to others and then seeing the railway in the hands of creditors. On the other hand, he saw bonding as the best way to recover a part of his investments without endangering the FEC. Actuarially, a bonded debt read better on the ledger than an unsecured personal loan from Flagler because it did not appear as a current debt against operating expenses.

Flagler's enterprises in Florida depended on the economic leverage the railway gave him. The FEC provided the major means for his obtaining land. Flagler saw his hotel chain as the handmaiden of the railway. He remarked on the interconnection of his hotel and transportation network, "I don't know of a hotel that I would want to take as a gift except I owned the transportation lines that reached it." On another occasion he emphasized the subordinate role that the hotel chain played in the Flager System: "My Hotels in Florida are regarded by me merely as auxiliaries to my Railroad interests in that State."[30] Since Flagler often refused offers to build hotels in areas other than the Florida east coast, these statements have the ring of truth. However, during his lifetime his hotels were almost profitable—which is more than one can say for the railroad.

It is best to view the Flagler System as a single unit. Flagler realized that a variable railway schedule was necessary during the tourist season in order to provide frequent and convenient connections with his hotels. On the other hand, if Parrott's report to the state railway commission is to be accepted at face value, then the hotel clientele was indispensable to the railway's passenger service.

The Flagler hotels were the center of Florida east coast resort life. The Florida East Coast Hotel Company continued its public relations campaign so ably begun when Flagler first developed St. Augustine. The FEC published brochures and booklets such as "Three Casinos in One Book" and "Seven Centers in Paradise." FEC publicity outlets placed pictures of the hotels on Hamburg-American Line steamers to encourage the line's clientele to consider vacationing on America's Winter Riviera. By 1899, the system had built golf courses at all its major resorts. Entertainment casinos were available in St. Augustine, Palm Beach, and Miami. The hotels offered a wide range of prices for winter visitors. In 1910, a visitor could stay in St. Augustine for as little as $4.00 a night at the Alcazar. Charges for the Ponce de Leon, which included breakfast, began at $6.00. The other hotels in the system were either on a $5.00 or a $6.00 base rate. Summer visitors to the Continental paid as little as $4.00 a night.[31]

It is difficult to draw precise conclusions about the financial success of the Florida East Coast Hotel Company from the data available. For the 1899 season, the hotels did very well. As early as March 16, Clarence B. Knott, superintendent of the hotel system, sent $120,000 above immediate expenses to the New York office. By April 1, the hotels had a credit balance on Flagler's book of over $30,000. At the end of each season, Flagler charged the excess or deficit to the "profit and loss" account, and the hotels began the next season with a clean slate. The total indebtedness of the hotel system to Flagler as of July 1, 1901, stood at $2,638,655. The company gave Flagler a note for the amount.[32]

Flagler's correspondence during 1901–2 allows one to follow the financial status of the hotel company during that season. The hotel company had a debit balance on Flagler's books of $120,854.18 as of November 20, 1901. This increased to over $150,000 by the following February. It remained fairly steady through the first half of March. By March 17, 1902, the hotel company had paid Flagler $60,000 on his advances and another $100,000 due to profits. With this amount, the company was showing a credit balance on Flagler's books of over $33,000 by the end of the month. At the end of the fiscal year, the hotel company had a credit balance of over $143,000. Flagler assessed the relative strength of his hotels. He did this by dividing each hotel's seasonal profit by its house count totals. The results were a daily profit per person of:

Royal Poinciana	$3.03
Breakers	2.16
Ponce de Leon	2.12
Royal Victoria	1.07
Alcazar	.84
Royal Palm	.62
Ormond	−.07
Colonial	−.32

He was more concerned with the small profits of the Alcazar and the Royal Palm, since he thought they could make handsome profits, than he was with the deficits of the Colonial and Ormond.[33]

The season-to-season financing of Flagler's railway and hotel operations required the financial expertise of William H. Beardsley, his longtime secretary who supervised the New York office. Using portions of Flagler's 30,000 shares of Standard Oil (New Jersey) stock as collateral, Beardsley would begin in the late summer of each year to borrow money needed to prepare the Florida operations for the coming season. Beardsley preferred to use "call loans" (a banker could "call for payment" at any time and the loan could either be repaid or renegotiated) or "demand loans" (a banker could "demand" immediate payment of the loan). These methods allowed more flexibility than did conventional time loans. The rates of interest fluctuated from as low as 2.5 percent to as high as 12 percent. In 1890, it took 500 shares of Standard Oil stock to secure a $50,000 loan. With the increase in the value and stability of Standard Oil stock brought about by the formation of Standard Oil (New Jersey) as a holding company in 1899, Beardsley borrowed $100,000 in 1901 with only 200 shares of Standard Oil (New Jersey) stock as collateral. At times, Beardsley even borrowed short-term funds from Standard Oil itself, usually when it offered a lower rate of interest than the banks. During the late spring and early summer months, the loans would be paid out of income from Flagler's Florida businesses. Any deficit remaining was paid from the dividend income of Flagler's Standard Oil stock. Flagler's Standard Oil Company dividends amounted to about $1,200,000 a year during the first decade of the twentieth century.[34]

Flagler's business interests, in and of themselves, do not support the term "domain" for his relationship with Florida; but his concerns—and power—along the east coast of Florida went far beyond his railway, land, and hotel interests. Flagler attempted to shape the character of the population in several ways. He instructed Ingraham to be more concerned with the character of the colonists coming to the area than with the number of people sought. As Flagler wrote to one inquirer concerning the people along the east coast, "I feel that these people are wards of mine and have a special claim upon me." Thus, he tried to meet the needs of the people of this area before contributing to other causes. In view of his bequests, he seemed to have seen their needs as, first, a basic education and then Christian training. To assure himself that requests to build community structures were sincere, he required residents to raise as much money as the community could afford; then, and only then, would he contribute the amount necessary to complete the planned structure. Flagler disapproved of too many churches: "I haven't a drop of denominational blood in my veins, and feel like assisting all worthy enterprises. I am a firm believer in doing business on christian principles, and equally firm in my belief that we should do the Lord's business on business principles. In small communities such as yours [Fort Pierce], a new church ordinarily means another place to starve a poor Pastor in." Flagler's youth in modest Presbyterian parsonages of upstate New York surely molded opinions such as these. Also, he thought that too many churches were simply inefficient. After watching railroad building for over twenty-five years, Flagler declared that he also recognized the temporal value of churches: "I am not ignorant of the fact that churches are not only the conservation of public morals but business interests. . . . I have always said to the Officials of these roads [in the United States northwest], that there was no better way of serving their interests than to aid in the establishing of churches along their Lines."[35]

In giving financial help to individuals, Flagler personally determined the worthiness of each request. When one young lady requested a $60.00 loan in order to complete a stenographic course, Flagler was moved, although it was "but one of hundreds received by me, 99% of which I turn down, there is something about this letter which commands my attention." He continued this analysis by giving the qualities that he wished to see in the lady before the loan was to be granted: "If the young girl is energetic, intelligent and deserving, I do not know but I would make the small loan." After fully checking the request, Flagler did just that.[36]

Although Flagler himself drank alcohol in moderation, he thought that most persons of the lower classes could not handle strong drink. He opposed the sale of liquor in public places. When one former employee wrote Flagler that he was now free of his addiction to alcohol, Flagler wrote him an encouraging letter, although Flagler confided to John McGuire, one of his builders, that he had no recollection of the man. At other times, Flagler thought he could have a direct beneficial effect. When several FEC employees on one occasion reported to Flagler that the FEC auditor was on one of his periodic drunken sprees in Jacksonville, Flagler instructed them to try to help him: "Before taking any summary steps in this matter, we must make another effort to save him."[37]

Flagler offered special inducements to his personal servants to improve their financial status. He bought Standard Oil stock for those wishing to invest in the company, to be repaid from their dividends and wages at the rate of 5 percent annual interest on the unpaid balance. In 1909, one Whitehall employee had just paid off a share of stock worth $660 and was beginning the repayment of a $685 purchase. Another Whitehall employee had already secured two shares of the stock.[38] Since Standard Oil stock was appreciating and dividends amounted to $40 a year, Flagler offered his employees something valuable, while attempting to instill in them his Presbyterian principles of sacrifice and thrift.

Florida colleges also benefited from Flagler's philanthropy. In 1899, Flagler pledged to Rollins College (established in Winter Park in 1885) that he would endow a chair at the rate of $1,000 per year for a period of five years. He stipulated that his friend, Dr. George W. Ward, president of the college, be the first occupant of the chair as Professor of Economics and Law. Amid the Flagler divorce controversy of 1901, Flagler made a contribution of $20,000 to the Florida Agricultural College at Lake City for a gymnasium. It was rumored that this was a payoff for the legislative action on his behalf. While that was entirely possible, it was more likely due to his friendship with college trustees George W. Wilson, editor of the *Florida Times-Union*; Frank Harris, editor of the *Ocala Banner*; and Parrott, who had been on the college's board of trustees since 1899.[39]

A controversy over the leadership at Stetson University erupted at the time Flagler gave that school $60,000 to build a hall of science, eventually named Flagler Hall. In 1901, he had promised the donation to the school because of his friendship with President J. F. Forbes. Forbes became involved in a bitter contest to keep his job. John B. Stetson accused Forbes of immoral conduct with a female co-worker and attempted to have him removed. Flagler told Parrott to bring pressure on certain trustees of the institution to allow Forbes the benefit of an open hearing. Forbes resigned under Stetson's pressure during the spring of 1902, but then withdrew the resignation. Flagler was confident that only one trustee other than Stetson would oppose Forbes. Throughout the controversy between Stetson and Forbes, Flagler could well have been thinking of his own situation. Ida Tarbell later recalled that, while doing research in 1902 on her muckraking book on Standard Oil, she encountered a great deal of hostility toward Flagler in his own social circles as a result of his divorce and remarriage.[40] Flagler may well have seen Forbes as one being pilloried by Stetson in a similar manner.

Flagler was more than a partisan spectator in the Stetson-Forbes battle. One Florida newspaper stated that Flagler's $60,000 donation for a hall of science had triggered the controversy since it undermined the power of Stetson over Forbes. In any case, other powerful personages in the state came to Forbes's aid, including Governor Jennings and Jacksonville Mayor Duncan U. Fletcher, both members of Stetson's board of trustees. As a result of this publicity, Mrs. Stetson finally withdrew her threat to deny a gift to the university. In December 1902, Flagler arranged a trip to DeLand to see the new science hall. The next spring, he could not restrain the desire to take a last, friendly jab at Forbes's position: "I note that the envelope containing your letter bore the imprint of the President's office of the Stetson University." It would seem that Flagler would then congratulate Forbes on his perseverance. But Flagler continued, "I think it would be more prudent if you would do as I do,—use plain envelopes."[41]

In order to have command of his domain, Flagler thought it necessary to control newspapers. Publicly, he detested the press. In 1890, when rumors circulated that he planned to buy a Florida paper, he announced, "There is not a particle of truth in the rumor that I am about to start a newspaper. If I had to take my choice between a den of rattlesnakes and a newspaper, I think I would prefer the snakes." Less than a year later, during the spring of 1891, Flagler, Plant, and H. R. Duval of the Florida Central and Peninsular Railway bought the Jacksonville *Florida Times-Union*. Flagler's purpose was to establish a powerful "Standard" newspaper in Florida. This paper, coupled with other purchases and loans, consolidated tight control of the daily press along the Florida east coast. When the Atlantic Coast Line and the Seaboard Air Line systems absorbed the Plant System and the Florida Central and Peninsular Railway, respectively, one-third interests in the *Florida Times-Union* also passed to the larger roads. Flagler even made personal loans to George W. Wilson, its editor. Wilson accommodated Flagler by printing special requests, such as "Trusts" and "The Future of Railroads" from the New York *Sun*. At times, Flagler loaned money to other papers, including the Gainesville *Sun* and the Pensacola *News*.[42]

Flagler usually did not involve himself in Florida politics unless it directly affected his business interests. During 1899 and again in 1901, friends and pro-Flagler newspapers lobbied the state legislature to elect Flagler to the United States Senate. Flagler, not desiring such a position, cautioned associates that the best way to quell such movements was a conspiracy of silence. There would have been little to be gained from a senatorial chair. Flagler had become friends with James P. Taliaferro when the latter was serving as chairman of the Florida Democratic Executive Committee in 1890. He probably was instrumental in, or at least supported, the state legislature's election of Taliaferro to the United States Senate in 1899. When bills affecting Flagler's interests came up in the Senate, he advised Taliaferro on the proper action, whether it was to be absent for a vote or to oppose filibustering efforts by fellow Democrats. Flagler made no effort to "retain" politicians during the Progressive Era, for he realized that the politics of the situation made it impossible for a politician to stay in office if he voted the corporate line all the time. On the other hand, he was not adverse to bribing officials when it was necessary to defeat certain proposals, such as an anticorporation bill before the Florida legislature in 1903. He wrote Parrott, "I wish you would take pains to examine it, and if it can be done at a moderate expense, see that the Bill is sent to the proper 'pigeon hole.' "[43]

Flagler supported the racial policies of conservative southern politicians. When the Lodge Force Bill, which would have allowed for federal supervision of elections in the South, was being discussed in Congress in 1890, Flagler announced his opposition to the measure. He wrote a Florida banker lamenting that the extremists on both sides of the issue were stirring up an unnecessry controversy. He leveled a barb at Benjamin Brewster, one of his Standard Oil associates: "There would be no question as to the passage of [compromise legislation] if it were not for the efforts *you* Black Republicans are making to force upon the South the Force Bill." Flagler wrote William McKinley before the latter's nomination for president that the best policy for the Republican party to follow toward the South was one of excluding blacks from patronage. In 1901, Flagler advised Parrott to send a similar message to Theodore Roosevelt.[44]

Just because Flagler had southern sympathies on some issues did not mean that southern politicians dealt kindly with the Standard Oil magnate. During 1894, Governor James Hogg of Texas, as a part of his campaign against Standard Oil, sent papers to Florida Governor Henry L. Mitchell requesting that Flagler be extradited to Texas for trial. At first Mitchell, wanting to avoid charges of favoritism, agreed to comply with the request since the papers seemed to be in order. But friends of Flagler pressured against the action. It was rumored that Parrott dictated a telegram to Hogg that Taliaferro signed. The message cautioned Hogg to use more care in his handling of the matter. Finally, Mitchell issued an executive order on January 3, 1895, stating that Hogg had to prove that Flagler was a fugitive from

Texas before he would agree to extradite him. Mitchell, not even waiting for the opinion he had requested from his attorney general, had yielded to the pressure of Flagler's friends.[45]

Although most of Flagler's later career did center on Florida, he took an interest in national events. He was a Republican, but he showed little interest in most national campaigns. Two exceptions were the James G. Blaine–Grover Cleveland contest of 1884 and the William McKinley–William Jennings Bryan race of 1896. In the 1884 election, although Cleveland was not seen as an enemy of business, Blaine seemed so much a businessman's candidate that Flagler contributed heavily to his campaign. Flagler, always seeking good public relations, offered Cleveland his services when the president vacationed in Florida in 1888. The 1896 presidential campaign, however, was a war between conservative business interests and Bryan's populistic silver platform. After Bryan's third defeat for the presidency in 1908, he announced that he would continue to be available if the people chose to nominate him. Flagler feared that Republicans would not be rid of Bryan until the day the Democratic orator died.[46]

The only politician Flagler truly despised was Theodore Roosevelt. The two had had an amicable relationship while Roosevelt was governor of New York, and Roosevelt invited Flagler to a social function at the White House in 1901. But there was one thing that Flagler could not tolerate: he thought that, as president, Roosevelt had rejected the business community, which had been instrumental in making him vice-president. At the time that Roosevelt was attacking Standard Oil and Rockefeller, Flagler wrote an associate, "I have no command of the English language that enables me to express my feelings regarding Mr. Roosevelt. He is ———. Some time I will tell you a good many things regarding him and the Standard Oil Co. which we cannot make public, which will surprise you." Although Flagler never publicly documented his charges, he never ceased to fume about Roosevelt's alleged betrayal. When Roosevelt announced after leaving office in 1909 that he was planning to visit Africa, Flagler wrote: "I am glad that Teddy is going to Africa soon, for I want to spare him the humiliation of knowing that he has been 'all wrong' in his persecution of the Standard. I would like to keep him swelled up as much as possible, so that when a lion swallows him, he won't be able to disgorge him."[47]

When William Howard Taft became president, Flagler was elated, for he thought there would be a major change in policy: "Thank God the 'Muck Raker's' job will soon come to an end, and if the President-elect will carry out Mr. Roosevelt's policies in the same way that Ananias and Sophira [Sapphira] were treated, viz,—'carry them out and *bury* them,' the country will rejoice." Flagler had good reason for celebration. When Taft replaced Elihu Root as Roosevelt's secretary of war, he had proved valuable to Flagler's Florida railroad. J. R. Parrott, Flagler's second-in-command in Florida, was Taft's friend, the president's brother Harold having been Parrott's Yale classmate. On at least one occasion while Taft was still secretary of war, Parrott urged him to expedite paperwork in Washington to help the Flagler railroad in right-of-way matters, since navigable river crossings needed the approval of the War Department. The Parrott-Taft correspondence stopped, however, after Taft became president. In fact, Taft proved a disappointment. When a proposed corporation tax bill emerged with Taft's support, Flagler regarded him as a turncoat like Roosevelt.[48]

Flagler used the *Florida Times-Union* to express his points of view on national issues. His main goal was to combat the trust-busting rhetoric of Progressive Republican and Democratic politicians In 1899, he wrote George W. Wilson, editor of the paper: "Both parties seem to vie with each other in declaring hostility to trusts. This thing however, will wear out after a voter realizes, as he must, that these foolish declarations are the life blood of demagogues." Flagler proudly told his Standard Oil friends that Wilson had voted for McKinley in 1896, "and has been a consistent supporter of his policy to the fullest extent possible, consistent with being a Democratic paper in a southern State."[49]

While Flagler often criticized the policies of both parties, he was especially concerned when businessmen could not control the process. When an associate noted in 1903 that the political control of New York City had once again fallen into the hands of Tammany Hall, Flagler expressed disappointment. However, Cleveland Mayor Tom Johnson's socialist tendencies worried Flagler more than the evils of machine politics: "I do not think however, that Tammany's ascendency will exercise one-tenth the influence that Tom Johnson's victory [in the governor's race] in Ohio would have done. The success of Johnson would have been a great National misfortune."[50]

Although Flagler took more than a passing interest in national politicians and political issues, his major concern throughout his later years was in business. He served on the board of directors of former United States Vice-President Levi P. Morton's trust company, along with John Jacob Astor, James B. Duke, Elihu Root, and other prominent business leaders. In 1910, when Morton's company merged with two other New York City firms, Flagler resigned his directorship. He also sought to rid himself of other directorships. In 1909, he wrote John Archbold, by now the managerial head of Standard Oil: "Notwithstanding my long connection and large pecuniary interest in the Company, I feel that my years and absence each year from New York, render me unfit to take any active part in the management of the Company." But it was not until the reorganization of Standard in 1911 that the company accepted Flagler's resignation. In addition to these offices, Flagler held directorships in the Western Union and the Union Theological Seminary. In 1895, Thomas S. Hastings, Flagler's former pastor and now president of Union Seminary, appointed Flagler to the seminary board. Although Flagler attended only one board meeting in his first five-year term, he was reelected to another term in 1900. In 1902, he finally resigned from the seminary board.[51]

Although Flagler made some investments in national companies other than Standard Oil, they were small and infrequent. On the stock market he speculated in railways, especially the Southern Railway, Reading, and the Canadian Pacific. Flagler was one of the persons in the United States Steel syndicate, which bought Andrew Carnegie's operations and gave Flagler a $15,000 profit from his $150,000 investment in the six-month venture. At one time, he had a large securities investment in the American Bank Note Company, but soon sold the issue to Morton Plant.[52] Florida interests took up too much of Flagler's time and money to allow him to invest heavily on Wall Street, despite his belief in the stock market as the quickest way to a fortune.

During the last years of his life, Flagler placed day-to-day control of his Florida empire in the hands of subordinates. J. R. Parrott first became president of the Florida East Coast Hotel Company in 1899. He also became head of the Peninsular and Occidental Steamship Company during its first year of operation. In Flagler's 1901 will, he designated Parrott as the next president of the FEC. As it happened, Parrott assumed this office four years before Flagler's death. When Parrott became president of the FEC in 1909, Flagler retained his position as chairman of the board, but relinquished responsibility for the daily operation of his road.[53]

The large amounts of capital and time that Flagler spent on his Florida ventures disprove the conclusion that Florida was just his "playground," satisfying a capricious nature. But neither should Florida represent the failure of Flagler to understand the complexities of developing a frontier region. When he began investing heavily in Florida during the late 1880s and early 1890s, he had chosen to build and develop an area that he thought had vast potential. In doing so, he realized that this would mean that he would not be able to build an even greater financial fortune by plowing back Standard Oil dividends into new stock. But Flagler's nature led him to new adventures rather than to consolidation of his position. He enjoyed being the "Florida resort king," rather than merely another "Gilded Age prince." However, Flagler was still aware that Floridians thought he often—if not always—had ulterior motives for his every action. Although he never consciously stated the motive for his building of the Key West Extension of the FEC, his lifelong desire was to be remembered in history as a "builder," not a destructive force. What better way to fulfill his destiny than to build the impossible, a railroad across the sea.

Key West:
"America's Gibraltar"

STANDING AT THE STRATEGIC ENTRANCE to the Gulf of Mexico, Key West served for many years as America's Gibraltar. Stephen S. Mallory, a United States Senator from Florida, had given it that title during the 1850s while serving as chairman of the Senate's Rivers and Harbors Committee. By the mid-1890s Key West had a population of almost 20,000. In fact, for almost fifty years it had been Florida's most populous city. The economic base of this small island was diverse, with the marine trades—fishing, sponging, shipbuilding, and wrecking—predominating. The cigar industry was the largest single employer on the island, most of the workers being Spanish and Cuban émigrés. Key West also served as a coaling station and naval port. Two geographic advantages were responsible for the port city's naval significance. First, it had a natural harbor with four entrances, ranging from fourteen to thirty-three feet in depth, which would allow the navy's largest ships to anchor there. Second, by traveling only ten miles from the harbor, a ship was in a direct line to its next port anywhere in the Gulf area.[1]

For many years, Floridians had speculated that a railroad could be built from the mainland to Key West. As early as the 1830s, Key West newspapers were discussing the possibilities. The International Ocean Telegraph Company conducted a survey for the construction of a telegraph line across the Keys in 1866. It was over a decade later before someone actually attempted to make the railroad vision a reality. In 1883, Florida granted former Confederate General John B. Gordon, who became governor of Georgia in 1886, the first charter for a Key West railroad. He built fifty miles of road on the mainland; however, he stopped the project before the road reached the coast.[2]

As Flagler's own railroad building inched down the east coast of Florida, he became concerned about possible competition in the southern area of the state. In 1891, ironically during a visit to Henry B. Plant's Tampa Bay Hotel, Flagler laid the initial groundwork for what would eventually become his railroad's Key West Extension. Flagler's political partner in the early maneuverings was Jefferson B. Browne. A Florida state senator from isolated Key West, Browne was a politician whom a railroad developer would wish to cultivate. Flagler sent the Key West senator a note requesting that Browne visit him.[3]

Browne and Flagler discussed a number of issues in that initial conference, but the Key West senator was most taken with Flagler's argument that the goal of all Florida railroads was a deep-water port as far south on the peninsula as possible. Flagler convinced Browne that the three railroads holding Key West Extension charters at that time would be financially unable to build such an extension.[4] What was understood was Flagler's financial ability for such an undertaking.

From his position as president of the Florida senate, Browne acted as Flagler's informal legislative agent in defeating the renewal of these charters in the 1891 legislative session. Browne even went so far as to leave the rostrum to speak to the issue from the floor. When a senator from Jacksonville with a personal interest in one of the affected railroads sought to interfere, Browne sent a note to him that halted the effort.[5]

Browne was personally convinced that, at that early date, Flagler was fully dedicated to the building of his railroad to Key West. In reality, Flagler just wished to keep his options open—and close such options to others. It was not until 1895, with the official name change from the Jacksonville, St. Augustine and Indian River Railway to the Florida East Coast Railway, that Flagler gave any official indication that Key West might become the final destination of his road.[6]

Jefferson Browne may also have played a role in Flagler's 1895 decision to push for a Key West Extension charter. In 1894, Browne, then serving as the United States Collector of Customs of the Port of Key West, wrote an essay that presented data on the feasibility of a Key West railroad. Flagler did not blindly follow the suggestions of Browne, who after all was but a local politician and Key West booster. In 1902, Flagler hired William J. Krome, a respected civil engineer, to lead an expedition across an alternative route in the swampy Cape Sable area. Krome came back with a negative report.[7]

With the Cape Sable route an impossibility, Flagler turned to Browne's plan. Browne had stated that Key Largo, a thirty-mile-long island connected on its north side with the mainland, was the most likely point of departure from the east coast. From there, the road would travel over Plantation Key, Umbrella Key, and Upper Matecumbe Key, with no more than 100 yards separating any two of these islands. The first major project would be a two-mile trestle between Upper and Lower Matecumbe. A trestle 3½ miles long would connect Lower Matecumbe with the 4-mile Long Key, and a 2½-mile trestle would then run from Long to Grassy Key. From Grassy to Knights Key, thirty miles away, no extensive bridgework would be necessary.[8]

According to Browne's estimate, the most expensive section of the road would be from Knights Key to Bahia Honda, a distance of eight miles. It would be necessary to use the small keys and sand bars in order to avoid the deep water between the two points. Along this southern detour to Pigeon Key, a drawbridge would be constructed at the Moser Channel. The thirty miles from Bahia Honda to Key West could be bridged easily from the Bahia Honda channel to Big Pine Key, no two islands in this area being separated by more than seven feet of water. Big Pine Key could provide all the trestles and ties that would be needed for the road. From Big Pine Key, construction crews could easily trestle the short distances between the remaining islands to Key West.[9]

Browne was confident that Flagler would provide Key West with a land connection. Its mild climate, he predicted, would make it the "Newport of the South." Appealing to Flagler's vanity, Browne continued, "The building of a railroad to Key West would be fitting consummation of Mr. Flagler's remarkable career, and his name would be handed down to posterity linked to one of the grandest achievements of modern times." In 1895, a *Railway World* article furthered speculation by announcing that Flagler had bought the lower half of Key Largo. It also indicated that a Flagler agent had bought parts of the other islands between the mainland and Key West. This property followed earlier route plans closely.[10]

If others were confident of Flagler's plans, he was not. In his 1901 will, he specifically forbade the use of his estate for the building of a railroad extension south of Miami. This did not keep Flagler himself from inching toward the project. In January 1903, he began extending the FEC from Miami to Cutler, twelve miles to the south. At the same time, a survey was made south of Cutler to determine if it was feasible to continue construction. In 1904, the line was built to a temporary terminus, and the town of Homestead was established there, twenty-eight miles south of Miami.[11]

In 1905, Flagler added a codicil to his will that not only allowed for the Key West Extension project after his death, but actively promoted it. The primary reason for this enthusiastic turnabout was the federal government's decision to construct the Panama Canal. Key West was America's nearest port to the canal. It was 850 miles closer than New Orleans or Pensacola and 250 miles nearer than Tampa, its most likely deep-water competitor. With a railway terminus and dock facilities at Key West, Flagler could take advantage not only of Cuban and Latin American trade but also of the western connection that the canal provided. In January 1905, Flagler and a party of associates cruised along the route of the proposed railway extension. When he arrived in Key West, he assured its citizens that he would be extending his railroad into their city.[12]

A lawmaker introduced a bill in the Florida legislature in the wake of President Theodore Roosevelt's 1905 Panama Canal announcement. The bill encouraged the building of the Key West Extension by requiring fair taxation for the road and fair rates for its users. It allowed three months for an existing railway to show a plat of a proposed route, with work on the road beginning within six months of passage. The promised tax assessment for the road was to be as low as any in the state; the assessment for the Extension would be no more than mainland costs. A 5 percent profit earning ceiling on the bonded debt of the road was set, a sinking fund of 3 percent was established, and the freight rate would not exceed the maximum in force as of April 1, 1905. The corporation's books would be open for railroad commission inspection, and a $25,000 bond would be secured with the state before letting contracts and hiring labor. A 200-foot right-of-way was to be established for the Extension.[13]

After favorable committee action, the House added two amendments. One provided that the road's assessment rate was to be the average rate for railroads in the state. The other changed the closing date for the tariff rate from April 1 to May 1. With the passage of the bill, Alex St. Clair-Abrams, a politician from Key West, categorized opponents to the measure as prejudiced, ignorant, and/or mercenary. Calling their disease "Flagler-phobia," he praised Flagler's business and personal integrity, especially his building of the FEC. St. Clair-Abrams also noted his own prophetic vision: "In the matter of the extension of the road from the mainland to Key West, twenty-five years ago I marked with blue pencil a map of this State in the office of Gov. Bloxham and penciled four lines of railroad running north and south, one of them from Jacksonville to Key West. . . . I have lived to see nearly all these lines constructed and in operation."[14]

During the summer of 1905, the *New York Herald* announced the Extension plans. In addition to the Extension itself, Flagler was going to build twelve 800-foot piers at the Key West harbor. Between each 200-foot-wide pier there would be a slip of equal width capable of harboring four ocean-going vessels. He planned to complete his project by the first part of 1908.[15]

After Flagler requested bids for the project, he discovered that the only contractor who responded insisted on a cost-plus contract. Flagler refused this offer in favor of his own organization. He chose Joseph C. Meredith as chief engineer for the project. Meredith had been in charge of building the Tampico, Mexico, docks for the Missouri Valley Bridge Company. The first phase of the Extension construction ended with the opening of the Knights Key Dock for commerce on February 6, 1908. During this portion of the building, the Long Key viaduct was the prized engineering accomplishment. The viaduct, located ninety miles south of Miami, was 2¾ miles long and was supported by 180 arches, each eighty feet high, of reinforced concrete. Flagler wished to use the best available materials, even bringing tap rock for the concrete mixture from Clinton, New York.[16]

The project encountered major difficulty when the Navy would not allow Flagler to dredge the Key West harbor for material to build up the dock area. This dredge work would have not only provided additional land for the terminal area but also deepened the harbor area for oceangoing commerce. Without these improvements, Flagler did not wish to expend the capital for an extension all the way to Key West.[17]

Because of this unforeseen problem, Flagler established a terminus for the road at the Knights Key Dock eighteen miles beyond Long Key. Knights Key provided the railway with excellent steamship connections to Key West and Havana. It could accommodate ships with a nineteen-foot draw. The Knights Key terminus allowed daily steamship service to Havana rather than the Miami-Havana route, which ran only three times weekly. With the additional mileage of the Knights Key Extension, the Post Office Department increased its yearly payment to the FEC by approximately $15,000.[18]

Flagler's plans to construct the "overseas railway" coincided with a period of chronic labor shortage in the state. Many growing trades and industries—turpentining, cigar manufacturing, and lumbering, to name a few—competed for Florida's small labor supply. Hence, one of the most critical problems that Flagler faced during the early stages of construction was finding reliable laborers. When work began in May 1905, the labor force was composed entirely of black Americans; by midsummer their numbers had dwindled to 150. The FEC, unable to maintain effective control over blacks, gradually replaced them with white immigrant laborers.[19]

The railway hired most of its immigrant work force from Philadelphia and New York. Technically, this was done through an independent Miami labor office. One of the methods the railway used to attract workers from New York was the padrone system in the Italian community. By this method, a padrone, functioning as a labor agent, contracted with the railway for a certain number of workers to be delivered to Miami. In return for this, the FEC granted him a commission, which might take the form of cash or a land grant. Railway officials carefully noted that the labor recruiter was not an FEC employee: "They [laborers] are boarded [in Miami] by a man by the name of Lewis, as a private enterprise, the Company not recognizing in any way, except when an employee calls for settlement, he is required to be present to collect his board accounts." The FEC took the $16.00 New York–to–Miami transportation charge out of the laborer's first monthly check. Although the railway by law could not recruit laborers in foreign countries, some foreign laborers did volunteer for the project. Laborers from Spain's northern coast came to the Extension via Havana. Most of these men worked for Spanish foremen on boats along the Keys. They would work continuously for two years and then return home. The FEC also hired natives of the Cayman Islands of the Caribbean. Usually Caymanians worked steadily for a year, went home for Christmas, and then returned for another year's work.[20]

The FEC Extension managers attempted to improve the harsh existence along the Keys. They used two types of housing for boarding workers. The quarters in land-based camps consisted of long, unpainted wooden buildings containing four-high berths along the walls. Some of the larger buildings held 300 to 400 men, although the capacity of a normal-sized building was 30 to 50 men. The mess hall was in a separate building at each camp. There were no wells. As a result, trains had to bring drinking water along the Keys twice daily from the mainland. Two trained orderlies at each camp maintained an emergency hospital. The men used pyrethrum powder to combat mosquitoes, the great nuisance of the land-based camps. When the time came to put finishing touches on a portion of the project, the FEC placed a crew of 150 men on a quarterboat, a barge approximately 100 by 30 feet. The greatest single loss of human life on the Extension project occurred during a 1906 hurricane when Quarterboat Number Four broke from its moorings and 50 of its 150-man crew died.[21]

The railway experienced many labor problems. Although the FEC sought to curb the practice, "booze boats" were a part of the payday scene along the Keys. Carl Zapf, the West Palm Beach liquor merchant, was one of the first entrepreneurs to exploit the Keys' trade. Some of the stewards in the camps also participated in the smuggling. Beginning in July 1907, railway officials at Long Key attempted to stop whiskey sales, but only on company property could the officials effectively discourage "booze boat" landings. One internal report, although never implemented, even suggested that the FEC establish its own canteen system as a means of stopping illicit sales.[22]

The primary labor problem during the construction of the Key West Extension was keeping recruits. Many potential laborers deserted the labor trains even before they arrived in Jacksonville; others left enroute to Miami. Unscrupulous labor agents used deceptive tactics. One agent arranged with the railway to receive $1.00 for each worker he delivered for Extension work. The FEC also promised him a head foremanship if he could deliver 300. He only brought seventeen workers, and these few complained he had failed to deliver on promised wages of $1.75 per day. The railway had made no such arrangement. In fact, an internal FEC investigation reported that the agent's "subsequent operations would lead to the belief that the claims of misrepresentations made against him are well founded."[23]

The problems of labor recruitment and retention were compounded when the federal government began investigating charges of peonage in Florida. Mary Grace Quackenbos obtained an appointment as a special assistant United States attorney during 1906, working for—as she called it—"The People's Law Firm." The government gave her the assignment on the strength of her earlier research into possible peonage violations in Florida.[24]

After several successful prosecutions, Quackenbos turned her attention to an investigation of rumors of peonage practices in the building of Flagler's Key West Extension. What emerged from the investigation was a story of fraud, intimidation, and corruption. Her investigation centered on Francesco Sabbia's German-Italian Exchange in New York. Max Lipetz, a disenchanted labor contractor, exposed the inner workings of the organization in his affidavit to Otto F. Klinke, a United States Secret Service agent. Sabbia had promised Lipetz half of the amount the exchange collected for all laborers signed for Key West Extension work except for Italians; that ethnic group had already been committed to A. G. Lapiporo. Flagler gave the Exchange $3.00 for each person delivered to the Extension. The FEC deducted $2.00 of that amount from the worker's pay, and the worker was led to believe it was just part of his transportation payment. With the first group of workers being sent on November 7, 1905, Sabbia made a $10,000 profit in the first seven weeks of this activity.[25]

The labor agent for the FEC was E. J. Triay, former secretary to Florida

Governor Frances P. Fleming. Triay also profited from the arrangement. When Lipetz approached Triay with an offer to deliver laborers for only $2.00 a head, Sabbia's "counteroffer" of a $1,000 bribe caused Triay to renew the contract with Sabbia. According to Lipetz, Triay had told him that, although the laborers were told they would have to repay the advance for their transportation, they were actually getting free transportation. Although Lipetz may have been confused as to exactly how the transportation arrangements were made, he was aware that he got his fee from each of the "transportation advances."[26]

Lipetz and Sabbia preyed on the destitute of New York City. They handed out FEC circulars in various places—on the streets, to charity organizations, in parks and lodging houses—anywhere they felt they could locate persons desperate for work. Once potential workers came to the German-Italian Exchange office, Sabbia would begin his talk, with Triay present. Sabbia promised each person, from plumbers to blacksmiths, that his skill would be put to good use on the Extension. He would give men letters of introduction, with their job description, to be given to Meredith when they arrived in Miami. The promised positions, such as foremanships and interpreters, would vanish once the laborer got to Miami. Sabbia and Triay kept their New York colleagues as ignorant as possible concerning the conditions of the railroad construction project. For example, Lipetz did not discover until reports began to filter back to New York from the first group of laborers that the work was on islands. At one point, Lipetz asked Sabbia what had gone wrong, since some of the reports indicated that laborers were refusing to work. Before Sabbia could answer, Triay noted that if laborers would not work off their transportation advance, then they would be put on a local chain gang for violating their contract. Sabbia nodded, adding that their only other option would be a sixty-mile swim.[27]

Some of the laborers, however, made their way back to New York and gave Quackenbos or other government employees their stories. One typical case was that of Samuel Rosen. Around the first of November 1905, Sabbia promised Rosen employment on the Key West Extension. Sabbia told Rosen he would receive $1.25 per day for his labor, with a transportation charge of $10.00 being deducted from his wages at the rate of $.50 a week. In addition, another $2.50 a week would be deducted for his room and board. After having worked on the Extension for three weeks, Meredith told Rosen that not only did he have $12.00 in wages coming to him, but he also had a $13.50 transportation debt from New York to erase. When Rosen disputed the transportation figure, Meredith reminded him who was in charge. Rosen continued to refuse to pay the transportation amount, and Meredith had him put in the Miami jail.[28]

When Rosen's case came before a judge, he was given the option of going back to the Keys or ten days in jail. Rosen opted for jail. Two blacks served as Rosen's guards on a street-cleaning detail. After five days of what he considered a humiliating situation, Rosen escaped, only to be rearrested in the Palm Beach area. The second time around, the Miami judge sentenced him to fourteen days, but he was released after only ten days for good behavior. Ironically, Rosen was so desperate for work that he accepted a pipe laying job in Miami with the FEC. After this job ended in two weeks, FEC officials once again told Rosen he owed $13.50 for transportation from New York to Florida. Rosen paid the amount, but Meredith refused to give him a receipt. Shortly thereafter, Rosen returned to New York penniless.[29]

According to affidavits from other government witnesses, the FEC forced workers to remain on the job and would not allow them access to transportation off the islands. They reported that FEC personnel locked the dock gates at Miami, preventing Extension workers' entry into that city without railway permission. Some who did escape were arrested on vagrancy charges and returned to the Extension project either as state convicts or as paid workers. They described the construction camps as unbearable, with inadequate eating and sleeping conditions. After hearing some of this testimony, a New York federal grand jury issued an indictment on March 27, 1907. It charged three FEC employees and the New York labor agent Francesco Sabbia with violating an 1866 slave-kidnapping law.[30]

Flagler sought in various ways to minimize the problem. The FEC published its own "Report on Labor Conditions on the Florida East Coast Railway Extension." The Florida State Board of Trade, Florida legislature, and others who sought to protect the state's reputation supported the FEC. The railway obtained a list of prosecution witnesses in order to investigate their backgrounds.[31]

In February 1907, A. V. S. Smith, Flagler's Jacksonville attorney, began to prepare the railway's defense. He instructed Meredith to obtain affidavits stating that no worker was detained on the Keys for nonpayment of transportation or for any other reason. Smith also told Meredith to obtain evidence that vessels other than those of the railway were in the area, thereby permitting workers the opportunity to leave at any time. An August 14, 1905, letter from Parrott to Meredith contained important material in the railway's favor. Parrott's letter clearly outlined the proper handling of laborers, which included specific regulations against peonage-type abuses. Meredith had posted copies of this letter throughout the Keys. As Smith carefully noted during pretrial preparations, testimony concerning the letter was needed in order to clear the chief engineer's office of any charge of peonage conspiracy. The railway took photographs of the dock and railway facilities at Miami as evidence of free travel through the Miami terminal. A Catholic priest from Mobile agreed to testify that labor conditions, as he saw them on his travels along the Keys, were not of a peonage nature.[32]

Both sides accused the other of illegal tactics. Quackenbos alleged that Flagler forces were buying grand jury information and bribing witnesses. In one instance, the FEC lawyer suggested to Meredith that he advance $100 in wages to a boat captain who was to serve as a government witness. On the other hand, three blacks told FEC officials they had been promised $150 each to testify against the railway and a $250 fine if they did not. Although FEC personnel did accompany government investigators along the Keys, it is doubtful that either side extensively engaged in illegal practices during the investigative process. When he went to testify at the trial, W. J. Krome reported to Meredith that there were ten other witnesses traveling with him: "Of these Smith and Neal are the only two who will give much adverse testimony. Both of them are very bitter for personal reasons."[33] There was no evidence in Krome's correspondence to suggest that there was any ill feeling toward these men or any intimidation to change their testimony.

The case came to trial November 10, 1908. Before the proceedings began, the government added a list of thirty-four additional instances of peonage to its original allegations. The railway witnesses were not always of the highest quality; Meredith reported to Smith that he was sending workers to New York by the Mallory Line—rather than by rail, with its many stops— "this to avoid any possible means of their getting incapacitated by over indulgence in liquor." Before the trial began, the government dropped its charges against Krome and Meredith, probably to strengthen its case against the labor agents. From the beginning of the trial, the prosecution was in a defensive position for the indictment was defective. The presiding judge stated that, since the case was being decided on an 1866 slave-kidnapping statute, the prosecution had to prove that the workers had actually been enslaved, not merely involved in a peonage situation. After the first day of hearings, he adjourned the day's proceedings, noting that the prosecution had failed to establish a prima facie case of conspiracy. A week

219

later the judge directed the jury to return a not-guilty verdict since the government had not improved its case over the first day's performance. The judge dismissed indictments on separate charges remaining against Sabbia the following day when the prosecution withdrew its charges.[34]

Flagler was pleased but puzzled over this sudden halt in the case. When government attorneys asked on November 20 for the dismissal of all charges against the FEC, Flagler was suspicious: "There is however, an air of mystery about this thing that we do not understand." He was disappointed that the FEC did not have an opportunity to present its case, but he fully expected the government to formulate another peonage case against his company; this eventuality did not occur. The defense had cost Flagler approximately $80,000. He was convinced that the affair was part of a governmental attack on Standard Oil and its owners.[35] There is evidence to show that instances of peonage by overzealous foremen did occur and that the FEC was prepared to conceal these incidents during the trial. But it is also correct that no system of peonage was in operation on the Keys.

With the peonage case settled, the year 1909 dawned as the most promising in the construction of the Key West Extension. During the first three months of the year, the actual work was costing only slightly over half Meredith's estimates. Then Meredith died on April 20. Although Extension employees were aware that he had been very ill, they did not know he was so near death.[36]

Fortunately for the project, W. J. Krome, a graduate of the University of Illinois and Cornell University, had been ably assisting Meredith. Krome and his three division engineers were members of the Society of American Engineers. He was only thirty-two years old when Flagler appointed him as Meredith's replacement. Although Krome had left the project during the spring of 1908 for health reasons, he returned before Meredith's death. Flagler had great faith in Krome's ability: "Mr. Krome is a very efficient man, and we have no anxieties about his being able to prosecute the work successfully."[37]

Under Krome's direction, the Extension construction continued to move forward rapidly. The first concrete pier for the Knights Key viaduct, to the west of the island, was completed at 3 P.M. on February 27, 1909. Always a person for noting speed, Flagler also recorded the last pier as being completed at 5 P.M. four months and one day after the first one. In August 1909, Flagler announced confidently that trains would be running to Key West by February 1910.[38]

A devastating hurricane ruined Flagler's timetable. A report to construction headquarters at 5:40 A.M. on October 10, 1909, indicated that a hurricane was heading for the Keys. The storm, which hit on the eleventh, destroyed the western portion of the Extension and caused major damage above Knights Key. Although approximately 3,000 workers were exposed to the hurricane, the only loss of life was a crew of thirteen on the tug *Sybil*. Flagler estimated the monetary loss of the Extension north of Knights Key to be $200,000. He told associates the damage was "very discouraging, but to the general public we must all keep a stiff upper lip and admit nothing." His motto throughout the crisis was "Nil Desperadum, Keep the Flag Waving." The FEC quickly reinstated train service to Knights Key, with passenger, construction, and supply trains beginning to arrive on November 8.[39]

Flagler learned a valuable lesson from the experience. When it was discovered that marine marl, composed of coral rock, held better against the hurricane than did rock fill, he instructed Krome to build a structure to last, "even though it costs a little more money and takes considerable more time. I would rather be two years completing the Line to Key West and have it permanent, than a repetition of the disaster of the hurricane of the 11th ult." Where the hurricane destroyed wooden trestles, they were replaced with sturdier material. Although concrete arches were more expensive, Flagler used them in many places, rather than steel atop concrete piers, since the arches were more permanent. Flagler's engineers had also discovered that the railroad needed to be as high as the water beneath it was deep. Engineers installed automatic devices that blocked trains from crossing bridges over which the wind velocity was over fifty miles per hour. The engineers also limited trains to fifteen miles per hour when crossing the longer bridges. Krome estimated that the cost for the completion of the Extension itself would now be $9 million, with another $1 million required for construction of the Key West terminal facilities. The Extension now represented a Flagler commitment of $20 million, approximately 40 percent of his total Florida investment.[40]

The building of the Extension did not cause Flagler to ignore other aspects of his system. During the fall of 1906, he followed the suggestion of one of the Extension workers that a boarding camp be established at Long Key for the families of skilled workers and mechanics. Flagler later converted it into the Long Key Fishing Camp for sportsmen among his hotel clientele. By January 2, 1909, workers had completed all the cottages and dormitory facilities at the camp. Although it was already accepting guests, the Long Key Fishing Camp did not officially open until January 11.

Flagler also bought the Russell House in Key West and renamed it the Hotel Key West. Open year-round, it functioned as an ordinary hotel rather than the typical Flagler luxury resort.[41]

The state law under which Flagler constructed the Key West Extension stipulated that it had to be completed by May 1912. More than 2,500 men were working on the project as of June 1911. Toward the end of the year, crews worked around the clock, with the marl train running throughout the night. The major reason for the haste was not the May deadline, but Krome's deadline of January 22, 1912, twenty days after Flagler's eighty-second birthday. As early as February 1911, Krome contemplated finishing by the following January, but it was not until a newspaper report in July that Flagler discovered Krome's plans. Enthusiasm began to mount, and Frank Clark, a United States congressman from Florida and former Flagler foe, proposed a resolution in the House praising Flagler and the Extension project. During August 1911, members of the Key West Extension Celebration Committee asked Flagler about plans for a January 22 celebration. Flagler modestly declined to endorse any such effort. In spite of this, the movement continued. FEC employees had a telegram cast in solid gold plate to present to "Uncle Henry" when the celebration occurred.[42]

Flagler's relationship to Key West was not limited to the Extension project. He had had business interests in Key West for over a decade. In 1899, he had purchased the local newspaper. At the time, probably recalling some Standard Oil experiences, he had instructed Parrott to keep the enterprise secret, since "If it leaks out that we are interested, somebody will surely start an opposition paper in the expectation that we will buy them out." After the 1909 hurricane, he sent supplies to Key West from Port Tampa and Miami to relieve the suffering and authorized Mayor Fogerty of Key West to use $5,000 from Flagler's Key West bank account if needed. In order to help the economy of the city, Flagler had volunteered to contribute half the needed $50,000 to induce a large cigar manufacturer to leave Tampa and relocate in Key West.[43]

January 22, 1912, the official opening of the Key West Extension, was probably the highest moment in Henry Flagler's Florida career. On the morning of January 21, he left his home in Palm Beach for the trip to Key West, located more than 220 miles over land and sea from West Palm Beach. The only thing that might mar the occasion was a strike of railway firemen, which was in progress. To prevent any possibility of sabotage, the FEC placed men with shotguns along the entire route. There were no incidents, and Flagler, after spending the night in Miami, arrived in Key West

Flagler with a group on an inspection tour of the Key West Extension, 1908. The party includes (left to right) J. R. Parrott, J. C. Meredith, C. D. Vanaman, Captain Marcotte, Senator J. P Taliaferro, T. V. Porter, H. M. Flagler, Major General J. R. Brooke, R. T. Goff, William R. Kenan, Jr.

at 9:30 A.M. to a most unusual birthday celebration. Joining him in the event was a large delegation of United States congressmen and senators. Other dignitaries included military personnel, foreign ambassadors, and Florida officials. Governor Albert Gilchrist was Florida's official representative. The music of military bands filled the air; and bunting-laden buildings added vivid color to the festivities. The program of speeches, banquets, and tours lasted for several days. Speakers acclaimed the Extension as the "Eighth Wonder of the World."[44]

As events were to prove, however, the Key West Extension was a failure. It never earned the expected revenue before the Labor Day hurricane of 1935 destroyed it. Even after the federal government replaced the railroad with a modern highway, Key West remained relatively isolated from the mainland. In the period from 1910 to 1980, the city added less than 5,000 to its population, while the rest of the state boomed.[45] Contrary to the statements of the Flagler engineer, "business economy" did not dictate the sinking of 40 percent of Flagler's Florida investment in the Key West Extension. However, one should not view the Key West Extension as a business

223

investment. As Flagler's 1901 will indicated, he knew the risks involved in such a venture.

Henry Flagler built the Key West Extension as his enduring monument. It also functioned to endear him to the people of a state that he felt had not appreciated his past accomplishments for Florida and its citizens. Many regarded the Extension project as "Flagler's Folly." Yet, the people would realize that he was not doing it to enhance his personal wealth or position. There was no way an aging man would reap a profit from the venture. One must view the Key West Extension simply as Henry Flagler's gift to Florida—and his desire to be immortalized.

13

The Florida Baron's Estate

DURING THE LAST ten years of his life, Henry Flagler was in declining health with problems associated with age. However, being the active man he was, he would not publicly admit to such a possibility. In a note to an acquaintance in 1903, Flagler bragged about his good health:

> I was born with a live oak constitution, and it is only within a year or two that I have known of the possession of any organs. My diet has always been simple, and the only excess I believe I have indulged in has been that of hard work. I have however one ailment (old age) which is incurable, and that I am submitting to as gracefully as possible. I am quite sure however, that I possess as much vitality and can do as much work as the average man of forty-five.

The Key West Extension project certainly supported Flagler's argument; but, the aging process was already taking its toll at the very time of that letter. In a letter to his New York physician less than a month later, Flagler was admitting to the infirmities of old age:

> Won't you please give me the name and address of the physician whom you recommended I should call upon with regard to my deafness. I have been using the instrument very faithfully for a month past, and instead of benefiting me, I do not hear as well as I did.

Mary Lily and George Ward had an audiophone (also known as an ear trumpet) installed in the Royal Poinciana Chapel to help Flagler better hear the services. However, Flagler told Ward that it caused him too much embarrassment to use it. By 1909, as Flagler had indicated six years earlier, the ailments associated with old age were gaining on him. He wrote to a cousin, "My general health is very good. I too however, have lost my eyesight to such an extent that it is difficult for me to do more than sign the letters I dictate."[1]

During this period of declining health, Ward often read to Flagler from books ranging from philosophy and science to the Bible. Ward recalled, "Many of the books I treasure most dearly are books he first discovered and read." Ward freely admitted, "History he did not care for. You see it was the past. His only interest was in the present, and above all, the future. He literally lived in the future." With the completion of the Key West Extension, Ward feared that Flagler would lose his will to live: "I wanted him to see his undertaking completed, but I dreaded the withdrawal of this spur to living."[2]

Flagler had always been a man of few words. On one occasion, when he had been listening to one of the men at Palm Beach in what he considered idle conversation with some ladies, he turned to Ward and asked, "Doctor, how *do* you suppose he finds so much to say?" With his loss of hearing, Flagler became more withdrawn—and lonely. He would spend long afternoons in silence in a rocking chair on a porch or riding in an "Afromobile" with his dog Bobby.[3]

As Flagler advanced in years, he became very concerned with his own immortality. His last gift to Ward was a Bible in which he had underlined the promises of eternal life. The two men often disagreed about the nature of God's relationship with man. Once Ward preached a sermon on God's plan for every man's life. Flagler reacted to it with the announcement that he had too much work to do to allow God's "will be done" before he reached 100 years of age. He later asked Ward if Ward thought Flagler's physical problems were a part of God's plan for him. After a serious fall on Whitehall's grand staircase on January 15, 1913, Flagler informed Ward, "Doctor, I do not want to go, but I can say, and say honestly, I am ready to do His will."[4]

As a response to Ward's complaint that he was too concerned with conserving time, Flagler once replied, "Why, time is life, and you say life is a part of eternity." Flagler, the man so determined to help "conserve" eternity, had lived a full life. On May 20, 1913, Flagler, at the age of eighty-three, died quietly at Nautalis, his cottage on the ocean side of Palm Beach. Although his fall had hastened his demise, the general cause of death was old age. His wife, pastor, physician, and several servants visited him frequently during his last illness. Flagler's staff had kept a close watch on their employer's condition, sending coded messages from Palm Beach to the New York office. Although his son Harry had been called, Flagler was in a coma when he arrived. Harry later bitterly recalled the situation, hinting that the Kenan family had intentionally delayed calling him until his father was so far gone that he would be unable to recognize his son.[5]

On the morning of May 23, Flagler's body arrived at St. Augustine from Palm Beach. It laid in state in the rotunda of the Ponce de Leon until shortly before 3 o'clock, when the pallbearers, leading the processional, carried it the few short blocks to the Memorial Presbyterian Church. Among the pallbearers were J. R. Parrott, William H. Beardsley, James E. Ingraham, James A. McGuire, John A. McDonald, E. J. Triay, and W. J. Krome. Notable for their absence, both among the pallbearers and attending the funeral itself, were members of the Standard organization, none of whom seemed to have come to the funeral. The service itself was a simple affair, with George Ward giving the eulogy. Later, Flagler was entombed in his crypt, next to his first wife Mary, in the Memorial Presbyterian Church mausoleum.[6]

Flagler's 1901 will provided that the bulk of his estate would go to Mary Lily Kenan Flagler. After a trust period of at least five years, Mary Lily would then receive the amount in the estate after Flagler's specific bequests were fulfilled. The trust provided Mary Lily with a yearly income of $100,000. Flagler granted $3,000 a year during the trust period to the Memorial Presbyterian Church in St. Augustine. At the end of the trust period, Harry Flagler was to receive 5,000 shares of Standard Oil Company (New Jersey) stock. Flagler explained his reasoning for granting a relatively low inheritance to his son. First, he noted that he had already given Harry "securities which yielded him an average of $75,000 per annum in income." Furthermore, "my son has not shown for me the filial regard that would make me inclined to do more for him now than is done by this item of my will." Flagler's attitude toward his son did not cause him to deny his granddaughters an inheritance: Harry's three daughters equally divided another 8,000 shares of Standard Oil stock.[7]

Flagler rewarded his most faithful associates. Joseph Parrott, who had served as Flagler's close confidant in the Florida venture, received $100,000. James Ingraham received $20,000. Hotel managers Fred Sterry, John Anderson, Joseph D. Price, and Henry W. Merrill received $10,000 each, as did Flagler's builders, McGuire and McDonald. R. T. Goff, the FEC general superintendent, received $10,000, as did Flagler's private secretary J. C. Salter. A 1904 codicil raised William H. Beardsley's portion of the estate from $10,000 to $50,000. The only institutions to receive monies from the Flagler estate were Hamilton College, $100,000, and the Memorial Presbyterian Church, $75,000.[8]

Flagler's beloved Mary Lilly suffered an untimely death. She had married Robert W. Bingham, a Kentucky politician, on November 16, 1916. Less than a year later, on July 27, 1917, Mary Lily died. Members of her family reported that she had died of an "acute heart disturbance."[9]

The tenor of the stories in the press quickly changed when Bingham, who had originally signed a prenuptial agreement foregoing any gains from his wife's estate, announced that Mary Lily Bingham had added a codicil to her will on June 17 that gave him $5 million. Her brother and sisters were outraged. Suspecting foul play in the arrangement, especially since the codicil was handwritten on the stationery of the Bingham family physician, the Kenans had Mary Lily's body exhumed and her vital parts were taken from Kenansville, North Carolina, to New York's Bellevue Hospital for a private autopsy. In the ensuing furor, the Kenans promised to make the results public—they never did. That helped fuel stories that Mary Lily had been a frequent user of laudanum (a polite Victorian way of saying she was addicted to opium products) and may have died of an accidental or induced overdose. In any case, Bingham got his $5 million and used it as the principal financial means to establish a newspaper empire with the *Louisville Courier-Journal* as its cornerstone.[10]

Mary Lily Flagler's will gave most of her estate to her brother and two sisters. In addition, her brother, W. R. Kenan, Jr., and the other trustee received $50,000 a year for managing the trust during its twenty-one-year life. In honor of her father and uncles who had attended the University of North Carolina, she gave $75,000 to the university to create an endowment for academic positions. She gave to her niece, Louise Wise Lewis, who had married and was living in Cincinnati, the strand of pearls which Flagler had given her as an engagement gift. In addition, Mary Lily's three homes, Lawn Beach, Kirkside, and Whitehall, became Louise's. Until the age of forty, Louise would receive $200,000 a year from the estate, and then she would get $5 million at her fortieth birthday.[11]

For the most part, the Kenans did well with their inheritance from the Flagler estate via Mary Lily. Louise Wise, however, was the exception. She found it impossible to survive on a yearly allowance of $200,000. Therefore, in 1919 she sold Satanstoe (Lawn Beach) to D. W. Griffith, the silent screen movie mogul. He converted the mansion into a movie studio and set, and the place became known as Oriental Point. He shot all the interior scenes of his movie "Way Down East" there. Five years later, again needing cash, Louise sold Whitehall. A group of investors added a tower of rooms to the rear and converted it into a hotel. As for her $5 million inheritance, Louise had the full amount for only a short time, for she died in 1937, two years after her fortieth birthday.[12]

Members of the older generation lived much longer and died much richer than Louise. When a court declared Sarah Graham Kenan, one of Mary Lily Flagler's sisters, incompetent during the mid-1960s, her financial status became public record. It revealed that her estate included $56 million of Standard Oil of New Jersey stock. Upon the death of W. R. Kenan, Jr., in 1965, his estate created a trust, which through its endowments, began a number of academic positions named in his honor. Therefore, Flagler's fortune had benefited a number of academic institutions through Kenan's generosity. When Jessie Kenan Wise, Louise's mother, died in 1968, her estate was estimated at $300 million. It included the Peninsular and Occidental Steamship Company, Miami's Ingraham Building, and one-third of the stock of the Florida Publishing Company (owner of Jacksonville's two daily newspapers). Lawrence Lewis, Jr., the son of Louise Wise Lewis, continues the family tradition of service and philanthropy as chairman of the board of trustees of Flagler College, which is housed in what had been Flagler's Ponce de Leon hotel.[13]

Certainly, a case can be made that Flagler's money has assisted many individuals and institutions over the years through the generosity of members of the Kenan family. But that is not the same as Flagler himself having made these bequests. Flagler's was a rags-to-riches story. As such, he believed that others were equally capable, if self-motivated enough, to accomplish the same status in life he had attained. He was not, therefore, willing to just give money to persons or institutions he did not know. The Kenans, also, did not give away *too* much. Therefore, we find that in the 1960s the Flagler fortune, for the most part, was still virtually intact.

229

Epilogue: "Time is Life"

HENRY MORRISON FLAGLER is an example of the fulfillment of the American Dream. Rising from respectable but humble beginnings, he began earning his livelihood at the age of fourteen. Flagler emerged from this background with a drive toward success and a yearning for accomplishment. The direction of Flagler's business ventures continually changed. Once he successfully completed a project, it lost its attraction for him. He then turned over its daily operations to his management team. Although he kept a watchful eye on their activities, he turned his attention to yet another innovative project. In a 1906 interview, reflecting upon his early career, he said: "I have always been contented, but I have never been satisfied. To be dissatisfied means that you are ambitious to progress, to do things, not that you may be richer, but that you may be useful and take a part in the work of the world."[1] This ambivalent statement may not satisfy us, but coming from Flagler, it seems a good explanation of his motives.

When Henry Flagler began his developments along the Florida east coast, he could not have foreseen how the area would develop over the next thirty years. By the time of his death, Flagler had built a railway which connected with lines serving the eastern seaboard and the Midwest; he had improved agricultural opportunities as a result of the work on the experimental farms of the Flagler System; and he had established a chain of luxury hotels whose wealthy clientele journeyed south each winter. One cannot determine Flagler's motivation for this development by just analyzing the normal processes of the business community. It could not have been only a desire for profit; Standard Oil offered Flagler great opportunities in that area. In spite of his statements, it was not philanthropy, at least not as the word is usually defined. One can find better examples of this type of motivation in John Rockefeller, Andrew Carnegie, James B. Duke, and others.[2]

To understand Flagler's plan for his Florida empire, one must return to his explanation of satisfaction versus contentment. He once confided to Richard H. Edmonds, editor of *Manufacturer's Record*, that he realized that, if he had concentrated his efforts on accumulating wealth, he would have probably been one of the richest men in the world. Flagler, however, was an individualist. Although he would not have indicated his dissatisfaction to anyone, his type of personality did not easily lend itself to the consensus decision-making process in the Standard Oil boardroom, especially after Standard had gained absolute dominance of the industry by 1882. In spite of Rockefeller's praise of Flagler's abilities, the Standard Oil Trust had the stamp "Made by Rockefeller." Flagler needed a project, a vision, that he could claim as uniquely his own. He told Edmonds that he saw in his Florida career the opportunity to help humanity by opening up limitless opportunities for persons to advance themselves. Although this type of comment was obviously to some degree self-serving, Flagler had always been an optimist. He told Edmonds, "This country has entered upon an era of boundless expansion in trade and commerce, and though business may at times have its temporary setbacks, the future is destined to surpass what has been achieved in railroad advancement and business activity in my lifetime."[3]

When he began his St. Augustine venture, Flagler probably did not realize his need to be remembered as an important contributor to the nation's development. But as the project progressed, his actions moved from the whim of a wealthy man to the search for immortality. The first public indication of this was his 1886 comment that the Ponce de Leon would be standing long after he was gone. His yearning for lasting fame reached its logical conclusion with the decision to build the Key West Extension.

A great strength—and weakness—of Flagler as a businessman was his ability to dream. This ability became a weakness due to its overpowering effect on his judgment. He constantly stretched his credit rating to the limit in order to expand his empire, while failing to consolidate what was already in operation. There was no logical reason for buying the Casa Monica in St. Augustine, for instance, when the Alcazar Hotel was due to open the same season. Of course, in the case of the Key West Extension, Flagler embarrassingly turned to other sources for credit. In many respects, he was a visionary in businessman's clothing.

In his relationship with the people of Florida, Flagler did not see himself as a despotic baron, but a paternalistic lord. He thought he provided the people of the Florida east coast with economic opportunity. After all, they could leave if they had paid their debts and found better situations elsewhere. In his opinion, control of the press did not control the minds of people; it only allowed him to present his positions and interpretations on various issues affecting his system. He felt that paying occasional bribes to governing officials in Tallahassee and lobbying efforts in Washington merely satisfied his desire to control his own destiny.

Flagler attempted to modify the Middle Ages for modern conditions. He invited other businessmen to see his domain from their palace cars and hotel rooms. They could see that he had provided for the welfare of his wards by building institutions for their special social, governmental, and religious needs. In return for this generosity, he expected the people along the Florida east coast to give him their loyalty and allegiance. Although he did not own all the land in his domain, Flagler sought to control the character of the people through both his land sales policies and such documents as antiliquor deeds. He financed his empire from the "tribute" received from the rich during their visits to his unusual kingdom and the money paid for the transport of agricultural produce.

Regardless of motivation, Flagler had a major impact on the development of the east coast of Florida. Few men of his era would have undertaken so great a task. Although it is possible that the area could have capitalized on its climate and geography without Flagler, it is highly improbable that it could have developed as rapidly as it did. To Flagler's credit, he built up a region that had been sparsely populated, rather than pushing the will of a vast public to his own desires. Business leaders such as Julia Tuttle, Mary Brickell, and George Miles realized that they would benefit from any concessions they gave to Flagler. They wished to give him a portion of their holdings, knowing the remainder would increase in value once he accepted their offers. Development of underdeveloped regions always has a cost. Few areas in the post–Civil War United States were developed as rapidly at less cost to its inhabitants than Henry Flagler's development of Florida's east coast. A prime example of the cost of the FEC to *stockholders* is the fact that it did not pay its first dividend until 1980. In other words, not only did Flagler not receive any return on his railroad investment, but with the Depression-era bankruptcy and other events, many other investors lost money in the FEC before it finally became a truly profitable business institution.[4]

Flagler hoped his able associates would continue to run the Flagler System. He was fortunate in having men who served him consistently and well. Bequests made in his will reflect this. This was especially true of Parrott, Beardsley, and Ingraham. A trust, with Parrott, Beardsley, and William R. Kenan, Jr., as trustees, was to operate for five years after Flagler's death. Afterward, if the Flagler companies were solvent, an election of officers could take place and reorganization could occur. Flagler stipulated that, in the meantime, Parrott was to be president and Beardsley vice-president and treasurer of the operations.[5]

Flagler's plans for his businesses were dealt a major blow with the death of J. R. Parrott only five months after that of Flagler. William H. Beardsley became president of the Florida East Coast Railway and the other Flagler enterprises and remained in those positions until 1923, when William R. Kenan, Jr., assumed the presidency of the FEC. Beardsley remained chairman of the board until his death in 1925.[6]

Kenan, as president of the FEC, directed the company through the 1920s, during first the Florida boom and then the bust. During the boom period, Kenan had the FEC line double-tracked from Jacksonville to Miami in 1925. The boom, and the FEC's inability to fully meet the demand, caused the Seaboard Air Line to move into the Miami area in 1927. Meanwhile, between a major hurricane of 1926 and the collapse of the boom in the late 1920s, the FEC was already in a depression in 1929. During the Depression years of the 1930s, declining revenues forced the road into receivership. Ironically, the federal judge's September 1, 1931, order came in response to a creditor's petition filed by another company that Flagler had helped organize years before, the Standard Oil Company of Kentucky. The federal court appointed Kenan and former United States Senator Scott Loftin as the FEC's receivers. Meanwhile, Edward Ball, trustee for the Alfred I. duPont estate (Ball's sister having been duPont's wife), bought the mortgage debt at a fraction of its face value. After extended litigation, Ball gained complete control of the railway in 1961.[7]

The period of the 1920s was a time of prosperity for the Florida East Coast Hotel Company. Business was booming, and when the second Breakers burned in 1925, the company immediately constructed a new palatial structure on the oceanfront site. The Villa Medici and the Boboli Gardens of Florence inspired the Breakers and its grounds. The company brought seventy-five artists from Europe to work on the Breakers paintings. The $6 million hotel contained 450 master bedrooms, 50 guest servants' rooms, and 250 service rooms for hotel employees. It opened on December 29, 1926, just in time for the collapse of Florida's boom economy.[8]

The Great Depression forced the hotel company to close all but the most profitable of its hotels. In 1932, the Cordova and Poinciana shut their doors. Only the Ponce de Leon, Ormond, the Breakers, and the Long Key Fishing Camp opened two years later. The hotel company razed the once-regal Poinciana in 1936. The citizens of St. Johns County converted the Cordova into the St. Johns County Courthouse; the Alcazar's hotel section became the St. Augustine City Hall; and the casino portion of the Alcazar became the Lightner Museum. The Ponce de Leon closed its doors as a hotel in 1967, but it continued to function in a new role as Flagler College. During the 1960s, the revitalized Flagler Systems, Incorporated, built hotels in Gainesville, St. Augustine, and New Providence (Bahamas).[9]

The Breakers, under Flagler Systems control, continued to be popular with Palm Beach's winter resort visitors. It was the only hotel in the system to show good earnings during the 1930s. During the 1954–1955 season, rates ranged from $16.00 to $49.00 per couple on the American plan. The management openly advertised: "The clientele of the Breakers is restricted and satisfactory social references must be submitted." This policy resulted in the first lawsuit under the 1964 Civil Rights Act, an action brought by the Anti-Defamation League. The plaintiffs charged the hotel with systematic exclusion of Jews. The Breakers and the League reached an out-of-court settlement favorable to the League's position. By 1971, the Breakers had dropped all social requirements, increased its rates, doubled its capacity, and beginning in 1973, stayed open throughout the year. At that time, the *Philadelphia Enquirer* described it as "the last resort."[10]

The influence of Henry Flagler lives on in our nation's business. He played an important role in Standard Oil's rise to prominence as the world's first great trust. Exxon, the direct corporate descendent of Standard Oil (New Jersey), is among the richest corporations in the world today—and that does not include the other Standard Oil subsidiaries which are now independent corporations. However, the Florida east coast provides the best examples of the lasting monuments to Flagler's career. One of its counties now bears his name; there is a statue of him on an island at the mouth of the Miami River; and the rails from the Key West Extension are used as guard rails for the "Overseas Highway." Examples could be multiplied, but they would still fail to show the influence that Flagler exercised on Florida's east coast. By building the Florida East Coast Railway and providing connections with northern cities, he diverted to Florida winter tourists who would have gone to Europe or southern California. If Henry Flagler has a business claim to immortality, it is his development of the east coast of Florida—that land which, from the time of Ponce de Leon, allowed people to dream—and Flagler made his a reality.

Map showing route of Florida East Coast Railway to Key West Extension, ca. 1913

Notes

THE PURPOSE of this documentation is to assist readers attempting to broaden their scholarly inquiry. Every effort has been made to credit properly secondary sources and refer back to the location of original source materials, giving close attention to where primary materials may be found. In order not to overburden the manuscript, I have taken the liberty of reducing the length of the notes section in the following ways: First, since often five or more business letters are cited as source material for one sentence of a narrative, citations have been clustered in one end note for each paragraph within the text. Source material has been placed in direct relationship to its placement in the textual passage. When it is unclear which source is being quoted, a parenthetical statement follows the citation. Second, abbreviations for some citations which are used frequently and in several chapters are given below. These abbreviations are used throughout the notes; consult individual sets of chapter notes to find the meaning of other specific abbreviations.

The bibliography was designed for those wishing to pursue this particular area of inquiry. It is not intended either to show the author's prowess in accumulating data or to be an exhaustive compendium on late nineteenth- and early twentieth-century Americana.

Abbreviations Used in Notes

CCL   Camden Consolidated Oil Co. letter book (contained in JNCP, see below)
FHQ   *Florida Historical Quarterly*
FLb   Flagler letter book (Flagler Papers, The Henry Morrison Flagler Museum, Palm Beach, Fla.)

FP	Flagler Papers (The Henry Morrison Flagler Museum, Palm Beach, Fla.)
FT-U	Jacksonville *Florida Times-Union*
HCR	New York State Committee on Railroads, *Proceedings of the Special Committee on Railroads* (New York, 1879). (The report was commonly referred to as the *Hepburn Committee Report*, after the committee's chairman, Alonzo B. Hepburn.)
HTI	House Committee on Manufactures, *Report on Investigation of Trusts: The Standard Oil Trust*, 50th Cong., 1st sess., 1888, H. Rept. 3112 (or, simply, *House Trust Investigation*).
JDRL	John D. Rockefeller letter book (Rockefeller Archive Center, North Tarrytown, N.Y.)
JNCP	Johnson Newlon Camden Papers (West Virginia University Archives, Library, West Virginia University, Morgantown, W.Va.)
lb.	letter book
PKY	P. K. Yonge Library of Florida History (Research Library, University of Florida, Gainesville, Fla.)
RAC	Rockefeller Archive Center (North Tarrytown, N.Y.)
RA&F	Rockefeller, Andrews & Flagler letter book (Rockefeller Archive Center, North Tarrytown, N.Y.)
SAHS	St. Augustine Historical Society Library (St. Augustine, Fla.)

Preface

1. The 1978 Pulitzer Prize for history went to Alfred D. Chandler, author of *The Visible Hand: The Managerial Revolution in American Business* (Cambridge, Mass., 1977). The 1985 Pulitzer Prize for history went to Thomas K. McCraw, author of *Prophets of Regulation: Charles Francis Adams, Louis D. Brandeis, James M. Landis, Alfred E. Kahn* (Cambridge, Mass., 1984).

2. Several fine business history textbooks to appear recently include Keith L. Bryant, Jr., and Henry C. Dethloff, *A History of American Business* (Englewood Cliffs, N.J., 1983); and Mansel G. Blackford and K. Austin Kerr, *Business Enterprise in American History* (Boston, 1986). For our purposes, a general economic history of America is excellent: Stanley Lebergott, *The Americans: An Economic Record* (New York, 1984), especially pp. 322–36.

3. Henry Demarest Lloyd, "The Story of a Great Monopoly," *Atlantic Monthly* 47 (March 1881): 317–34.

4. Henry Demarest Lloyd, *Wealth against Commonwealth* (1894; rpt. New York, 1899).

5. For a pro-Standard interpretation of the reception of the Lloyd work, see Allan Nevins, *Study in Power: John D. Rockefeller, Industrialist and Philanthropist* (New York, 1953), 2:140–44 (on the *Atlantic* article) and 2:330–34 (on *Wealth against Commonwealth*).

6. David M. Chalmers, Introduction to *The History of the Standard Oil Company*, by Ida M. Tarbell, Briefer Version (New York, 1966), xiv–xv; Ida M. Tarbell, *All in the Day's Work: An Autobiography* (New York, 1939), 205–11.

7. Tarbell, *All in the Day's Work*, 211–53.

8. Ibid.

9. W. O. Inglis's methods constituted a rather crude form of oral history/reminiscence. He would quote passages from either Ida Tarbell's *The History of the Standard Oil Company* or Henry Demarest Lloyd's *Wealth against Commonwealth* and then allow Rockefeller to react to them. The value of the material is somewhat lessened in that it does tend to become hyperbolic at times. On the other hand, it is the nearest we will come to Rockefeller's true feelings about the men and events around him. Within that framework, Nevins did an excellent job of integrating the Inglis materials into his own biographies of Rockefeller.

10. John T. Flynn, *God's Gold: The Story of Rockefeller and His Times* (New York, 1932), viii.

11. In comparing the Inglis documents at the Rockefeller Archive Center with Nevins's *John D. Rockefeller: The Heroic Age of American Enterprise*, 2 vols. (New York, 1940), there is no doubt that the Inglis material contributed heavily to Allan Nevins's interpretation of Rockefeller in this first two-volume biography of Rockefeller. On the other hand, Nevins did continue a similar interpretative framework relying less on Inglis in the two volumes of *Study in Power*, published in 1953. The basic point I wish to convey is that Nevins tended to take Rockefeller's interpretation of crucial events and personalities uncritically at times.

12. Nevins, *Study in Power* 1:vii–ix.

13. Ralph W. Hidy and Muriel E. Hidy, *Pioneering in Big Business, 1882–1911*, vol. 1 of *History of Standard Oil Company (New Jersey)*, ed. Henrietta M. Larson (New York, 1955).

14. Jerome Thomas Bentley, *The Effects of Standard Oil's Vertical Integration into Transportation on the Structure and Performance of the American Petroleum Industry, 1872–1884*, Energy in the American Economy, ed. Stuart Bruchey (New York, 1979).

15. Bruce Bringhurst, *Antitrust and the Oil Monopoly: The Standard Oil Cases, 1890–1911* (Westport, Conn., 1979).

16. David Freeman Hawke, *John D.: The Founding Father of the Rockefellers* (New York, 1979).

17. Sidney Walter Martin, *Florida's Flagler* (Athens, Ga., 1949); David Leon Chandler, *Henry Flagler: The Astonishing Life and Times of the Visionary Robber Baron Who Founded Florida* (New York, 1986)

Prologue: Young Entrepreneur

1. *FT-U*, January 23, 1912; from author's observation of various photographs of Flagler in The Henry Morrison Flagler Museum, Palm Beach, Florida.

2. In Sidney Walter Martin, *Florida's Flagler* (Athens, Ga., 1949), the chapter on the Key West Extension is appropriately entitled "Flagler's Folly." See *Miami Herald*, January 22, 1913, for a glowing report of the Extension upon its completion.

3. Kermit J. Pike, *A Guide to the Manuscripts and Archives of the Western Reserve Historical Society* (Cleveland, Ohio, 1972), inside cover.

4. For a general overview of the Erie Canal's place in the transport revolution, see George Rogers Taylor, *Transportation Revolution, 1815–1860* (New York, 1951). For more detail concerning the canal itself, see Ronald E. Shaw, *Erie Water West: A History of the Erie Canal, 1792–1854* (Lexington, Ky., 1966).

5. Bill Oddo, *Stories of Old Bellevue, Book II: December 1984–December 1986* (privately printed, 1986), 149.

6. Ibid.

7. Ibid. For a summary of Stephen's career, see J. H. Kennedy, "Stephen Vanderburg Harkness," *Magazine of Western History* 9 (November 1888–April 1889): 188.

8. This material was gleaned from the genealogical writings on Flagler's ancestry by Robert Pierce. His articles are as follows: "The Germanic Origin of the Flagler Family in Dutchess County," *Year Book: Dutchess County Historical Society* 57 (1972): 12–35; "The Seed is Planted in American Soil," ibid., 59 (1974): 30–38; "Over Hill; Over Dale," ibid., 60 (1975): 71–78; and "A Wandering Preacher I," ibid., 61 (1976): 79–86. Much of this material is also included in the appendixes in David Leon Chandler, *Henry Flagler: The Astonishing Life and Times of the Visionary Robber Baron Who Founded Florida* (New York, 1986), 272–89. The information on Isaac Flagler's first wife and family was provided in a letter from Charles B. Simmons, director of The Henry Morrison Flagler Museum, to the author, August 23, 1986.

9. Pierce, "A Wandering Preacher I," 86–87

10. Ibid., 87; Hammondsport Presbyterian Church (New York), Original Session Book, September 14, 1831–December 31, 1835 (also contains registry of members through 1883), Box 41-A, FP; Clark Waggoner, *History of Toledo and Lucas County, Ohio* (Toledo, 1888), 669.

11. Oddo, *Bellevue, Book II*, 150. For a concise biographical sketch of Dan Harkness, see W. W. Williams, *History of the Fire Lands, Comprising Huron and Erie Counties, Ohio* (Cleveland, Ohio, 1879), 116–17.

12. Oddo, *Bellevue, Book II*, 150.

13. Williams, *Fire Lands*, 390–91; Harriet Taylor Upton, *History of the Western Reserve* (Chicago, 1910), 1:439–41; Williams, *Fire Lands*, 416.

14. Oddo, *Bellevue, Book II*, 150. For more on Stephen, see Kennedy, "Stephen Vanderburg Harkness," 188; Thomas W. Latham, "Revelations of an Old Account Book," *Firelands Pioneer* 22 (Fall 1920): 133–34.

15. Oddo, *Bellevue, Book II*, 150; Flagler interview with James B. Morrow, New York *Tribune*, December 23, 1906.

16. Flagler quoted in Jacksonville *Metropolis*, May 21, 1913. Flagler's exact words with regard to the French five-franc piece were, "The five-franc piece is at home in my desk. I have kept it all these years, imitating the man in the Bible who had but one talent." The true import of this comment may have passed over his interviewer. Since the one-talented biblical character went out and hid his talent and was thus scolded, it may have been that Flagler used this as an illustration of the person who is not willing to risk and thus has no gain.

17. Flagler interview with Morrow.

18. Williams, *Fire Lands*, 416; Flagler interview with Morrow.

19. "Marriage Records of Huron County, Ohio," vol. 3, Old Series, May 14, 1846, to June 12, 1855, WPA Project, 105, 133; Williams, *Fire Lands*, 416.

20. Latham, "Old Account Book," 134–35; Williams, *Fire Lands*, 414–15; *Huron Reflector*, January 30, 1844; Williams, *Fire Lands*, 417.

21. Flagler Family Records, FP; "Necrology—Mr. William Lamont Harkness," *Transactions, The Western Reserve Historical Society* 102 (October 1920): 25–26; Williams, *Fire Lands*, 416. Bell Harkness died when William was eight, probably in 1866; Dan Harkness died August 5, 1896.

22. Williams, *Fire Lands*, 400; Allan Nevins, *Study in Power: John D. Rockefeller, Industrialist and Philanthropist* (New York, 1953), 1:56.

23. Latham, "Old Account Book," 135; Williams, *Fire Lands*, 403.

24. Williams, *Fire Lands*, 403; Flagler interview with Morrow. According to Clark Wag-

goner, Isaac Flagler served as the first president of the Toledo City Temperance Society (" 'on the tee-total plan,' with a pledge agreeing not to use or traffic in intoxicating liquors") in 1838. By the end of April 1838, the temperance society had gotten the city council to pass a mild prohibition ordinance. See Waggoner, *Toledo and Lucas County, Ohio*, 809.

25. Kennedy, "Stephen Vanderburg Harkness," 188; Latham, "Old Account Book," 136–37.

26. Williams, *Fire Lands*, 54–55. In addition to S. V. Harkness, the income,tax statements in Williams's volume show both Lamon Harkness and Dan Harkness to have had 1864 earnings in excess of $21,000 each.

27. Oddo, *Bellevue, Book II*, 10.

28. Ibid.

29. Norwalk (Ohio) *Reflector*, August 19, 1862. I appreciate David Chandler sending me his photocopies of clippings from the *Reflector*. Both Chandler and I wish full credit for much of the Bellevue research to go to Bill Oddo. Oddo's full account of the incident is in his *Bellevue, Book II*, 10. He ends his account by noting that upon the death of Dan Harkness in 1896, General Buckland sent a contingent of officers to the funeral to serve as an honor guard and pallbearers.

30. Williams, *Fire Lands*, 416–17; Bell Harkness to Mary Flagler, [date unclear, but obviously while Dan was in uniform], Box 43, FP; Pierce, "A Wandering Preacher I," 88; Bell Harkness to Mary Flagler, [date unclear], 1862, Box 43, FP.

31. Sunday School meeting minutes, Bellevue Congregational Church, Bellevue, Ohio, July 25 and December 11, 1862, and January 10 and April 15, 1863, in Box 41-A, FP.

32. Bill Oddo, "The Harkness Family Mark on Bellevue," *Stories of Old Bellevue, Book I: January 1983-December 1984* (privately printed, 1984), 92; clipping from Norwalk *Reflector*, n.d. (but the Flagler & Vail notice of dissolution was dated February 2, 1863); Deed Book 15, Huron County, Ohio, 103, 169–70; Williams, *Fire Lands*, 116–17; Deed Books, County of Saginaw, Mich., Libre 30, p. 584.

33. *Saginaw Courier*, January 19, 1880; *Saginaw Enterprise*, February 3, 1859.

34. *Saginaw Courier*, January 19, 1880; *Saginaw Enterprise*, March 31 and April 14, 1859.

35. *East Saginaw Courier*, August 10, 1864; Deed Books, County of Saginaw, Mich., Libre 31, p. 222, and Libre 46, pp. 62–64. The deed book listing states that Flagler and York purchased their first property on October 23, 1862, with the final recording on December 20.

36. *East Saginaw Courier*, August 10, 1864.

37. Ibid., April 7, 1863. Although there was always some variation, the typical salt manufacturing operation in Saginaw went something like this: Wells were sunk 700 to 1,000 feet at a cost of $5,000. Typically, one man would be employed at the $1,000 engine house on the surface to run the operation. He would use a cord of wood a day, at a cost of $2.00, and would bring enough brine to the surface to supply three blocks of kettles. A block would produce fifty barrels of salt a day, using 6½ cords of wood to heat the three blocks of kettles.

38. *East Saginaw Courier*, February 10, 1864.

39. *History of the First Presbyterian Church of Saginaw, Michigan, 1838–1938* (n.p., 1938), 25–26; *Manual of the First Congregational Church and Society of East Saginaw with Historical Sketch and Catalogues* (East Saginaw, Mich., 1873), 4–6, 9, 65.

40. *Saginaw Weekly Enterprise*, March 2, 1865, and January 25, 1866.

41. *Pioneer Directory [city directory] of the Saginaw Valley*, 1866–1867; *Saginaw City Directory*, 1866; *East Saginaw Courier*, September 21, 1864; *Pioneer Directory*, 26–27; *Saginaw Weekly Enterprise*, January 19, 1865. To give some idea of the explosive growth of the

east side of the Saginaw River, in the 1866 city directory twenty-eight pages were devoted to Saginaw itself, while East Saginaw had forty-nine, and Salina had seven, giving the two communities on the east side of the river a decided edge over the parent community.

42. *Saginaw Weekly Enterprise,* March 15, 1866; *Pioneer Directory,* 28; *Saginaw Weekly Enterprise,* February 16, 1865.

43. Deed Books, County of Saginaw, Mich., Libre 38, p. 57; *East Saginaw Courier,* May 4, 1864.

44. Mary Harkness to Mary Flagler, June 19 and December 13, 1865, Box 43, FP.

45. Oddo, *Bellevue, Book II,* 153.

46. *Saginaw Weekly Enterprise,* October 5, 1865; *Saginaw Daily Enterprise,* December 20, 1866. During the later months of 1865, producers, accustomed to the high prices of the war years, simply refused to sell at lower prices. The large number of small firms engaged in the salt business compounded this crisis. In 1865, there were sixty-seven salt companies in the Saginaw area, with a total capital investment of $2,269,500. *Pioneer Directory,* 47.

47. *Saginaw Courier,* January 19, 1880.

48. *Saginaw Daily Enterprise,* December 20, 1866; *Saginaw Enterprise,* January 27, 1867.

49. *Saginaw Enterprise,* January 17 and February 7, 1867. The Saginaw Salt Company was a thinly veiled combination. Article VII of its articles of incorporation reads:

> The Company shall manufacture salt by making contracts for a period of one year with the proprietors of salt manufactories at present in Saginaw Co., and such others as the Board may determine, to manufacture salt on the Company's account, in the manner hereafter provided. Each contract shall stipulate that the manufacturer shall make salt solely on the Company's account, of the best quality of the kind manufactured by him— that he will not sell or pledge any salt made by him, but deliver the same to the Company, upon the terms offered by the said Company in accordance with its Charter and By-laws. . . . [*Saginaw Enterprise,* January 17, 1867]

50. *Saginaw Weekly Enterprise,* January 18, 1866. In a graph of 1868 Saginaw Valley salt manufacturers, Flagler & York was credited with 4 blocks and 208 kettles, with invested capital of $75,000. But its kettles had not been run in 1868. In the overall statistics for Saginaw County, it was shown that there were 111 blocks with 4,154 kettles, representing an invested capital of $2,217,000. George F. Lewis and C. B. Headley, *Annual Statement of the Business of Saginaw Valley and "The Shore," for 1868* (East Saginaw, 1869), 19. In their report a year later, Lewis and Headley had the same report on Flagler & York, except to note that the firm was down to 2 blocks and 128 kettles. Ibid., *for 1869* (East Saginaw, 1870).

51. The Flagler house was sold to Emma A. Ripley on March 21, 1866, for $5,500. Deed Books, County of Saginaw, Mich., Libre 44, p. 83. For a description of the 1866 Bellevue experience, see Chandler, *Henry Flagler,* 43. By tracing deeds, we can establish that the Flaglers were in Cleveland by the end of July 1866, but that the Yorks did not move to Cleveland until sometime between the fall of 1866 and the summer of 1867. Deed Books, County of Saginaw, Mich., Libre 45, pp. 381 and 539, and Libre 46, pp. 496–97. Interestingly, Flagler and York sold much of their Saginaw area holdings to their father-in-law for $15,000 in the spring of 1866; Lamon Harkness in turn gave the property to his daughters, their wives. Deed Books, County of Saginaw, Mich., Libre 44, pp. 129–31. The Flagler and York properties were still in the family as late as 1877. "Saginaw Atlas," *Records,* City of Saginaw, Mich. (1877), 77. More than likely, the $15,000 was used to help erase Saginaw debts; therefore, Chandler's depiction of Flagler's return to Bellevue in a condition of poverty still rings true.

52. For the local perspective on the salt producers' meeting, see Cleveland *Leader,* March 25, 1871.

53. *Manufacturers' Record,* January 26, 1922, p. 60, in James E. Ingraham Papers, MS Box 1, SAHS. For a look at Daniel Drew, see Clifford Browder, *The Money Game in Old New York: Daniel Drew and His Times* (Lexington, Ky., 1986).

Introduction to the Standard Years

1. Robert H. Wiebe, *The Search for Order, 1877–1920* (New York, 1967); Allan Nevins, *John D. Rockefeller: The Heroic Age of American Enterprise* (New York, 1940), 1:147–52.

2. Nevins, *Rockefeller* 1:157–65.

3. Ibid., 172–80

4. Allan Nevins, *Study in Power: John D. Rockefeller, Industrialist and Philanthropist* (New York, 1953), 1:20–36.

5. For the best explication of this thesis, see Jerome Thomas Bentley, *The Effects of Standard Oil's Vertical Integration into Transportation on the Structure and Performance of the American Petroleum Industry, 1872–1884,* Energy in the American Economy, ed. Stuart Bruchey (New York, 1979), 8–9.

1 Rockefeller, Andrews & Flagler

1. Deed Books, County of Saginaw, Mich., Libre 45, p. 381; *Cleveland City Directory,* 1866–67; Session Minutes, 1867, First Presbyterian Church, Cleveland, Ohio (in offices of the Old Stone Church); Allan Nevins, *Study in Power: John D. Rockefeller, Industrialist and Philanthropist* (New York, 1953), 1:56–57; Wilfred Henry Alburn, *This Cleveland of Ours* (Chicago, 1933), 2:608; Charles Melbourne Higgins recollections to W. O. Inglis, Inglis book 3, RAC. David Chandler makes much of the return to Bellevue as a humiliating experience for Flagler. David Leon Chandler, *Henry Flagler: The Astonishing Life and Times of the Visionary Robber Baron Who Founded Florida* (New York, 1986), 43. Both Flagler's naturally optimistic personality and the short duration of the experience suggest that it had little effect on him. Deed records, as previously cited, indicate that Flagler was still in Saginaw on March 21 and in Cleveland by July 26. The actual move to Cleveland could have been even earlier.

2. Flagler interview with James B. Morrow, New York *Tribune,* December 23, 1906; *Cleveland City Directory,* 1868–69.

3. Nevins, *Study in Power* 1:58–59.

4. John D. Rockefeller, *Random Reminiscences of Men and Events* (New York, 1909), 12–15.

5. New York to Cleveland, October 15, 1867, RA&F 393. Although most New York office correspondence is assumed to be from William Rockefeller and most Cleveland correspondence from Flagler or John Rockefeller, only correspondence that can be specifically identified will be attributed here. Otherwise, "New York" or "Cleveland" must suffice. If simply referred to as "Rockefeller," the reference means "John Rockefeller."

6. New York to John Andrews, August 26 and 31, 1868, Cleveland to J. L. Pierce & Co., September 27, 1868, and William Rockefeller to John Andrews, November 2, 1868, RA&F 1.

7. Rockefeller letters to Flagler and John Andrews, November 5, 1867, RA&F 393.

8. Rockefeller to Flagler, November 5 (first quotation), and November 11, 1867, RA&F 1.

9. New York to Cleveland, November 26, 1867 (quotation), and Cleveland to New York, December 6, 1867, RA&F 393. It should be mentioned that, according to John Rockefeller in his *Random Reminiscences* (pp. 12–13), he and Flagler worked closely together in those years. Other testimony indicates that they would pass correspondence back and forth between themselves until they had the wording just right. Therefore, it should be assumed that letters from Cleveland were the joint work of John Rockefeller and Flagler unless clearly identified.

10. William Rockefeller to Cleveland, January 20, 1868, RA&F 1.

11. New York to Cleveland, September 10, 12, 16, and 21, 1867, RA&F 393; William Rockefeller to Cleveland, October 19 and November 11, 1867, RA&F 1.

12. New York to Cleveland, August 22, 1867, RA&F 1; Cleveland to New York, August 27, and September 7 and 9, 1867, RA&F 393.

13. New York to John Andrews (in Oil City), March 20 and 26, and April 20, 1868, RA&F [00]. The [00] designation indicates no letter book number.

14. William Rockefeller to Cleveland, January 30 and 31 (quotation), 1868, RA&F 1; New York to Cleveland, February 24 and 26, 1868, RA&F 393; ibid., March 23, 25, and 26, and April 27 and 29, 1868, RA&F [00]; George Girty to Cleveland, May 2 and 12, 1868, RA&F [00]; Cleveland to New York, September 10, 1867, RA&F 393.

15. New York to Cleveland, January 28, 1868, RA&F 1; ibid., February 28, 1868, RA&F 393; New York to Flagler, March 12, 1868, RA&F 393; Harold F. Williamson and Arnold P. Daum, *The American Petroleum Industry: The Age of Illumination, 1859–1899* (Evanston, Ill., 1959), 337.

16. New York to Cleveland, April 11, 16, 1868, and March 23, 26, and April 27, 1868, RA&F [00].

17. New York to Flagler, April 22, 1868 (first quotation), William Rockefeller to Cleveland, April 27 and 29, 1868, RA&F [00]. The first quotation given seems to be Flagler's. This is deduced from the fact that New York, probably William Rockefeller, stated in the letter of April 22 that John was in New York and continued: "Your new maxims, 'Sell when others. . . .' "

18. This attitude by the RA&F partners, and continuing at Standard Oil, will become more evident as the story unfolds.

19. New York to Cleveland, August 23, 1867, RA&F 393; New York to John Andrews, August 29, 1867, RA&F 1; Cleveland to New York, October 25, 1867, Cleveland to John Andrews, November 2, 1867, and to New York, November 13, 1867, RA&F 393; New York to Cleveland, December 12, 1867, RA&F 1.

20. New York to Cleveland, February 4, 12, and 8 (quotation), 1868, RA&F 393.

21. New York to Cleveland, February 12, 1868, RA&F 393.

22. New York to Cleveland, January 20–24, 27, February 5, 14, and March 20, 1868, RA&F 393.

23. Cleveland to John Andrews, November 2, 1867, RA&F 1; New York to John Andrews, September 11, 1867, and New York to Cleveland, September 24, 1867, RA&F 393; Rockefeller to Flagler, November 1 and 2, 1867, RA&F 1; New York to Cleveland, March 3, 1868, RA&F 393; New York to Sam Andrews, March 25, 1868, RA&F 2.

24. New York to Cleveland, February 26, 27, 28, and March 4, 6 (quotation), and 15, 1868, RA&F 393.

25. New York to Cleveland, March 21 and 27, 1868, RA&F [00]; ibid., March 30, 1868,

RA&F 2; ibid., April 5, 1868, RA&F [00]; ibid., April 11, 1868, RA&F 2; ibid., April 18, 1868, RA&F [00].

26. New York to Cleveland, May 4, 1868, RA&F [00]; New York to John Andrews, June 17, 1868, and New York to Cleveland, June 22 and 27, 1868, RA&F [00].

27. William Rockefeller to Cleveland, May 9, 1868, RA&F 2; New York to John Andrews, June 17, 1868, RA&F [00].

28. Chester McArthur Destler, "The Standard Oil, Child of the Erie Ring, 1868–1872: Six Contracts and a Letter," *Mississippi Valley Historical Review* 33 (June 1946): 89–91. For an intense historical debate over this issue, see the letter from Julius Grodinsky, the Jay Gould biographer, and Destler's reply under the general heading "A Variance of Views on the Standard Oil and the Erie Ring," *Mississippi Valley Historical Review* 33 (March 1947): 617–28.

29. Destler, "The Standard Oil," 92–93. The agreement itself reproduced in ibid., 103.

30. Ibid., 93–95. Copy of the agreement in ibid., 104–6. Maury Klein has recently written an excellent biography of Gould. However, he and I disagree on the specific impact of Gould's alliance with the oil refineries of Cleveland. See Maury Klein, *The Life and Legend of Jay Gould* (Baltimore, 1986), 95.

31. The June 5th agreement, as reproduced in Destler, "The Standard Oil," 106–10.

32. Destler credits Flagler with the change, ibid., 109, n. 31.

33. Edward H. Mott, *Between the Ocean and the Lakes: The Story of the Erie* (New York, 1908), 181.

34. *Dictionary of American Biography*, s.v. "Amasa Stone."

35. Flagler interview with Morrow.

36. Paul H. Giddens, *The Birth of the Oil Industry* (New York, 1938), 153ff.

37. From my calculations from RA&F correspondence over that period.

38. Nevins, *Study in Power* 1:77–80.

39. Standard Oil Company original minute book, January 10, 1870, RAC.

40. Ibid.

41. Ibid., February 12, 1870; *Dictionary of American Biography*, s.v. "Amasa Stone." Allan Nevins, in both his biographies of Rockefeller, mistakenly thought there were two Amasa Stones, junior and senior. In reality, there was only one, the point of confusion being that he was sometimes referred to simply as "Amasa Stone" and at other times as "Amasa Stone, Jr."

42. Amasa Stone testimony, "Appendix: Report of Special Committee on Railroads," *Ohio Senate Journal* 63 (1867): 76.

43. Nevins, *Study in Power* 1:86.

2   Cleveland Company, National Business

1. Allan Nevins, *Study in Power: John D. Rockefeller, Industrialist and Philanthropist* (New York, 1953), 1:88.

2. James H. Devereux affidavit, *Standard Oil v. William C. Scofield et al.*, Court of Common Pleas, Cuyahoga County, Ohio, as Appendix 3, in Ida Tarbell, *The History of the Standard Oil Company*, 2 vols. in 1 (1904; rpt. New York, 1950), 1:277–79. David Freeman Hawke is to be given full credit for first noting the difference between Standard's capacity and its commitment to the Lake Shore. David Freeman Hawke, *John D.: The Founding Father of the Rockefellers* (New York, 1980), 67–68.

3. Devereux affidavit cited in note 2. At the time of the Standard contract with the Lake Shore, Devereux wrote to William H. Vanderbilt on February 10, 1870: "The magnitude and regularity of the business of R. A. and Co. [RA&F] makes a low rate profitable with the results of the whole year." Two weeks later, on February 25, Devereux wrote Vanderbilt again: "The peculiar point of the business of the Standard Oil Company is its assured regularity and evenness." Thomas C. Cochran, *Railroad Leaders, 1845–1900: The Business Mind In Action* (Cambridge, Mass., 1953), 311.

4. Ibid.

5. Nevins, *Study in Power* 1:94; Standard Oil original minute book, 1871, RAC.

6. Standard Oil original minute book, 1872, RAC.

7. Ibid.

8. Ibid.

9. Charles Tucker recollections to W. O. Inglis, Inglis book 3, RAC.

10. Isaac L. Hewitt testimony, before the Hepburn Committee (1879), quoted in Nevins, *Study in Power* 1:137; Alexander testimony before 1872 House investigating committee, quoted in Tarbell, *The History of the Standard* 1:65.

11. George O. Baslington affidavits, *Standard Oil* v. *William C. Scofield et al.,* Court of Common Pleas, Cuyahoga County, Ohio, as Appendix 7, in Tarbell, *The History of the Standard* 1:290–91; John D. Rockefeller, "Random Reminiscences of Men and Events," *World's Work* 17 (November 1908): 10881 (quotation).

12. Nevins, *Study in Power* 1:102–3; JDR to wife, December 1, 1871, quoted in Nevins, *Study in Power* 1:100.

13. Nevins, *Study in Power* 1:105–6; Tarbell, *The History of the Standard* 1:58. Tarbell was unaware of Watson's secret alliance with the Standard. Nevins was aware of it, but that did not keep him from presenting a skewed version of South Improvement's power relationships: "No city held a controlling interest, and Watson's presidency would provide neutral leadership and protect the railroads" (p. 106).

14. Nevins, *Study in Power* 1:106–10.

15. Contract between the South Improvement Company and The Pennsylvania Railroad Company, January 18, 1872, as Appendix 5, in Tarbell, *The History of the Standard* 1:281–88; Rockefeller conversation with W. O. Inglis, Inglis book 1, RAC.

16. See contract cited in n. 15.

17. For Flagler's explanation of the 10 percent "commission/drawback," see his testimony, *HTI,* 774–75. Flagler's explanation also in Appendix 27 in Tarbell, *The History of the Standard* 1:369–70.

18. Nevins, *Study in Power* 1:110–11.

19. Ibid., 112–13.

20. Rockefeller conversation with W. O. Inglis, Inglis book 1, RAC.

21. Nevins, *Study in Power* 1:120.

22. Tarbell, *The History of the Standard* 1:89–93.

23. Nevins, *Study in Power* 1:128.

24. Tarbell, *The History of the Standard* 1:95–96. Rockefeller telegram quoted in full on page 96.

25. Nevins, *Study in Power* 1:146.

26. Ibid., 128.

27. Flagler testimony, Ohio legislative committee, 1879, as Appendix 14 in Tarbell, *The History of the Standard* 1:332–33. In her text, Tarbell identifies the contract specifically on page 100. As she states, it is interesting to note that Standard had already signed the Lake

Shore contract on March 25, 1872, a couple of weeks before Rockefeller's telegram denying any contracts existed between Standard and transportation agencies. Cleveland refiners were to pay $.50 a barrel to get crude oil from the Regions and then another $1.50 to ship refined to New York. Producers, under the March 25, 1872, agreement, were able to ship crude to New York at a $1.35 rate.

28. Tarbell, *The History of the Standard* 1:104–9; Nevins, *Study in Power* 1:162–63.

29. Flagler testimony, as Appendix 14 in Tarbell, *The History of the Standard* 1:333.

30. Ibid., 333–34.

31. Ibid.

32. Ibid., 329–35.

33. Nevins, *Study in Power* 1:192.

34. Ibid., 196.

35. Paul H. Giddens, *The Birth of the Oil Industry* (New York, 1938), 67; Jewett testimony, *HCR* 2:463.

36. New York *Tribune*, July 11, 20, 31, and August 3 and 4, 1874; The Rutter Circular, *HTI*, 363. The Rutter Circular rates were $1.85 a barrel from every refining point to Philadelphia and $2.00 from every refining point to New York.

37. Agreement of 1874 between the railroads and pipelines, as Appendix 22 in Tarbell, *The History of the Standard* 1:354–58.

38. Nevins, *Study in Power* 1:203–6.

39. March 10, 1875, and January 5, 1875, meetings, Standard Oil minute book, RAC.

40. Ibid., March 10, 1875; Walter F. Taylor, "History of the Standard Oil Company," RAC.

41. *HTI*, 223–26.

42. New York *Tribune*, February 6, 1875.

43. For a full biographical treatment of Camden, see Festus P. Summers, *Johnson Newlon Camden: A Study in Individualism* (New York, 1937).

44. Taylor, "History of the Standard Oil Company," 105.

45. Nevins, *Study in Power* 1:228–29.

46. Ibid., 229–30.

47. Tarbell, *The History of the Standard* 1:181; Nevins, *Study in Power* 1:229–30.

3   The Supreme Evener of Oil Transport

1. [Joseph D. Potts], *Theory and Practice of the American System of Through Fast Freight Transportation as Illustrated in the Operations of the Empire Transportation Company* (Philadelphia, 1876), 45.

2. For a background on the Empire and other fast-freight lines and their contribution to business, see Alfred D. Chandler, *The Visible Hand: The Managerial Revolution in American Business* (Cambridge, Mass., 1977), 127–78. Note that Chandler tends to agree with the Standard Oil argument that many of these fast-freight operations were only a means for officers of railroads to enrich themselves.

3. Allan Nevins, *Study in Power: John D. Rockefeller, Industrialist and Philanthropist* (New York, 1953), 1:231–32.

4. Rockefeller conversation with W. O. Inglis, Inglis book 1, RAC; Cassatt testimony,

Pennsylvania v. *The Pennsylvania Railroad Company, et al.* (1879), excerpted in *HTI*, 175–76. All the Cassatt testimony contained in the *HTI* was excerpted from the *Pennsylvania* case.

5. Nevins, *Study in Power* 1:237.

6. Rockefeller conversation with W. O. Inglis, Inglis book 1, RAC; *HCR* 2:1466. Tarbell indicated that only one hundred copies of the testimony were printed, and none were used as official documents; see *The History of the Standard Oil Company,* 2 vols. in 1 (1904; rpt. New York, 1950), 1:228. I was able to use volumes 2–5, located in the New York Public Library system (the first volume being lost).

7. Chandler, *The Visible Hand,* 153.

8. H. J. Jewett testimony, *HCR* 2:1463–66; A. J. Cassatt testimony, excerpted in *HTI*, 174–207.

9. Rockefeller conversation with W. O. Inglis, Inglis book 1, RAC; Nevins, *Study in Power* 1:238–39.

10. Cassatt testimony, excerpted in *HTI,* 176; William Brough to Camden, April 24, 1877, Box: Standard Oil correspondence, JNCP.

11. B. B. Campbell testimony, *Pennsylvania* v. *The Pennsylvania Railroad Company, et al., HTI,* 134–35; Nevins, *Study in Power* 1:242–43.

12. Standard Oil Company Executive Committee minute book, 1877, RAC; Tarbell, *History of the Standard* 1:190–91.

13. John T. Flynn, *God's Gold: The Story of Rockefeller and His Times* (New York, 1932), 196; Payne to Cleveland office, August 16, 1877, JDRL 180.

14. Nevins, *Study in Power* 1:244; William Rockefeller to Payne, September 22 and 29, 1877, JDRL 180.

15. Cassatt testimony, excerpted in *HTI,* 179; William Rockefeller to O. H. Payne, September 18, and to John D. Rockefeller, October 17, 1877, JDRL 180.

16. Flagler statement on agreement with Sone & Fleming, October 18, 1877, William Rockefeller to John D. Rockefeller, October 15, and to Payne, October 18, 1877, JDRL 180.

17. Cassatt testimony, excerpted in *HTI,* 179; R. C. Vilas to George I. Vail, October 24, 1877, JDRL 180. Nevins gives a rather intricate presentation of the purchase amounts, which may at first seem at variance with this presentation. Nevins, *Study in Power* 1:246. However, in his presentation, Nevins missed an opportunity to show how exactng the Standard Oil leaders were in their business dealings, for the $3,394,441.67 check represented the $3.4 million purchase price minus the amount of interest for 17 days on the $3.4 million. This was due to the fact that the Standard had stood ready to pay for the properties on October 1 (so they said—the facts contradict that sanguine assessment).

18. Vilas to Vail, October 24, 1877, JDRL 180.

19. Cassatt testimony, excerpted in *HTI,* 208–9.

20. Nevins, *Study in Power* 1:249.

21. Flagler to Joseph Bushnell (treasurer, Empire Pipe Co.), October 22, 1877, JDRL 180; Flagler to George Chester, December 8, 1877, JDRL 181; Flagler to Camden, October 27, 1877, JDRL 180.

22. Flagler to Cassatt, October 13 (telegram), and October 19, 1877, and to A. D. Hepburn (the past president of the Empire Transportation Co.), October 27, 1877, JDRL 180; Flagler to Cassatt, November 26 and 28, 1877, JDRL 181.

23. Flagler to Cassatt, December 3, 1877, and to George Vail, December 26 (two letters, quotation from the second), 1877, JDRL 181.

24. Flagler to Cassatt (marked "confidential"), January 23, 1878, JDRL 182.

25. Flagler to George Chester, November 17, and to Camden, November 19, 1877, JDRL 181.

26. Flagler to J. H. Rutter, November 12, 1877 (second of two letters on that date), Flagler to Chester, December 8, 1877, JDRL 181.

27. Flagler to William Brough, December 5, 1877, JDRL 181. The three companies that combined to make up the United Pipe Lines were American Transfer Company, Columbia Conduit Company, and Empire Pipe Company.

28. Copy of September 20, 1877, Windsor House agreement, JDRL 180. Under the October 1, 1877, rate structure, Standard and its allies paid only $.895 per barrel for refined oil shipped to New York and $.76 for oil bound for Baltimore and Philadelphia. These rates were based on a published rate of $1.50 per barrel to New York and $1.35 to the other two ports. From that open rate, all shippers received an arbitrary allowance as a crude rebate of $.455. In addition, Standard received its usual 10 percent commission. Crude oil moved to the seaboard at $1.00 a barrel, again with Standard receiving a 10 percent commission on all shipments.

29. Tarbell, *The History of the Standard* 1:47–49 (although her argument is periodically stated throughout volume 1, this is her most succinct expression); Flagler testimony, *HTI*, 774–75; Flagler telegram to Cassatt, October 13, 1877, JDRL 180; Flagler to Vail, November 5, 1877, and Flagler to John Newell, December 5, 1877, JDRL 181. For examinations of the widespread use of rebates and drawbacks as early as the 1860s, see Pennsylvania Senate Committee on the Judiciary, "Report to the Senate (January 21, 1868)," in *Journal* (1868), 121–31; and Ohio Senate, "Appendix: Report of Special Committee on Railroads," in *Journal* 63 (1867): 2–27.

30. Flagler to Rutter, September 21, 1877, JDRL 180.

31. Flagler to Vail, November 9, 1877, JDRL 181; Flagler to Rutter, September 21, 1877, JDRL 180. In his letter to Vail, Flagler also advised his auditor to collect at least $.895 for all shipments, since it would be easier to rebate to the railroads for oil having come under the old agreement than to attempt a second collection from shippers on oil falling under the new contract.

32. Flagler to Vail (marked "confidential"), December 18 and December 3, 1877, JDRL 181. Flagler, in the same tight-fisted vein, advised Ambrose McGregor with regard to the subleasing of tank cars: "I recommend we try and accommodate our friends in the business, of course, conditioned, that they are not used in any business competing [*sic*] with ours." Flagler to McGregor, October 27, 1877, JDRL 180.

33. Flagler to Rutter, October 31, 1877, JDRL 180.

34. Ibid., November 1, 1877, JDRL 180; ibid., November 12, 1877, JDRL 181.

35. Rate to take effect December 1, recorded on p. 166 of JDRL 181.

36. Flagler to J. N. Camden, October 31, 1877, JDRL 180.

37. Flagler to Jewett, November 8, 1877, JDRL 181.

38. Camden telegram to Flagler, November 6, 1877, CCL 33; Flagler to Camden, November 17 (first quotation) and 19, 1877, JDRL 181.

39. Andrew Anderson to Camden, December 10, 1877, Box 1, JNCP; Flagler to Camden, December 12, 15, 17, and 18, 1877, JDRL 181.

40. Flagler to Camden, December 18, 1877, JDRL 181.

41. Ibid., December 20, 1877, JDRL 181; Camden to Flagler, December 26, 1877, CCL 33; Flagler to Camden, January 21, 1878, JDRL 182.

42. Flagler to Camden, January 30, 1878, JDRL 182.

43. Flagler to Vail, January 18, 1878, JDRL 182; Flagler to George Vilas, January 22, 1878, JDRL 182.

44. Flagler to Ambrose McGregor, January 23, 1878, JDRL 182; Flagler to Rutter, January 2, 1878, JDRL 181.

45. Flagler to Vail, January 24, 1878, and copy of Cassatt to Flagler, February 1, 1878, JDRL 182.

46. Flagler to Cassatt, April 18, 1878, JDRL 183; Flagler to Andrew Anderson, February 21, 1878, JDRL 182.

47. Flagler to Rutter, February 23, 1878, JDRL 182.

48. Flagler to Daniel O'Day, February 26, 1878, JDRL 183.

49. Flagler to American District Telephone Co., October 31, 1877, JDRL 180; Flagler to Vail, November 16, 1877, JDRL 181.

50. Cleveland City Directory, 1870–71; The Reverend and Mrs. Arthur Clyde Ludlow, *History of Cleveland Presbyterianism* (Cleveland, Ohio, 1896), 731; Grace Goulder, *John D. Rockefeller: The Cleveland Years* (Cleveland, Ohio, 1972), 95. According to Goulder, when the Russian Grand Duke Alexis visited Cleveland in 1872, Amasa Stone invited Flagler—but not Rockefeller—to a dinner party in the Duke's honor (p. 109).

51. Harry Harkness Flagler's marginal comments in his personal copy of Sidney Walter Martin, *Florida's Flagler* (Athens, Ga., 1949), FP. According to Flagler letter to O'Day (May 24, 1878, JDRL 184), Hinckley was working with H. H. Rogers. When George Chester retired in 1880, Flagler requested Rockefeller to appoint Hinckley to the position. Flagler to Rockefeller, August 17, 1880, RG 1, Box 15, folder 112, RAC.

52. Harry Harkness Flagler's marginal comments in his personal copy of *Florida's Flagler;* Flagler to D. D. Tompkins, his builder, December 31, 1877, and January 10, 1878, JDRL 181; Thomas S. Hastings's obituary was the only personal item Flagler had in his statistical diary at the time of his own death; Flagler to Jewett, May 8, and to George H. Vaillant, May 9, 1878, JDRL 184. Flagler and Jennie did not offically join West Presbyterian until March 25, 1882, about a year after the death of Mary Flagler. See Membership Book, First Presbyterian Church (Old Stone Church), Cleveland, Ohio.

53. Flagler to Jewett, February 11, 1878, JDRL 182; Flagler to Amasa Stone, February 25, and to Daniel O'Day, February 26, 1878, JDRL 183.

54. Flagler to Daniel O'Day, February 26, 1878, JDRL 183.

55. Martin, *Florida's Flagler,* 77–78.

56. Flagler to Vail, March 26, 1878, JDRL 183. Since Flagler was ill upon coming back from Florida, he did not make it into the Standard offices until March 26.

4   The Great Pipeline Battle

1. J. N. Camden to Flagler, January 4, 1878, CCL 33; Flagler to Camden, January 10, 1878, JDRL 182.

2. Allan Nevins, *Study in Power: John D. Rockefeller, Industrialist and Philanthropist* (New York, 1953), 1:289–90.

3. Flagler to Daniel O'Day, January 22, 1878, JDRL 182.

4. Flagler to Camden, January 25, 1878, JDRL 182.

5. Ibid., January 31 (first quotation), and February 14, 1878 (second quotation), and Flagler to O. H. Payne, February 7, 1878, JDRL 182.

6. Flagler to J. H. Devereux, December 31, 1877, JDRL 181; Flagler to Payne, February 7, and to Camden, February 14, 1878, JDRL 182.

7. Flagler to Payne, February 7, and to Camden, February 14, 1878, JDRL 182. Although

Flagler had established a working relationship with the trunk lines, such was not the case with the numerous short line roads scattered about the Regions. While he vacationed in Florida in early March, entrepreneurs contemplated a new pipeline that would be shorter than the Seaboard, but just as dangerous to Standard. It would be built from the Regions to Buffalo, where the crude could thence be sent by canal to New York for refining. In order for the pipe to get to Buffalo, it had to go across the right-of-way of the Buffalo and Jamestown Road. Rockefeller, in Flagler's absence, suggested that O'Day either purchase the right-of-way for such activity from the Buffalo and Jamestown, or give the road enough of Standard's refined business to keep it in opposition to the pipe threat. In any case, Rockefeller gave O'Day a direct order, "Don't let them get a pipe to Buffalo." Rockefeller to O'Day, March 14, 1878, JDRL 183.

Standard officials prepared for an all-out offensive on the Buffalo pipeline matter. The objective was the protection of Standard's critical refining center at Cleveland. Rockefeller even suggested that Standard would now be willing to enter a combination with the producers of the country in which Standard would promise to refine all the nation's production. This was an overly ambitious ploy designed to thwart activities such as the Buffalo refinery plans of Lewis Emory, one of the planners of the Bradford-Buffalo pipeline. Emory's plans were especially disconcerting. Worrying about crude by canal to New York refiners was bad enough, without having to be concerned about a new refining center at Buffalo. Rockefeller had had enough; he stated in a letter to Charles Lockhart, "There seems to be refineries in the air." Rockefeller to J. J. Vandergrift (marked "confidential"), March 16, and to Lockhart, March 19, 1878, JDRL 183.

8. Flagler to Andrew Anderson, March 28, 1878, JDRL 183

9. Rockefeller to H. J. Jewett, March 30, 1878, JDRL 183.

10. Flagler to Payne, April 20, 1878, JDRL 183.

11. Flagler to A. J. Cassatt, April 18, 1878, JDRL 183; Rockefeller to Payne, April 20, 1878, JDRL 183.

12. Flagler to Camden, April 29, 1878, JDRL 184; Flagler to Cassatt, April 20, 1878, JDRL 183.

13. Identical letters from Flagler to W. K. Vanderbilt (New York Central), John W. Garrett (B&O), Cassatt (Pennsylvania), and R. C. Vilas (general freight agent, Erie), April 23, and Flagler to H. L. Davis, April 26, 1878, JDRL 183. Present at the meeting were: Flagler, W. K. Vanderbilt and J. H. Rutter (New York Central), Cassatt (Pennsylvania), George R. Blanchard and R. C. Vilas (Erie), and Andrew Anderson (B&O).

14. Flagler to Camden, April 29, 1878, JDRL 184.

15. Ibid.

16. Camden to Flagler, May 1, 1878, CCL 33.

17. Flagler to Vail, March 28, 1878, and Flagler to Cassatt, March 30 and April 1, 1878, JDRL 183. The exact amount of the initial Seaboard Pipe account was $2,671.87.

18. Flagler to Cassatt (marked "confidential") and to Brough, April 6, 1878; Flagler to Cassatt, April 9, and Flagler to O'Day and to Brough, April 10, 1878, JDRL 183.

19. Flagler to Cassatt, April 12, 1878, JDRL 183.

20. Flagler to Payne and to Cassatt, April 20, 1878, JDRL 183.

21. Flagler to Cassatt and to Payne, April 20, 1878, JDRL 183.

22. Flagler to Blanchard, April 22, 1878, JDRL 183.

23. Flagler to Smith M. Weed, April 24, and to Jewett (personally handwritten), April 25, 1878, JDRL 183.

24. Flagler to Blanchard and to Cassatt, April 29, 1878, JDRL 184.

25. Flagler to W. G. Warden, May 24, 1878, JDRL 184. The Benson abandonment did take the pressure off Flagler with regard to the actions of the Pennsylvania legislature. The Pennsylvania road lobbyists did a better job than those of the Central. Although a free-pipeline measure did pass the Pennsylvania house on Tuesday, April 30, the senate killed it a week later. With the Benson party now out of the Maryland picture, the likelihood that a Baltimore pipeline would be constructed in the near future was remote. In spite of this alleviation of the immediate problem with free pipelines in Pennsylvania, Flagler did not want to jeopardize Standard's future position with regard to any pipeline questions. Therefore, he counseled associates to watch for new seaboard pipeline proposals that might later surface. Nevins, *Study in Power* 1:298; Flagler to Jewett, May 8, to H. L. Davis, May 14, and to Smith M. Weed, May 15, 1878, JDRL 184.

26. Flagler to Jewett, May 8, to Cassatt, May 2, and to Smith M. Weed, May 15, 1878, JDRL 184. The activities of independent pipelines and railroads did not necessarily guarantee Flagler cooperation from all trunk lines. Relations between Standard and the B&O continued to deteriorate during May. John D. Rockefeller expressed to a Standard associate his great disappointment in Garrett: "He is evidently not our friend and I regret very much our committals to him for building that transfer at Pittsburgh." Rockefeller even intimated to Charles Lockhart that Flagler was also disappointed in the decision to push for the pipeline connection with the B&O. While it was true that Flagler continued to have trouble with both the B&O and the Pittsburgh pipeline connection, there is no evidence to indicate that Flagler lost confidence in the pipeline project. Rockefeller to Payne, May 4 (quotation), and to Charles Lockhart, May 2 (marked "strictly confidential"), 1878, JDRL 184.

27. Flagler to Cassatt, April 29, 1878, JDRL 184.

28. Flagler to Rutter, May 18 (both quotations) and 29, and to Rockefeller, May 29, 1878, JDRL 184.

29. Flagler to Rutter, May 29, 1878, JDRL 184.

30. Flagler to Camden, May 21, 1878, JDRL 184. Also see Flagler to Horace Stone, May 16, 1878, JDRL 184.

31. Flagler to Rockefeller, May 23, 1878, JDRL 184.

32. Ibid., May 23 and 25, 1878, JDRL 184. Even before the Executive Committee of the trunk lines took their action, Flagler could not hide his antagonism toward Garrett. Flagler wrote Charles Lockhart on May 23, advising him not to bring up a minor local problem with the B&O, since the rate matter was such a sensitive issue: "The old man [John Garrett] feels that we are after him in every possible shape and form. It seems to me that before long we shall either come to a complete understanding with the Baltimore and Ohio people or else break with them." On the other hand, Flagler was confident that should the rift between Standard and the B&O be bridged, he would be able to carry out a policy he had desired for some time, the obtaining of rebates by Standard on its domestic traffic. Flagler to Lockhart, May 23, 1878, JDRL 184. Just in case, Flagler went ahead and began to reroute shipments to Philadelphia instead of to Baltimore. Flagler to William Frew, May 24, 1878, JDRL 184.

33. Flagler to Rockefeller, May 27, and to Payne, June 3, 1878, JDRL 184.

34. Flagler to Rockefeller, June 4, 1878, JDRL 184.

35. Ibid.

36. Ibid., May 29, 1878, JDRL 184.

37. Nevins, *Study in Power* 1:215; Flagler to Rockefeller, June 3 (first quotation), May 27, and May 25 (second quotation), and to Rutter, May 31, 1878, JDRL 184.

38. Flagler to Rockefeller, June 3, 1878, JDRL 184.

39. Articles of Incorporation of the Tidewater Pipe Line, as Appendix 37 in Ida Tarbell,

Notes to Chapter 5

The History of the Standard Oil Company, 2 vols. in 1 (1904; rpt. New York, 1950), 2:295–97; Harold F. Williamson and Arnold R. Daum, *The American Petroleum Industry: The Age of Illumination, 1859–1899* (Evanston, Ill., 1959), 440. Even before the successful Tidewater venture, Flagler had fought off an attempt by former Empire employees. In April 1878 J. H. Dilks headed a team that intended to build a pipeline from the Bradford District to Williamsport. Flagler presumed that Dilks planned to connect the pipe with the Reading Railroad terminal at Williamsport. Flagler suggested to the Pennsylvania's Cassatt that Col. Joseph Potts might be able to dissuade Dilks. There is no evidence to connect Dilks with the later, successful venture that used the route. Flagler to Cassatt, April 8 and 20, 1878, JDRL 183.

40. Williamson and Daum, *The Age of Illumination,* 440ff.

41. Rockefeller to Flagler, May 13, 1879, JDRL 185; Nevins, *Study in Power* 1:349–50.

42. Flagler testimony, *HTI,* 783; *Oil, Paint & Drug Reporter,* August 3, 1879.

43. Walter F. Taylor, "History of the Standard Oil Company," 391–95, RAC; Nevins, *Study in Power* 1:352.

44. Warden to Rockefeller, April 27 and 29, 1881, JDRL 186.

45. Nevins, *Study in Power* 1:355–56.

46. Camden to Flagler, December 17, 1878, CCL 33; William Drough to Rockefeller, March 6, 1879, JDRL 185; Rockefeller to P. H. Judd (Standard purchasing agent), November 29, and to Jewett, December 16, 1879, and O'Day to Rockefeller, January 21 and February 13, 1880, JDRL 186. The office letters for the critical summer and fall of 1879 are not contained in the letter books.

47. O'Day to Rockefeller, March 11, 1880, JDRL 186; Nevins, *Study in Power* 1:353–54; Warden to [Rockefeller], [November 1880], quoted extensively in ibid., 361–62.

48. Nevins, *Study in Power* 1:363–65.

49. Rockefeller to Payne, December 10, 1879, and J. J. Vandergrift to Rockefeller, March 7 and May 18 (telegram), 1880, JDRL 186; Taylor, "History of the Standard Oil Company," 381, 391–92, 205.

50. U.S. Commissioner of Corporations, *Report on the Petroleum Industry, Part I, Position of the Standard Oil Company in the Petroleum Industry* (Washington, 1907), 339ff.

51. Bruce Bringhurst, *Antitrust and the Oil Monopoly: The Standard Oil Cases, 1890–1911* (Westport, Conn., 1979), 108.

52. Ralph W. Hidy and Muriel E. Hidy, *Pioneering in Big Business, 1882–1911,* vol. 1 of *History of Standard Oil Company (New Jersey),* ed. Henrietta M. Larson (New York, 1955), 197–98.

5 Standard's "Lawyer"

1. Quoted in Allan Nevins, *John D. Rockefeller: The Heroic Age of American Enterprise* (New York, 1940), 2:61.

2. Flagler to Charles Lockhart, February 15, 1878, JDRL 182; Flagler to Rockefeller, May 31, 1882, RG 1.2, Box 56, folder 414, RAC.

3. Allan Nevins, *Study in Power: John D. Rockefeller, Industrialist and Philanthropist* (New York, 1953), 1:307; Flagler to A. J. Cassatt (marked "confidential"), March 27, 1878, JDRL 183.

4. Flagler and Rockefeller to R. P. Ranney, April 8, 1878, JDRL 183.

5. Flagler to Rockefeller, June 1, 1878, JDRL 184; Nevins, *Study in Power* 1:307.

6. Copy of Pennsylvania Auditor General's letter to "J. H. Flagger, Treas of SOC," Febru-

ary 4, 1878, in JDRL 182, p. 322. The follow-up correspondence, after Flagler's formal reply: Flagler to W. G. Warden, February 20, and Rockefeller to George I. Vail, March 7, 1878, JDRL 182.

7. Flagler to Warden, and to J. F. Temple, February 14, 1878, JDRL 182; Ida Tarbell, *The History of the Standard Oil Company,* 2 vols. in 1 (1904; rpt. New York, 1950), 1:225.

8. Tarbell, *The History of the Standard* 1:225–27; New York *Sun* quotation in John T. Flynn, *God's Gold: The Story of Rockefeller and His Times* (New York, 1932), 216.

9. J. J. Vandergrift to D. McIntosh, March 20, Flagler to Payne, March 14, and John D. Archbold to T. O. Barstow, March 10, 1879, JDRL 185; *New York Times,* April 30, 1879; Nevins, *Study in Power* 1:313–14; Rockefeller to H. L. Davis, and to Chauncey Depew, April 25, 1879, JDRL 185.

10. Flagler to Rockefeller, May 10, 1879, RG 1.2, Box 56, folder 414, RAC.

11. Nevins, *Study in Power* 1:315ff.

12. O. H. Payne to W. P. Thompson, April 14, 1879, JDRL 185.

13. Flagler to Rockefeller, May 14, 1879, RG 1.2, Box 56, folder 414, RAC. For a copy of Flagler's testimony before the Ohio legislative committee, see Appendix 14 in Tarbell, *The History of the Standard* 1:329–35.

14. Rockefeller to Flagler and to Warden, May 8, and Flagler to Rockefeller, May 12, 1879, JDRL 185; Flagler to Rockefeller, May 9, 1879, RG 1.2, Box 56, folder 414, RAC.

15. Rockefeller to J. N. Camden, to Payne, and to J. J. Vandergrift (quotation), May 19, and to Payne, May 23, 1879, JDRL 185; Camden to Rockefeller, June 23, 1879, Box: Standard Oil Correspondence, JNCP.

16. Nevins, *Study in Power* 1:309–10.

17. Flynn, *God's Gold,* 218–20. Archbold quotation to the Hepburn committee contained in this passage.

18. Ibid.

19. George D. Rogers to Dodd, November 18, 1879, Rockefeller to Judge J. P. Bishop (attorney for Standard), November 26, to Vandergrift, December 2, and to R. C. Vilas, December 10, 1879, JDRL 186; Standard Oil Company Executive Committee minute book 1880, RAC.

20. Standard Oil Company Executive Committee minute book, 1880, RAC.

21. Ralph W. Hidy and Muriel E. Hidy, *Pioneering in Big Business, 1882–1911,* vol. 1 of *History of Standard Oil Company (New Jersey),* ed. Henrietta M. Larson (New York, 1955), 35.

22. Ibid., 58, 61.

23. Walter F. Taylor, "History of the Standard Oil," 21–22, RAC.

24. Nevins, *Study in Power* 1:384–85.

25. Dodd to Flagler, July 23, 1881, quoted extensively in Nevins, *Study in Power* 1:391–92; Hidy and Hidy, *Pioneering in Big Business* 51, 56.

26. Rockefeller conversation with W. O. Inglis, Inglis book 1, RAC.

27. Ibid.

28. Tarbell, *All in the Day's Work: An Autobiography* (New York, 1939), 219.

29. Some comments over time: In 1886, Rockefeller sent Flagler an old envelope, marked "Rocefelder, Flagler and Co.," just as a reminder of the "old days." George D. Rogers to Flagler, October 26, 1886, JDRL 190. In 1902, Flagler wrote to Rockefeller:

> Dr Shelton spent the night with me recently and told me of a conversation with you at Lakewood and of your kind expression of regard for me. I hope I have brains and heart

enough left to appreciate and be thankful for all you said to the Doctor in my favor and I want you to know that I appreciate every word you told him. You and I have been associated in business upwards of thirty five years, and while there have been times when we have not agreed on questions of policy I do not know that one unkind word has ever passed or unkind thought existed between us. It is a record that affords me very great pleasure. I feel that my pecuniary success is due to my association with you, if I have contributed anything to yours I am thankful. You and I have been in a number of battles but always on the same side. In saying all this I hope I do not incur the suspicion that I am indulging in a fit of hystrics [*sic*]. As the years go by I see these things more plainly than I did twenty years ago, and I thank you for your confidence in me and esteem for me [personally handwritten note, Flagler to Rockefeller, June 22, 1902, RG 1.2, Box 56, folder 416, RAC].

The feelings seemed to be mutual, as indicated by this Rockefeller telegram to Flagler's wife upon Flagler's death:

I have just learned with great sorrow of the death of Mr. Flagler, my lifelong business associate and friend. He will be greatly missed in our association, where his wise counsels and prompt and decisive action, coupled with his faithful devotion, made him most valuable in the conduct of our affairs. His memory will be cherished by us as an upright man, a true and loyal friend, and a master mind among men of great affairs. Be assured of the sympathy of each member of my family, for you. We all mourn his loss [Rockefeller telegram to Mrs. Flagler, May 20, 1913, JDRL 242].

30. Flagler testimony, *HTI*, 307.

31. Sidney Walter Martin, *Florida's Flagler* (Athens, Ga., 1949), 84; "Molly Maguires," in *The Concise Columbia Encyclopedia*, ed. Judith S. Levey and Agnes Greenhill (New York, 1983), 556.

32. Flagler testimony, *HTI*, 307.

33. Ibid.

34. Rockefeller to Flagler, July 3, 1885, JDRL 189; Flagler to Rockefeller, October 8, 1885, quoted in Hidy and Hidy, *Pioneering in Big Business*, 177.

35. Hidy and Hidy, *Pioneering in Big Business*, 56, 51, 223–24, 314.

36. Henry Demarest Lloyd, *Wealth against Commonwealth* (1894; rpt. New York, 1899).

37. For the impact on Standard Oil of both the activities of states and the United States government in the area of antitrust, see Bruce Bringhurst, *Antitrust and the Oil Monopoly: The Standard Oil Cases, 1890–1911* (Westport, Conn., 1979), 40–88. For an excellent summary of the path of state and national legislation on the subject during the 1880s and 1890s, see Joseph E. Davis, *Trust Laws and Unfair Competition* (Washington, D.C., 1916), 1–21.

38. David Chalmers, Introduction to Ida M. Tarbell, *The History of the Standard Oil Company*, Briefer Version (New York, 1966), xiii–xiv.

39. Ibid., xiv–xv. Most of this information is also contained in Ida M. Tarbell, *All in the Day's Work: An Autobiography* (New York, 1939).

40. Chalmers, Introduction to Tarbell, *History of the Standard*, xiv.

41. Tarbell, *All in the Day's Work*, 204.

42. Ibid., 210–11; Bringhurst, *Antitrust and the Oil Monopoly*, 188–89.

43. Nevins, *Study in Power* 1:339–43 (quotation from page 339); Chalmers, Introduction to Tarbell, *History of the Standard*, xvii–xviii.

44. Bringhurst, *Antitrust and the Oil Monopoly*, 133–36.

45. Ibid., 145–52.
46. Ibid., 154–57, 180–81, 188–89.
47. Martin, *Florida's Flagler*, 78, 79; and Harry Harkness Flagler's marginal comments on those pages in his personal copy, FP.
48. *New York Times*, February 10, 1924; Flagler ledger, Mamaroneck property, FP; Harry Harkness Flagler conversation with Sidney Walter Martin, reported in *Florida's Flagler*, 79–80.
49. *New York Times*, December 14, 1925.
50. Bringhurst, *Antitrust and the Oil Monopoly*, 76.
51. Hidy and Hidy, *Pioneering in Big Business*, 314.
52. Earlier references to Flagler's holdings in the 1870s; Flagler statistical diary, FP; George Sweet Gibb and Evelyn H. Knowlton, *The Resurgent Years, 1911–1927*, vol. 2 of *History of the Standard Oil Company (New Jersey)*, ed. Henrietta M. Larson (New York, 1956), 37. The Gibb and Knowlton table is deceptive, for Flagler had already given his wife 15,000 of his shares before the dissolution.

The Florida Years

1. See Charlton W. Tebeau, *A History of Florida* (Coral Gables, 1971), especially chap. 17, "New Directions in Economics and Society, 1865–1880," for a picture of Florida's level of development at the time of Flagler's arrival.
2. Herbert J. Doherty, Jr., "Florida" in *The Encyclopedia of Southern History*, ed. David C. Roller and Robert W. Twyman (Baton Rouge, 1979), 456.
3. Tebeau, *A History of Florida*, 142–43, 188–89.
4. Ibid., 189–90.
5. Ibid., 190.
6. Ibid., 278.
7. J. E. Dovell, "The Railroads and the Public Lands of Florida, 1879–1902," *FHQ* 34 (January 1956): 237–43.
8. Roland H. Rerick, *Memoirs of Florida*, ed. Francis P. Fleming (Atlanta, 1902), 1:360; *Minutes of the Trustees of the Internal Improvement Fund*, State of Florida 7 (1907–1908): 532. According to Dovell, the IIF trustees had deeded all but 3,076,904.69 acres of their 20,133,837.41-acre obligation by August 1902. Dovell, "The Railroads and the Public Lands of Florida," 256.

6   St. Augustine: "Newport of the South"

1. Flagler to Dr. Andrew Anderson, November 27, 1885, FLb.
2. Cleveland Amory, *The Last Resorts* (New York, 1952), 19.
3. Sidney Walter Martin, *Florida's Flagler* (Athens, Ga., 1949), 90–91, and Harry Harkness Flagler's marginal comments on those pages of his copy, FP.
4. Ibid., 99.
5. John Temple Graves, *The Winter Resorts of Florida, South Georgia, Louisiana, Texas, California, Mexico, and Cuba: Containing a Brief Description of Points of Interest to the Tourist, Invalid, Immigrant, or Sportsman, and How to Reach Them* ([New York], 1883), 33; *Health Resorts of the South: Containing Numerous Engravings Descriptive of the Most De-*

sirable Resorts of the Southern States, Together with Some Representative Northern Resorts (Boston, 1892), 7–53.

6. Joseph W. Howe, *Winter Homes for Invalids: An Account of the Various Localities in Europe and America, Suitable for Consumptives and Other Invalids during the Winter Months, with Special Reference to the Climatic Variations at Each Place, and Their Influence on Disease* (New York, 1875), 50–51 (quotation); *Appleton's Illustrated Handbook of American Winter Resorts for Tourists and Invalids* (New York, 1877), 7, 11–13.

7. Martin, *Florida's Flagler,* 104–7. Much of this gleaned from Flagler diary entries. The best entry is for March 27, 1888, when he comes up with the idea for the Ponce de Leon.

8. Flagler to F. W. Smith, October 16, 1885, FLb.

9. Deed Book EE, St. Johns County, Florida, 16–19, 136–39; *St. Johns Weekly,* May 23, 1885, clipping in Ponce de Leon file, SAHS; Flagler to Osborn D. Seavey, September 1, 1885; Flagler to William Crafts, September 1, 1885; Flagler to C. M. Cooper, September 2 and 3, 1885; Flagler to Dr. Anderson, December 30, 1885; Flagler to C. M. Cooper, September 3, 1885; Flagler to F. W. Smith, September 5, 1885, FLb.

10. Flagler to Dr. Anderson, November 16, 1885, FLb. Flagler continued to have difficulty with the Ball property. The sale of Mrs. Ball's property to Flagler was transacted as a quit-claim, rather than a warranty deed. Therefore, Flagler was liable for the items against the property. See Flagler to F. W. Wildes, April 26, 1886, FLb.

11. Flagler to W. G. Warden, September 1, 1885 (quotation); Flagler to F. W. Smith, September 1, 1885, FLb.

12. Flagler to W. W. Dewhurst, September 11, 21, and 29, 1885; Flagler to Dr. Anderson, November 23 and 27, 1885; Flagler to John G. Long, September 1, 1885; Flagler to F. W. Smith, September 8, 1885 (quotation); Flagler to Long, September 29, 1885, FLb.

13. Flagler to C. M. Cooper, October 3, 1885, FLb; Boston *Evening Transcript,* August 20, 1886, clipping, Box 5-B.2, FP.

14. Flagler to R. McLaughlin, January 22, 1886, FLb.

15. Flagler to Dr. Anderson, January 9, 1886 (both quotations); Flagler to Dr. Anderson, January 2 and 9, 1886; Flagler to John H. Flagg, January 18, 1886; Flagler to Dr. Anderson, January 18, 1886, FLb.

16. Flagler to Dr. Anderson, April 30, 1886; ibid, July 6, 1887 (quotation), FLb; Deed Book 4, St. Johns County, Florida, 182.

17. Edwin Lefevre, "Flagler and Florida," *Everybody's Magazine* 22 (February 1910): 182 (quotation); Charles B. Reynolds, *A Tribute: The Architecture of the Hotel Ponce de Leon in Its Relation to the History of Saint Augustine* (privately printed, 1889). For more information on the Paris art scene at this time, see H. Wayne Morgan, ed., *An American Art Student in Paris: The Letters of Kenyon Cox, 1877–1882* (Kent, Ohio, 1986).

18. Flagler to McGuire & McDonald, November 19, 1885, FLb; Thomas Graham, "Flagler's Magnificent Hotel Ponce de Leon," *FHQ* 54 (July 1975): 2–3; Flagler to Smith, November 6, 1885, FLb.

19. Flagler to Smith, August 1885; Flagler to Flagg, September 12, 1885; Flagler to Dr. Anderson, November 16, 1885; Flagler to McGuire & McDonald, November 23, 1885 (quotation); Flagler to Dr. Anderson, November 18, 1885; Flagler to W. W. Dewhurst, November 27, 1885; Flagler to Flagg, January 18 and April 7, 1886, FLb.

20. Flagler to Dr. Anderson, December 28, 1885; ibid, December 23, 1885 (quotation); Flagler to McGuire & McDonald, January 21, 1886, FLb.

21. Flagler to McGuire & McDonald, December 26, 1885; Flagler to Smith, December 26, 1885, and January 15, 1886; Flagler to John T. Devine, April 22, 1886, FLb.

22. Reynolds, *A Tribute*, [1]; Charles B. Reynolds, *The Standard Guide: St. Augustine* (St. Augustine, Fla., 1891), 28; John Carrère and Thomas Hastings, *Florida, the American Riviera; St. Augustine, the Winter Newport: The Ponce de Leon, the Alcazar, the Casa Monica* (New York, 1887), 24; Graham, "Flagler's Magnificent Hotel," 4; *Florida's East Coast: The Winter Resort Section of America*, 1902–1903, in Box: Florida East Coast Railway annuals, 1902–1910, PKY; "Ponce de Leon," *Home Journal*, December 9, 1887, as quoted in *Early Years of the Ponce de Leon*, comp. Louise D. Castleden (n.p., 1957), 15.

23. Carrère and Hastings, *Florida, The American Riviera*, 28; "The Ponce de Leon," *Home Journal*, December 9, 1887, as quoted in Castleden, *Early Years*, 13; Reynolds, *The Standard Guide*, 38. None of the published sources reveal that the cupola atop the rotunda was really a facade. This was discovered in a tour I made some time ago of the structure, which now houses Flagler College. The top side of the cupola is supported by a wooden structure on the fourth floor.

24. Carrère and Hastings, *Florida, The American Riviera*, 28, 30, 32; Joseph McAloon interview with Thomas Graham, St. Augustine, Fla., August 2, 1974. Mr. Graham is a professor at Flagler College, and Mr. McAloon was an employee of the Ponce de Leon from 1904 to 1960.

25. "The Ponce de Leon," *Home Journal*, December 9, 1887, as quoted in Castleden, *Early Years*, 16; New York *Evening Post*, January 13, 1888, as quoted in ibid, 12.

26. Carl W. Condit, *American Building Art: The Nineteenth Century* (New York, 1960), 228; Reynolds, *The Standard Guide*, 22–28; Graham, "Flagler's Magnificent Hotel," 7–8.

27. Castleden, *Early Years*, 31–33. Other personnel of the Ponce de Leon during its first seasons include Romer Gillis, chief clerk; Clarence B. Knott, cashier; Henry Merry, night clerk; Anna McKay, housekeeper; Charles W. Bickford, steward; Joseph Grizzetti, chef; Max Urlan, pastry chef; and Edward McGuire, chief engineer. B. R. Howe to R. O. Riddle, March 22, 1935, MS Box 6, FP. Knott eventually became the superintendent of Flagler's hotel company, the Florida East Coast Hotel Company. McKay served in her capacity until after Flagler's death.

28. Flagler to Smith, October 16, 1885; Flagler to C. A. Bennett, September 15, 1885; Flagler to W. G. Ponce, October 3, 1885; Flagler to Smith, November 10, 1885; Flagler to Dr. Anderson, November 12, 1885; Flagler to Smith, January 2, 1886, FLb.

29. Doris C. Wiles, "Report on the history of the St. Johns County Courthouse building to Bacon, Hartman and Vollbrecht, Inc., March 18, 1968," St. Johns Courthouse Bldg. file, and the Hotel Cordova, 1889, file, SAHS; Carrère and Hastings, *Florida, The American Riviera*, 41–47.

30. Flagler to Dr. Anderson, November 7 and 10, 1885, FLb.

31. Flagler interview with James B. Morrow, New York *Tribune*, December 23, 1906; St. Augustine *Tatler*, March 23, 1901; Carrère and Hastings, *Florida, The American Riviera*, 34; "The Ponce de Leon," *Home Journal*, December 9, 1887, quoted in Castleden, *Early Years*, 16; Flagler to B. W. Angell, September 20, 1890, FLb.

32. "Three Casinos in One Book," a Flagler System publication, ca. 1898, MS Box on FEC Rwy., SAHS; William H. Beardsley (Flagler's treasurer) to James E. Ingraham, February 17, 1903, FLb 138-A.

33. Flagler to Seavey, July 2, 1890; Flagler to E. N. Wilson, July 2, 1890; Flagler to C. S. Beerbower, September 15, 1890, FLb; Reynolds, *Standard Guide*.

34. Martin, *Florida's Flagler*, 127, and Harry Harkness Flagler's marginal comments in his personal copy, FP.

35. Martin, *Florida's Flagler*, 127; John C. Poppelier, "Report on the Memorial Presbyter-

ian Church, St. Augustine, March 1965," HABS, FLA-170; David A. Redding, *Flagler and His Church* (Jacksonville, 1970), 24–30; Flagler to Pottier, Stymus & Co., August 22, 1890, FLb.

36. Redding, *Flagler and His Church,* 3, 24, 27.

37. Flagler to G. W. Bentley, January 19, 1886; John C. Poppelier, "Report on the Grace Methodist Church, March 1965," HABS, FLA-167; personal observations; Flagler to McGuire & McDonald, January 30, 1886, FLb.

38. Flagler to Dr. Anderson, November 19 and 26, 1890; Flagler to DeWitt Webb, July 21, 1890; Flagler to W. G. Warden, November 17, 1890, FLb; Flagler to S. D. Paine, February 21, 1891, Box 40, FP.

39. Lease, H. M. Flagler to City of St. Augustine, for the City Market, including jail and office space, May 21, 1890, copy in Box 5-B.1, FP; Flagler to McGuire & McDonald, October 3 and December 11, 1890, FLb.

40. Flagler to Crichlow, August 2, 1890, FLb; W. H. Beardsley to Flagler, February 14, 1903, FLb 138-A; Flagler to E. N. Wilson, August 2, 1890, Flagler to Crichlow, July 10, 1890, FLb.

41. Deed, H. M. Flagler to City of St. Augustine, July 12, 1889, copy in Box 5-B.1, FP; Committee on Streets' report in answer to Flagler's July 12, 1889, deed, copy in ibid.

42. B. C. Rude to Flagler, December 15, 1891, MS Box 5-B.1, FP; unidentified clipping, "Railway Ordinance," Box 5-B.2, FP. The envelope containing the newspaper clipping stated the ordinance passed the council July 25 and was signed by the mayor July 26, 1895.

43. Flagler to Sister M. Sazarus, April 27, 1886, FLb; W. H. Beardsley to W. H. Chambers, August 9, 1909, FLb 176; James Ingraham, rough draft of "A Man's Work [1884–1909]," for May 26, 1909, speech, MS Box 1, James Ingraham Papers, SAHS.

44. Flagler to Dismukes, August 7 and 19, 1890; Flagler to J. E. Ingraham, June 25, 1890, in folder "Cigar Factory Agreement Dismukes & Carcaba," Box 5-B.2, FP.

45. St. Augustine *Tatler,* March 4, 1893.

46. Ibid., February 6, 1892.

47. Martin, *Florida's Flagler,* 126; J. A. McGuire to Harry H. Flagler, November 26, 1894, January 14, 1895, December 30, 1894, and January 14, 1895; C. B. Knott to Harry H. Flagler, December 17 and 26, 1894; Joseph P. Greaves to Harry H. Flagler, January 4 and 5, 1895; C. B. Knott to Harry H. Flagler, January 7, 1895, all letters in Box 45-E, FP.

48. Martin, *Florida's Flagler,* 126 n. 49.

49. Ponce de Leon House Counts, 1888–1913, FP; Graham, "Flagler's Magnificent Hotel," 6; *Florida East Coast Railway and Hotels,* 1902–1903, Box: Florida East Coast Railway annuals, 1902–1913, PKY.

50. Flagler to Dr. Anderson, January 16 and 11, 1886; Henry James, *The American Scene* (1907; rpt. Bloomington, Ind., 1968), 459.

7 Railroads: From Short Lines to East Coast Lines

1. Flagler to Robert McLaughlin, April 28, 1886, FLb.

2. Ruby Leach Carson, "William Dunnington Bloxham, Florida's Two-Term Governor" (M.A. thesis, University of Florida, 1945), 251; *A Chronology of American Railroads* (Washington, D.C., 1957), 7.

3. *Poor's Manual of Railroads* 16 (1883): 482 (hereinafter, *Poor's*).

4. Ibid., 480–81.

5. Flagler to Charles Green, October 13, 1885; W. H. Beardsley to Flagler, December 10, 1885; Flagler to McGuire & McDonald, November 28, 1885, FLb.

6. Flagler to G. W. Bentley, December 19 and 22, 1885; Flagler to Charles C. Deming, May 5, 1886; Flagler to W. L. Crawford, December 13, 1885; Flagler to W. G. Warden, September 30, 1885; Flagler to Charles Green, December 26 and 30, 1885, FLb.

7. Flagler to J. B. Higbee, February 6, 1886; Flagler to Dr. Anderson, January 15, 1886, FLb.

8. Flagler to Robert McLaughlin, September 5, 1885, FLb.

9. Flagler to J. B. Higbee, February 6, 1886, FLb; *Poor's* 18 (1885): 452; ibid., 19 (1886): 767–68; ibid., 21 (1888): 595. Deming later became vice-president of both roads. Ibid., 24 (1891): 1307.

10. Robert H. Coleman to Flagler, May 16, 1888, JT&KW February 1888–December 1888 lb., Carton 3, Robert Coleman Papers, Lebanon County Historical Society, Collection, MS 182, Division of Archives and Manuscripts, Pennsylvania Historical and Museum Commission, Harrisburg (hereinafter, RCP).

11. W. L. Crawford to Flagler, November 29, 1888, Box 14-F.1, FP; unidentified July 4, 1937, newspaper clipping, H. M. Flagler file, SAHS; Florida East Coast chronological chart, FP.

12. *Daytona Beach Winter Resorter,* December 31, 1937.

13. Flagler to J. R. Parrott, November 16, 1903; Flagler to J. A. McGuire, September 26, 1904, Box 40, FP; "Florida East Coast Hotel Company: Ormond Plant, Ormond, Florida (Schedule Showing Plant Values & Accrued Depreciation Period January 1, 1900, to December 31, 1931)," FP.

14. W. L. Crawford to D. F. Jack, February 1, 1890, Box 14-F.1, FP; Crawford to Flagler, November 23, 1889, Box 14-H, FP; Crawford to D. F. Jack, February 1, 1890, Box 14-F.1, FP; Florida East Coast Railway chronological chart, FP; "Corporate History of the Florida East Coast Railway Company, Flagler System, Compiled as of June 30, 1918; As Filed with Bureau of Valuation," 12, Box 14-I, FP; Flagler statistical diary, FP.

15. G. Hutchingson Smythe, *Henry Bradley Plant* (New York, 1898), 120–21, 134–35, 138–39.

16. Ibid., 162–65.

17. *Poor's* 19 (1886); 768; ibid., 20 (1887): 595; ibid., 21 (1888): 595; Flagler to Charles C. Deming, December 6 and September 2, 1890; Flagler to Crawford, November 22 and December 10, 1890; Flagler to W. J. Jarvis, December 10, 1890, FLb.

18. Flagler to Deming, July 31, 1890; Flagler to J. E. Starke, August 2, 1890; Flagler to J. F. Freeman, July 30, 1890; Flagler to Deming, July 3, 1890; Flagler to Mason Young, July 7, 1890, FLb. The JT&KW did cease to press its claims against the ECL. Flagler to J. E. Starke, August 8, 1890, FLb.

19. Flagler to Mason Young, July 26, 1890; Flagler to W. J. Jarvis, July 31, 1890; Flagler to Young, October 3, 1890, FLb.

20. Biographical sketch of Coleman done in 1891, Carton 11, RCP; Coleman to Flagler, August 17, 1889, JT&KW 1889 lb., Carton 3, RCP.

21. Coleman to Flagler, December 11, 1890, JT&KW 1890 lb., Carton 3, RCP.

22. Coleman to Flagler, June 19 and July 1, 1891, JT&KW 1891–May 1892 lb., Carton 3, RCP.

23. *FT-U,* February 29, 1892; Juno *Tropical Sun,* July 14, 1892 (quotation); general announcement by Henry M. Flagler, September 29, 1892, Box 14-F.1, FP.

24. *Poor's* 26 (1893): 792; ibid., 27 (1894): 175; ibid., 28 (1895): 193–94.

25. Joseph R. Parrott transcript (on microfilm) and miscellaneous pamphlets in MS Box "Yale University Class of 1883," all in University Archives, Sterling Library, Yale University, New Haven, Conn.

26. Sidney Walter Martin, "Flagler's Associates in East Florida Developments," *FHQ* 26 (January 1948): 259–61. See Wayne Flynt, *Dixie's Reluctant Progressive: Duncan Upshaw Fletcher* (Tallahassee, Fla., 1971).

27. *Laws of Florida,* chap. 4260, 1893; Flagler to W. J. Jarvis, September 1, 1893, Box 14-F.5, FP; Florida East Coast Railway chronological chart, FP.

28. Juno *Tropical Sun,* November 24, 1892.

29. *FT-U,* April 25 and 10, 1893.

8 Palm Beach: "Queen of Winter Resorts"

1. Cleveland Amory, *The Last Resorts* (New York, 1952), 333–34, 330; Juno *Tropical Sun,* May 25, 1893. Lang was killed in 1870 by two Fort Pierce men, probably during a brawl. Charles Moore died in 1888. *Lake Worth News,* Christmas, 1900. For a good eyewitness account of the pre-Flagler Lake Worth area, see Charles W. Pierce, *Pioneer Life in Southeast Florida,* ed. Donald Walter Curl (Coral Gables, Fla., 1970).

2. *Palm Beach News,* 1903 Souvenir Number.

3. *Lake Worth News,* Christmas, 1900; Juno *Tropical Sun,* May 25 and 4, 1893. M. W. Dimick, one of the original colonists, was elected to the state legislature in 1890 and the state senate in 1896, and again in 1900. In 1893, he founded the Dade County State Bank.

4. Juno *Tropical Sun,* May 25, 1893 (first quotation); ibid., April 20, 1893; Savannah (Ga.) *Morning News,* quoted in Juno *Tropical Sun,* April 6, 1893; Flagler to W. R. Moses, August 27, 1893, FLb.

5. Juno *Tropical Sun,* April 20, 1893; West Palm Beach map, 1893, FP (note that the date is before the settlement of the town); Flagler statistical diary, FP.

6. Juno *Tropical Sun,* November 1, 1894; Beardsley to George S. Scofield, September 18, 1911, FLb 186-N; West Palm Beach *Tropical Sun,* December 5, 1903.

7. Flagler to Ingraham, October 24, 1902, and August 2, 1909; Flagler to Parrott, January 7, 1901; Beardsley to Flagler, December 26, 1901, FLb 133; Flagler to A. S. Botsford, October 8, 1901 (quotation); Flagler to Ingraham, August 14, 1901, FLb.

8. Ingraham to F. P. Forster, August 9, 1894, MS Box 40, FP; J. C. Salter to John P. McKenna, August 15, 1911, FLb 186-N.

9. Juno *Tropical Sun,* May 25, 1893.

10. Ibid., April 6 and May 25, 1893; U. Grant Duffield, *Souvenir of the Royal Poinciana, Palm Beach (Lake Worth)* (New York, 1894), PKY (copy also in MS Box 10, FP).

11. Duffield, *Souvenir; FT-U,* April 10, 1893; "Florida East Coast Hotel Company: Palm Beach Plant, Palm Beach, Florida (Schedule showing Plant Values & Accrued Depreciation for each Year for the Period January 1, 1900, to December 31, 1931)," FP.

12. *FT-U,* April 10, 1893; Amory, *The Last Resorts,* 339 and frontispiece.

13. Flagler to Harry Harkness Flagler, January 23, 1895, Box 40, FP; Juno *Tropical Sun,* May 25, 1893; *Florida East Coast* brochure [1895–1897], [14], PKY; *Florida East Coast Homeseeker* 3 (January 1901): 8; *The Florida East Coast Hotel Company* (1900), and *East Coast of Florida: The New Florida* (1901–1902), MS Box: Florida East Coast Railway annuals 1893–1901, PKY.

14. West Palm Beach *Tropical Sun,* June 10, 1902; Flagler to J. N. Mulford, August 21, 1903; West Palm Beach *Tropical Sun,* June 10 and 24, 1903; Flagler to J. A. McGuire, June 15, 1903, MS Box 40, FP; Flagler to D. O. Wickham, September 12, 1903, FLb.

15. Florida East Coast Railway annuals, PKY; *Palm Beach Life,* April 2, 1907; *Lake Worth News,* Christmas, 1900.

16. *Palm Beach Life,* April 2, 1907. The other cottagers: Eugene M. O'Neill, Mr. and Mrs. William P. Snyder of Pittsburgh, Mrs. George W. Miller of Buffalo, Mr. and Mrs. George H. Christian of Minneapolis, Mr. and Mrs. Charles Bingham of Buffalo, and the "Bachelor Quartet" (Chase, Love, Campbell, and Evans).

17. George C. Shelton Testimony in Flagler Divorce Proceedings, 1901, Florida Seventh Circuit Court, 40–41.

18. Ibid.

19. Ibid., 42; Carlos McDonald Affidavit, August 8, 1901, in New York City, in Flagler Divorce Proceedings, 1901.

20. Alvaretta Kenan Register, comp., *The Kenan Family and Some Allied Families of the Compiler and Publisher* (Statesboro, Ga., 1967), 47–52.

21. *New York Tribune,* August 25, 1901; Flagler to Pembroke Jones, July 7 and 19, 1890, FLb 99-A.

22. Sidney Walter Martin, *Florida's Flagler* (Athens, Ga., 1949), 192; Flagler to Pembroke Jones, July 7 and 19, 1890, FLb; Beardsley to W. R. Kenan, Sr., April 3, 1899, FLb 99-A. Thomas Kenan III, in an interview with David Chandler, stated that Flagler also gave Mary Lily a million dollars worth of jewelry in 1899. David Leon Chandler, *Henry Flagler: The Astonishing Life and Times of the Visionary Robber Baron Who Founded Florida* (New York, 1986), 189–90.

23. Bill of Divorce: Henry M. Flagler, complainant, vs. Ida A. Flagler, defendant, in Flagler Divorce Proceedings, 1901 (on my 1977 research trip to Miami, this material was in a county-owned warehouse).

24. Samuel Proctor, "Napoleon Bonaparte Broward: The Portrait of a Progressive Democrat" (M.A. thesis, University of Florida, 1942), Appendix A.

25. Frank Clark to A. S. Mann, April 22, 1901, Box 1892–February, 1905, Austin Shuey Mann Papers, PKY; Samuel Proctor, *Napoleon Bonaparte Broward, Florida's Fighting Democrat* (Gainesville, Fla., 1950), 168; Beardsley to Parrott, August 27, 1901 (two letters), FLb 131. The law was repealed in 1905, amid continuing rumors that Flagler had spent $100,000 to get the legislature to pass the "Flagler divorce law." *New York Times,* April 19, 1905. Flagler was entirely capable of bribery, but he would have found it offensive to think he would have had to spend so large a sum on a legislature—he had spent much less for similar activities during his Standard Oil days. (I fear I have inadvertently contributed to the "$100,000" legend. In taking notes for my dissertation, I failed to put a decimal point in Flagler's expense payment to George P. Raney. Therefore, the amount came out as $106942, when it should have read $1,069.42. I compounded the factual error by hinting that surely such a large amount of money would have been the Flagler "bribery fund." There is no documentary evidence to support the $100,000 figure. That does not, however, negate the rumor mill; it merely means we are unaware of any factual basis for the rumors.)

During Flagler's divorce and remarriage year of 1901, another possible scandal surfaced. He was named in an "alienation of affection" suit in New York. Flagler was accused of keeping a mistress during 1896 and 1897. Just as quickly as the charges surfaced, accompanied with a blanket denial by Flagler's lawyer, they disappeared. *New York Times,* May 10, 1901. What are we to make of the situation? First, the fact that it came just after Flagler's divorce law

262

passed the Florida legislature suggested "blackmail," as indeed Flagler's lawyer stated when confronted by a reporter. An attempt at blackmail, however, often indicates a factual basis for the allegation. Since this situation has a close relationship with the Henry Flagler–Mary Lily Kenan liason, a plausible explanation, if indeed the allegations were true, seems to be that Flagler did conform to the Victorian standards of the day with regard to sexual conduct—*until* Ida Alice Flagler became hopelessly insane.

26. Martin, *Florida's Flagler*, 193–94; *Lake Worth News*, Christmas, 1900: Beardsley to Flagler, December 26 and 27, 1901, FLb 133; Flagler to Carrère & Hastings, February 12, 1901, FLb. Charles B. Simmons, director of The Henry Morrison Flagler Museum and an architect by training, assisted me greatly in a letter of August 23, 1986, in getting my facts straight regarding the building of Whitehall. In the same letter, Simmons also offered the plausible explanation that Flagler presented the Whitehall deed to his bride on their wedding day, although it was not officially deeded until December 21, when Whitehall neared completion.

27. Personal observation of The Henry Morrison Flagler Museum (formerly Whitehall).

28. Ibid.; Simmons to author, August 23, 1986; Henry James, *The American Scene* (1907; rpt., Bloomington, Ind., 1968), 447; Henry James to Mrs. Frederic R. Jones, February 24, 1905, MS Harvard, quotes from Leon Edel's notes in reprint edition.

29. Simmons to author, August 23, 1986; Martin, *Florida's Flagler*, 201; Flagler to Annie MacKay [Anna McKay], September 25, 1901; Flagler to Dr. Andrew Anderson, September 7, 1910, FLb; Martin, *Florida's Flagler*, 200–201; Beardsley to Flagler, December 27, 1901, FLb 133; personal observations during guided tour of The Henry Morrison Flagler Museum, 1974.

30. Flagler to Louise Wise, August 7, 1911, FLb 186N.

31. Mrs. Douglas C. Scott to Charles B. Simmons, May 8, 1982, FP. Mrs. Scott is Priscilla Spalding Scott, the granddaughter of Arthur Spalding. The letters referred to in this manuscript from Arthur Spalding have been edited by her. She stated: "These are as they were written, with my only changes the elimination of personal remarks having no bearing on life at Whitehall and the substitution of 'colored' for 'niggers.' "

32. Arthur C. Spalding to his mother, January 19, 20 (first quotation), and February 3, 1907 (second quotation), Spalding letters, FP (hereinafter, SL).

33. *Florida's East Coast: The Winter Resort Section of America* (1902–03), 83, MS Box: FEC annuals, 1902–1910, PKY; Flagler to C. L. Myers, January 9, 1901, FLb; *Palm Beach Life*, April 5, 1910.

34. *Lake Worth News*, Christmas, 1900.

35. Spalding to his mother, February 22 and 23, 1907, SL.

36. West Palm Beach *Tropical Sun*, March 8, 1905; J. C. Salter to F. B. Squires, January 28, 1901, FLb 127; Flagler to J. D. Archbold, February 14, 1901, FLb; Beardsley telegrams to J. D. Rahner and Fred Sterry, February 8, 1902, and Beardsley to Sterry, February 27, 1902, FLb 133; *Palm Beach Life*, January 17, 1911; Flagler to C. S. Cory, September 17, 1902; FLb.

37. *In Memoriam: Henry Morrison Flagler* (Buffalo, N.Y., 1914), 12, 7.

38. *Palm Beach Life*, March 7, 1911, January 28, 1908, March 16, 1909.

39. Amory, *The Last Resorts*, 339–40.

40. Spalding to his mother, January 23, February 13 and 9, 1907, SL; Beardsley to R. C. Rathbone & Son, April 8, 1903, FLb 138-A.

41. Spalding to his mother, January 25, 1907, SL.

42. Amory, *The Last Resorts*, 340–41.

43. Spalding to his mother, February 8, 1907, SL.

44. *Palm Beach Life*, January 12, 1907 (quotation); ibid., March 7, 1911.

45. C. B. Knott to J. Dunbar Wright, December 26, 1896, Box 6, FP; *Palm Beach Life,* January 28, 1907, and January 24, 1911.

46. *Lake Worth News,* Christmas, 1900 (quotation); Flagler to Parrott, July 29, 1899; Flagler to J. A. McGuire, June 26, 1899, FLb; T. W. Travers, *History of Beautiful Palm Beach* (West Palm Beach, Fla., 1928), 89, 93.

47. Spalding to his mother, March 12, 1907, SL.

48. Amory, *The Last Resorts,* 340–41.

9 Miami and Nassau: "American Riviera"

1. Harry G. Cutler, *History of Florida, Past and Present,* 3 vols. (Chicago, 1923), 1:396. See also Sidney Walter Martin, *Florida's Flagler* (Athens, Ga., 1949), 154–55.

2. Thelma Peters, *Biscayne Bay Country 1870–1926* (Miami, Fla., 1981), 6–9; Jane Wood, "Mary Bulmer Brickell: A Mother of Miami," *Miami News,* undated clipping, Box 2-C, FP. The Wood account differs from the Peters account that I used in the text in that Wood stated Mary Bulmer and William Brickell met in Ohio, and that they bought 640 acres in the Biscayne Bay area in 1868. I simply have more faith in the Peters account.

3. Peters, *Biscayne Bay Country,* 6–9; E. V. Blackman, *Miami and Dade County, Florida* (Washington, D.C., 1921), 58–60; *Florida East Coast Homeseeker* 3 (January 1901): 3 (hereinafter, *Homeseeker*). For an account of the Tuttle-Rockefeller connection, see Edward N. Akin, "The Cleveland Connection: Revelations from the John D. Rockefeller–Julia D. Tuttle Correspondence," *Tequesta* 42 (1982): 57–61.

4. Akin, "The Cleveland Connection," 57–61.

5. Cutler, *History of Florida* 1:396; Flagler to Julia D. Tuttle, April 27, 1893, Tuttle Family Papers, MS Box 22, Historical Museum of Southern Florida, Miami.

6. James Ingraham, rough draft of speech delivered to Miami Women's Club, November 12, 1920 (appeared in *Miami Herald,* November 13, 1920), Box 1, James E. Ingraham Papers, SAHS.

7. Martin, *Florida's Flagler,* 154; George L. Bradley to A. P. Sawyer, April 30, 1895, and Flagler to A. P. Sawyer, June 5, 1895, Box 1, Albert P. Sawyer Papers, Florida State Library, Tallahassee (hereinafter, ASP). Since there seems to be no confirmed documentation as to exactly what kind of blossoms or flowers were contained in Mrs. Tuttle's bouquet, I have taken no particular position on the matter. However, it has been the subject of much speculation. Most recently, Seth Bramson has added his thoughts. According to Bramson, a booklet published in 1911 stated that the blossoms were those of lime trees. Bramson then speculates that the FEC may have changed the story in later years to orange blossoms, to go along with the public perception of a sweeter fruit. Seth H. Bramson, *Speedway to Sunshine: The Story of the Florida East Coast Railway* (Erin, Canada, 1984), 58 (see n. 77).

8. Flagler to Julia D. Tuttle, April 22, 1895, copy in Box 21-A, FP; Parrott to Flagler, July 29, 1895, Box 24-F.0, FP; Martin, *Florida's Flagler,* 159; Flagler statistical diary, FP.

9. W. S. Graham to Parrott, February 24, 1895, Box 14-F.9, FP.

10. Flagler to Mrs. Julia D. Tuttle, August 10 and 27, and December 5, 1896, Tuttle Family Papers, MS Box 22, Historical Museum of Southern Florida, Miami; Beardsley to L. McBride, administrator of the Julia D. Tuttle estate, February 18, 1899, FLb 99-A; Flagler to R. C. Rathbone & Son, November 18, 1899; Flagler to McBride, November 16, 1899; Robbins & Graham to Ingraham, April 3, 1897, Box 21-A.1, FP; Flagler to Ingraham, July 15, 1899, FLb.

11. *Miami Herald,* May 14, 1964; William Mark Brown, "The Raising and Razing of the Royal Palm" in *Miami Women's Club Souvenir Book* 1:33, in Box 12, FP; *Miami Herald,* May 14, 1964.

12. *Miami Metropolis,* June 4, 1897, and December 23, 1898.

13. "Florida East Coast Hotel Company: Miami Plant, Miami, Florida (Schedule showing Plant Values & Accrued Depreciation for each Year for the Period January 1, 1900, to December 31, 1931)," FP; *Miami Metropolis,* February 24, 1898; *Miami Herald,* May 14, 1964.

14. *Miami Metropolis,* November 5, 1897; *Homeseeker* 3 (January 1901): 5; *Miami Metropolis,* October 8, 1897; Hotel Biscayne stationery, August 29, 1898, Florida East Coast Hotel System file, SAHS.

15. Fort Dallas Land Company ledger, 1895–1903, p. 53, FP; *Homeseeker,* no. 13 (March 1898): 15; *Miami Metropolis,* July 9, 1897; Beardsley to J. B. Reilly, March 20, 1899, and Beardsley to Ingraham, April 18, 1899, FLb 99-A.

16. J. C. Salter to Louis Larson, January 17, 1901, FLb 127; J. B. Reilly to E. V. Blackman, April 26, 1899, in *Homeseeker* 1 (May 1899): 11; Flagler to Ingraham, November 5 and October 31, 1902, FLb.

17. *Miami Herald,* July 25, 1934, *Homeseeker* 3 (January 1901): 3; ibid., no. 13 (March 1898): 4; *Miami Metropolis* and *Miami Herald,* June 4, 1897; "John Sewell, Pioneer Miami Citizen, Dies Suddenly at Home," unidentified newspaper clipping, in Box 2-C, FP; *Homeseeker* 3 (January 1901): 4.

18. *Homeseeker,* no. 16 (December 1898): 9; Fort Dallas Land Company journal, 1895–1903, p. 75, FP; J. A. McDonald to J. Dunbar Wright, January 5, 1897, Box 12-A, FP; C. D. Boice to A. V. S. Smith, April 20, 1909, FLb 173; Carleton J. Corliss interview with author, Tallahassee, Florida, October 6, 1973.

19. *Homeseeker* 3 (January 1901): 7; Flagler to Ingraham, June 3, 1899 (first quotation); *Homeseeker* 3 (January 1901): 7; ibid. 1 (February 1899): 3.

20. Flagler telegram to Parrott, September 25, 1899; Flagler telegram to J. B. Reilly, September 27, 1899; Flagler to Ingraham, October 23, 1899; Flagler telegram to Parrott, October 30, 1899; Flagler to Parrott, November 2, 1899, FLb; Martin, *Florida's Flagler,* 167.

21. Martin, *Florida's Flagler,* 167–68.

22. *Homeseeker,* no. 16 (December 1898), 10; Flagler to H. W. Davis, August 23, 1911 (quotation), FLb; *The Voice* (Jesuit periodical), December 1, 1972; Flagler to Century Co., July 10, 1899; Flagler to Stymus, October 13, 1899; Flagler to J. B. Reilly, September 1, 1899, FLb.

23. Golden anniversary section, *Miami Daily News,* May 12, 1946; *Miami Metropolis,* June 4, 1897; W. S. Graham to Parrott, February 24, 1896, Box 14-F.9, FP; Flagler to Parrott, September 28 and November 13, 1899, FLb; West Palm Beach *Tropical Sun,* January 4, 1905.

24. Flagler to Father Thomas Slevin, May 19, 1909 (first quotation); Flagler to Parrott, August 23, 26, and September 9, 1910 (second quotation), FLb; Blackman, *Miami and Dade County,* 50.

25. Nassau *Guardian,* April 24, 1897, quoted in *Miami Metropolis,* May 14, 1897.

26. Ibid.; *Miami Metropolis,* January 7, 1898.

27. *Laws of the Bahamas* (from 15th March to 26th August, 1898), copy in Box 12½, FP.

28. Map of Nassau properties bought by Flagler, Box 12½, FP; Flagler to H. E. Bemis, February 4, 1901; Flagler to Parrott, February 14, 1901; Flagler to Fred Sterry, October 8, 1903, FLb. See boxes of FEC promotional material, PKY.

29. *Bahama News,* quoted in *Miami Metropolis,* February 11, 1898; Flagler to Parrott,

May 22, 1899; Flagler to McDonald, July 27 and 29, 1899, FLb; Hotel Colonial brochure, Box 12½, FP; Flagler to H. E. Bemis, December 12, 1900, FLb.

30. Hotel Colonial brochure, Box 12½, FP; Flagler to Sir William Van Horn, November 6, 1902, FLb.

31. Beardsley to Flagler, March 7, 1902, FLb 133; ibid., April 23, 1902, FLb 134.

32. Flagler to Van Horn, September 30, 1902 (quotation); ibid., December 8, 1903; Flagler to Parrott, March 11, 1909, FLb.

33. Parrott to Flagler, August 23, 1897, lb. #10, Box 14-H, FP; *Miami Metropolis,* October 22, 1897; timetable of the Florida East Coast Railway, No. 16, corrected to November 10, 1898, Box 19, FP; *Miami Metropolis,* December 13, 1897, and January 7, 1898; William H. Harbaugh, *The Life and Times of Theodore Roosevelt,* rev. ed. (London, 1975), 108.

34. Timetable No. 16, Box 19, FP; Flagler to McDonald, August 21 and October 9, 1899, FLb.

35. *Miami Metropolis,* August 27, 1897; Flagler to M. S. Quay and to Boies Penrose, November 20, 1899; Flagler to Marcus Hanna, October 30, 1901, FLb; *Miami Metropolis,* February 24, 1899.

36. Flagler to Parrott, July 27, 1899 (quotation); Flagler to C. M. Depew and to James McMillan, December 24, 1900; Flagler to Parrott, May 29, 1902; Flagler letters to James P. Taliaferro, Stephen B. Elkins, and James McMillan, June 4, 1902, FLb; *Homeseeker* 4 (June 1902): 8, 10.

37. Flagler to J. M. Hall, FLb 131; J. C. Salter to C. L. Myers, February 5, 1902, FLb 127; Salter to J. Victor Wilson, August 27, 1902, and Salter to George F. Carpenter, September 7, 1901, FLb 131; Flagler to Parrott, June 25 and July 3, 1902, FLb.

38. Flagler to Parrott, June 4 and 5, 1902; ibid., June 4, 1902 (separate letter from one just cited).

39. Flagler to Parrott, November 28, 1903 (quotation), FLb; Flagler statistical diary, FP; Flagler to Parrott, December 7, 1908; Flagler to J. P. Beckwith, January 5, 1909, FLb.

40. Flagler to R. W. Parsons, March 20, 1909; Flagler to H. E. Bemis, September 4, 1909, FLb.

41. Flagler to J. A. McGuire, September 4 and October 27, 1900, MS Box 40, FP.

42. Continental Hotel brochures for 1902, 1906, and 1908, MS Box 9, FP.

43. Flagler to Parrott, September 6, 1901, June 17, 1902, and August 15, 1905 (quotation), FLb; packet of pictures, Box 9, FP; Flagler to H. E. Bemis, October 11, 1909, FLb; *FT-U,* March 3, 1957.

10 Land Baron

1. *FT-U,* April 27, 1893; Miles to A. P. Sawyer, November 11, 1896, Box 1, ASP. Fleming statement quoted in Wallace Martin Nelson, "The Economic Development of Florida, 1870–1930" (Ph.D. dissertation, University of Florida, 1962), 149–50.

2. Lands granted by state to railroads incorporated in FEC Ry Co., Box 14, FP.

3. *Laws of Florida,* chap. 4260, 1893; *Minutes of the Trustees, Internal Improvement Fund (MIIF),* State of Florida 4 (1889–1899): 273; Flagler to Parrott, June 28, 1902, FLb; *MIIF* 4:433.

4. *MIIF* 5 (1900–1904): 264–65.

5. Ibid., 265–68, 281–82.

6. *MIIF* 6 (1905–1906): 114–15; *FT-U,* August 24, 1906; original draft of the letter in MS Box 14-F.9, FP. Flagler and two other railroad owners, Henry Plant and H. R. Duval, bought the *Times-Union* in 1891 (discussed in chapter 11).

7. Flagler to Ingraham, July 19, 1909, FLb; "List of lands deeded by Florida Commercial Company to Florida East Coast Railway Company," March 30, 1896, #L8, Flagler Enterprises Papers, Robert M. Strozier Library, Florida State University, Tallahassee, Florida; *MIIF* 8 (1909–1910): 415–19. Robert Coleman, the owner of the JT&KW Railroad discussed in chapter 7, was also principal owner of the Florida Commercial Company.

8. *MIIF* 9 (1911–1912): 598–619.

9. Ora L. Jones, comp., "Some Glimpses of Pompano History," unpub. MS, Box 3-A, FP; "General announcement of the incorporation of the Boston and Florida Atlantic Coast Land Company, November 24, 1891," Box 1, ASP. Officers of the company were Sawyer, president; George L. Bradley, vice-president; and George W. Piper, treasurer. The directors were Sawyer, Bradley, Piper, George F. Miles, and Thomas B. Bailey. On letterhead of A. P. Sawyer to George T. Mason, February 13, 1893, Box 1, ASP.

10. George L. Bradley to Flagler, August 12, 1892; George F. Miles to A. P. Sawyer, October 18 and 24, 1892, and January 31, 1893; Bradley to A. P. Sawyer, January 23, 1893; and Sawyer to George T. Mason, February 13, 1893, Box 1, ASP.

11. Unsigned note dated July 20, 1895, Flagler to A. P. Sawyer, June 5, 1895, and Miles to A. P. Sawyer, October 23, 1896, Box 1, ASP. In January 1895, the canal company deeded almost 10,000 acres to Flagler as part of its donation for the extension to Lake Worth. Another grant from the canal company in 1897 added almost 100,000 acres to Flagler's land holdings. List of lands deeded by the Florida Coast Line Canal and Transportation Company to Florida East Coast Railway Company, January 11, 1895, #L6, Flagler Enterprises Papers; Ingraham to Parrott, June 30, 1897, Box 21-A.1, FP.

12. Miles to A. P. Sawyer, February 15, 1896, with enclosure of copy of Ingraham-to-Miles letter of February 15, 1896, Box 1, ASP; Ingraham to A. P. Sawyer, October 20, 1897, Box 2, ASP; Ingraham to Miles, September 18, 1896, Box 1, ASP.

13. Miles to A. P. Sawyer, January 28, 1897, Box 1, ASP; Otto Zetterlund to Ingraham, November 17, 1899, Box 21-A, FP; F. Jacobson to Ingraham, February 2, 1897, Box 1, ASP.

14. Ingraham to Miles, December 14, 1897, Box 1, ASP.

15. *Miami Metropolis,* July 2, 1897.

16. Frederick S. Morse to A. P. Sawyer, November 30, 1895, Box 1, ASP; Miles to Bradley, January 17, 1902, and Miles to Haydn Sawyer, October 26, 1904, Box 3, ASP.

17. Miles to A. P. Sawyer, September 15, 1898, Box 2, ASP; Miles to Bradley, April 17, 1905, Box 3, ASP.

18. West Palm Beach *Tropical Sun,* November 25 and December 9, 1905.

19. Miles to Haydn Sawyer, April 30 and May 13, 1906, Box 3, ASP; West Palm Beach *Tropical Sun,* May 12, 1906.

20. Miles to Haydn Sawyer, June 3, 1906, Box 3, ASP; West Palm Beach *Tropical Sun,* May 19, 1906; Haydn Sawyer to Miles, September 5, 1906, Box 3, ASP; West Palm Beach *Tropical Sun,* November 24, 1906.

21. West Palm Beach *Tropical Sun,* November 24, 1906.

22. Ingraham to Miles, April 18, 1906; Miles to Haydn Sawyer, April 19 (quotation), January 11 and July 4, 1906, Box 3, ASP.

23. On Ingraham's career: an unidentified newspaper clipping, Box 14-A, FP. For the life of Henry Sanford, see Joseph A. Fry, *Henry S. Sanford: Diplomacy and Business in*

Nineteenth-Century America (Reno, Nev., 1982). Chapters 5 and 6 (pp. 87–131) are especially illuminating concerning his Florida investments. See also Richard James Amundson, "The American Life of Henry Sheldon Sanford" (Ph.D. diss., Florida State University, 1963).

24. Juno *Tropical Sun,* November 24, 1892.

25. Model Land Company stock certificate book, FP; Model Land Company journal (1895–1903), pp. 31, 32, and 79, FP.

26. W. H. Beardsley to W. J. Russell, November 23, 1903, FLb 142; Beardsley to Ingraham, July 14, 1909, FLb 174; Flagler to W. J. Russell, July 2, 1909, FLb. Deeds executed in 1911 transferred the following amounts of land in each county to the MLC: Dade, 75,549.66 acres; Palm Beach, 106,856.97 acres; Brevard, 1,211.76 acres; Volusia, 34,768.29 acres; and St. Lucie, 18,044 acres. In 1914, another major transaction deeded 196,734.95 acres to the MLC, over half of it in Monroe County. List of deeds from Florida East Coast Railway to Model Land Company, January 3, 1911, and April 18, 1914, #L8, Flagler Enterprises Papers.

27. J. E. Dovell, "The Railroads and the Public Lands of Florida 1879–1902," *FHQ* 34 (January 1956): 245; *Miami Herald,* September 2, 1948. Chartering dates of the Flagler land companies: Model Land Company (February 6, 1896), Fort Dallas Land Company (March 17, 1896), Perrine Grant Land Company (May 6, 1899), and Chuluota Land Company (1912). Martin, *Florida's Flagler,* 240.

28. *Homeseeker* 1 (July 1899): 14; ibid. 3 (January 1901): cover; ibid. 8 (January 1906): 22; S. H. Richmond to Ingraham, April 3, 1896, Box 21-A.1, FP.

29. *Miami Metropolis,* November 11, 1898; J. C. Salter to W. W. Dewhurst, August 14, 1899, FLb 99-A; Flagler to Ingraham, May 19 and June 24, 1902; Flagler to Parrott, June 4, 1902; Flagler to L. Larson, December 10, 1903, FLb.

30. Parrott to Ingraham, March 28, 1901, Box 21-A.2, FP.

31. F. Jacobson to Ingraham, March 26, 1897, Box 21-A.1, FP Ingraham to Flagler, August 8, 1900, Box 21-A.2, FP.

32. Unsigned letter from the Travellers' Information Company to Ingraham, November 2, 1899, "Florida on Wheels Tours U.S.," unidentified clipping inserted with letter to Ingraham, April 30, 1894, and Wanton S. Webb to Parrott, May 25, 1895, all in Box 21-A.1, FP. Locations of the Travellers' offices: New York, Boston, Buffalo, Philadelphia, Cleveland, Cincinnati, Chicago, St. Louis, St. Paul, Baltimore, Pittsburgh, Detroit, and Washington, D.C. *Homeseeker* 2 (February 1900): 29.

33. C. M. Sturges to Ingraham, November 24, 1899 (first quotation), Box 21-A.1, FP; Flagler to Ingraham, October 4, 1900, Box 21-A.2, FP.

34. *Homeseeker* 7 (October 1905): 17; ibid. 8 (January 1906): 25; unsigned letter from the Travellers' Information Company, Detroit office, to Ingraham, January 13, 1900, Box 21-A.2, FP; *Homeseeker* 9 (April 1907): 134; ibid. 7 (October 1905): 15; Ingraham to F. O. Williams, January 2, 1900, Box 21-A.2, FP; Ingraham to Parrott, June 30, 1897, Box 21-A.1, FP. In early November 1905, the Flagler road and cooperating railroads offered excursion rates from Chicago for one-half the round trip, first-class fare plus $2.00. This ticket was good for twenty-two days, allowing stops along the Florida east coast. Another opportunity Flagler's road presented in mid-November was that the cost of a round trip homeseeker ticket was 80 percent of the regular one-way, first-class ticket, also good for twenty-one days. Homeseeker rates to Florida from other midwestern cities were comparable. *Homeseeker* 7 (October 1905): 17; ibid. 8 (January 1906): 25; ibid. 7 (October 1905): 16.

35. George E. Pozzetta, "Foreign Colonies in South Florida, 1865–1910," *Tequesta* 24 (1974): 48, 51–52.

36. Flagler to Louis Larson, July 16, 1909; Flagler to Beckwith, June 30, 1909 (quotation),

FLb; Henry Y. Ozaki to George E. Pozzetta, June 3, 1975, in Pozzetta's possession. Ozaki had interviewed George Morikami, one of Yamato's original colonists.

37. Flagler to Ingraham, February 20 and July 22, 1900, Box 21-A.2, FP; Flagler to Thomas H. Hastings, August 19, 1890, FLb; Ingraham to S. W. Crichlow, August 15, 1894, and Ingraham to Flagler, June 8, 1899, Box 21-A.1, FP; Beardsley to Ingraham, June 18, 1902, FLb 134; James Ingraham, "A Man's Work [1884–1909]," rough draft of speech of May 26, 1909, Box 1, James Ingraham Papers, SAHS.

38. Beardsley to Ingraham, March 4, 1899, FLb 99-A; *Homeseeker* 2 (April 1900): 14; Flagler to Ingraham, August 13, 1901, FLb; Beardsley to Ingraham, August 19, 1901, FLb 131; Beardsley to A. V. S. Smith, November 30, 1901, FLb 133; *Homeseeker* 1 (February 1899): 6; Flagler telegram to Ingraham, February 5, 1901, FLb; Beardsley to Ingraham, October 28, 1901, FLb 131; Flagler to Ingraham, January 4, 1902; Flagler to J. P. Beckwith, November 15, 1909, FLb.

39. Flagler to George W. Carver, May 24, 1902; Flagler to William Fremd, May 24, 1902, FLb; H. E. Stockbridge to Ingraham, June 10, 1899, in *Homeseeker* 1 (June 1899): 8; ibid., June 17, 1899, in *Homeseeker* 1 (July 1899): 11–12.

40. Flagler to Frederick S. Morse, February 7, 1901; Flagler to Ingraham, December 27, 1901, and January 3, 1902, FLb; West Palm Beach *Tropical Sun*, December 27, 1905.

41. Comparative statement of oranges handled by East Coast Line for month of January, 1890, 1891, 1892, 1893, 1894, and 1895, lb. #9, Box 14-H, FP; *FT-U*, January 16, 1893.

42. *FT-U*, December 29 and 30, 1894, and January 3, 1895; Jacksonville, St. Augustine and Indian River Railway Company Circular 307, December 31, 1894, W. J. Jarvis to Parrott, January 26, 1895, both in Florida East Coast Railway Collection, St. Augustine, Florida (microfilm copy in PKY; since this collection was microfilmed in 1954, much of it is now in the FP); *FT-U*, February 8, 1895; W. J. Jarvis to Parrott, January 29, 1896, lb. #9, Box 4-H, FP.

43. Ingraham to [Louis] Larson (agent, Ft. Dallas Land Company), February 16, 1899, MS Box 21-A.1, FP; Flagler to Ingraham, August 5, 1909, FLb.

44. U.S. Bureau of the Census, *Fourteenth Census of the United States, 1920: Population,* vol. 1 (Washington, 1921), 97–98.

45. *Homeseeker* 1 (August 1899): 9; ibid. 4 (July 1902). 2, ibid., no. 16 (December 1898): 5–6.

46. U.S. Bureau of the Census, *Twelfth Census of the United States, 1900: Population,* vol. 1, pt. 1 (Washington, 1901), 496–97, Flagler to Ingraham, November 12, 1902.

47. U.S. Bureau of the Census, *Twelfth Census,* vol. 1, pt. 1, xl; U.S. Bureau of the Census, *Fourteenth Census,* 1:97–98.

11 "My Domain"

1. Flagler to John Addison Porter, McKinley's private secretary, February 15, 1898, William McKinley Papers, Library of Congress (microfilm copy).

2. Beardsley to Flagler, April 3 and 7, 1899, FLb 99-A; Flagler to Parrott, May 22, 1899, Flagler to E. M. Ashley, May 25, 1899; Flagler to Mrs. J. J. Vandergrift, August 8, 1911, FLb; Beardsley to Beckwith, August 11, 1911, FLb 186-N.

3. R. T. Goff to G. A. Miller, August 2, 1898, Box 14-F.9, FP; R. T. Goff to Parrott, August 24, 1898, lb. #11, Box 14-H, FP; Florida East Coast Railway Co., Flagler System, Steam Locomotives Original Cost to June 30, 1915, #14, Flagler Enterprises Papers.

4. Flagler to Parrott, November 24, December 4, and November 28, 1902; Flagler to Beckwith, November 15, 1909.

5. February 1895 statistics of the Parlor cars "Gov. Perry" and "Gov. Bloxham," by W. L. Crawford, lb. #2, Box 14-H, FP; Parrott to Flagler, August 28, 1895, lb. #8, Box 14-H, FP; J. T. Van Campen to D. E. Kottke, March 22, 1946, Box 14-F.9, FP; Flagler to Wayne MacVeagh, November 5, 1908; Flagler to W. H. Chambers, November 24, 1909; Flagler to Beckwith, September 7 and 23, 1909, FLb.

6. Flagler statistical diary, FP; Flagler to Beckwith, April 17, 1909.

7. Parrott to Flagler, August 12, 1895, lb. #8, Box 14-H, FP; Flagler to Parrott, June 15, 1899, FLb.

8. Flagler to H. S. Haines, August 20, 1890; Flagler to Parrott, August 17, 1899, FLb.

9. Beardsley telegram to Flagler, April 4, 1902, FLb 134; Beardsley to Bankers Trust Company, August 6, 1909, FLb 176. Flagler asked for, and received, the Plant Investment Company charter. He was considering purchasing it for use by his businesses. Flagler to R. G. Erwin, November 17, 1902; Flagler to Parrott, November 26, 1902, FLb.

10. Statement of special and limited trains for 1902 season, lb. #12, Box 14-H, FP; Flagler to Beckwith, July 30, 1909, FLb; unidentified newspaper clipping, Flagler statistical diary, FP.

11. W. L. Crawford to Flagler, January 8, 1893, lb. p. 22, Box 14-F.2, FP; R. T. Goff to T. A. Phillips, January 15, 1895, lb. #10, Box 14-H, FP; H. R. Duval telegram to Flagler, December 19, 1894, and Flagler telegram to Duval, December 19, 1894, lb. #4, Box 14-H, FP.

12. Flagler to William H. Baker, December 20, 1901; Flagler to Robert C. Clowry, October 16, 1909; Flagler to John Wells, January 13, 1902; Flagler to M. J. O'Brien, April 2, 1909, FLb; Beardsley to J. D. Rahner, March 11, 1902, FLb 133; Flagler to Charles M. Hays, February 5, 1901, FLb; J. C. Salter to Flagler, December 31, 1901, and January 6, 1902, and Beardsley telegram to Parrott, February 19, 1902, FLb 133.

13. Private car movements, 1901–1902 season, Box 32, FP; Flagler to W. A. Patton, December 15, 1903, FLb; Beardsley to William Scott, June 30, 1902, FLb 134; Beardsley to Parrott, April 23, 1903, FLb 138-A.

14. Flagler to Parrott, July 27, 1899, FLb; Kathryn T. Abbey, "Florida Versus the Principles of Populism, 1896–1911," *Journal of Southern History* 4 (November 1938): 467; Durward Long, "Florida's First Railroad Commission, 1887–1891," Part 1, *FHQ* 42 (October 1963): 106–8.

15. Long, "Florida's First Railroad Commission," Part 1, 120; Abbey, "Florida Versus the Principles of Populism," 467; Durward Long, "Florida's First Railroad Commission, 1887–1891," Part 2, *FHQ* 42 (January 1964): 253.

16. J. C. Slater to Parrott, January 8, 1903, FLb 138-A; Flagler to Beckwith, August 30, 1909; Flagler to Julien T. Davies, December 10, 1909, FLb.

17. Abbey, "Florida Versus the Principles of Populism," 467.

18. Flagler to D. H. Elliott, December 12, 1890, FLb.

19. Abbey, "Florida Versus the Principles of Populism," 467; Florida, [Second] Railroad Commission, *Annual Report* (1897–98), 1:17–32 (hereinafter, *RCR*).

20. New York *Post*, quoted in *FT-U*, May 4, 1897, and *FT-U* comment; *Railway Age*, June 4, 1897, quoted in *FT-U*, June 7, 1897.

21. Abbey, "Florida Versus the Principles of Populism," 470–71, 473.

22. Flagler to H. R. Duval, June 23, 1899; Flagler to G. S. Baxter, July 10, 1899; Flagler to E. G. Erwin, July 18 and 28, 1899; Flagler to Parrott, August 17, 1899; Flagler to Samuel

Spencer, June 5, 1902, FLb; Roland H. Rerick, *Memoirs of Florida,* ed. Francis P. Fleming, 2 vols. (Atlanta, Ga., 1902), 2:209.

23. Parrott to R. H. M. Davidson, September 3, 1898, *RCR* 2 (1898–99): 38–41.

24. Ibid., 6 (1902–1903): 17; Louis C. Massey to Florida Railroad Commissioners, February 26, 1908, in ibid., 11 (1907–1908): 14–15; ibid., 7 (1908–1909): 12; ibid., 11:7; ibid., 10 (1906–1907): 42; ibid., 16 (1912–1913): 43, 48–50.

25. Ibid., 6:9–11; ibid., 14 (1910–1911): 15–16; ibid., 15 (1911–1912): 7–8; ibid., 16:18.

26. *Poor's* 29 (1896): 210; ibid., 30 (1897): 161.

27. Ibid., 46 (1913): 411; Flagler to Beckwith, January 12, November 29, and December 3, 1909, FLb.

28. Beardsley to Flagler, February 20 and 27, 1899, FLb 99-A; ibid., January 26, 1903, FLb 138-A; Flagler to William B. Walker & Co., October 31, 1902, FLb.

29. Beardsley to Flagler, April 19, 1909, FLb 173; Flagler to Julien T. Davies, November 30, 1908, FLb; Beardsley to F. W. Stevens (of J. P. Morgan & Co.), June 7, 1909, FLb 173; Beardsley to J. N. Babcock, July 16, 1909, FLb 174; Flagler to George W. Perkins, June 10, 1909; Flagler to U. S. Mortgage & Trust Co., September 14, 1911, FLb. The principal on one series of the 1909 offering came due January 1, 1933, while the due date on two other series was May 1, 1949. Beardsley to W. H. Chambers, June 14, 1909, FLb 173.

30. Flagler to John C. Blair, November 2, 1903 (first quotation); Flagler to W. D. Morgan (Georgetown, S.C.), June 26, 1899, FLb. A similar comment was made in Flagler to T. Skelton Jones & Co. (Macon, Ga.), June 26, 1899, FLb.

31. Flagler to Parrott, October 10, 1901 and November 28, 1903, FLb; *America's Hotel and Resort Bureau Booklet* [n.p., penciled date of 1910, 1911], FEC Hotel System file, SAHS; *Homeseeker* 1 (January 1899): flyleaf; "Three Casinos in One Book," FEC booklet, Box: FEC Railway, SAHS.

32. Beardsley to Flagler, March 16, 1899, and Beardsley to Clarence B. Knott, April 18, 1899, FLb 99-A; Beardsley to Florida East Coast Hotel Company, December 27, 1900, FLb 127; Beardsley to W. H. Chambers, October 16, 1901, FLb 131.

33. Beardsley to W. H. Chambers, November 20, 1901, FLb 132; ibid., February 18 and March 12, 1902, FLb 133; Beardsley to Flagler, March 17, 1902, FLb 133; Beardsley to Chambers, April 24 and June 9, 1902, FLb 134; Flagler to Parrott, November 13, 1902, FLb.

34. Beardsley to Flagler, September 15, 1902, FLb 138; ibid., February 27, 1902 and December 13, 1902, FLb 133; Flagler to Frank Dean, December 9, 1890, FLb; Beardsley to Dean, November 13, 1901, FLb 132; Flagler to Beardsley, December 20, 1901, FLb; Beardsley to Flagler, February 3, 10, and 17, 1902, FLb 133; ibid., April 2, 1903, FLb 138-A; ibid., March 1 and 4, 1902, FLb 133; ibid., March 14, 1903, FLb 138-A; ibid., April 29, 1909, FLb 173; ibid., December 17, 1901, FLb 133; ibid., December 15, 1902, FLb 138.

I calculated Flagler's Standard Oil stock ownership by computing on the basis of the $150,000 dividend for September 1902. Beardsley to Flagler, September 14, 1902, FLb 138. The Flagler statistical diary reveals this to be $5 a share. Therefore, he and Mary Lily Flagler owned at least 30,000 shares. Also, the Flagler diary reveals a 40 percent annual dividend rate from 1905 through at least 1909; therefore, giving the $1,200,000 dividend income figure. In mid-1909, Flagler and his wife had 31,030 shares of Standard Oil (New Jersey). Beardsley to Flagler, June 25, 1909, FLb 173. I earlier stated that Henry and Mary Lily Flagler owned "at least" 30,000 shares; we are never sure of Flagler's total holdings, for he often had Beardsley hold stock for him in Beardsley's name.

35. Flagler to Rev. Charles S. Stevens, September 4, 1901 (first quotation); Flagler to W. T.

Laine, September 16, 1899 (second quotation), and June 2, 1902 (third quotation), FLb.

36. Flagler to Parrott, May 24, 1900 (both quotations), FLb; A. J. Kitching to J. C. Salter, July 1, 1900, Box 40, FP.

37. Flagler to J. W. West, September 5, 1899; Flagler to Charles E. Layton and to McGuire, July 1, 1907; Flagler to Beckwith, August 27 and 30, 1909, FLb.

38. Beardsley to George A. Cooper, June 11, 1909, and Beardsley to Ingraham, May 24, 1909, FLb 173.

39. Flagler to George M. Ward, November 9, 1899, and November 12, 1903, FLb; Beardsley to Flagler, January 15, 1902, FLb 133; Flagler to George W. Wilson, June 20, 1902; *Florida Agricultural College Catalogue,* 1898–99, 1899–1900, 1900–1901, in PKY.

40. Flagler to J. F. Forbes, October 4, 1901; Flagler to Parrott, June 4, 1902, FLb; Ida Tarbell, *All in the Day's Work: An Autobiography* (New York, 1939), 219. Tarbell stated: "Henry Flagler was not an acceptable figure even to Wall Street in those days. There were scandals of his private life which, true or not, his fellow financiers did not like. Bad for business." For a full discussion of the Stetson-Forbes battle, see Gilbert L. Lycan, *Stetson University: The First 100 Years* (DeLand, Fla., 1983), 92–100. Although Lycan presents a very balanced account, he tends to believe Forbes may have indeed been guilty of sexual misconduct.

41. West Palm Beach *Tropical Sun,* April 8, 1903; Flagler to Forbes, October 10 and December 10, 1902; Flagler to Parrott, December 8, 1902; Flagler to Forbes, May 18, 1903, FLb.

42. Flagler to James Jahns, July 30, 1890, FLb; Beardsley to Flagler, April 8 and 15, 1891, and Beardsley to Parrott, April 17 and 20, 1891, FLb 62; Flagler to George W. Wilson, November 8, 1899; Flagler to H. R. Duval, November 20, 1899; Flagler to Beardsley, January 19, 1891, FLb; Beardsley to John T. Dismukes, June 28, 1902, FLb 134; Flagler to George W. Wilson, May 31 and June 13 and 17, 1899, FLb; Beardsley to Parrott, September 30, 1901, FLb 131; ibid., April 14, 1902, FLb 134.

43. Flagler to W. H. Sharpe, May 31, 1899, FLb; *Ocala Banner,* June 7, 1901; *Pensacola Journal,* June 1, 1901; Flagler to George W. Wilson, May 31, 1899; Flagler to James P. Taliaferro, September 17, 1890, and June 18, 1909; Flagler to Parrott, February 6, 1901; Flagler to J. D. Archbold, December 7, 1901; Flagler to Parrott, May 19, 1903, FLb.

44. Flagler to John T. Dismukes, August 19, 1890; Flagler to Benjamin Brewster, July 17, 1890; Flagler to Parrott, November 7, 1901; Flagler to F. B. Squires, January 7, 1901, FLb.

45. *FT-U,* December 26, 1894, and January 4, 1895.

46. Sidney Walter Martin conversation with Harry Harkness Flagler, reported in Sidney Walter Martin, *Florida's Flagler* (Athens, Ga., 1949), 254; Thomas Graham, "Flagler's Magnificent Hotel Ponce de Leon," *FHQ* 54 (July 1975), 8; Flagler to Dr. Anderson, August 18, 1896, cited in Martin, *Florida's Flagler,* 255; Flagler to Dr. George G. Shelton, November 18, 1908, FLb. Grover Cleveland returned to the Ponce de Leon in 1893, 1899, 1903, and 1905. Other presidents enjoying the hotel during Flagler's lifetime included William McKinley in 1895, while still governor of Ohio, and Theodore Roosevelt for a special out-of-season opening in October 1905. See Graham, "Flagler's Magnificent Hotel," 8.

47. Flagler diary, December 12, 1904, cited in Martin, *Florida's Flagler,* 255; Flagler to Theodore Roosevelt, July 20, 1899; Flagler to George W. Wilson, November 23, 1899; Flagler to B. Smith, November 4, 1908 (first quotation); Flagler to Julien T. Davies, March 11, 1909, FLb. Flagler chose not to accept Roosevelt's White House invitation. He wrote to Parrott: "I have your personal favor of the 5th inst., and note the account of your meeting with President Roosevelt; also your desire that I should stop in Washington and make a call upon him. I don't

believe there is a man in America who dreads such a thing as much as I do. I am glad you saw him, for I am sure I don't want to do it." Flagler to Parrott, November 7, 1901, FLb. It may have been Flagler's introverted nature that led him to that statement, but it may have involved his knowledge of Roosevelt's previous political stands, which were already being recognized as progressive.

48. Flagler to John A. Sleicher, January 2, 1909 (quotation), FLb; William H. Taft to Parrott, July 24 and 29, 1906, and May 4 and August 16, 1907, William Howard Taft Papers, Library of Congress (microfilm copy); J. C. Salter to W. M. Ball, November 16, 1909, FLb 178.

49. Flagler to George W. Wilson, June 3, and to John H. Flagg, August 23, 1899, FLb.

50. Flagler to E. T. D. Myers, November 5, 1903, FLb.

51. Levi P. Morton form letter to "Gentlemen," May 16, 1900, Box 40, FP; Flagler to Beardsley, January 8, 1910; Flagler to John D. Archbold, April 21, 1909, FLb; George Sweet Gibb and Evelyn H. Knowlton, *The Resurgent Years, 1911–1927*, vol. 2 of *History of the Standard Oil Company (New Jersey)*, ed. Henrietta M. Larson (New York, 1956), 16; Beardsley to A. R. Brewer, March 6, 1903, FLb 138-A; Flagler to E. M. Kingsley, November 5, 1902, FLb; Robert T. Handy to author, October 18, 1984. Professor Handy, church historian at Union, is now writing a history of the seminary.

52. Beardsley to Flagler, December 12, 1902, FLb 138; ibid., January 5, March 13, and April 23, 1903, FLb 138-A; ibid., February 18, 1902, FLb 133; Flagler to M. F. Plant, November 8, and to Cleodennin Eckert, November 11, 1902; FLb.

53. Martin, *Florida's Flagler*, 229–30; *Last Will and Testament of Henry M. Flagler*, copy in Box 41-A, FP (hereinafter, *Flagler's will*); Flagler to Beardsley, April 10, and to Beckwith, April 17, 1909, FLb. The 1909 directors of the FEC, when the board was expanded from five to seven members, were Flagler, Parrott, Ingraham, Beckwith, Dr. Andrew Anderson, W. R. Kenan, Jr., Beardsley, and George W. Perkins. Flagler to W. H. Chambers, August 17, 1909, FLb.

12 Key West: "America's Gibraltar"

1. Carlton J. Corliss, "The Iron Horse on the Florida Keys," *Tequesta* 29 (1969): 17–26 (this was a speech that Corliss had delivered at the dedication of a historical marker at Marathon, Florida, January 25, 1969); Jefferson B. Browne, "Across the Gulf by Rail to Key West," unpublished MS, copy in Box 17, FP. Seth Bramson noted that this manuscript appeared as an article in an 1894 issue of *National Geographic*. Seth H. Bramson, *Speedway to Sunshine: The Story of the Florida East Coast Railway* (Erin, Ontario, 1984), 76.

2. Corliss, "The Iron Horse"; Browne, "Across the Gulf"; Harry G. Cutler, *History of Florida, Past and Present*, 3 vols. (Chicago, 1923), 1:60.

3. *Miami Herald*, September 22, 1935. This was a letter from Jefferson B. Browne to the *Herald* just after the devastating hurricane of that year.

4. Ibid.

5. Ibid.

6. Ibid.; "Corporate History of Florida East Coast Railway, 1916," unpublished MS, MS Box 14.1, FP.

7. Browne, "Across the Gulf"; Bramson, *Speedway to Sunshine*, 68.

8. Browne, "Across the Gulf."

9. Ibid. The only drawbridges constructed were at Jewfish Creek, Indian Key, Moser

Channel west of Knights Key, and Key West. For this and other route details, see George M. Chapin, *Official Souvenir: Key West Extension of the Florida East Coast Railway* (St. Augustine, Fla., [1912]), map.

10. Browne, "Across the Gulf"; *Railway World,* April 6, 1895, 274, clipping, Box 17, FP.

11. *Flagler's will;* E. Ben Carter to A. A. Dooley, January 31, 1903, Parrott to R. T. Goff, April 15, 1903, and E. Ben Carter to W. J. Krome, November 5, 1903, Box 14-G, FP; *St. Augustine Record,* May 30, 1913.

12. *Flagler's will;* William Mayo Venable, "Importance of the Railway to Key West," *The Engineering Magazine* [1908], 63; *Miami Metropolis,* February 2, 1905.

13. West Palm Beach *Tropical Sun,* April 15, 1905.

14. Ibid., May 10, 1895.

15. Ibid., June 28, 1905; Bob Phillips, Raleigh, North Carolina, correspondent for the *New York Herald,* reported Flagler's plan to the public, and the *Tropical Sun* reprinted his article.

16. E. V. Blackman, *Miami and Dade County, Florida* (Washington, D.C., 1921), 54; William Mayo Venable to Carlton J. Corliss, January 17, 1952, Box 17, FP; Venable, "Importance of the Railway," 57–58.

17. Venable, "Importance of the Railway," 57–58.

18. Chapin, *Official Souvenir,* 15; Flagler to Butler Ames, July 12, 1909. See William Mayo Venable, "The Long Key Viaduct; Description of a Two-Mile Reinforced Concrete Railway Viaduct," *Engineering Record* 56:558–60, copy in Box 17, FP.

19. Data concerning Key West Extension operations, Key West Extension (KWE) file 1184, FP; Carlton J. Corliss interview with author, Tallahassee, Florida, October 6, 1973 (Corliss was the chief clerk in the office of the chief engineer of the Key West Extension, Marathon, Florida); Chapin, *Official Souvenir,* 13.

20. George E. Pozzetta, "A Padrone Looks at Florida: Labor Recruiting and the Florida East Coast Railway," *FHQ* 54 (July 1975), 74–84; Data concerning Key West Extension operations (quotation), KWE file 1184, FP; Corliss interview with author, Tallahassee, Florida, October 6, 1973, and April 28, 1973.

21. Corliss interview with author, April 28, 1973; Chapin, *Official Souvenir,* 13–14; Corliss interview with author, April 28, 1973.

22. Corliss interview with author, April 28, 1973; enclosure in William Mayo Venable to J. C. Meredith, January 9, 1908, KWE file 7036, FP.

23. Data concerning Key West Extension operations, KWE file 1184, FP.

24. Pete Daniel, *The Shadow of Slavery: Peonage in the South, 1901–1969* (Urbana, Ill., 1971), 83.

25. Ibid., 95–98, 103. Daniel's account suffers from a failure to consult the Flagler Papers. Edward J. Triay had a definite ethnic bias. In 1902, he sent Flagler a book entitled *Anglo-Saxon Superiority.* Flagler to Triay, November 22, 1902, FLb. Also note, from chapter 11, that it was the 1891 nomination of Triay, Governor Francis P. Fleming's secretary, as a railroad commissioner which caused the end of Florida's first railroad commission.

26. Max Lipetz deposition to Otto F. Klinke (agent, U.S. Secret Service), March 12, 1907, Department of Justice, RG 60, National Archives (NA).

27. Ibid.

28. Samuel Rosen affidavit, [n.d.], Department of Justice, RG 60, NA.

29. Ibid.

30. Affidavits of the following: John J. Kegan, George Marris, Frank Meany, Winifield Ronald, Robert Murray, Edward Maher, and Charles Zinke (March 6, 1907), all except Zinke with no date, all in Department of Justice, RG 60, NA.

31. Triay to Parrott, March 17, 1907, A. V. S. Smith to J. C. Meredith, April 6, 1907, Meredith to Smith, March 25, 1907, KWE file 2517, FP.

32. A. V. S. Smith to Mr. Day, April 16, 1907, Smith to Meredith, November 7 and 13, 1908, Meredith telegram and letter to Father P. J. Kennedy, November 4, 1908, Kennedy to Meredith [received November 9, 1908], KWE file 2517, FP. Although the 1905 Parrott-Meredith letter is not extant, another along similar lines was written in 1906:

> There seems to be at this time, a great deal of agitation by the United States Government over the question of peonage, and I cannot impress upon you too strongly the necessity of exercising through all of your forces the greatest care possible to relieve the Company from the slightest possibility of claims of this character.
>
> The basis upon which this claim is made primarily is a debt. You know that we have a great many cases of debt. The debt basis being made, any attempt to hold a man whether by threats, the use of force, or otherwise, makes the offense. Any use of force would be construed probably as being an attempt to hold the man for the payment of the debt so we cannot be too careful.
>
> You will recall that more than a year ago I had occasion to advise you that some one had reported to me that some of our men on the extension work were using guns for making the men work and I told you at that time as a humane proposition it must not be done, and our men must be treated kindly, and if we had any foremen who could not work and supervise labor without the use of force or threats, or violent language they must be relieved. Apart from the humane idea, it is a business proposition that men work better and they are better men if treated like men should be. While we may have some men among us who are not fit to be treated like men, I think it is best to discharge them even though it is an expense to us. [Parrott to Meredith, November 21, 1906, KWE file 9253, FP]

33. Daniel, *Shadow of Slavery*, 105; A. V. S. Smith to Meredith, November 6, 1908, Meredith telegram to Smith, October 28, 1908, and W. J. Krome to Meredith, November 8, 1908, KWE file 2517, FP.

34. *U.S. vs. Francesco Sabbia, F. J. Triay, Harkey, and Huff*, prosecution brief pursuant to October 19, 1908, court order, Southern District of New York, copy in KWE file 2517, FP; Meredith to A. V. S. Smith, October 30, 1908, Meredith to W. P. Dusenbury, October 23, 1908, KWE file 2517, FP; Daniel, *Shadow of Slavery*, 105–6; A. V. S. Smith telegram to Meredith, November 14, 1908, and George S. Scofield telegrams to Meredith, November 18 and 19, 1908, KWE file 2517, FP. The greatest travesty of justice during the entire proceedings was the refusal of the presiding judge to allow interpreters for foreign-born workers in order for them to present their testimony.

35. Flagler to John A. Sleicher (quotation), and Flagler to Dr. Andrew Anderson, both on November 20, 1908; Flagler to Elihu Root, November 25, 1908; Flagler to J. Blake White, November 12, 1908, FLb.

36. Beardsley to Flagler, April 12, 1903, FLb 173; Beardsley to Alex St. Clair Abrams, July 8, 1909, FLb 174. In the letter of April 12, 1903, Beardsley informed Flagler of the following:

	Estimates	*Actual Expenditures*
January	$155,000	$ 60,000
February	255,000	118,000

	Estimates	*Actual Expenditures*
March	185,000	100,000
Totals	$465,000	$278,000

37. W. R. Hawkins diary, April 20, 1909, FP (Hawkins was one of the white-collar workers at the Marathon headquarters); Flagler to Dr. Anderson, April 21, 1909; Flagler to E. T. D. Myers, April 22, 1909, FLb. In 1935, after a lengthy illness, Krome died at his beloved town of Homestead at the age of 52. The immediate cause of death was attributed to the shock of learning that the Key West Extension had been destroyed by the Labor Day hurricane. Until his death, he had continued a lifelong interest in horticulture, especially avocado production. He had been president of the South Dade County Fruit Growers' and Truckers' League since 1914. He was elected vice-president of the Florida Horticultural Society in 1916. He headed the eradication of the citrus canker in 1914–15. Unidentified clipping, Box 17, FP.

38. Flagler statistical diary, February 27 and July 28, 1909, FP; Flagler to Major General John A. Brooke, August 14, 1909, FLb.

39. Hawkins diary, October 10–12, 1909, and Flagler statistical diary, October 11, 1909, FP; Flagler to Frederick Guest, October 18, 1909; Flagler to Ingraham, October 27, 1909 (first quotation); Flagler to A. C. Spalding, October 16, 1909, and Flagler to George W. Allen, October 18, 1909 (the second quotation appears in both letters), FLb; Flagler statistical diary and Hawkins diary, November 8, 1909, FP.

40. Flagler to Beckwith, October 15, 1909; Flagler to Krome, November 8, 1909, FLb; Chapin, *Official Souvenir,* 9–12, 18; Flagler to John Carrère, January 4, 1910; Chapin, *Official Souvenir,* 21. The viaducts were the most expensive part of the project. The Niles Channel viaduct cost $207,418.20 and required over 150 workers, most of them skilled. "Report on Niles Channel Viaduct," pp. 21–23, Box 17, FP.

41. Walter Olsen to Flagler (copy), September 7, 1906, enclosed in Flagler to Meredith, September 11, 1906, KWE file 5739, FP; Flagler to Beckwith, August 11, 1909, FLb; A. R. MacMannis to Carlton J. Corliss, December 21, 1965, and Meredith weekly progress report, both in Box 12, FP; *East Coast of Florida Hotel List and Information Folder, 1900–1901,* p. 27, PKY.

42. Flagler to Krome, November 22, 1909, FLb; total force on work for week ending June 20, 1911, Box 17, FP; Hawkins diary, September 20, 1911, FP; Flagler to Krome, December 24, 1911, KWE file 25800, FP; Chapin, *Official Souvenir,* 19; Flagler to Beckwith, July 26, 1911; Flagler to Frank Clark, August 15, 1911, FLb; J. C. Salter to Elgin E. Curry, August 15, 1911, FLb 185-N; Hawkins diary, December 5, 1911, FP.

43. Flagler to Parrott, November 18 and August 4, 1899 (quotation); Flagler telegrams to George W. Allen, October 16, C. L. Myers, October 18, and Beckwith, October 19, 1909, FLb.

44. Corliss interview with author, April 28, 1973; *FT-U,* January 23, 1912; Chapin, *Official Souvenir,* 77; *Miami Herald,* January 22, 1912.

45. Cutler, *History of Florida* 1:60; U.S. Bureau of the Census, *Twentieth Census of the United States, 1980: Population,* vol. 1 (Washington, D.C., 1983), 124.

13   The Florida Baron's Estate

1. Flagler to Hugh T. Birch, Aug. 29, 1903, Flb 138-A; Flagler to Dr. G. C. Shelton, Sept. 25, 1903, FLb S21-D17, 03; George W. Ward, 1914 eulogy to Flagler, in *In Memoriam, Henry*

Morrison Flagler (Buffalo, N.Y., 1914), 14; Flagler to Mrs. Laura A. Ford, Aug. 26, 1909, FLb 175.

2. Ward eulogy, *In Memoriam*, 16–17, 14.

3. Ibid., 14.

4. Ibid., 19.

5. Ibid., 14; *New York Times*, April 2, 1913; *St. Augustine Evening Record*, May 30, 1913; Harry Harkness Flagler, marginal comments in his personal copy of Sidney Walter Martin, *Florida's Flagler* (Athens, Ga., 1949), FP.

6. *St. Augustine Evening Record*, May 30, 1913.

7. *Flagler's will.*

8. Ibid.

9. *New York Times*, July 28, 1917.

10. Photocopy of original codicil, obtained from Mr. Donald Jahn of Jacksonville, Florida; *New York Times*, August 12 and September 21, 22, 24, 25, and 26, 1917; David Leon Chandler, *Henry Flagler: The Astonishing Life and Times of the Visionary Robber Baron Who Founded Florida* (New York, 1986), 189, 266. For the specific charges and the course of the scandal, see the Louisville *Evening Post*, August 27, 1917, for the initial contest by Louise Lewis of Bingham's right to any of the estate. The New York *American*, September 20, 1917, was able to obtain some of the deposition testimony which had been taken regarding the making of the codicil. Attorneys at that time asked questions concerning the possible use of drugs as inducement. Nothing was conclusive. The London *Daily Mail* on April 9, 1918, reported that the suit between Louise Wise and Robert Bingham had been settled out of court, with Bingham getting his $5 million.

11. *Last Will and Testament with Codicils Thereto of Mary Lily (Flagler) Bingham Deceased*, copy in Box 50, FP.

12. *New York Times*, February 10 and March 5, 1924.

13. *Miami Herald*, July 29, 1965; Palm Beach *Post-Times*, September 23, 1979; *Miami Herald*, April 18, 1965, and January 6, 1968.

Epilogue: "Time is Life"

1 Flagler interview with James B. Morrow, New York *Tribune*, December 23, 1906.

2. For a discussion of these men's philanthropy, see Robert F. Durden, *The Dukes of Durham, 1865–1929* (Durham, N.C., 1975); Allan Nevins, *John D. Rockefeller: The Heroic Age of American Enterprise* (New York, 1940); and Joseph F. Wall, *Andrew Carnegie* (London, 1970).

3. Richard H. Edmonds, Baltimore *Sun*, reprinted in *St. Augustine Evening Record*, May 30, 1913, Memorial edition.

4 Seth H. Bramson, *Speedway to Sunshine: The Story of the Florida East Coast Railway* (Erin, Canada, 1984), 167.

5 *Flagler's will.*

6. Bramson, *Speedway to Sunshine*, 93, 102.

7. Ibid., 102, 107; Circular No. 1 of the FEC Rwy in receivership, September 1, 1931, Box 14-F.9, FP. See Alexander R. Stoesen, "Road from Receivership: Claude Pepper, the du Pont Trust, and the Florida East Coast Railway," *FHQ* 52 (October 1973) 132–56. See also Leon Odell Griffith, *Ed Ball: Confusion to the Enemy* (Tampa, Fla., 1975). Although a popular

history and poorly documented, this is the closest we have come to unraveling the mystique of Ed Ball. Beardsley had first entered the employ of Flagler at Standard headquarters at the age of 30, the year the Trust was formed. Climbing up the ladder from stenographer to second in command at Parrott's death, Beardsley remained in New York throughout his career. *New York Times,* December 14, 1925.

8. *Palm Beach Times,* July 6, 1973; Palm Beach *Daily News,* December 19, 1926.

9. Annual report of the Florida East Coast Hotel Company, fiscal year ending December 31, 1933, FP. Flagler System Hotels brochure, 1934, Box 6, FP; Palm Beach *Post,* July 9, 1934; personal observation of St. Augustine structures; information on the present Flagler Systems, Incorporated, provided in John T. Morris interview with author, St. Augustine, Florida, May 23, 1974. Mr. Morris was the last manager of the Hotel Ponce de Leon, and in 1974, was the manager of the Ponce de Leon Motor Lodge in St. Augustine.

10. Breaker's room rates, 1954–55 season, and Philadelphia *Enquirer,* April 1, 1973, clipping, Box 11, FP.

Selected Bibliography

I. Primary and Contemporary Sources

A. Manuscript Sources

Broward, Napoleon Bonaparte. Papers. P. K. Yonge Library of Florida History, University of Florida, Gainesville, Florida.

Cleveland, Grover. Papers. Library of Congress. (Research Library, University of Florida. Microfilm.)

Coleman, Robert H. Papers. Lebanon County Historical Society. On deposit, Pennsylvania Archives Department, Harrisburg, Pennsylvania.

Devereux, James H. Family Papers. Western Reserve Historical Society. Cleveland, Ohio.

Flagler, Henry M. Papers. The Henry Morrison Flagler Museum, Palm Beach, Florida.

Flagler, Henry M. Related files. St. Augustine Historical Society Library, St. Augustine, Florida.

Flagler Enterprises. Papers. Robert L. Strozier Library, Florida State University, Tallahassee, Florida.

Florida East Coast Railway Annuals, 1893–1901, 1902–1910. P. K. Yonge Library of Florida History.

Florida East Coast Railway Collection. Originally housed at the Florida East Coast Railway headquarters in St. Augustine; most of the material is now in The Henry Morrison Flagler Museum, Palm Beach, Florida (P. K. Yonge Library of Florida History. Microfilm).

Gilchrist, Albert Walker. Papers. P. K. Yonge Library of Florida History. Microfilm.

Gleason, William H. Papers. P. K. Yonge Library of Florida History.

Harrison, Benjamin. Papers. Library of Congress. (Research Library, University of Florida. Microfilm.)

Inglis, William O. Conversations with John D. Rockefeller. Typescripts. Rockefeller Archive Center, North Tarrytown, New York.

Ingraham, James E. Papers. St. Augustine Historical Society, St. Augustine, Florida.

Jennings, William Sherman. Papers. P. K. Yonge Library of Florida History.

McKinley, William. Papers. Library of Congress. (Research Library, University of Florida. Microfilm.)

Mann, Austin Shuey. Papers. P. K. Yonge Library of Florida History.

Parrott, James R. Biographical information. University Archives, Sterling Library, Yale University, New Haven, Connecticut.

Rockefeller, John D. Papers. Rockefeller Archive Center, North Tarrytown, New York.

Rockefeller, Andrews & Flagler. Papers. Rockefeller Archive Center, North Tarrytown, New York.

Roosevelt, Theodore. Papers. Library of Congress. (Research Library, University of Florida. Microfilm.)

Sanford, Henry Sheldon. Papers. General Sanford Memorial Library, Sanford, Florida. (P. K. Yonge Library of Florida History, Microfilm.)

Sawyer, Albert P. Papers. State Library, Tallahassee, Florida.

Standard Oil Company. Executive Committee Minute Books. Rockefeller Archive Center, North Tarrytown, New York.

Standard Oil Company. Stockholder Meetings Minute Books. Rockefeller Archive Center, North Tarrytown, New York.

Taft, William Howard. Papers. Library of Congress. (Research Library, University of Florida. Microfilm.)

Trammell, Park. Papers. P. K. Yonge Library of Florida History.

Tuttle Family. Papers. Historical Museum of Southern Florida. Miami, Florida.

B. Other Contemporary Sources

American Resorts 1 (January and February, 1896).

Appleton's Illustrated Handbook of American Winter Resorts; for Tourists and Invalids. New York: Appleton, 1877.

Blackman, E. V. *Miami and Dade County, Florida.* Washington, D.C.: V. Rainbolt, 1921.

A Brief History of the Florida East Coast Railway and Associated Enterprises: Flagler System, 1885–86—1935–36. St. Augustine, Fla.: Record Co., 1936.

Selected Bibliography

Browne, Jefferson B. *Key West, the Old and the New*. St. Augustine, Fla.: Record Co., 1912.

Carrère, John, and Thomas Hastings. *Florida, the American Riviera; St. Augustine, the Winter Newport: The Ponce de Leon, the Alcazar, the Casa Monica*. New York: Gilliss Brothers & Turnure, 1887.

Chapin, George M. *Florida, 1513–1913, Past, Present, and Future: Four Hundred Years of Wars and Peace and Industrial Development*. Vol. 2, 683–86. Chicago, Ill.: S. J. Clark, 1914.

————. *Official Souvenir: Key West Extension of the Florida East Coast Railway*. St. Augustine, Fla.: Record Co., [1912].

Cleveland [Ohio] City Directory 1866–67; 1867–68; 1868–69; 1870–71.

Dodd, S. C. T. *Trusts: An Address Delivered before the Merchants' Association of Boston*, [1899].

Duffield, U. Grant. *Souvenir of the Royal Poinciana, Palm Beach (Lake Worth)*. New York, 1894.

First Presbyterian Church, Cleveland, Ohio (now, Old Stone Church). Membership and Session Books, n.d.

Florida Agricultural College Catalogue, 1898–1899; 1899–1900; 1900–1901.

Florida East Coast Homeseeker no. 13 (March 1898); no. 16 (June 1898); 1–5 (1899–1904); 7–10 (1906–1909); 12–14 (1911–1913). Some of the numbers within these volumes are missing.

Graves, John Temple. *The Winter Resorts of Florida, South Georgia, Louisiana, Texas, California, Mexico, and Cuba: Containing a Brief Description of Points of Interest to the Tourist, Invalid, Immigrant, or Sportsman, and How to Reach Them*. [New York: C. G. Crawford], 1883.

Hammondsport Presbyterian Church, Hammondsport, New York. Original Session Book, Box 41-A, FP.

Health Resorts of the South; Containing Numerous Engravings Descriptive of the Most Desirable Resorts of the Southern States, Together with Some Representative Northern Resorts. Boston: G. H. Chapin, 1892.

Howe, Joseph W. *Winter Homes for Invalids: An Account of the Various Localities in Europe and America, Suitable for Consumptives and Other Invalids during the Winter Months, with Special Reference to the Climatic Variations at Each Place, and Their Influence on Disease*. New York: G. P. Putnam's Sons, 1875.

In Memoriam, Henry Morrison Flagler. [Buffalo, N.Y.: Matthews-Northrup, 1914].

Kenan, William R., Jr. *Incidents by the Way, Lifetime Recollections and Reflections*. Lockport, N.Y.: [Privately printed], 1946.

Kennedy, J. H. "Stephen Vanderburg Harkness," *Magazine of Western History* 9 (November 1888): 288–92.

Lewis, George F., and C. B. Headley. *Annual Statement of the Business of Saginaw Valley and "The Shore," for 1868*. East Saginaw, Mich., 1869.

————. *Annual Statement of the Business of Saginaw Valley and "The Shore," for 1869.* East Saginaw, Mich., 1870.

Lloyd, Henry Demarest. "The Story of a Great Monopoly." *Atlantic Monthly* 47 (March 1881): 317-34.

————. *Wealth against Commonwealth.* New York: Harper & Brothers, 1894.

Marchman, Watt P., ed. "The Ingraham Everglades Exploring Expedition, 1892." *Tequesta* 7 (1947): 3-43.

"Marriage Records of Huron County, Ohio." Vol. 3, Old Series. May 14, 1846, to June 12, 1855. WPA project.

Moffett, Samuel E. "Henry Morrison Flagler." *The Cosmopolitan* 33 (August 1902): 416-19.

Montague, Gilbert H. *The Rise and Progress of the Standard Oil Company.* New York and London: Harper and Brothers, 1903.

————. "The Rise and Supremacy of the Standard Oil Company." *The Quarterly Journal of Economics* 16 (February 1902): 265-92.

Moody, John, and George K. Turner. "The Masters of Capital in America: The Standard Oil Company, Bankers." *McClure's Magazine* 36 (March 1911): 564-77.

Morgan, H. Wayne, ed. *An American Art Student in Paris: The Letters of Kenyon Cox, 1877-1882.* Kent, Ohio: Kent State University Press, 1986.

Palm Beach Life. 1907-1913.

Pierce, Charles William. *Pioneer Life in Southeast Florida.* Edited by Donald Walter Curl. Coral Gables, Fla.: University of Miami Press, 1970.

Poor's Manual of Railroads, 13-46 (1885-1913).

[Potts, Joseph D.] *Theory and Practice of the American System of Through Fast Freight Transportation as Illustrated in the Operations of the Empire Transportation Company.* [Philadelphia, 1876].

Rerick, Roland H. *Memoirs of Florida.* Edited by Francis P. Fleming. 2 vols. Atlanta, Ga.: Southern Historical Association, 1902.

Reynolds, Charles B. *The Standard Guide: St. Augustine.* St. Augustine, Fla.: E. H. Reynolds, 1891.

————. *A Tribute: The Architecture of the Hotel Ponce de Leon.* [Privately printed, 1889.]

Rockefeller, John D. *Random Reminiscences of Men and Events.* New York: Doubleday, Page, 1909 [1933 Doubleday, Doran edition used here].

————. "Random Reminiscences of Men and Events." *World's Work* 17 (November 1908): 10878-10894.

Saginaw [Mich.] City Directories, 1866, 1866-67.

Seavey, Osborn Dunlap. *The Early Years of the Ponce de Leon: Clippings from an Old Scrap Book of Those Days Kept by the First Manager of this "Prince of Hotels."* Compiled and edited by Louise Decatur Castleden [St. Augustine, Fla.: np, 196?]

"Sketch" [of Henry M. Flagler]. *Outlook* 104 (May 31, 1913): 231-32.

Smythe, G. Hutchinson. *Henry Bradley Plant*. New York and London: G. P. Putnam's Sons, 1898.

Tarbell, Ida M. *The History of the Standard Oil Company*. 2 vols. New York:
McClure, Phillips, & Co., 1904. Reprint (2 volumes in 1). 1950 [Used for this
book].

———. "The History of the Standard Oil Company: Chapter V: The Price of Trust
Building." *McClure's Magazine* 20 (March 1903): 493–508.

———. "The History of the Standard Oil Company: Chapter VI: The Defeat of the
Pennsylvania." *McClure's Magazine* 20 (April 1903): 606–21.

———. "The Oil War of 1872." *McClure's Magazine* 20 (January 1903): 248–60.

———. "The Rise of the Standard Oil Company." *McClure's Magazine* 20 (December 1902): 115–28.

———. "An Unholy Alliance." *McClure's Magazine* 20 (February 1903): 390–403.

Veblen, Thorstein. *The Theory of Business Enterprise*. New York: Charles
Scribner's Sons, 1904.

———. *The Theory of the Leisure Class: An Economic Study in the Evolution of
Institutions*. New York: The Macmillan Co., 1899.

Venable, William Mayo. "Importance of the Railway to Key West." *The Engineering Magazine* [1908].

———. "The Long Key Viaduct: Description of a Two-Miles Reinforced Concrete
Railway Viaduct." *Engineering Record* 26:558–60. [Copy located in MS Box 17,
Flagler Papers.]

C. Newspapers

East Saginaw Courier, April 1863–1864.

Huron Reflector, January 30, 1844.

Jacksonville *Florida Times-Union*, 1885–1913; March 3, 1957.

Juno *Tropical Sun*, 1891–January 3, 1895.

Lake Worth Historian, 1896.

Lake Worth News, Christmas number, 1900.

Miami Daily News, May 12, 1946.

Miami Herald, January 1911–August 1913; September 22, 1935; May 14, 1964;
July 29, 1965.

Miami Metropolis, May 1897–1910.

New York Herald, April 3, 1911.

New York Times, May 10, 1901; April 19, 1905; April 1, 1913; July–September
1917; December 14, 1925.

New York *Tribune*, July 11–August 4, 1874.

Norwalk (Ohio) *Reflector*, August 19, 1862; February 1863.

Ocala Banner, June 7, 1901.

Oil, Paint & Drug Reporter, August 3, 1879.

Palm Beach *Daily News,* 1902–1913; December 19, 1926.

Palm Beach Life, 1907–1913.

Palm Beach *Post,* July 9, 1934.

Palm Beach Post-Times, September 23, 1979.

Palm Beach Times, July 6, 1973.

Pensacola Journal, June 1, 1901.

Royal Poinciana *Daily Program,* 1903–1907.

Saginaw Courier, January 19, 1880.

Saginaw Daily Enterprise, December 20, 1866.

Saginaw Enterprise, 1859, 1867.

Saginaw Weekly Enterprise, January 19, 1865–January 18, 1866.

St. Augustine Record, 1899–1913.

St. Augustine *St. Johns County Weekly,* April 24, 1886; March 12, 1887; April 16, 1887.

St. Augustine *Tatler,* March 23, 1901.

The Voice [Jesuit periodical], December 1, 1972.

West Palm Beach *Tropical Sun,* 1895–1906 [broken files].

D. Public Documents

Florida. [First] Railroad Commission. *Annual Report.* 1–4 (1887–1888 to 1890–1891).

Florida. [Second] Railroad Commission. *Annual Report.* 1–15 (1897–1898 to 1911–1912).

Florida. Flagler Divorce Proceedings, 1901. Seventh Circuit Court. Miami, Fla. [housed in a Dade County warehouse].

Florida. *Laws of Florida.* Chap. 3166. 1879.

Florida. *Laws of Florida.* Chap. 4260. 1893.

Florida. Internal Improvement Fund. *Minutes of the Trustees.* 1–9 (1855–1872 to 1911–1912).

Huron, County of. Deed Records. Bellevue, Ohio.

New York, Committee on Railroads. *Proceedings of the Special Committee on Railroads.* 5 vols. New York, 1879.

Ohio. Senate. "Appendix: Report of Special Committee on Railroads.". In *Journal* 63 (1867).

Pennsylvania. Senate. Committee on the Judiciary. "Report to the Senate (January 21, 1868)." In *Journal* (1868).

Saginaw, City of. Records, Atlas. Saginaw, Mich.

Saginaw, County of. Deed Records. Saginaw, Mich.

St. Johns, County of. *Certified Copy of Last Will and Testament with Codicils Thereto of Henry M. Flagler, Deceased, And Probate Proceedings Thereon before the Hon. M. R. Cooper, County Judge of St. Johns County, Florida, Including Petition for Probate of Will and Codicils, with Proofs, Affidavit of Execu-*

tors, Order Admitting to Probate, Oath of Executors, Letters Testamentary, Etc. St. Augustine, Fla., [1913].

_____. Deed Books. St. Augustine, Fla.

U.S. Bureau of the Census. *Twelfth Census of the United States, 1900: Population.* 1, pt. 1, xl. Washington, D.C., 1901.

_____. *Thirteenth Census of the United States, 1910: Agriculture.* 6:306–10. Washington, D.C., 1913.

_____. *Fourteenth Census of the United States, 1920: Population.* 1:97–98. Washington, D.C., 1921.

_____. *Twentieth Census of the United States, 1980: Population.* 1. Washington, D.C., 1983.

U.S. Commissioner of Corporations. *Report on the Petroleum Industry, Part I, Position of the Standard Oil Company in the Petroleum Industry.* [Washington, 1907].

U.S. Congress. House. Committee on Manufactures. *Report . . . on the Standard Oil Trust.* 50th Cong., 1st sess., 1888, H. Rept. 3112.

U.S. Congress. Senate. *Perrine Grant.* 54th Cong., 2d sess., 1892, S. Rept. 1574.

U.S. Department of Commerce. Prepared by Joseph E. Davis. *Trust Laws and Unfair Competition.* Washington, D.C., 1916.

U.S. Department of Justice. *U.S. v. Francesco Sabbia, E. J. Triay, Harkey, and Huff* [files]. RG 60, NA.

E. Interviews and Letters

Corliss, Carlton J. Interview with author. Tallahassee, Florida, April 28, 1973; October 6, 1973.

Flagler, Henry M. "Flagler in Florida." Interview with Edwin Lefevre. *Everybody's Magazine* (February 1910): 168–86.

_____. Interview with James B. Morrow. New York *Tribune*, December 23, 1906.

McAloon, Joseph. Interview with Thomas S. Graham. St. Augustine, Florida, August 2, 1974.

Morris, John T. Interview with author. May 23, 1974.

Curry, Lamar Louise. Letter to author, June 26, 1975.

Handy, Robert T. Letter to author, October 18, 1984.

Ozaki, Henry Y. Letter to George E. Pozzetta, June 3, 1975.

Simmons, Charles B. Letter to author, August 23, 1986.

II. Secondary Materials

A. Books

Allen, William H. *Rockefeller, Giant, Dwarf, Symbol.* New York, 1930.

Selected Bibliography

Amory, Cleveland. *The Last Resorts.* New York, 1952.

Bartlett, Richard A., ed. *Gilded Age America, 1865–1900: Interpretative Articles and Documentary Sources.* Reading, Mass., 1969.

Beard, Charles A. *Contemporary American History, 1877–1913.* New York, 1914.

Blackford, Mansel G., and K. Austin Kerr. *Business Enterprise in American History.* Boston, 1986.

Bramson, Seth H. *Speedway to Sunshine: The Story of the Florida East Coast Railway.* Erin, Canada, 1984.

Bringhurst, Bruce. *Antitrust and the Oil Monopoly: The Standard Oil Cases, 1890–1911.* Westport, Conn., 1979.

Browder, Clifford. *The Money Game in Old New York: Daniel Drew and His Times.* Lexington, Ky., 1986.

Bryant, Keith L., Jr., and Henry C. Dethloff. *A History of American Business.* Englewood Cliffs, N.J., 1983.

Burgess, George H., and Miles C. Kennedy. *Centennial History of the Pennsylvania Railroad Company, 1846–1946.* Philadelphia, 1949.

Cabell, Branch, and A. J. Hanna. *The St. Johns: A Parade of Diversities.* New York, 1943.

Cash, W. T. *The Story of Florida.* 4 vols. New York, 1938.

Chandler, Alfred D. *The Visible Hand: The Managerial Revolution in American Business.* Cambridge, Mass., 1977.

Chandler, David Leon. *Henry Flagler: The Astonishing Life and Times of the Visionary Robber Baron Who Founded Florida.* New York, 1986.

A Chronology of American Railroads. Washington, D.C., 1957.

Cochran, Thomas C. *Railroad Leaders, 1845–1890: The Business Mind in Action.* Cambridge, Mass., 1953.

Cochran, Thomas C., and William Miller. *The Age of Enterprise: A Social History of Industrial America.* New York, 1942.

Condit, Carl W. *American Building Art: The Nineteenth Century.* New York, 1960.

Cutler, Harry G. *History of Florida, Past and Present.* 3 vols. Chicago, 1923.

Daniel, Pete. *The Shadow of Slavery: Peonage in the South 1901–1969.* Urbana, Ill., 1971.

Davis, T. Frederick. *History of Jacksonville, Florida and Vicinity, 1513 to 1924.* Jacksonville, Fla., 1925.

DeSantis, Vincent P. *The Shaping of Modern America, 1877–1916.* Boston, 1972.

Dictionary of American Biography. 10 vols. New York, 1936.

Durden, Robert F. *The Dukes of Durham, 1865–1929.* Durham, N.C., 1975.

Faris, John T. *Seeing the Sunny South.* Philadelphia and London, 1921.

Faulkner, Harold U. *The Decline of Laissez Faire, 1897–1917.* New York, 1951.

———. *Politics, Reform, and Expansion, 1890–1900.* New York, 1959.

Florida Statistical Abstract. 8. Gainesville, Fla., 1974.

Flynn, John T. *God's Gold: The Story of Rockefeller and His Times.* New York, 1932.

Selected Bibliography

Flynt, Wayne. *Duncan Upshaw Fletcher: Dixie's Reluctant Progressive*. Tallahassee, Fla., 1971.

Fry, Joseph A. *Henry S. Sanford: Diplomacy and Business in Nineteenth-Century America*. Reno, Nev., 1982.

Garraty, John A. *The New Commonwealth, 1877–1890*. New York, 1968.

Gaston, Paul M. *The New South Creed: A Study in Southern Mythmaking*. New York, 1970.

Gibb, George Sweet, and Evelyn H. Knowlton. *The Resurgent Years, 1911–1927*. Vol. 2 of *History of Standard Oil Company (New Jersey)*. Edited by Henrietta M. Larson. New York, 1956.

Giddens, Paul H. *The Birth of the Oil Industry*. New York, 1938.

Goulder, Grace. *John D. Rockefeller: The Cleveland Years*. Cleveland, Ohio, 1972.

Graham, Thomas. *The Awakening of St. Augustine: The Anderson Family and the Oldest City, 1821–1924*. St. Augustine, Fla., 1979.

Griffith, Leon Odell. *Ed Ball: Confusion to the Enemy*. Tampa, Fla., 1975.

Grodinsky, Julius. *Jay Gould: His Business Career, 1867–1892*. Philadelphia, 1957.

Hanna, Kathryn Abbey. *Florida: Land of Change*. Chapel Hill, N.C., 1941.

Harbaugh, William H. *The Life and Times of Theodore Roosevelt*. Rev. ed. London, 1975.

Hawke, David Freeman. *John D.: The Founding Father of the Rockefellers*. New York, 1980.

Hidy, Ralph W., and Muriel E. Hidy. *Pioneering in Big Business, 1882–1911*. Vol. 1 of *History of Standard Oil Company (New Jersey)*. Edited by Henrietta M. Larson. New York, 1955.

History of the First Presbyterian Church of Saginaw, Michigan, 1838–1938. N.p., 1938.

Hungerford, Edward. *The Story of the Baltimore & Ohio Railroad, 1827–1927*. New York, 1928.

Josephson, Matthew. *The Robber Barons: The Great American Capitalists, 1861–1901*. New York, 1934.

Joubert, William W. *Southern Freight Rates in Transition*. Gainesville, Fla., 1949.

Kirkland, Edward C. *Dream and Thought in the Business Community, 1860–1900*. Ithaca, N.Y., 1956.

———. *Industry Comes of Age: Business, Labor and Public Policy, 1860–1897*. New York, 1961.

Klein, Maury. *The Life and Legend of Jay Gould*. Baltimore, Md., 1986.

Kolko, Gabriel. *Railroads and Regulation, 1877–1916*. Princeton, N.J., 1965.

Lane, Wheaton J. *Commodore Vanderbilt: An Epic of the Steam Age*. New York, 1942.

Lebergott, Stanley. *The Americans: An Economic Record*. New York, 1984.

Lee, W. Howard. *The Flagler Story and Memorial Church*. St. Augustine, Fla., 1949.

Ludlow, The Reverend Arthur Clyde and Mrs. Arthur Clyde Ludlow. *History of Cleveland Presbyterianism*. Cleveland, Ohio: 1896.

Lycan, Gibert L. *Stetson University: The First 100 Years*. DeLand, Fla., 1983.

Manual of the First Congregational Church and Society of East Saginaw with Historical Sketch and Catalogues. East Saginaw, Mich., 1873.

Martin, Sidney Walter. *Florida's Flagler*. Athens, Ga., 1949.

McCraw, Thomas K. *Prophets of Regulation: Charles Francis Adams, Louis D. Brandeis, James M. Landis, Alfred E. Kahn*. Cambridge, Mass., 1984.

Mills, James Cooke. *History of Saginaw County Michigan*. Saginaw, Mich., 1918.

Morgan, H. Wayne, ed. *The Gilded Age*. Syracuse, N.Y., 1970.

Mott, Edward H. *Between the Ocean and the Lakes: The Story of the Erie*. New York, 1899.

Mowry, George E. *The Era of Theodore Roosevelt, 1900–1912*. New York, 1958.

Nevins, Allan. *John D. Rockefeller: The Heroic Age of American Enterprise*. 2 vols. New York, 1940.

———. *Study in Power: John D. Rockefeller, Industrialist and Philanthropist*. 2 vols. New York and London, 1953.

Oddo, Bill. "The Harkness Family Mark on Bellevue." *Stories of Old Bellevue, Book I: January 1983-December 1984*. Privately printed, 1984.

———. *Stories of Old Bellevue, Book II: December 1984-December 1986*. Privately printed, 1986.

Peters, Thelma. *Biscayne Bay Country, 1870–1926*. Miami, Fla., 1981.

Pettengill, George W., Jr. *The Story of the Florida Railroads, 1834–1903*. Boston, 1952.

Pike, Kermit J. *A Guide to the Manuscripts and Archives of the Western Reserve Historical Society*. Cleveland, Ohio, 1972.

Proctor, Samuel. *Napoleon Bonaparte Broward: Florida's Fighting Democrat*. Gainesville, Fla., 1950.

Redding, David A. *Flagler and His Church*. Jacksonville, Fla., 1970.

Shannon, Fred A. *The Farmer's Last Frontier: Agriculture, 1860–1897*. New York, 1945.

Shaw, Ronald E. *Erie Water West: A History of the Erie Canal, 1792–1854*. Lexington, Ky., 1966.

Summers, Festus P. *Johnson Newlon Camden: A Study in Individualism*. New York, 1937.

Tarbell, Ida. *All in the Day's Work: An Autobiography*. New York, 1939.

Taylor, George Rogers, and Irene D. Neu. *The American Railroad Network, 1861–1890*. Cambridge, Mass., 1956.

Tebeau, Charlton W. *A History of Florida*. Coral Gables, Fla., 1971.

Trachtenberg, Allan. *The Incorporation of America: Culture and Society in the Gilded Age*. New York, 1982.

Travers, J. W. *History of Beautiful Palm Beach*. West Palm Beach, Fla., 1928.

Upton, Harriet Taylor. *History of the Western Reserve*. 2 vols. Chicago, 1910.

Waggoner, Clark. *History of Toledo and Lucas County, Ohio*. Toledo, Ohio, 1888.

Wall, Joseph F. *Andrew Carnegie*. London, 1970.

Wiebe, Robert H. *Businessmen and Reform: A Study of the Progressive Movement*. Cambridge, Mass., 1962.

_____. *Search for Order, 1877–1920*. New York, 1967.

Williams, W. W. *History of the Fire Lands, Comprising Huron and Erie Counties, Ohio*. Cleveland, Ohio, 1879.

Williamson, Harold F., and Arnold R. Daum. *The American Petroleum Industry: The Age of Illumination, 1859–1899*. Evanston, Ill., 1959.

Woodward, Comer Vann. *Origins of the New South, 1877–1913*. Baton Rouge, La., 1951.

B. Theses and Dissertations

Akin, Edward Nelson. "Southern Reflection of the Gilded Age: Henry M. Flagler's System, 1885–1913." Ph.D. dis., University of Florida, 1975.

Amundson, Richard James. "The American Life of Henry Sheldon Sanford." Ph.D. dis., Florida State University, 1963.

Carper, N. Gordon. "The Convict-Lease System in Florida, 1866–1923." Ph.D. dis., Florida State University, 1964.

Carson, Ruby Leach. "William Dunnington Bloxham: Florida's Two-Term Governor." M.A. thesis, University of Florida, 1945.

Clark, Morita Mason. "The Development of the Citrus Industry in Florida before 1895." M.A. thesis, Florida State University, 1947.

Graham, Thomas S. "Charles S Jones, 1848–1913: Editor and Progressive Democrat." Ph.D. dis., University of Florida, 1973.

Johnson, Dudley Sady. "The Railroads of Florida, 1865–1900." Ph.D. dis., Florida State University, 1965.

Johnson, Kenneth R. "The Administration of William Dunnington Bloxham, 1881–1885." M.S. thesis, Florida State University, 1953.

Nelson, Wallace Martin. "Economic Development of Florida, 1870–1930." Ph.D. dis., University of Florida, 1962.

Pavlovsky, Arnold Marc. "We Busted Because We Failed· Florida Politics, 1880–1908." Ph.D. dis., Princeton University, 1973.

Prince, Sigsbee Carlton. "Edward Alysworth Perry: Florida's Thirteenth Governor." M.A. thesis, University of Florida, 1949.

Proctor, Samuel. "Napoleon Bonaparte Broward: The Portrait of a Progressive Democrat." M.A. thesis, University of Florida, 1942.

_____. "The University of Florida: Its Early Years, 1853–1906." Ph.D. dis., University of Florida, 1958.

Staid, Mary Evangelista. "Albert Walter Gilchrist: Florida's Middle of the Road Governor." M.A. thesis, University of Florida, 1950.

Williamson, Edward C. "The Era of the Democratic County Leader: Florida Politics, 1877–1893." Ph.D. dis., University of Pennsylvania, 1953.

Selected Bibliography

C. Articles

Abbey, Kathryn T. "Florida Versus the Principles of Populism, 1896–1911." *Journal of Southern History* 4 (November 1938): 462–75.

Akin, Edward N. "The Cleveland Connection: Revelations from the John D. Rockefeller–Julia D. Tuttle Correspondence." *Tequesta* 42 (1982): 57–61.

———. "The Sly Foxes: Henry Flagler, George Miles, and Florida's Public Domain." *Florida Historical Quarterly* 58 (July 1979): 22–36.

Amundson, Richard J. "The Florida Land and Colonization Company." *Florida Historical Quarterly* 44 (1966): 153–68.

Berthoff, Rowland T. "Southern Attitudes toward Immigration, 1865–1914." *Journal of Southern History* 17 (August 1951): 328–60.

Bridges, Hal. "The Robber Baron Concept in American History." *Business History Review* 33 (Spring 1959): 1–13.

Carson, Ruby Leach. "Miami: 1896–1900." *Tequesta* 16 (1956): 3–13.

Cash, W. T. "The Lower East Coast, 1870–1890." *Tequesta* 8 (1948): 57–71.

Chandler, Alfred D. "The Beginnings of 'Big Business' in American Industry." *Business History Review* 33 (Spring 1959): 1–31.

Clark, Patricia. " 'A Tale to Tell from Paradise Itself': George Bancroft's Letters from Florida, March 1885," *Florida Historical Quarterly* 48 (1970): 264–78.

Conrad, Mary Dauthit. "Homesteading in Florida during the 1890's." *Tequesta* 17 (1957): 3–30.

Corliss, Carlton J. "Building the Overseas Railroad to Key West." *Tequesta* 13 (1953): 3–21.

———. "Henry M. Flagler, Railroad Builder." *Florida Historical Quarterly* 38 (1960): 195–205.

———. "The Iron Horse on the Florida Keys." *Tequesta* 29 (1969): 17–26.

Covington, James W. "The Tampa Bay Hotel." *Tequesta* 26 (1966): 3–20.

Craven, Avery. "The 'Turner Theories' and the South." *Journal of Southern History* 5 (August 1939): 291–314.

Crofts, Daniel W. "The Warner-Foraker Amendment to the Hepburn Bill: Friend or Foe of Jim Crow?" *Journal of Southern History* 39 (August 1973): 341–58.

Curti, Merle, Judith Green, and Roderick Nash. "Anatomy of Giving: Millionaires in the Late Nineteenth Century." *American Quarterly* 15 (Fall 1963): 416–35.

Davis, T. Frederick. "The Disston Land Purchase." *Florida Historical Quarterly* 17 (January 1939): 200–210.

Daytona Beach Winter Resorter, December 31, 1937.

Destler, Chester McArthur. "The Standard Oil, Child of the Erie Ring, 1868–1872: Six Contracts and a Letter." *Mississippi Valley Historical Review* 33 (June 1946): 89–114.

Doherty, Herbert J., Jr. "Florida." In *The Encyclopedia of Southern History,* edited by David C. Roller and Robert W. Twyman. Baton Rouge, La., 1979, 441–58.

Selected Bibliography

Graham, Thomas. "Flagler's Magnificent Hotel Ponce de Leon." *Florida Historical Quarterly* 54 (July 1975): 1–17.

Kendrick, B. B. "The Colonial Status of the South." *Journal of Southern History* 8 (February 1942): 3–22.

Kennedy, J. H. "Stephen Vanderburg Harkness." *Magazine of Western History* 9 (November 1888–April 1889): 188–92.

Klein, Maury. "Southern Railroad Leaders, 1865–1893: Identities and Ideologies." *Business History Review* 42 (Fall 1968): 288–339.

Klein, Maury, and Kozo Yamamura. "The Growth Strategies of Southern Railroads, 1865–1893." *Business History Review* 42 (Winter 1968): 358–77.

Kolko, Gabriel. "The Premises of Business Revisionism." *Business History Review* 33 (Fall 1959): 330–44.

Latham, Thomas W. "Revelations of an Old Account Book." *Firelands Pioneer* 22 (Fall 1920): 133–38.

Lively, Robert A. "The South and Freight Rates: Political Settlement of an Economic Argument." *Journal of Southern History* 14 (August 1948): 357–84.

Long, Durward. "Florida's First Railroad Commission, 1887–1891." Parts 1, 2. *Florida Historical Quarterly* 42 (October 1963, January 1964): 103–24, 248–57.

McClelland, Peter D. "New Perspectives on the Disposal of Western Lands in Nineteenth Century America." *Business History Review* 43 (Spring 1969): 77–83.

Marks, Henry S. "Earliest Land Grants in the Miami Area." *Tequesta* 18 (1958): 15–21.

———. "Labor Problems of the Florida East Coast Railway Extension from Homestead to Key West: 1905–1908." *Tequesta* 32 (1972): 28–33.

Martin, S. Walter. "Flagler's Associates in East Florida Developments." *Florida Historical Quarterly* 26 (January 1948): 256–63.

———. "Flagler Before Florida." *Tequesta* [5] (1945): 3–15.

———. "Henry Morrison Flagler." *Florida Historical Quarterly* 25 (January 1947): 257–76.

———. "One of the Great Names in the Building of Florida Is—Flagler." *Suntime* 5 (September 5, 1953): 4–7.

Mercer, Lloyd C. "Land-grants to American Railroads: Social Cost or Social Benefit?" *Business History Review* 43 (Summer 1969): 134–51.

———. "Taxpayers or Investors: Who Paid for the Land-grant Railroads?" *Business History Review* 46 (Fall 1972): 279–94.

Merrick, George E. "Pre-Flagler Influences on the Lower Florida East Coast." *Tequesta* 1 (1941): 1–10.

Nash, Gerald D. "Research Opportunities in the Economic History of the South after 1880." *Journal of Southern History* 32 (August 1966): 305–24.

"Necrology—Mr. William Lamont Harkness." *Transactions, The Western Reserve Historical Society* 102 (October 1920): 25–26.

Owsley, Frank L. "The Pattern of Migration and Settlement on the Southern Frontier." *Journal of Southern History* 11 (May 1945): 147–76.

Patrick, Rembert W. "The Mobile Frontier." *Journal of Southern History* 29 (February 1963): 3–18.

Pierce, Robert. "A Wandering Preacher I." *Year Book: Dutchess County Historical Society* 61 (1976): 79–87.

_____. "Over Hill; Over Dale." *Year Book: Dutchess County Historical Society* 60 (1975): 71–78.

_____. "The Germanic Origin of the Flagler Family of Dutchess County." *Year Book: Dutchess County Historical Society* 57 (1972): 128–35.

_____. "The Seed Is Planted in American Soil." *Year Book: Dutchess County Historical Society* 59 (1974): 30–38.

Poppelier, John C. "Report on the Grace Methodist Church." March 1965. Historic American Buildings Survey, FLA 167.

_____. "Report on the Memorial Presbyterian Church, St. Augustine, March 1965," HABS, FLA-170.

Pozzetta, George E. "Foreign Colonies in South Florida, 1865–1910." *Tequesta* 34 (1974): 45–56.

_____. "A Padrone Looks at Florida: Labor Recruiting and the Florida East Coast Railway." *Florida Historical Quarterly* 54 (July 1975): 74–84.

Robinson, T. Ralph. "Henry Perrine: Pioneer Horticulturist of Florida." *Tequesta* 1 (1942): 16–24.

Saunders, William H. "The Wreck of Houseboat No. 4, October 1906." *Tequesta* 19 (1959): 15–21.

Scott, Roy V. "American Railroads and Agricultural Extension, 1900–1914: A Study in Railway Development Techniques." *Business History Review* 39 (Spring 1965): 74–98.

Sessa, Frank B. "Miami in 1926." *Tequesta* 26 (1956): 15–36.

Stoesen, Alexander R. "Road from Receivership: Claude Pepper, the duPont Trust, and the Florida East Coast Railway." *Florida Historical Quarterly* 52 (October 1973): 132–56.

Tipple, John. "The Anatomy of Prejudice: Origins of the Robber Baron Legend." *Business History Review* 33 (Winter 1959): 510–23.

Wagner, Henry J. "Early Pioneers of South Florida." *Tequesta* 9 (1949): 61–72.

Wiles, Doris C. "Report on the History of the St. Johns County Courthouse Building to Bacon, Hartman and Vollbrecht, Inc., March 18, 1968." In: St. Johns Courthouse Bldg. file, St. Augustine Historical Society Library, St. Augustine, Fla.

Wilson, F. Page. "Miami, from Frontier to Metropolis: An Appraisal." *Tequesta* 14 (1954): 24–49.

Woodruff, William. "History and the Businessman." *Business History Review* 30 (September 1956): 241–59.

Zimmerman, Jane. "The Penal Reform Movement in the South during the Progressive Era." *Journal of Southern History* 17 (November 1951): 462–92.

Acknowledgments

WHEN ONE HAS BEEN involved in a project for fifteen years—such as, indeed, is the case with this one—a number of debts are created. My only hesitation in writing this section is the fear that I may leave out someone who made an important contribution to any success the final product may enjoy. Any errors contained in this book are mine and mine alone. I hope to be forgiven for any errors of omission which may occur in this section, for I have received many kindnesses, and from "strangers" on more than one occasion.

I wish to thank the administration and my fellow history teachers at Mississippi College. At small liberal arts colleges such as mine, historical research and writing are not part of the job description. However, the administrative staff, from president Lewis Nobles to the fine head of secretarial services, Pat Turner, has fully supported my research and writing efforts over the years. My colleagues within the history department, Ed McMillan, Bill Hicks, Ron Howard, and Kirk Ford, have always been not only associates but friends.

A special thanks goes to those who have attempted to understand the early Standard Oil years. Ida M. Tarbell set a high standard with her early twentieth-century study of Standard Oil. This was followed by Allan Nevins's masterpiece biography of John D. Rockefeller. Others have contributed over the years to the literature on Standard Oil. Most recently, David Freeman Hawke and David Leon Chandler have written biographies of John Rockefeller and Henry Flagler, respectively. Both these gentlemen have encouraged and assisted my own efforts. To them I owe a debt of appreciation.

Three persons share my tremendous gratitude for their intellectual guidance on the Flagler project. Samuel Proctor directed the Florida phase of this project as a doctoral dissertation at the University of Florida (completed in 1975). His skill can be seen by the fact that Wayne Flynt and Bertram Wyatt-Brown, my other "intellectual creditors," suggested few changes to that section of the Flagler biography.

Acknowledgments

Since the Florida days, Sam Proctor has continued his steadfast interest in and support of my career. Wayne Flynt has been teacher, friend, and confidant to me since the first course I took under his guidance when I was a freshman at Samford University in the late 1960s. Although he left Samford for Auburn University in the mid-1970s, he has maintained a strong interest in my career, so much so that he was willing to read through a rather rough draft of my Flagler manuscript. Bertram Wyatt-Brown also read a later version of the manuscript, but he came to me from a different direction. Although he is now at the University of Florida, I did not have the privilege of having his instruction during my graduate student years at that institution. Wyatt-Brown volunteered to read the manuscript for me, a most gracious gesture; and he spent much more time than this "stranger" had a right to expect from such a brilliant stylist and generous scholar.

Historians are heavily dependent on librarians and archivists in plying their craft. I am indebted to those professionals in locations throughout the eastern half of the nation, ranging from the Saginaw (Michigan) Public Library to the Sterling Library of Yale University. There are three collections which were most critical to the Flagler project. During the graduate school years, Elizabeth Alexander and her staff at the P. K. Yonge Library of Florida History at the University of Florida offered me not only a home base but also shared their knowledge of Florida history with a non-Floridian. Charles Simmons and his staff at The Henry Morrison Flagler Museum in Palm Beach, Florida, guided me through the Flagler papers housed there—and then left me to my own reflections and interpretations. Especially helpful to me during the major phase of research at the museum was Cathy McElory. Even after leaving the museum to become a curator for the William Penn State Museum in Harrisburg, Pennsylvania, she sent me a detailed analysis of my dissertation. Joseph Ernst (since having returned to the teaching of history at York University in Toronto) and his staff at the Rockefeller Archive Center in North Tarrytown, New York, worked closely with me during a month's research in the Rockefeller papers as I retraced the steps of Allan Nevins, Rockefeller's biographer, and looked at new material in the collection, especially the papers of Rockefeller, Andrews & Flagler, the partnership which formed the Standard Oil Company in 1870. A number of other librarians and archivists assisted me in my efforts; I hope my notation of their institution in the appropriate note material will be partial repayment of that debt.

Throughout the past decade or so, I have been financially assisted by a fellowship and several travel grants. During my last year in graduate school, as I was writing my dissertation on Flagler's Florida years, the Lincoln Educational Foundation granted me a John E. Rovensky Fellowship in Business and Economic History. Later, a grant from Rockefeller University allowed me to spend time at the Rockefeller Archive Center in North Tarrytown, New York, working in Flagler's Standard Oil correspondence. Penrose Grant #9145, awarded by the American Philosophical Society in 1982, allowed me to travel throughout the eastern half of the nation on four critical trips as I completed the final primary research for the full biography of Flagler.

Acknowledgments

Throughout the years, old friends and new acquaintances have assisted me in various ways. Some offered me a place to stay and, more importantly, encouragement during some of my lonely days on the road. Jerry and Brenda Weeks, now in Chattanooga, were there for me in West Palm Beach during 1974, and have been dear friends ever since. In later research trips, various friends provided places of respite: Linda Vance and David and Jean Chalmers in Gainesville, Florida; Emil Hardin in New Haven, Connecticut; Evelyn Shields in Saginaw, Michigan; and Cathy McElroy in Harrisburg, Pennsylvania. In the last, critical stage of preparation for publication, friends provided quick responses to my harried requests: Tom Graham (history professor, Flagler College); Joan Runkel (curator, The Flagler Museum); Randy Nimnicht (executive director, The Historical Association of Southern Florida); and Dan Hobby (executive director, Ft. Lauderdale Historical Society).

One gentleman needs to be singled out for special praise: Bill Oddo. This "amateur" historian has dedicated his spare time to the history of his town, Bellevue, Ohio. His newspaper articles on local historical subjects, which he later compiled into two privately printed books, have added to my understanding of Henry Flagler's formative business experience on the Western Reserve frontier of the 1840s and 1850s.

The Flagler manuscript was the winner of the 1985 Manuscript Award of Phi Alpha Theta, the international history honorary society. I appreciate Donald Hoffman, international secretary-treasurer of the organization, and the awards committee members for their assistance and constructive criticism. Phi Alpha Theta financially assisted in the publication of the Flagler biography. John T. Hubbell and his staff at Kent State University Press have been most understanding and supportive as I went through the growing pains of producing my first book. Hubbell became director of the Press—giving up the life of the history classroom teacher, but continuing as editor of *Civil War History*—just before negotiating the contracts with me and Phi Alpha Theta. I hope that this has been a good transition for him, for it has been an enjoyable experience for me.

My most intimate friends throughout the Flagler project have been my wife and son. Gail, during the graduate school years, was my typist, editor, and strongest critic and supporter. As she entered her own career path as a law student and then lawyer, the day-to-day interest in the project waned, needless to say, but her faith in me never did. My son, David, was born in 1971, the same year I began thinking of Henry Flagler as a dissertation topic. This book is dedicated to them, not as a repayment of the many lost hours with them, but as a means of honoring their contribution. As for daughter Jennifer: I'll dedicate the next one to you.

It is most appropriate that these acknowledgments be written during

Thanksgiving, 1986

295

Index

305